Compassion Or Apocalypse

A comprehensible guide to the thought of René Girard

Compassion Or Apocalypse

A comprehensible guide to the thought of René Girard

James Warren

CHRISTIAN
ALTERNATIVE

Winchester, UK
Washington, USA

First published by Christian Alternative Books, 2013
Christian Alternative Books is an imprint of John Hunt Publishing Ltd.,
Laurel House, Station Approach,
Alresford, Hants, SO24 9JH, UK
office1@jhpbooks.net
www.johnhuntpublishing.com
www.christian-alternative.com

For distributor details and how to order please visit the 'Ordering' section on our website.

ISBN: 978 1 78279 073 0

A CIP catalogue record for this book is available from the British Library.

Printed and bound by CPI Group (UK) Ltd, Croydon, CR0 4YY

Contents

Acknowledgments

Many thanks to John Linton at the Oregon Extension in Lincoln for first turning me onto Girard (not to mention so many other wonderful authors). And thanks to those who graciously read the manuscript and gave feedback, and encouragement: James Alison, Anthony Bartlett, Mel Leaman, David Leaman, Liz Richners, and Dr. Jose Ramirez-Rivera. Special thanks to David Leaman, who first called me over to his lunch table at a Theology And Peace conference and challenged me to write this book, with a vote of confidence that I was the one to do it. Without that kind of encouragement I would never have undertaken the task.

This book is dedicated to my wife Sally, who in deep understanding and purity of devotion gave me space to write it, and was always supportive of the process; and to Nate, who lost some daddy-time because of it.

Foreword
By Brian McLaren

I first met Jim Warren, not as a writer and not as a scholar of the work of René Girard, but as a magician. That's right – a pull-a-rabbit-out-of-your-hat magician (except that no actual rabbits were harmed, or even used, in his show). Jim was very good and I was fascinated by his show. But someone kept wanting to talk to me and kept whispering in my ear, and I was torn between being rude to the person beside me and being intrigued by Jim's magic.

Finally I surrendered to my persistent, whispering neighbor and I missed the end of the show. People told me it was excellent and that I shouldn't have missed it. I agree!

My next introduction to Jim was through the manuscript that became this book, and I am glad I had the chance to read it in private, free of whispered interruptions, for this too was an excellent performance from beginning to end.

My two experiences with Jim have me thinking about the relationship between good writing and good magic. There's no shortage of either in the pages you're about to read.

As for good writing, Jim writes in a down-to-earth, conversational style – which will be especially welcome to readers who've tried to read serious philosophy, anthropology, psychology, and theology in the past and found them impenetrable. Jim Warren magically transforms dauntingly complex material into simple, graspable sentences, and he does so with so much ease that you'll wonder, "Hey, how did he do that?"

The magic you'll encounter in this book is not illusion or trickery, not sleight of hand or deception, but the opposite. Jim doesn't hide anything up his sleeve, but shows you what's in his mind and heart with a kind of disarming transparency – a magical quality that delights and intrigues as it inspires awe and wonder. What will he make appear next?

Of course, to many, there is nothing more "old hat" than the Bible. For Jim to reach into the Bible and, without so much as an "abracadabra" or "presto," pull out a live rabbit would be quite a trick. But he does it again and again – making one live-and-kicking insight appear after another, pulled from old familiar stories that you'll never see the same way again.

If Jim has a magic wand at his disposal, it would be the thought of a French intellectual named René Girard. Girard's insights, though, don't work like alchemy: they don't turn humdrum Biblical materials into gold. They work more like paint remover. When Jim applies Girardian solvent to the Biblical text, we see that beneath layers of paint, there was gold there all along.

Again, this (re)discovery has a certain magic to it, especially these days, when religions – and especially the Abrahamic/monotheistic ones – have lost their luster for many, due to their adherents' tendency to use their religions to justify their unjustifiable behaviors. In a world like ours, shaken as it is by religious violence, the Bible is as suspicious as an abandoned suitcase at an airport. Observers suspect that it has "loaded verses" inside, verses that tick like time bombs, because they have been used and will be used again to inspire hate, fear, killing, even mass murder. To many of us, the Bible seems complicit in the world's religious violence, so one hardly expects anyone to open it up and pull out not swords but plowshares, not spears but pruning hooks, not terrorism but a movement for peace and reconciliation.

But that is precisely what René Girard did in the last half of the last century. He read the Bible from a fresh perspective that disarmed it. And Jim, having been indoctrinated (as I was) under the influence of less charitable, more fundamentalistic readings of the Bible, is able to wave the Girardian wand over the Biblical text so that you too can see the old book in a new light.

Ever since I began reading Girard, and ever since I began re-reading the Bible in light of Girard, I've wished someone could make Girard's insights more widely accessible. I tried to do so in one chapter in one of my books,[1] but Girard has far too much magic for just one chapter, which is why I'm so glad for Jim's performance in these pages.

But Jim doesn't simply rehash Girardian thought. He integrates Girard with his own wide reading. So along with Girardian insight, you'll gain insight from Jim's reading of Dostoevsky, Shakespeare, Aeschylus, Charles Taylor, Nietzsche, W.B. Yeats, and – of course – Dr. Seuss, among others. And Jim brings in other resources too – contemporary movies like Gran Torino, for example, and the Twelve Steps of Alcoholics Anonymous. Put it together, and you have a truly unique magic potion that can give you a kind of magical power, the power to see through things.

That "through-sight" isn't simply X-ray vision that penetrates steel or stone. It's the ability to see what's going on behind the headlines in world affairs, or behind the surface in a classroom or family or church or gang. It will even enable you to see through the surface of the Christian religion – especially in its most popular forms – to something dark and dangerous underneath. And then, if you look deeper still, you'll see through to something more ... something that is pure, luminous gold.

Put it all together, and you'll see why I think the book you are holding is a treasure.

It all begins, not with the waving of a wand, but with the simple turning of a page. So, ladies and gentlemen, get ready for your world to be shaken.

Brian D. McLaren
Marco Island, FL
Advent 2012

---

[1] *Why Did Jesus, Moses, the Buddha, and Mohammed Cross the Road? [Christian Identity in a Multi-Faith World]* (Jericho, 2012). See especially the chapter on the Eucharist.

Introduction

Is God violent? No question, it seems to me, is more important for our era than this one. Another, related question is: What is the relation between violence and religion? What are we to make of so-called "sacred violence?" For Christian and Jewish readers of the Bible, there are all the questions that arise in connection with page after page of sometimes horrifically violent episodes. What are believers to make of such texts? Is God really like this?

Never have questions about violence burned with such existential urgency as at the present moment of entry upon the twentieth century. We are positioned on the edge of apocalypse – and that by our own doing. We will need no assistance from the divinity to bring about the end of history. Our capacity for violence has skyrocketed in the last century to unimaginable dimensions. And, at the same time, violence has become "democratized," no longer the more or less exclusive prerogative of governments, states, kings, Popes, or the wealthy. As Jacques Ellul wrote:

> *Previously only the rich had horses and carriages and could sometimes cause accidents to pedestrians. . . . Today most people have automobiles. And it has often been noted what a change comes over gentle and polite people when they begin driving powerful vehicles. . . . relations of vanity, scorn, competition, and anger expressed in insults and finally leading to fatal accidents. . . . [T]hose who hated their neighbors might once have attacked them with a stick, but they would have done so far less effectively than if they had a submachine gun. But everybody today in many different areas has the equivalent of a submachine gun. . . . Years ago [drugs] could be had only by the wealthy, by artists, and by half-mad intellectuals. Now they have been democratized, and they recruit their victims among the people. . . . We might also mention the ease with which explosives are obtained. A century ago attacks with explosives were difficult and dangerous. Nihilists were heroes who were ready to die with their bombs or dynamite. In fact we now find*

plastic and other explosives everywhere, and attacks, the taking of hostages, and the seizing of airplanes occur all the time."[1]

Ellul wrote these words almost 25 years ago – but the situation he described has intensified exponentially since then. If the modern situation is inflammable with insane, anarchic violence, the question is also raised as to how we can avoid or control this by means other than a lapse into a different kind of violence: namely, totalitarian, "top-down" violence. This latter violence is just as horrific as the former, as the entire twentieth century has testified.

Always, everywhere, the issue of violence is in our face today, within our local communities no less than on an international scale, and nobody feels safe. What makes it a particularly frightful issue is that the solutions proposed by various factions generally seek to use the poison as a remedy. They reframe, re-label, and re-package violence so that it becomes acceptable, a kind of "good" violence, which will limit and control "bad" violence. Nothing is taken seriously as a solution unless it includes some dosage of violence – and that includes the religious solution. Much of the world's population is gripped by varieties of fundamentalist religion that praise and worship a violent God, seeing their salvation in the fact that God's violence is greater than the enemy's violence, and looking fervently toward the day when God will give the evil ones their just deserts. They see themselves protected by the love and mercy that God bestows upon them; but they reckon God's love quite useless unless backed up by the power to defeat their enemies. And that power, wreaking vengeance on Judgment Day, differs from human violence only in the purity of its justification and the infinity of its power. Believers in such a deity have seldom hesitated regarding the desirability of exercising their own violence in defense of God's values and theirs, or in aggression against their and God's enemies – who are always clearly profiled.

But is God violent? This is a hugely important question, and irresistible for those who can no longer take God's violence for granted, because they can no longer take *violence* for granted. Violence has always been the age-old solution to human problems, including the problem of violence itself. The reliability of the simple schema of using violence to control and punish violence is falling apart in today's world, which is witnessing the nightmarish unleashing of every person's ability, through access to technology, to turn their petty resentments and rivalries into national, even international, concerns. Is the Bible simply irrelevant to this situation? Or does it make matters worse by enflaming imaginations and supplying religious justifications? Or does the Bible in fact offer a radical alternative to our violent ways of thinking? Does it reveal a God positioned utterly outside the human cycles of violence, despite the numerous biblical passages that portray God as vengeful and violent? To anyone who burns with questions such as these, the perspective of René Girard offers intelligent and relevant commentary.

I remember the excitement, more than a decade ago, when I picked up a copy of Gil Bailie's book, *Violence Unveiled*,[2] and began to learn about René Girard and mimetic theory. Everything I read rang true intellectually and gripped me existentially, and yet it was just the appetizer. After finishing that book I jumped immediately into Girard himself, chowing down on *Violence and the Sacred* as a main entrée. This is not an easy book for a beginner in Girardian studies, but it is absolutely foundational, and can profitably be reread as one grows in understanding. What was it that gripped me so, and has held my earnest attention for over a decade? More than anything else, I would say that it was the way in which the Girardian "lens" illuminated the scriptures, its amazing ability to multiply meaning – profound, relevant meaning – from text after text after text. Girard shed new light on the Bible, and at a time when I was searching for a reason to continue to call myself a "Christian." The narrow Evangelicalism of my seminary years was no longer an option for me, but neither was the liberal, "social gospel" approach, which seemed to me to offer little more than ethical clichés about social justice, and scriptures stripped of personal, spiritual meaning. I have since come to see how, at its best, the social gospel theological tradition can be deeply meaningful for some, and humbly acknowledge the deeply compassionate and dedicated ministry of those for whom Christianity is summed up in advocacy for the poor and oppressed.

Nevertheless, I remain one who feeds on "meaning" as much as bread. The "higher criticism" of the Bible upon which social gospel theology is based destroys the kind of meaning that excites and feeds me.

A Girardian perspective does not exclude biblical criticism, and indeed sometimes makes use of it.[3] Mostly, however, Girard is concerned with the meaning of the biblical text *as it stands written*. He is not interested in creating a portrait of the "historical Jesus," for instance, based upon a reconstruction that accepts some texts as the *ipsissima verba* – the very words of Jesus – and throws out others as interpolations of the early church. He reads the Bible as a literary critic, concerned primarily with the text as it has come down to us, regardless of how it came into existence or took the form it now possesses.

This was highly congenial to me, because the biblical text had always been what excited me. I loved the Bible and its stories even as a kindergartener, and began an earnest attempt to understand the biblical text during my first year in college. But after years of searching, so much about the Bible still seemed like a mystery to me, and some aspects of it appeared downright scandalous (like the genocide stories in Joshua). When I discovered Girard, a whole new world opened up before me. If I can liken the Bible to an underground cavern, it was as though in place of my flashlight, Girard supplied central illumination. Mimetic theory lit up obscure and difficult biblical passages, and did so in the most significantly relevant way possible for the new millennium. In this new light I was enabled to see that the cavern contained treasures, pearls of insight that spanned the entire range of human history from the beginning to the contemporary, possessing great relevance both for individuals and society. And Girard attributes this light to the Bible itself. The text, taken just as it stands, is revelatory: it reveals the truth that humanity has long attempted to hide. But, as Girard has pointed out, since this could not happen within the closed-system of human culture, the text must have its source, and its fundamental structuring, in something outside that system – that is, in God.

Most likely, the person who purchases and begins to read this book will have done so for one of two reasons. There will be the reader who knows nothing about Girard or his thinking, but whose interest in this book has been piqued because of the *themes* it addresses. This is the reader who is looking for answers to questions about the relevance of Christianity for the twenty-first century, and is concerned especially with questions regarding the relationship between religion and violence, the disturbing frequency and intensity of violence in the Bible, and how such texts can be reconciled with any viable view of God and spirituality. These are important questions, and one meets with them frequently among our contemporaries. To such readers, Girard has much to offer.

There will also be the reader who, having heard of René Girard and been exposed to some basic knowledge about his thinking, has found it fascinating and insightful, but difficult. Such a reader may have attempted to read Girard directly and found it daunting, and is looking for a more straightforward and clear exposition of his thought. I wish to say right at the beginning that while this book attempts to do something like that, the reader must constantly bear in mind that, as an author, I have put a lot of *myself* into this book. Indeed, in the very process of trying to explain some of Girard's concepts, I found myself exploring them in greater depth than I had before, and making many new discoveries. Sometimes this was a matter of realizing and tracing out implications of ideas that I had not previously thought through in a nuanced way. Sometimes the discoveries were at the practical level, as I searched for examples to illustrate abstract concepts.

The important point for the reader to understand is that this book is mine, not Girard's, and nothing I say in its pages should be taken as reflecting in any straightforward manner what Girard would say, unless I specifically quote him or indicate otherwise. I have made the Girardian perspective my own – and "my own" is what the reader is getting herein. Often, when an author writes an introductory book about a great thinker, he or she will take pains to present nothing but the thinker's own ideas, using the thinker's own illustrations, examples, terminology and language (albeit simplified for ease of understanding), and will attempt to present a balanced picture of the thinker's entire body of work. This book is not a classic, textbook introduction to René Girard in that sense. It is much more personal than that. It is also the result of my integration of the work of many other scholars who have built upon Girard's work. What I present here, therefore, should not be considered a textbook outline of the thought of René Girard; it is, rather, my attempt to help readers grasp the general Girardian point of view, which I have compounded from many years of study and broad reading in the field.

That said, I do hope the book will be of value for anyone curious about or struggling with Girard's ideas, and will prepare them to read Girard himself (or any number of other "Girardian" writers) with greater understanding. This book attempts to take some very complicated concepts and present them as clearly and intelligibly as possible, so that newcomers to Girard will be able to grasp some of the meaning and significance of mimetic theory and its application to biblical interpretation. This does not mean, however, that I take a simplistic approach. The challenge for me in writing the book has been to steer a path between shallow shoals and deep ocean. The intention from the beginning has been to avoid mere snorkeling; at the same time, however, this is a book for relative beginners, so deep sea diving was out of the question. That leaves scuba. We shall dive deep, but only to a level at which the newcomer can hopefully withstand the pressure. The criterion throughout has not been the avoidance of depth, but the achievement of clarity (thus the word "comprehensible" in the subtitle of this book). I have wanted to give the reader more than a mere superficial acquaintance with mimetic theory of the sort one finds in books offering short and overly dense introductions to the subject – usually before plunging off into complex and specialized applications. I have not been afraid to provide the reader a rather nuanced understanding of some complex Girardian notions; but I will have failed in my purpose if, in attempting to do so, I have sacrificed clarity.

There is, however, another danger, apart from the issue of obscurity. Even if I have been able to explain the more theoretical aspects of mimetic theory in a "user-friendly" way, some readers may lack the patience for a sustained theoretical investigation. There are some for whom practical application is everything, who may find themselves at points asking (as I often did in my seventh grade algebra class), "Why do we have to study this?" No matter how intelligibly I (hopefully) render the concepts, some may not long tolerate breathing a purely conceptual air. Therefore I have had to make choices regarding how nuanced to make the explanations. I frankly admit, however, that I would rather err on the side of too much than too little. I should like to think that not only have I achieved depth without sacrificing clarity, but that I have also achieved theoretical depth without sacrificing the interest of readers short on patience for the theoretical. But, of course, the reader must judge for him or herself the answers to both those questions. I do hope that anyone interested enough in René Girard to purchase this book will be prepared to sustain a theoretical outlook for a few pages here and there in the interests of a deeper grasp of what the Girardian perspective is all about.

For some, the Girardian perspective on the human condition in general, and on the Bible and Christian revelation in particular, has come with the engaging force of a revelation, issuing in a palpable excitement and sense of conviction. I share much of that excitement myself. At the same time, however, it is possible to avoid some of the "totalizing" language that Girard himself sometimes uses, and see mimetic theory as one lens among possible others for illuminating the world and the scriptures. And it is possible to be deeply impacted by Girard's thinking, without thereby becoming a "Girardian." When discussing Marxism in the seventh volume of his magisterial history of philosophy, Frederick Copleston says that while Marxism is a living faith or creed (he was writing in the early 1960's), one might rather take it as simply an interesting "vision" of the world – in which case pedantic criticism of the details is not the main point. For, he says, "Philosophers who provide striking visions of the world are inclined to take one aspect of reality and to use it as a key to unlock all doors. And detailed criticism, it may be said, is out of place. For it is the very exaggeration involved in the vision which enables us to see the world in a new light. When we have done so, we can forget about the exaggeration: the vision has accomplished its purpose."

"And it is largely," Copleston continues, "because of the exaggerations involved that it can have this effect, breaking the rigidity of other pictures or interpretations of the world."[4] This seems to me to make very good sense when dealing with the Girardian interpretation of the world which I am attempting to explain in this book. The Girardian outlook does indeed form a kind of faith or creed for some people, especially since it claims to discover its truth in the biblical text – an ultimate authoritative source for many. Yet what Copleston says about Marxism can serve as a warning: "[T]he transformation of this philosophy into the dogmatic creed of a powerful Party has arrested the natural development of the different lines of thought to which its diverse aspects might otherwise be expected to have given rise."[5] As the annual international Girardian conference ("Colloquium on Violence and Religion") testifies, if Girardian thought is anything, it is amazingly fructifying for diverse fields and applications, and has offered scholars across many academic disciplines a lens through which to examine their subjects that continues to prove effective in yielding a plethora of new insights.

One would have to be quite closed-minded indeed to study Girard and not come away looking differently at the world. One may not perhaps be converted to a new creed, but any open mind will surely come away with at least an "interesting vision" that illuminates significant elements once hidden in shadow, and which, once perceived, will add lasting coloration to one's view of the world (and, perhaps, at the practical level, one's action toward the world). If one reckons this effect as due to Girard's "exaggeration," so be it: Oh happy exaggeration! My purpose here is not to make converts, but to sketch a view of the world (and a correlative vision of God) that I believe has tremendous value even for those who ultimately decline the full ride.

Part I
MIMESIS

Be imitators of me, just as I also am of Christ.
Paul (1 Cor.11:1)

Chapter One
Mimesis and Desire

Those conflicts and disputes among you, where do they come from? Do they not come from your cravings that are at war within you? You desire something and do not have it; so you commit murder. And you covet something and cannot obtain it; so you engage in disputes and conflicts. (James 4:1-2)

Oh, Hell! To choose love by another's eyes.
Hermia (Midsummer Night's Dream)

‡‡

Mimesis

Rubberbands used to be handy things to have around the house and office, very practical little gadgets, and very cheap – until the day my six year old son came home from school wearing some around his wrist. They weren't typical rubberbands, however, they were "Silly Bandz" – strangely shaped, neon-colored, rubberband-like things. When he took one off his wrist and threw it onto the table it instantly resolved into the shape of a guitar. I found out soon enough that Silly Bandz were not cheap. Nate wanted me to buy him a pack of twenty-four that cost almost five dollars! Mercifully, we discovered that the local dollar store sold a variety that cost only two dollars. (Why then did they call it a "dollar" store? Another of life's many conundrums.) Within a couple of weeks, Nate had become the owner of several dozen Silly Bandz, which he wore proudly displayed in a thick conglomerate around his wrist. At school the kids would show each other their bands and trade them, while parents across America forked out millions of dollars to satisfy their children's demands, and manufacturers laughed, as they say, all the way to the bank.

It's an old story, isn't it, and one we all know well. But nobody knows it better than the marketers, the promoters, and the advertising agencies. They are the experts who can work the magic that turns a rubberband into a national craze. Some readers might remember the 1970's craze called Pet Rocks. Mere stones sold in cardboard boxes cut with "breathing holes" so the "pet" could breath, these guys sold for almost four dollars back in 1975, and made their creator, Gary Dahl, a millionaire. There is no need to labor the point, because anyone living in our consumer culture is not only familiar with it, but has no doubt been taken in by such schemes many times over. None of us is immune. No matter how stupid or silly, sooner or later we all fall victim to the power of influence and live to laugh about it, or cry over it, as the case may be.

Although I said that no one knows this story better than the advertisers and promoters who know how to package these items in ways that will sell, advertisers do not truly understand the nature of the force they manipulate with sometimes amazing efficacy. There is someone, however, who *does* understand the force involved in such matters. His name is René Girard, and the force in question is what Girard calls *mimetic desire.* The term "mimetic desire" means desire shaped by mimesis (which, it turns out, is the only kind of desire there is). But what is mimesis? Before we get to the issue of desire itself, we need to understand a bit about mimesis.

"Mimesis" means imitation (think *mime*). Everybody is aware to some extent of the power of imitation in human life, and Girard is not the first great thinker to make it a major theme in the understanding of human nature. Imitation is at the very heart of Aristotle's *Poetics,* for example, where Aristotle uses imitation as the definition of what is common to all art, and what makes us human. Nor is imitation for Aristotle mere superficial mimicry, as in the copying of external shapes and sounds, but also involves the reproduction through art of human intentions and purposes, the stuff of which drama is made.

Another thinker who had much to say about imitation was Rudolf Steiner, the founder of Waldorf education. Steiner was clear that children learn by imitation: "At this age nothing is accomplished through admonition; commands and prohibitions have no effect at all. But the examples are most significant. What children see, what happens in their surroundings, they feel must be imitated. . . . Exhortations have no effect, but the way a person acts in the child's presence matters greatly. It is far more important to refrain from doing what the child is not permitted to do than to forbid the child to imitate it."[6] I was able to observe this process in my own child as I watched him picking up one habit after another, one interest after another, one mannerism after another – all by imitating elements in his environment. Everything that Nate is most passionate about, from Spiderman to karate to Taiko drum lessons, and everything that Nate has learned about how to be in the world, from tying shoelaces to brushing teeth to burping inappropriately (the way they do in the school cafeteria) to the desire for Silly Bandz – everything has been by way of imitation.

Researcher Andrew Meltzoff of the University of Washington in Seattle did experiments in 1977 with infants only a few hours old.[7] When Meltzoff stuck out his tongue, the babies would imitate the gesture and stick out theirs. One infant who did this was only a half-hour old and had not yet even seen its mother's face. Sometimes the imitation would happen immediately, but the infants also had the capacity for delay, so that the gesture would be remembered and imitated only at a later time. It is because of the child's incredible capacity to appropriate everything around her through imitation that Waldorf education is especially careful about protecting the child from the influences of television, motion pictures, computer images, and other such stimuli. It is too easy for the child to imitatively appropriate attitudes, behaviors, and images that are beyond the child's developmental level, leading to various difficulties and alienation from immediate experience.

René Girard developed the idea of imitation in directions undiscovered by any previous observers, and made it the lynchpin in a theory that goes far beyond child development. Girard calls it "mimesis" rather than imitation in order to avoid confusing his key idea with mere mimicry. Like Aristotle, Girard sees that mimesis runs much deeper than the mere copying of externalities such as repetition of sounds in language learning, or motor skills for mastering a sport -- although this kind of imitation is certainly ubiquitous in human experience. Mimicry of the other's gestures, sounds, movements, and so on, come as naturally to us as to chimpanzees. But our imitative gifts far exceed the chimp's, and as we begin to imitate, not just external gestures, but the other's unspoken intentions and unuttered desires, our very sense of self – how we experience ourselves and who we feel ourselves to be – comes to depend upon the "other." Girard saw that imitation of externals is a function of a much deeper imitation – the imitation of *desire*. When my son joins the Silly Bandz craze, he is not merely imitating the behaviors of wearing, trading, displaying, and so on, but, far more profoundly, he is imitating the *desire* for Silly Bandz that he senses in others; and at a deeper level still, he is imitating the desire to fit in, and the desire to stand out and be recognized (by having the coolest Silly Bandz). He sees that others desire these things, and then he wants them himself. Through mimesis, he develops the same desires, which leads him to pursue the same objects.

Mimetic Desire

The key to Girard's understanding of mimesis, therefore, and what gives his work its real depth and power, is his insight that *human beings copy each other's desires.* And we do this at levels of incredible subtlety, since desire is not something people always wear on their sleeve. We have a wonderfully sensitive ability to "sniff out" the other's desire, reading his or her intentions and feelings even before they become observable acts. This is because we are always quite anxious, if not downright desperate, to know what others desire. We come into this world naked not only of body, but naked also of any sense as to what should be valued, what should be *desired.*

Now, we must carefully distinguish this kind of cultural desire from what we might call "appetites," which are biologically already in place. We are programmed to seek and accept liquid when we are thirsty – we do not have to copy that appetite from anyone. But it is not long before the appetite to slack thirst becomes mingled with *desire,* which is for a particular *kind* of liquid, perhaps that specific cup of liquid which a child sees another enjoying. Perhaps the liquid is red, and it was its redness which first caught the child's eye; but now that it has her attention, she sees the other child drinking it and believes (rightly or wrongly) that the red liquid is something the other child desires. Then she experiences an incredibly powerful urge to have some for herself, even if other types of liquid refreshment are readily available. This urge is mimetic. Once she drinks it, if the red liquid turns out to be a highly sugared fruit punch, biology might kick in as the sugar stimulates further appetite without mimetic help. Even so, however, mimesis can modify and even overrule biology, as, for example, when a child throws a fit in a grocery store when mommy attempts to buy generic fruit punch that lacks the branding of the child's favorite cartoon character or superhero. Despite mommy's repeated attempts to explain that this punch is just as sweet and sugary, the child will have nothing to do with it. (No doubt if health food manufacturers made lucrative deals with Disney and George Lucas, children's food preferences – and their health – would be dramatically altered.)

A simple example often given to illustrate mimetic desire is the scenario every parent has witnessed (and had to deal with!) hundreds of times. A child is playing with a toy in a room full of toys. Your child enters the room, begins looking around, perhaps handles a few objects that seem interesting to him; but, eventually, the toy the other child is enjoying comes to look more and more desirable to your child. Sometimes gradually, sometimes immediately, your child edges his way closer to the object, and you already know what's coming. Without adult intervention there is likely to be trouble. You are going to have to intervene and talk with your child about boundaries and respecting other people's things; and the other parent will have to talk with her child about sharing.

Of course, the scenario I just sketched doesn't always materialize (thank God), because there may be other factors at work in the situation that steer the child into preferring a different toy. But even in this happy outcome, mimesis is probably at work. The child might defer her desire to possess the other kid's toy because she imitates her parent's admonition (heard a hundred times before) to wait until another child is finished playing with a toy before grabbing for it; or she might spot a different toy, which she recognizes as an even more powerful object of desire thanks to the influence of a television commercial, an older sibling, or a next-door neighbor.

Mimesis, therefore, is not a mechanical process. Mimesis is not the only force at work, since genetics and biology have their role to play in motivation as well, and there is a mutually modifying effect between mimesis and biological urges and needs. But mimesis does quite commonly distort and inhibit what would be the natural, biological response, leading people along even downright destructive paths. (An example that comes to mind would be ascetic practices involving mortification of the flesh, learned through imitation of the desires and practices of a religious order.) Various choices can be made about who and what to imitate, and Girard would affirm an element of freedom that allows us, to some extent at least, to choose what we will copy. Imitation of the desire of the other, however, is almost always an unconscious choice that we readily hide from ourselves. But more about that later.

Having brought up the issue of biology, some mention should be made here of the recent discovery of mirror neurons. Several decades after Girard had developed his theory of mimesis, a group of scientists experimenting with macaque monkeys in a laboratory in Parma, Italy, made the discovery of the decade in neuroscience – *mirror neurons* – thus providing what turns out to be a firm, experimental grounding for mimesis. When one performs any motor activity, what are called motor neurons fire in the brain; but these scientists made the amazing discovery that the brain also contains specialized neurons that fire when one merely *observes* an action being performed. This seems to be the physiological source of empathy, allowing me to feel sad when I see you cry, or get angry in response to your anger. It is the reason video games and movies can stimulate adrenaline rushes, as though I myself were performing the dangerous stunts I see on the screen. In all such activities, mirror neurons are firing away in response to my perception of the other's actions and feelings. Mirror neurons are now being accepted as the physiological mechanism underlying our capacity to imitate.[8]

Mimesis is a force rather like gravity. Jean-Michel Oughourlian points out that gravity's law of inverse proportion applies analogously to mimesis.[9] Once two desires are attuned, the force of attraction multiplies in power and it becomes easier to attract a third, in which case its power grows again, and so on as more "desirers" participate. I do not mean this as a strict mathematical function, only as a suggestive analogy; but it does seem to be the case that mimetic attraction grows with the size of a crowd.[10] Eventually we have the phenomenon of a "mimetic wave" – the so-called herd mentality characteristic of mobs, which at its peak exercises upon individuals an almost irresistible fascination. The more desires are focused upon a particular object, the more irresistibly desirable the object appears to everyone. The rises and plunges of the stock market are examples of mimetic waves: investors follow the numbers, which represent the desires of others for certain stocks. The stock market demonstrates the "snowball effect" of mimesis when it becomes a large scale group phenomenon, growing in power and seductiveness in proportion to the number of participating traders.

I often perform for schools, doing assembly programs that address the issue of bullying, and I use magic as a means of communicating the concepts in an entertaining way. In this setting I have often noticed the power of mimetic waves. Once I was doing a show for seven hundred middle school students in a large auditorium. I bring students up to the stage as helpers for various routines, and with middle school kids this is very easy to do since they generally love to assist the magician. Usually I ask for volunteers, but sometimes I simply grab someone's hand, yank them out of their seat, and say "thanks for volunteering!" It gets a laugh. On this occasion, however, it turned out that the girl I tried to get to volunteer was petrified of appearing on stage before her classmates, and she balked. I attempted to cajole her out of her seat, because I already knew what was likely to happen if she persisted in her stubborn refusal to volunteer. And I was right. When I tried to get the girl sitting next to her to volunteer, she exhibited *exactly* the same behavior as the first girl: facial expression, body language, and verbal expletives were all the same. It was as though she were a photocopy of the first girl.

Now I knew I was in trouble, because I had seen this happen before, and I know mimetic theory. Once the second girl chose to imitate the first girl's desire not to participate, the "gravitational" effect of mimesis set in: with two girls exhibiting the same desire/behavior, it was almost a certain bet that the next student would participate in the same imitation. Desire to "resist-the-magician" spread almost palpably like a wave throughout the auditorium, even though this age group is usually quite extroverted and enthusiastic in their desire to participate. I finally had to address the entire audience, asking for someone – anyone! – to raise his or her hand to volunteer – and only *two* people out of seven hundred went against the "wave" and raised their hands! This is how powerfully and quickly mimesis can control collective group behavior.

We will examine the Gospels in detail later, but I might mention here, in connection with mimetic waves, how the Gospels portray the actions of the "crowd" in relation to Jesus. News about Jesus spread contagiously throughout Judea, so that Jesus became a celebrity by word-of-mouth. When he entered Jerusalem on Palm Sunday, riding on a donkey, the crowds adored him and welcomed him as a king; but later those same crowds turned against him, shouting for his crucifixion. Both movements were mimetic waves. The reason it was so easy for the crowd to turn against Jesus (the famous "fickleness" of the crowd) is that the object of a crowd's desire can in principle be anything, because the crowd doesn't desire the object for its own sake; it looks desirable simply because everybody else is desiring it. Thus, like the child's toy in the playroom, the crowd will quickly discard its plaything when the mimetic fad changes – sometimes for the most trivial of reasons.

The Romantic Lie

Armed with some basic understanding of mimesis and mimetic desire, we move on to the crux of the matter for Girardian theory: the important ways in which mimesis plays itself out within human relationships. Let us remind ourselves that when we put the two words together – "mimetic" and "desire" – to form the term "mimetic desire," we are indicating a desire that is *copied*. We copy the desires of others. Not all the others, but certain others. Whom we copy, and why we choose (consciously or unconsciously) to copy that person's desire is not important here. What is crucial is the basic fact: *human beings copy the desires of others.* We are always on the lookout for the other's desire: it is our map, our clue for finding our way in the human world of culture and civilization. It is how we discover what is desirable, and therefore valuable. This idea is profoundly important because desire is the wellspring of what we might call psychological movement.[11] That is, it provides the basic impetus that moves us out into the world and into relation with others on levels of meaning that surpass simple biology, and whereby we create our sense of "self."

Imitating the other's desire is also of primary importance because *it is what creates rivalries,* bringing human beings into conflict over a desired object. In his 1976 book, *Deceit, Desire and the Novel,* Girard, writing as a literary critic, laid out his insights into how the mimetic nature of desire propels human beings into violent rivalries – insights he admittedly discovered by reading authors like Dostoevsky, Shakespeare, Flaubert, Proust, Stendhal, and Cervantes. These novelists seemed to grasp the essence of human relations in a manner quite different from the typical "romantic" view. What Girard calls the "romantic lie" might be characterized by Caesar's famous statement, "I came, I saw, I conquered." If we replace the word "conquered" with the word "desired" (which is implied anyway, since one would not typically conquer what one does not desire), we have the great romantic lie about desire: "I came, I saw, I desired." In other words, I came, I encountered an object, and I saw that it was wonderful and precious, and so I desired it. (And thus, in Caesar's case, *took* it.) This conception of desire is very flattering to Caesar, for it means that Caesar desires the object because of his ability to recognize value when he sees it. In this conception, Caesar's desire is not modeled from any other person. There is no third party involved, no "mediator," to use Girard's terminology, no one who displays that desire to Caesar as a model for imitation. No one needs to tell Caesar what to desire!

That Caesar's desire needs no model is a romantic myth. A true picture of Caesar's desire would bring out the reality of the mediator, or model. Just like everyone else, everything Caesar desires he has *learned* to desire, he has *copied* from a third party. Sometimes the third party is immediately present in mimetic interactions, as, for example, when Judy falls in love with Jon only after her best friend Susan has become enamored of him. Judy barely noticed Jon before, but now Susan's infatuation for Jon becomes "contagious" for Judy, who imitates it (but without being consciously aware that she is doing so). Judy "catches" desire for Jon directly from her friend, the mediator or model, almost as one would catch a cold.

On the other hand, the mediator or model might not be present at all, perhaps having long since passed from the scene; but the desire inherited from him or her continues for years. The term "mediator," by the way, is used by Girard to mean something similar to model. It is the model viewed specifically in relation to his or her role in mediating desire to another person. "Mediation" means the communication or passing of desire from one person to another: and as the channel for such communication, the model can be called the mediator.

Now, the mimetic situation can be subtle. It might be the case that the mediator is not even a real person. It could be a character in literature or legend, or a childhood hero admired on the movie screen whose attitudes, beliefs, gestures, and desires I spend the rest of my life unconsciously imitating. Also, there are times when what has been copied is not desire for a *particular* object (Jon), but for a certain *kind* of object ("hip" looking guys, for example). Judy desires Jon because he represents that type of male. No friend of

Judy's directly pointed to Jon and said, "Wow, I want that guy!" but that doesn't mean there is no mediator. Judy is already steeped in desire for a certain type of male, a desire she has picked up from many mediators in the cultural world she inhabits, including friends, romance novels, television and film, and so on. In cases like this, when there is no "Susan" immediately present as mediator, it is especially easy to claim that one's desire is original with oneself, buying into the romantic myth: "I came, I saw Jon's wonderfulness, and so I desired him." We are all little Caesars, promoting the myth of our own self-containment, yet all the while utterly saturated with what we have learned by imitating others – especially their desires.

Like Caesar, we do not wish to admit our dependence upon others when it comes to desire. But a true picture of Caesar's desire will detect that even the powerful ruler himself had a model: Alexander the Great. Julius Caesar reportedly wept at the age of thirty-two when he thought that his accomplishments were not as great as Alexander's. Alexander's body was one of the most sacred relics in the Roman Empire, and Julius paid homage to the tomb when he arrived in Alexandria. Alexander, and the entire Homeric tradition of the Greeks so envied by the Romans, was a model for Caesar's desire for conquest. But the buck doesn't stop with Alexander the Great, for he too had models for his desire for conquest, the two most powerful being his father, Philip of Macedonia, and the Homeric hero, Achilles. Alexander was so consumed by rivalry with his warrior father, that classics scholar Robin Lane Fox went so far as to call Alexander a "spark struck off Philip. . . more than a spark, it's a devouring flame."[12] And as we will see a bit further on, rivals always imitate each other.

My real point is not about Caesar or Alexander, remote as they are, but about ourselves: we little Caesars who indulge the romantic myth that we have desired the object independently of models. This often leads to the equally mythical idea that our desire has some right of priority, since we desired the object before the other person. It is flattering to my sense of independence and power to believe that I desire a woman simply because I came, I saw her beauty, and I desired her; and it might feel humiliating to admit that my desire for her flows in channels already cut by another, that my desire came to birth because of the influence of models I copied – even, perhaps, copying the desire of a *rival,* someone I consider beneath me, even an enemy! It also sounds denigrating to the object to say that I desire her because my friend (or even worse, my rival) desires her, and that should this fellow lose his interest in her, my *own* interest would also flag, and perhaps not even survive.

Of course, we are usually willing to admit our admiration for some remote hero (the way, for example, Napoleon and General Patton were quite willing to admit their admiration for Alexander the Great). There is no disgrace in not measuring up to the greatest of the great, and admitting our debt to them and admiration for them makes us appear flatteringly modest. But if the model is someone less remote, less universally acknowledged for greatness, someone of our own station and status, perhaps even an acquaintance – then it becomes very difficult to admit, even to ourselves, that this person is the secret model for our own desire. Besides, admitting the mediated nature of my desire would threaten my claim upon the object. If my desire is copied from you, how can I claim priority?

We are used to thinking of the "self" as a more or less self-contained entity, but mimesis indicates a different picture. Since it is desire that sets me in motion towards the cultural world, even as an infant, and since desire comes to me through the mediation of others, what I call my "self" is anything *but* self-contained. My whole sense of "I" is built up through my imitation of others. They are "in" me, and I "in" them. It is not that I have no self, but I am not self-possessed. I am permeable. There is what we might call a mutual inhabiting of selves in each other, what Girard and psychiatrist Jean-Michel Oughourlian call "interdividuality." With this unusual term, they seek to direct us away from the idea of the independent, self-contained individual, and have created a field of study and therapy called "interdividual psychology," based upon the dynamics of mimetic desire in human relationships.

The Model

Let us look more closely now at those dynamics, as Girard

himself discovered them in the great literature of the Western world. Mimetic desire was central for Shakespeare, who constantly portrays desire in just this manner.[13] Choosing love "by another's eyes," as Hermia says in the quote which opens this chapter, indicates Shakespeare's understanding of the role of the model. The following example will help us better to grasp the role of the model in mimetic dynamics, as well as the "contagiousness" of desire, how desire is "caught" from the model.

In his poem, *The Rape of Lucrece,* Shakespeare tells a tale that he adapts from Roman historian Livy, but he introduces an amazing and highly perceptive modification. In his *History of Rome* Livy tells about an evening gathering of high ranking warriors in the tent of Sextus Tarquinius, the king's son. Livy writes that "in their discourses after supper, every one commended the virtues of his own wife; among whom Collatinus extolled the incomparable chastity of his wife Lucretia." The old boys decide on a whimsy to test their wives' faithfulness, and the party breaks up as they ride to each one's home in turn, in order to surprise their wives. Only Collatinus' wife Lucretia is found dutifully spinning with her maids; the other wives are all found dancing or reveling or, as Livy says, in "several disports." Collatinus thus wins the victory, and his wife the fame. But when Sextus Tarquinius lays eyes on Lucretia for the first time at Collatinus' home, he is inflamed by her beauty. Livy says that he restrained his passions and rode back to camp, but shortly thereafter left again. He secretly rode back to Collatinus' home, where Lucretia entertained and lodged him as a royal guest. But that same night, says Livy, "he treacherously stealth into her chamber, violently ravish'd her, and early in the morning speedeth away..."

In his poetic version of the tale, Shakespeare stages the birth of Tarquin's desire for Lucretia in a very different manner. He has Tarquin leave the camp "lust-breathed," and "borne by the trustless wings of false desire," and the following verses tell how this desire came to birth:

> For he [Collatine] the night before, in Tarquin's tent
> Unlock'd the treasure of his happy state;
> What priceless wealth the heavens had him lent

In the possession of his beauteous mate;
Reck'ning his fortune at such high proud rate
That kings might be espoused to more fame,
But king no peer to such a peerless dame.

In other words, that night in the tent Collatine made the mistake of praising his wife's virtues to his fellow warriors, making a display of his enthused desire for Lucretia. This is what lit Tarquin's fire, who, in Shakespeare's version, *had at this point never even laid eyes upon the real Lucretia*. In Livy, Tarquin desires her the moment he sees her: I came, I saw, I desired. But Shakespeare retells it something along the lines of: I heard, I desired, I went. Tarquin's desire is lit because of the suggestive effect of the husband's own desire, imprudently displayed in the presence of potential rivals. A bit later in the poem, Shakespeare asks:

What needeth then apology be made
To set forth that which is so singular?
Or why is Collatine the publisher
Of that rich jewel he should keep unknown
From thievish ears because it is his own?[14]

Why, Shakespeare is asking, is Collatine so stupid as to publish his wife's beauty rather than just keep "that rich jewel" for himself, safe from "thievish ears?" Obviously, Collatine does not understand the mimetic nature of desire. He does not realize that his very bragging could itself inflame the desire of another, and create a rival. He is naively unaware of the danger involved in flaunting one's precious object before the eyes of others, how one's desire for that object becomes a model that entices the other to imitation. On the other hand, perhaps Collatine isn't so naïve. It may be that he is bent upon flaunting his desire for Lucretia because his desire for her is flagging. Collatine wants his male friends to ogle and salivate at his description of his wife because it will validate his own desire. As the others "catch" desire for Lucretia, Collatine will in turn be able to catch *their* desire, and so reinvigorate his own. He thus displays his desire to his buddies precisely because he wants them to imitate it; but he only wants them to imitate it to a certain extent, and no farther. He certainly doesn't intend to excite a rape. Whether Collatine operates simply from naivety, or the need for validation, the important point is that in having Tarquin become aroused and inflamed simply on the strength of Collatine's boasting, *before he has even seen the real Lucretia,* Shakespeare demonstrates his insight into mimetic desire. He knows, long before modern advertising (which is, in a sense, what Collatine was doing), that this is the way desire operates.

The Obstacle

I have explained the role of the "model" or "mediator" of desire. But as the Lucretia story illustrates, a model can be almost indistinguishable from a rival. No sooner did Tarquin take Collatine's desire as a model and begin to desire Lucretia for himself, than Collatine became his rival, an *obstacle* barring Tarquin's way to the prized object, an obstacle around which Tarquin had to sneak when secretly leaving the camp. If mimesis is the glory of humanity, as Aristotle thought, it is also its curse, because the model whose desire we imitate can quickly become the obstacle we must defeat in order to possess the desired object.

We see this dynamic played out time and time again among Jesus' disciples. They begin as models to one another who catch and reinforce each other's desire to follow Jesus. A perfect example is when Andrew, who followed Jesus because of the influence of his model, John the Baptist, goes to his brother Simon Peter and tells him enthusiastically, "We have found the Messiah!" (John 1:41)[15] The Gospel of John tells us that Andrew "brought him to Jesus." This is mimetic desire in action, as it spreads contagiously among the disciples: in this case from the Baptist to Andrew to Peter. They "turn each other on" to Jesus as an object of desire. However, it is not long before those who were each other's models become each other's obstacle, as over and over again we read about the disciples' competition with one another for Jesus' approbation, and rank and position in the kingdom of God.

We often see this model-turned-obstacle dynamic played out directly in master-apprentice relationships. When an aspiring artist apprentices under a master, everything goes well as long as the master is far above the apprentice's level of skill and knowledge. But as soon as the apprentice begins to match the master's abilities, there is likely to be trouble. For all along, although not consciously verbalized, the master has been saying to the apprentice, "Imitate me...*but only so far*. Imitate what I teach you, but do not imitate my success, do not imitate my popularity, do not imitate the profundity of my work, do not imitate me in any way that might threaten to diminish my image in the eyes of my admirers."

This prohibition is necessary because the apprentice is imitating far more than the master's skills. The master has found a way to use those skills to achieve recognition in society, and the apprentice wants the same thing. Seeing how important that recognition is to the master, the apprentice burns with the same desire. However, once the apprentice gains enough proficiency to compete with the master, his model will start to become an *obstacle.* In cases of exceptional maturity on the part of the master, conflict can be avoided; but if, as often happens, the master is imitating the apprentice just as much as the apprentice is imitating the master, there will be conflict.

How would a master imitate an apprentice? At the most profound level, by imitating his disciple's admiration. The master imitates the image of himself that he sees reflected in the disciple's admiring eyes. The adoring gaze of the apprentice makes him feel desirable, validates and revitalizes his opinion of himself. When models becomes obstacles, it is the end of the honeymoon.

The above is just one possible variation among the complexity of mimetic relations. The master/apprentice relationship shows us one way in which a model can become an obstacle and rival; but it also happens that *one can first encounter an obstacle who then becomes a model.* My favorite illustration for this is one Girard calls attention to from Dostoevsky's novelette, *The Underground Man.* The nameless protagonist of this story spends most of his time at home stimulating himself vicariously through reading, while plunging occasionally into secret debauchery with prostitutes, which leaves him sick with shame. Once constantly at loggerheads with his colleagues at work, he is now mostly a loner. One night he passes a small pub and witnesses a fight in which a man gets thrown through a window, and enters the pub with the hope of imitating the same thing: that is, he wants to get thrown through the window. A form of negative attention, this would at least add a touch of drama to his life, such as he enjoys in the books he reads. He doesn't mind being beaten up; what he minds is being ignored – which is precisely what happens in the pub, in a pathetic encounter with an army officer:

> *I was standing beside the billiard table and, in my ignorance, was blocking the way. As he* [the officer] *had to pass me, he took me by the shoulders and, without a word of warning or explanation, silently carried me bodily from where I was standing to another place and passed by as though he had not even noticed me. I could have forgiven him if he had given me a beating, but I could not forgive him for having moved me from one place to another as if I were a piece of furniture. I would have given anything at that moment for a real, a more regular, a more decent, and a more, so to speak, literary quarrel! But I had been treated like a fly. The army officer was over six foot, and I am a short, thin little fellow.*

How does our "hero" respond to this encounter? For the next several years he often sees that same army officer in the street, and stares at him with hatred and malice. He investigates and finds out everything he can about the officer, surreptitiously following him home and paying the landlord for information about the man's habits. He writes a story about the officer "in order to show him up for what he was." But the story is not published, which makes him even more resentful. Next, he decides to challenge the officer to a duel, writes a letter of challenge, and then doesn't send it. He has noticed that the officer makes way for generals and persons of important rank, but when it comes to people like himself:

> *. . . he walked straight at them as though there were just an empty space in front of him, and never in any circumstances did he make*

way for them. I gloated spitefully as I looked at him and – made way for him resentfully every time he happened to bear down on me. I was tortured by the thought that even in the street I could not be on the same footing as he. "Why do you always have to step aside first?" I asked myself over and over again in a sort of hysterical rage, sometimes waking up at three o'clock in the morning.

The upshot of all this obsessing is the "brilliant idea" to deliberately meet the officer on the street and *not* move aside, in order to defy him. The idea is not to give the officer a real shove, but simply to knock against him. "I shall only knock against him as much as he knocks against me." Preparation for this seemingly simple mission takes a long time, because our character (who is never named in the story) wants to be as well dressed as possible in order to put himself on an equal footing with the officer in the sight of any passersby. To afford the new wardrobe, however, he has to take an advance on his salary. He obsesses over the right color of dress gloves. He wants to change the raccoon collar of his overcoat for a classier beaver collar, which necessitates selling the raccoon collar and borrowing money from the head of his department – a shameful expedient that keeps him awake for three nights feeling feverish. Finally, having gone to all these lengths, there comes the moment of the attempted "knock-against" – which, however, fails miserably when he trips and falls a few feet in front of the officer, who proceeds to walk right over him and hurl him aside like a ball! After more nights of fever and obsessive delirium, he finally decides to give the whole thing up, and goes for a walk on Nevsky Avenue just to try to forget about it – and the officer appears on the street. This is how the affair ends:

Suddenly, only three paces from my enemy, I quite unexpectedly made up my mind, shut my eyes, and – we knocked violently against each other, shoulder to shoulder. I did not budge an inch and passed him absolutely on an equal footing! He did not even look round and pretended not to have noticed anything. But he was only pretending: I am quite sure of that. Yes, to this day I am quite sure of that! Of course I got the worst of it, for he was stronger. But that was not the point. The point was that I had done what I had set out to do, that I had kept up my dignity, that I had not yielded an inch, and that I had put myself publicly on the same social footing as he. I came back home feeling that I had completely revenged myself for everything. I was beside myself with delight.

With his extraordinary genius for caricature, Dostoevsky has given us a perfect illustration of how an obstacle becomes a model. The underground man represents no obstacle to the officer, of course, who merely lifts him by the shoulders and sets him aside like a piece of furniture. But the officer represents a huge obstacle to the underground man. He towers above him, stronger, richer, higher in social status and respectability, imperturbable. The officer is an absolute obstacle, like a mountain seemingly impossible to pass. But precisely because of this, the officer represents something our character wants: *power*. In order to blot out the voices of shame and self-revulsion that are his daily inner companions, power, and lots of it, appears very desirable to him. However, rather than become an apprentice to one who might actually help him achieve a modest measure of real power and success, he fixates on an obstacle and tries impossibly to imitate it. Why? Because he would consider unworthy of emulation anyone who deigned to notice someone as miserable as he. Just as he cannot love anybody who would love him, so he cannot choose anybody as a model who would have the bad taste to accept him as an apprentice. He can only make the self-defeating choice of selecting as model an impossible obstacle. In other words, it is precisely because the officer refuses to take notice of him that the officer becomes an object of fascination, seemingly worthy of imitation.

This entire brilliantly drawn episode is shot through with mimeticism. Dostoevsky emphasizes the imitative quality of all the protagonist's thoughts and deeds. Everything is about putting himself on an "equal footing" with the officer. He tries to copy what he perceives to be the officer's mannerisms, especially his aloofness and rudeness. He wants to match him in strength, which is impossible in reality but can be symbolically experienced through the ludicrous "knocking-against" test. He even dresses himself like the officer. Essentially, he wants to become the mirror image of the officer, wants to *become* the officer. But the underground character is "hyper-mimetic" long before his first encounter with the officer. What was he doing all that time he spent at home alone reading? Like Don Quixote, he was imitating heroes in his imagination (what we commonly refer to as "identification" is really a form of mimesis). In his first encounter with the officer in the billiard hall he is upset that things do not unfold more dramatically, like those scenes in the books that he daily imitates in his imagination. Had he been thrown through a window, it would have been an imitation of a truly "literary quarrel." But to be simply ignored, to be "treated like a fly"!

Yet by this ignoring the officer imposes himself upon the protagonist as an even greater object of fascination, like the coquette who becomes all the more seductive by her refusal to pay attention to her suitors, not even deigning to reject them outright. The coquette's attitude implies a tremendous power of self-possession that appears very seductive to anyone who cannot see through the game; that is, anyone who nurses a sense of personal lack and inadequacy, and thus envies the seemingly self-possessed. Like the coquette, the officer in our story becomes a model for imitation precisely by virtue of the obstacle he represents.

The Rival

Dostoevsky's story brings us to the theme of the rival within mimetic theory. A rival is always, of course, an obstacle; but an obstacle does not always turn into an actual rival in the sense of someone with whom I directly exchange hostilities. The rivalry may exist purely in the mind of one party, unreciprocated by the hated other, as in the case of the underground man's imaginative rivalry with the officer. But the potential for actual, reciprocal violence is always there.

Ideological differences often allow rivals to view themselves as entirely different, even opposites; yet there would be no rivalry if at some level there were not a mutually desired object – something concrete like a piece of land, or a lover; or abstract like fame, or status, or the desire to control. And as a matter of fact rivals actually *support* each other's desire for the object. Each becomes a kind of mirror in which the other can see his own desire reflected back – and thus reinforced. Rivalries sometimes start because of the need for such a mirror. I alluded to this in the tale of Collatine when I suggested that his bragging might have been born of an unconscious need for validation. Shakespeare makes this process explicit in his play, *Two Gentlemen of Verona,* in the relationship between Valentine and his best friend Proteus. These two men have been friends since childhood, imitating each others desires. They are used to feeling the security of knowing that they always agree with each other's choices, and share each other's enthusiasms. They are like tuning forks of the same frequency: start the one humming, and the other picks up the vibration and begins to hum along. In Girardian terms, the friends imitate each other's desires. When Valentine falls in love with Silvia, so does Proteus, despite the fact that Proteus has been in love with Julia. Proteus tries to resist: but in debating with Valentine the relative merits of Silvia and Julia, Proteus finally agrees to the superiority of Silvia. He falls now for Silvia, but cannot avoid a suspicion that his new love for Silvia has more to do with Valentine's desire for her than any intrinsic quality that Silvia herself may possess. He says:

> Is it mine eye, or Valentinus' praise,
> Her true perfection or my false transgression,
> That makes me reasonless, to reason thus?[16]

His suspicions are well founded. The play bears out that it was indeed Valentine's desire for Silvia that sparked Proteus' passion for her. But equally interesting is the fact that Valentine's own desire for Silvia *increases* once Proteus comes onboard. No doubt that was Valentine's motivation, albeit unconscious, for praising Silvia to Proteus. Valentine senses at some level that he needs the validation of his friend's agreement in order for him to be able to trust and enjoy his own desire. Valentine "deliberately" draws his friend into imitating his desire, in order that he, Valentine, might imitate what he sees in Proteus. He sees his own desire for Silvia reflected in Proteus as in a mirror, and since it appears to come from a source outside himself, it feels validating, and shores-up his own feeble subjectivity. Of course, Valentine does not wish to turn Proteus into an actual rival, much less to lose Silvia's affections to Proteus. Like Collatine, he wants imitation, but only enough so as to validate his own superiority. But Shakespeare reveals what his characters do not realize: that the same mimetic force that bonds friendships also tears them apart. Imitation of the other's desire is the basis for shared friendship, but it is also the basis for rivalry. Mimetic desire is at the bottom of both the best and the worst of human relations.

An important principle to understand is that as rivalries intensify, the object of desire over which the parties are fighting tends to become less and less central, as the rivals become more and more obsessed with each other. At a certain level of intensity the rivals will lose interest in what had been the original bone of contention (the desired object), and become obsessed with each other, scrutinizing and imitating each other with intense exactitude. This is because they always were – even from the very beginning of the competition, when their thoughts and feelings were so full of the beloved object – imitating each other's desire. For each of them – even from the very beginning – the object was so highly valued because the other held it in such high regard. As, during the course of their competition, the rivals naturally come to occupy more time and space in each other's mental and emotional life, rage, frustration, and fear stoke the desire to triumph over the opponent, until eventually that desire surpasses the original desire for the beloved object, sometimes suppressing it entirely – even *destroying* it for the sake of victory. At this point the object has ceased to be the real motivating factor. Each rival desires more than anything else the sweet savor of triumph over the other, and they reinforce this desire within each other just as they had the original desire. The more intensely each desires defeat of the other, the more intensely that same desire is copied and mirrored back by the other.

To use an ancient example, the battle portrayed in the Iliad had been provoked by the Trojan prince Paris absconding with Helen, wife of the Spartan king, Menelaus. But by the time the Illiad picks up the tale, the Greeks have already been encamped on the shores near Troy attempting to wage war on the Trojans for ten years! No doubt the war had long since ceased to be about Helen, even if her name continued to be invoked on the battlefield. The battle was now about rivalry pure and simple. As Homer makes plain, the Greeks desire more than anything the glory (*kudos*) that comes from crushing Trojans, and the Trojans desire the glory of crushing Greeks. Who among the Greeks or the Trojans other than a handful of privileged royalty had ever seen Helen, anyway? And even they last saw her ten years ago! Everything, once again, was advertising and reputation. "Helen" was a myth, in the sense that there never was a woman whose beauty was objectively and measurably beyond dispute; there was only a bragging husband who no doubt desired Helen because she was desired by others, and who by his own desire incited others also to desire her, as did Collatine. The more men who joined the ranks as admirers, the more the "Helen" craze gained in specific gravity of mimetic attraction. In that sense, the entire Trojan War might just as readily have been fought over Silly Bandz.

By now it will be clear that the designations "model" and "obstacle" are subject to change at any moment: like yin and yang, each contains the other. Every model is an obstacle waiting to happen, and every obstacle is an invitation to imitation. There exists a continuity, with extremes on either end, all the way from the stable and healthy imitation of a positive role model, to the pathology of the underground man, or the travesty of the Trojan war.

Mediation

Before we end this chapter, I must touch briefly once again on the idea of *mediation*, remembering that this designates the function of a model (or obstacle) in passing on – mediating – mimetic desire to an imitator. Girard delineates two types of mediation, *internal* and *external*. I have never liked these terms because they do not easily convey their meaning. But we could explain them in this way. There are many factors which make it likely, unlikely, or impossible that I should become entangled in an actual rivalry with someone, a rivalry involving a direct exchange of hostilities. For example, in the era before mass communication it was impossible for the average person to become involved in a direct rivalry with someone who lived any distance from one's home town. It would also have been impossible for a peasant to engage a king in an immediate personal rivalry, both because of lack of access, and because of deeply ingrained beliefs about the sanctity of royalty, and rigorously observed social protocols that kept the classes separated. For similar reasons it would have been most unlikely that a lower class individual could develop a rivalry with a nobleman.

These things were either impossible or very difficult because in order for a real rivalry to develop – that is, a series of ongoing, personal hostile encounters – there must be the possibility of direct exchange between the parties. And for exchange to take place, the parties must be on roughly the same level economically and socially, and able to have real, genuine contact. Of course, a peasant can build up resentment against a nobleman, like Dostoevsky's character in relation to the officer. But the rivalry there, as mentioned earlier, was all one-way, and existed only in the underground man's imagination. He could not develop a direct rivalry with the officer because of the vast social gulf that existed between them. They did not operate within the same immediate circle of exchange.

Which brings us to Girard's terms *internal* and *external mediation*. When a child extols and imitates, say, her heroine ballerina, the heroine exists outside of the child's circle of equal exchange within which a two-way, mutual rivalry could develop. Even if the child is in a direct relationship with the ballerina, who may, for example, be her instructor, the ballerina still exists in the eyes of the admiring child on an exalted plane that makes any thought of rivalry both ridiculous and taboo. This is what Girard means by external mediation: the mediator, the model, is *external* to one's circle of relationships based on equal exchanges, and so the child's imitation can safely proceed, at least for a while, without likelihood of the model turning into an obstacle/rival.

Another kind of external mediation is when the model doesn't even exist in real life, but is something like a character in a book or movie. Obviously, no exchange whatsoever is possible with such a character. Don Quixote's external mediator is the knight, Amadis of Gaul, whose great exploits he reads about in his collection of romance novels. Quixote will never come into direct rivalry with Amadis, not only because is Amadis an exalted being whom Quixote would never dream of challenging, but also because Amadis simply does not exist.

Internal mediation, on the other hand, occurs when the model exists *within* one's immediate circle of exchange: when, for example, the child decides to imitate a classmate's desire for a certain toy. Because she and her classmate move in the same circle of exchange, the possibility of a hostile encounter centered on the toy as object of desire is very real.

What begins as external mediation can develop into internal mediation. An example is the master-apprentice relationship mentioned earlier. Initially, the master is external to the lowly apprentice's circle of equal exchange, exalted by the admiring gaze of the inexperienced young apprentice. The relationship will be governed by rules, spoken and unspoken, meant to keep the apprentice "in his place," so that he cannot have with the master the same kind of intimacy he enjoys with friends, family, and others on his same level. These social rules serve to keep the relationship safe from violent exchanges (though they cannot, of course, prevent resentments and passive-aggressive strategies). But once the apprentice achieves a level of independence and recognition that moves him into the master's immediate circle, the worlds of mediator and imitator begin to mesh, and the relationship becomes vulnerable to violent exchange.

Chapter Two
Mimesis In Genesis 2 and 3

Mimeticism is the original source of all man's troubles, desires, and rivalries, his tragic and grotesque misunderstandings, the source of all disorder...

René Girard, *The Scapegoat* [17]

Now the serpent was more subtle than any other wild creature that the LORD God had made. (Gen. 2:1)

‡‡

We are now in a position to explore some of the insights the concept of mimetic desire can yield when used as a lens for the interpretation of biblical texts. The following interpretation of the second and third chapters of Genesis follows in broad pattern the approach of Jean-Michel Oughourlian in his excellent book, *The Genesis of Desire.*[18] Oughourlian is a practicing psychiatrist at the American Hospital of Paris, and professor of clinical psychopathology at the University of Paris. He has been a close collaborator of Girard's for over thirty years, and Girard's main dialogue partner in *Things Hidden Since The Foundation Of The World.* While Oughourlian may perhaps be called a Giardian, he is of course not Girard, nor am I Oughourlian. What follows is my own synthesis. Its purpose is not a faithful point for point reproduction of Girard's precise thoughts on the subject, but an attempt to demonstrate how fruitfully the mimetic concepts discussed in chapter one can be applied to biblical interpretation. Additionally, the reader should realize that what follows is not meant to eliminate or invalidate every other interpretive approach to the Genesis text, nor does it pretend to say everything that can be said about the text, even from a Girardian standpoint.

Desire is *Mimetic*

Mimesis is foundational for the Girardian perspective, and it also proves to be foundational for the Bible, which yields mimetic insight in its very first story about humanity in the Garden of Eden. The biblical text is savvy concerning mimetic desire to the point of positing it as the basic fact about the structure of human relations. For Oughourlian (and Girard), the Genesis story is not literal history. There never was a "once-upon-a-time" when human beings existed in a perfectly blissful state, and from which they subsequently "fell." Rather, Genesis describes allegorically what *happens* in human relationships everywhere and always, over and over again, as mimetic desire is birthed and unleashed, and leads to rivalry. Human beings do occasionally experience a kind of fusional bliss, an Edenic harmony, especially in romantic love relationships, when the partners are totally caught up in each other and unable to imagine life without the other. But this relational Eden is doomed, and does not last in the real world, as we are about to see.

> *Now the serpent was more subtle than any other wild creature that the LORD God had made. He said to the woman, "Did God say, `You shall not eat of any tree of the garden'?" And the woman said to the serpent, "We may eat of the fruit of the trees of the garden; but God said, `You shall not eat of the fruit of the tree which is in the midst of the garden, neither shall you touch it, lest you die.'" But the serpent said to the woman, "You will not die. For God knows that when you eat of it your eyes will be opened, and you will be like God, knowing good and evil." So when the woman saw that the tree was good for food, and that it was a delight to the eyes, and that the tree was to be desired to make one wise, she took of its fruit and ate; and she also gave some to her husband, and he ate.* (Gen. 2:1-6)

Something not commonly remarked is that this story offers nothing to indicate that in and of itself the tree was an exceptional enticement. We are told in 2:9 that "Out of the ground the LORD God made to grow every tree that is pleasant to the sight and good for food..." The tree of knowledge was thus not exceptional in providing pleasing, edible fruit and a pleasing appearance. In fact, it was just like all the rest. Now, the story could have been told in such a way as to make a big deal out of the tree's appearance, making it an object of extraordinary beauty or alluring enticement. Instead, there is nothing about this tree to distinguish it from the other trees, except perhaps that it is located in the middle of the garden, though nothing remarkable is made of that fact in the story. (Some translations say in the "midst" of the garden, meaning, presumably, in the thick of things but not necessarily in the precise center). The tree does possess the distinction of being named by God, who calls it the tree of the knowledge of good and evil, when he warns the humans not to eat of it, but the humans can have no understanding of what that means, nor does the name itself make the tree extraordinarily desirable. Bear in mind that when God first warns them about eating the fruit of the tree, Eve has not yet heard the suggestion that the tree will make her "wise" and godlike. All she knows is that God has told them not to eat of this tree, which he calls "the knowledge of good and evil."

Now, this should be an easy command to keep in view of the fact that the tree itself is unexceptional. Their hunger can easily be satisfied by any of the other lovely trees in the garden without the least sense of deprivation. But Genesis is telling the story of the origination of *desire,* which is cultural, not appetite, which is biological. Cultural desire is mimetic, and makes distinctions based on envy and rivalry. My appetite might be satisfied biologically by any breakfast cereal on the market, but *desire* wants only Wheaties. The main point, once again, is that we are dealing with an object unremarkable in itself, *but which is about to become extremely desirable to Eve,* and the birth of this desire is the point of the story.

To make this point as clearly as I can, since it is so important, consider once again how the Eden story might have been told. The tree of knowledge might have appeared like the cosmic tree of the

Upanishads, called Asvattha, with its roots in the sky and its branches growing downward to cover the earth. It might have been like the world tree of Norse myth, Yggdrasill, which grew like a pole through this world and the lower and upper realms. It might have been a tree guarded by an invisible dragon, such as one finds in traditional Persian myths. Or perhaps a talking tree similar to that of the Southwest American Yaquis. It might have displayed a unique, golden and shining fruit, which emitted a luscious fragrance. Had the story been told in some such way, however, it would have displayed an entirely different understanding of the nature of desire. The tree would have been an intrinsically captivating and alluring object, basically promoting the "romantic lie," discussed in the previous chapter, that the object possesses inherent desirability – which is why one desires it. In this kind of portrayal, desire originates within the self alone in direct response to the desirable object. But Genesis does not portray the tree in this way, because it has a radically different understanding of desire. That is why the story introduces a third party.

God as Obstacle and Rival

When God discovers the humans living in shameful awareness of their nakedness, he immediately asks "Who told you that you were naked?" God asks "Who?" because he knows that in order for desire to come to birth, a mediator is required. It could perhaps be said that the serpent is that mediator: the serpent desires the fruit, and Eve copies the serpent's desire. But the serpent's real role is to direct Eve's attention towards God, who, it is insinuated, has forbidden this particular tree because its fruit is very precious, able to confer upon God the knowledge that makes him divine. The serpent suggests that God is deliberately withholding the fruit of this tree from the humans, hording it in order to monopolize divinity. God has forbidden it not because he is concerned for human welfare, but simply in order to prevent them from grasping something he wants to keep for himself.

The logic is clear: if God is withholding the fruit of this tree it must be because he desires it for himself – and therefore the fruit must be highly desirable. *God,* then, becomes the primary mediator of desire; not by virtue of how God is in himself, but by how Eve perceives God thanks to the serpent's suggestion. It is a lie that God is in rivalry with the humans and therefore wants to withhold the fruit. (As if the creature could ever – fruit or no fruit – become the Creator!) God's prohibition expresses a loving desire to prevent creation's stable system of differences, which provide the basis for Adam and Eve's flourishing as creatures, from lapsing back into chaos. For if the creature becomes confused about the fundamental difference between itself and its Creator, the whole structure of creation is threatened.

But Eve comes to believe the serpent's suggestion that God is withholding something from her because he desires it for himself, and God thus becomes in her mind an obstacle; and it is for this very reason that the object, the fruit, begins to look desirable. In the Genesis text, Eve does not begin with the object, which by virtue of its exceptional beauty leads her to infer that God must desire it as much as she does; rather, she begins with the serpent's suggestion that God desires this otherwise rather undistinguished object, and is withholding it from Eve – *therefore* the object becomes transfigured in Eve's eyes into something so highly desirable that she is actually willing to violate the prohibition laid down by her own Creator, in order to possess it.[19]

Eve imitates the desire of her model-turned-obstacle – God – and now begins to imitate God (or what she takes to be God) as obstacle-turned-model. This is the very process we examined in the previous chapter when we discussed how desire is birthed and formed in the human self through mimesis, by imitating the desire of another. There we saw how the model can become an obstacle, and also how the obstacle can become in turn a model for imitation. Once Eve believes that the prohibition against eating the fruit is God's way of protecting his own ardent desire for the fruit, God immediately becomes in her mind an obstacle, and thus a rival. And she reproduces the rival's desire within herself.

Genesis shows us, therefore, the mimetic nature of desire: *in order for Eve to conceive desire within herself, that desire has to be modeled by another*. It does not matter that the modeling in this case is imaginary (since God really does not desire the fruit as Eve believes). It is enough that Eve believes it to be true, and thus constructs in her mind an image of a false God, making this, in a sense, the first instance of idolatry in the Bible. Eve creates an idol, conceived as a divine obstacle in rivalry with her over possession of a precious object. She has no idea that the fruit appears desirable to her only because she is copying the (imaginary) desire of a rival.

The fruit is a symbol for what we "eat" when we become mimetic consumers of the desires of others. As Oughourlian says,[20] it is a fruit that the human stomach will never be able to digest, and it will wreak havoc with our health. Models (even positive ones) will turn into obstacles and rivals, and obstacle-rivals will become models and gods.

Had the biblical narrative named it directly, it would probably have called the desire that arose within Eve covetousness or envy, following the tenth commandment of the Decalogue. By downplaying the extraordinariness of the tree itself, and elevating the role of the serpent and its suggestion that God is an obstacle, the story demonstrates its profound understanding that *the source of the desire called envy is not the coveted object*; the source is the *mediator*, who, by modeling desire, transforms the object in the eyes of the imitator, rendering it desirable. Thus Genesis shows an intuitive grasp of desire as a mimetic phenomenon.

(Let us recall once again that basic physiological needs and appetites are not mimetic. We do not need a model to make water desirable when we are thirsty, and Eve did not need a model to create desire for the satisfaction of hunger. But as soon as we enter the *cultural* realm – which is what this story in Genesis is really about – psychological momentum is initiated, and identity created, by the imitation of models of desire.)

Idolatry and the Serpent

God is God precisely because he exists beyond the possibility of entering into model-obstacle dynamics with human beings. From the standpoint of mimetic theory, that is why God is transcendent. The moment Eve imitates the serpent's suggestion and turns God into an idol-rival, transcendence collapses into immanence (Oughourlian's nice phrase[21]), which means that the infinite collapses into the finite, and the Creator becomes confused with the creation (in the mind of the creature, of course, not in actuality). From the standpoint of mimetic theory, what marks the relationship with the transcendent is that *God models desire and humans imitate, and there is no movement in the opposite direction*: humans do not model desire for God, and God does not imitate human desire. (Though in subsequent history pagan gods will do exactly that. Precisely because they are idols – i.e., projections of the human psyche – they will become involved in relationships with each other and with human beings that will display all the machinations of mimetic rivalry and violence.)

In relations among human beings, on the other hand, imitation is in *both* directions: one person models and the other imitates, but the imitator also becomes a model who reinforces the original model's own desire. (An example of this given earlier was the relationship between Valentine and Proteus in Shakespeare's *Two Gentlemen of Verona*.) This is the stuff of human relations, but it is not this way with God, who does not need human beings to reinforce his own desire, and who does not imitate human desire. But Eve's relationship with God has now taken on this purely human quality. She has pulled God, as it were, into the orb of human "interdividuality," where people reciprocally model and imitate each other, leading to the formation of rivalries. A God capable of such relations is not a transcendent God but an idol, a projection of mimetic rivalry. This story of the way in which human relations are knit together by desire leading to rivalry is Genesis' portrayal of how human beings are actually constituted within historical space and time. To emphasize the point, Genesis will go on to narrate important moments within that history, which turns out to be nothing less than a history of violent rivalries: Cain and Abel, Sarah and Hagar, Isaac and Ishmael, Esau and Jacob, Rachel and Leah, Joseph and his brothers, and so on. Genesis 3 shows us that the root of all these rivalries is the envious desire to which we spur one another as we play the mimetic model-obstacle game.

But what, then, is the serpent in this story? An allegory for mimetic rivalry itself. To listen to the voice of the serpent is to hearken to the urgings of mimetic rivalry. The fruit appears desirable to Eve when she is, as Oughourlian puts it, bitten and injected with the venom of mimetic rivalry. From this moment on, through all the history narrated in Genesis (and throughout the Bible), the serpent of mimetic rivalry will stealthily slither its way into all human relationships, ruining the Eden of perfect union before it can even get started. The self is constituted by rivalry born of desire before we even become aware of it: Genesis makes Esau and Jacob rivals even *in the womb!*

When God curses the serpent, he is cursing mimetic rivalry itself. He tells the serpent that he will put enmity between it and Eve's "seed." Life for human beings, in other words, will become a continual struggle against rivalrous desire. The real struggle is not with the rival – the real struggle is with mimetic rivalry as such, the serpent itself. God says in 3:15 that the serpent will strike at the heel. The venom reaches us through our most vulnerable spot ("Achilles heel"), and the only way to fight against this "subtle" or "crafty" creature that insinuates itself into even the most tender and vulnerable relationships is to crush its head (3:15), where the venom is. One cannot fight mimetic rivalry piecemeal. One cannot simply cut off its tail; one must resolutely crush its head. It was a wise reader of Scripture who first saw in this text an allusion to a Messiah who alone could accomplish such a victory.

The Opening of the Eyes

In Gen. 2:16 God tells Adam that eating of the tree of the knowledge of good and evil will result in death; but the serpent tells Eve that the result will not be death, but the opening of her eyes so that she will become like God (or like "the gods"), knowing good and evil. Gen. 3:7 confirms that eating the fruit does indeed result in an opening of the eyes ("Then the eyes of both were opened…"). But what is it that they perceive with those wonderful, new open eyes? That they are naked! What happened to the serpent's promise that they would become like gods, knowing good and evil? Was that simply a lie? Yes, it was a lie, but not *simply* a lie.

Adam and Eve do indeed become like gods, but the operative word is "like" – they have not become gods, they have only become *like* gods, in highly ironic fashion. They have become gods *to each other,* as Girard has said. Their godlikeness consists in the fact that they now mimic, in a perverted way, what God did "in the beginning." God had established a cosmos out of chaos by creating a system of stable differences, which constituted a perfect harmony and were not perceived as differences in any divisive or negative sense. But the humans create distinctions generated by the violence of mimetic rivalry, fracturing God's unified creation.

Mimetic rivalry does indeed generate "knowledge of good and evil" – meaning a knowledge constituted by violent oppositions. In Genesis 1, God pronounced what he had made "Good" – but this is not the same good as that generated by mimetic rivalry, which is a "good" that always stands antagonistically over against some "evil." In Genesis 1 God never pronounces anything evil. All is Good, all is perfect unity. What rivalry calls good, on the other hand, always stands in direct opposition to evil. This good and evil arise together as a distinctly human perception born of the machinations of mimetic desire.

Human history thus becomes the kaleidoscopic reflection of a thousand variations of this kind of "knowledge of good and evil," with human activity characterized by wars and interpersonal hostilities based upon each side's claimed possession of the "good," along with a labeling of the other side as evil. Utopian schemes, dictatorships, and even democracies will distinguish their own brands of good and evil, and seek to create the good society by eliminating evil-doers who threaten to pervert the structure. All over the planet human beings will gather themselves into associations large and small, defined by their perception of "good" and characterized by attempts, both crass and subtle, to exclude the evil other. All of this will be experienced as what we call "morality," which is a function of the fall into rivalrous desire.[22]

Unlike the stable, enduring differences-in-unity established by the Creator, the differentiations of morality will be shifting, unstable, subjective, confusing and unreliable. People who believe they possess knowledge of the good will kill others who think they possess it. Acts will be good in one context and evil in another, good if performed by the right person or at the right time, but evil if performed by the wrong person, or at the wrong time. Exceptions will multiply, casuistry will become an art. Good and evil will change from culture to culture, and from one time period to another, defined always from the point of view of the one who does the judging. People will undergo conversions and shift allegiances, taking what they once took as truth to be nothing but a lie, and what they once understood as an evil to be a good. They will even believe that in persecuting victims they are doing God's will. Circumstances will justify everything, yet claims to objectivity in judgment will be as numerous as they will be contradictory. Like Cain, humans will be doomed to wander as exiles through this landscape of shifting sand, never able to recover the real stability, security, clarity, and unity of Eden. Like Cain, they will establish communities and build cities sheltered behind huge walls in order to differentiate themselves from the enemy other, the rival, the one to be feared. From Hammurabi, sixth king of Babylon, to George W. Bush, "justice" will prevail against axes of evil defined by the interests of the king: "...Anu and Bel called me, Hammurabi, the exalted prince, the worshipper of the gods, to cause justice to prevail in the land, to destroy the wicked and the evil..."[23] Those "wicked and evil" will be defined, of course, in accordance with Hammurabi's own interests; and it is Hammurabi's power of violence that will create justice by destroying them.

Fear is one of the first results of mimetic rivalry. One lives in fear of the rival, which necessitates protecting oneself. One does not reveal one's vulnerabilities. Adam hides from God, his new rival, and explains, "I was afraid, because I was naked." (3:10) And just as they now fear God and hide themselves among the trees for cover, so Adam and Eve fear each other, and seek to "cover up" their vulnerable parts. Their unity is shattered; their differences have become oppositional. Even that which is most basic, sexuality, is now subject to rivalry. In an effort to make peace, and prevent the eruption of violence which is the natural result of rivalry, Adam and Eve cover over the differences with fig leaves. But it doesn't help. This just creates another obstacle that suggests something is being withheld – thus enflaming desire all the more. The unity of love becomes a clash of erotic powers.

The story of Eden is not relating literal history, as though human beings really did originally dwell in a paradisal state from which they fell, anymore than Eve was literally created from a rib. Historically, Girard understands hominization (the process of becoming human) as a process that occurred as a result of the operation of mimetic mechanisms among ape-like prehistoric creatures: and we will be examining that later in great detail. Genesis 3 is the story of how *every day* we humans turn the world into a theater of competing goods and evils, a world of clashing differences created by eyes turned covetous by the venom of mimetic rivalry. As an allegory, this story reveals to us how subtle are the machinations of mimetic desire (thus the serpent is said to be more subtle than any other creature), and how devastating are the consequences as it blossoms into rivalry even within our most intimate human relationships – and of course with God.

> *Then the LORD God said, "Behold, the man has become like one of us, knowing good and evil; and now, lest he put forth his hand and take also of the tree of life, and eat, and live for ever" – therefore the LORD God sent him forth from the garden of Eden, to till the ground from which he was taken. He drove out the man; and at the east of the garden of Eden he placed the cherubim, and a flaming sword which turned every way, to guard the way to the tree of life.* (Gen. 3:22-24)

The image of God portrayed in the early stories of Genesis are not, in my opinion, entirely free of violence. The deity they portray is not the God of love we meet in the New Testament. Nevertheless, in the story of Adam and Eve's expulsion from Eden, divine mercy rather than wrath seems to be God's primary motive. On first reading, we may almost be seduced, like Eve, to the view that we are dealing with a God fearful of human competition, a God in rivalry with humans, who is afraid of their accession to the power of divine knowledge, and seeks to block them from attaining an immortality that he would arrogate to himself alone. And, indeed, it may be that the Hebrew author began with a mythological tale that cast God in such terms (the rival-god occurs all the time in pagan myth); but if so, he significantly transformed it. It is difficult to imagine (even granted the highly anthropocentric images of God in Genesis 2 and 3) that the Hebrew writer and/or editors seriously conceive God as fearful of human competition. That perception was clearly hatched by instigation of the serpent. In fact, God mercifully *helps* the humans to cope with their new situation by clothing them. Even after their expulsion from the garden God continues in relationship with Adam and Eve: they worship him, and Eve begets children, she says, "with the help of the Lord." Just as God originally forbade the fruit, not to safeguard his own "stash," but to prevent Adam and Eve from tasting mimetic rivalry and its consequences, so God's barring of the Tree of Life is not the self-preserving act of a divine rival, but an act of *mercy*, lest the humans live forever ensnared within the nightmare of mimetic rivalry. Should that happen they would become gods like those of the ancient world: eternally subject to passions, lusts, and fear, and eternally involved in rivalry and reciprocal violence. Only a spiteful and vengeful God could desire and allow their achievement of such an eternity.

As it is, the humans have not become gods, and they do not possess immortality. But, God says, they have become "like one of us" in that they now possess the ability to make discriminations between good and evil. But such power cannot not lead them to the true Good (God's will, or God's *desire*), because "good" to them is now a function of mimetic rivalry: my desire is good, your desire is bad (even though, at bottom, we are really imitating each other's desire!). And here we are, living in time, not eternity; east of Eden, not in the Garden. There is a serpent among us which the Genesis story intuitively understands as a mimetic phenomenon giving rise to desire and issuing in rivalry and violence. Not even the most intense love affair can escape the fractures and divisions constantly introduced into human relationships by the serpent of mimetic rivalry. All we can do is become conscious of the serpent's stealth attacks, and practice an imitation of God rather than the idols of human desire. But within the closed-system of human reciprocity the knowledge of this practice is not something that arises naturally. We cannot possibly crush the serpent's head on our own. But we can, perhaps, attach ourselves to someone who has, as revealed in the New Testament Gospels.

Chapter Three
Scandal and Desire In the Gospels

Woe to the world because of scandals!
(Matt. 18:7)

The Gospels reveal all kinds of human relationships that at first seem incomprehensible and fundamentally irrational. These can and must ultimately be reduced to a single unifying factor: mimeticism.

René Girard, *The Scapegoat* [24]

‡‡

What is "Scandal?"

Although I chose to discuss Genesis first, the theme of mimetic desire is massively abundant in the New Testament and was central to Jesus' teaching and practice. In fact, it is in the light of Jesus that mimetic phenomena are truly revealed in their full significance. As Michael Hardin has convincingly argued in "The Jesus Driven Life,"[25] the Bible must be read through the "lens" provided by Jesus in his life and teachings, all of which center around themes related to mimetic phenomena. It is Jesus's understanding of mimetic desire and rivalry, and his nonviolent engagement with the violence resulting from such phenomenon, that provide for us a key for interpreting the entire Bible.

Jesus arrives upon the scene almost, one might say, like an alien from outer space, so disconnected does he seem from the mimetic realities that dominate and enslave human beings. His whole ministry was a revelation of people's bondage to mimetic desire, and a demonstration of the way out. Jesus' view of the human condition as characterized by mimetic enslavement is encapsulated in the New Testament by a single term, *scandal* (Greek: *scandalon*, σκανδαλον). Before moving to Jesus' solution, it will be helpful to examine in some depth his view of the problem.

> *Then he strictly charged the disciples to tell no one that he was the Christ. From that time Jesus began to show his disciples that he must go to Jerusalem and suffer many things from the elders and chief priests and scribes, and be killed, and on the third day be raised. And Peter took him and began to rebuke him, saying, "God forbid, Lord! This shall never happen to you." But he turned and said to Peter, "Get behind me, Satan! You are a hindrance to me; for you are not on the side of God, but of men."* (Matt. 16:20-23)

Jesus has "set his face" toward Jerusalem, determining to go there even though he knows it will mean his suffering and death. Why on earth their revolutionary leader would want to do that, the disciples cannot figure. Only Peter is bold enough to confront him directly: "God forbid, Lord! This shall never happen to you!" The response this draws from Jesus is astonishing: "Get behind me, Satan!" Of course, the Gospels present Jesus' death in Jerusalem as the climactic point and purpose of his ministry, so any attempt to frustrate his plans in that regard would certainly warrant a rebuke – especially since remaining faithful to such a mission would have been no easy matter. It must have required intense concentration and focus to maintain the view towards Jerusalem, and Jesus could allow no room for entertaining "escapist" fantasies. At every point, Jesus had to resist the power of suggestion which came to him from all who knew him, all those well-wishers who would rather have him live for them than die for God. In offering such a suggestion, Peter makes himself an obstacle, a hindrance, to Jesus. He positions himself in front of Jesus, whether physically or spiritually, blocking his way – thus the comment, "Get thee behind me…" We learned in the first chapter of this book how obstacles become objects of fascination, by the sheer fact of being an obstacle. When something blocks my path or my intention, it has (or sets itself up as having) power over me; and as much as I might despise it, I will be tempted to imitate it precisely because it this power. I recall the reader's attention to Dostoevsky's *The Underground Man,* and the protagonist's relationship with the officer whom he encountered initially as an obstacle.

What I am hinting at here is that the biblical story is showing us much more than Peter's sin of trying to block Jesus' journey to Jerusalem. It is giving us a paradigm case of mimetic relationality, and defining for us the very essence of mimetic rivalry. When Peter contradicts Jesus' prediction of suffering and death, he sets himself up as a *model* for Jesus to imitate. Peter wants Jesus to imitate his desire that Jesus should not suffer and die, should not follow through with his mission. Peter-the-obstacle is thus at one and the same time Peter-the-model. More accurately, he is a potential model: it remains for Jesus either to accept the model and begin imitating Peter, or to reject it. The essential nature of Peter's opposition to Jesus is that he puts his desire forward as an alternative to the Father's desire which Jesus faithfully imitates. And Jesus' response is so harsh because he is in danger of succumbing to the suggestive power of mimetic desire. He is in danger of accepting the offer, allowing Peter to become his model, in place of the Father. He is in danger of imitating his opposition. Jesus therefore deals with it sharply and immediately: "Get thee behind me, Satan!"

Jesus' point is not to label Peter as "Satan," but to name the mimetic dynamic that threatens to capture and enslave him, should he yield to it. The danger is defined in the comment that follows: "You are a stumbling block to me; for you are not setting your mind on God's interests, but man's." (NAS translation) Peter, in other words, is more interested in imitating other human beings than God. For the desire that Peter expresses to Jesus is not simply his own – our desires are never simply our own desires: they are borrowed, always, from others. Peter is merely echoing the sentiments of many others. He has set his mind on their interests, not God's. It is the "crowd" that speaks through Peter; and Jesus – alone, as always – must resist it in order to remain faithful to God his Father.

When Jesus tells Peter that he is being a hindrance, or "stumbling block," the Greek word, as mentioned earlier, is *scandalon* (σκανδαλον), which we may translate, with Girard, as *scandal.* "You are a scandal to me," says Jesus. Our contemporary society understands by "scandal" an outrageous event that shocks moral sensibilities. But Girard has seen that the New Testament's use of the word denotes something much more specific, and concerns mimetic desire and rivalry. We see that usage operating here when Jesus calls Peter a scandal. "You are a scandal to me!" Does Jesus mean that Peter has shocked his moral sensibilities? Probably not, since during his ministry Jesus encountered many ethically depraved people, and was not shocked by it; on the contrary, Jesus' behavior was shocking to many others precisely because he was willing to associate with characters considered unscrupulous or depraved. Does Jesus perhaps mean nothing more than that Peter wants to trip him up (stumbling block), or block his way? Yet Jesus encountered many who attempted to trip him up publicly in debate, or even to kill him, but he did not address them as Satan, or call them a scandal. So, what then is the meaning of this term "scandal?"

Girard gives us his understanding of the New Testament meaning of this term in *I See Satan Fall Like Lightning*: "...'scandal' means, not one of those ordinary obstacles that we avoid easily after we run into it the first time, but a paradoxical obstacle that is almost impossible to avoid: the more this obstacle, or scandal, repels us, the more it attracts us."[26] On the basis of this definition, we see that Jesus says Peter is a scandal to him because Jesus is repelled by Peter's suggestion – *and at the same time attracted to it and tempted by it.* Were Jesus not able to overcome this temptation, and put it decisively "behind" him, he would fall into what Girard calls a state of scandal; that is, he would be "scandalized." Dostoevsky's "underground man" is an extreme, caricatured portrait of a scandalized person, at once repelled and attracted by the obstacle/model (the officer), utterly obsessed with it, and unable to put it behind him. To be scandalized is thus to be in a double-bind state: both attracted and repelled at the same time. Model-obstacle relationships are like a Mobius strip – a strip of material that has been twisted before the ends are joined, so that if one starts "walking" on one side of the strip, one will end up on the opposite side upon returning to the starting point. Model and obstacle continuously depend upon and meld into one another. When I am attracted to a model and drawn in by it, I make a tacit admission that the Being of the model is higher than mine: that's why I wish to imitate it, so I can possess the same quality of Being as the model. But this "highness" of the model puts the imitator in a subordinate position, thus making the model a potential obstacle.

The opposite is also true: encountering an obstacle that blocks or challenges my way puts me in a subordinate position, and I may succumb to the need to overcome the obstacle, to cast it down. But in order to do so I will have to become just as powerful, cunning, or potent as the obstacle – thus turning it into a model which I imitate. To be in the state of scandal is thus to be locked in a double-bind condition, unable to find a way off the Mobius strip of model-obstacle bondage.

Rivals are always in this double-bind state of scandal, since they at one and the same time repel and fascinate each another. If Jesus allows Peter to become his rival, he will become scandalized by Peter. He will start to imitate Peter as model, while fighting Peter as obstacle – and this dynamic will only increase in its level of intensity and violence. To be truly free, Jesus must avoid rivalry with Peter, or anyone else. And he does this by imitating only his Father, for his Father (his "Abba") is not in rivalry with any human being.

Contemporary examples of scandal are easy to find. Wherever a rivalry exists, the participants are in a state of scandal: they have been "scandalized." Rivals are, by Girardian definition, scandalized by each other, and the more intense the rivalry, the more fascinated the rivals become with each other and the more impossible it becomes to break free from the double-bind. In really intense cases we are talking about something very much like addiction. In fact, addictions like gambling and sex can be understood as hyper-states of scandalization. In gambling, the fascinating obstacle is the *odds,* which must be overcome, and the more the gambler "stumbles" against the odds and is busted, the more fascinating the game becomes, and the more hold it has upon the addict. The addict desires the power she perceives her rival to possess. She wants to beat the odds, as the odds keep beating her. The personified odds becomes, then, the model to be imitated. Ultimately, what the scandalized gambler covets is not money, but triumph over the rival.

In certain forms of sexual addiction, the desirable woman is not the one most loving, or comfortable, or easy to obtain; rather, she is the unapproachable one, the coquette, the one hard-to-get. This type of woman stimulates a desire in her admirers that is inherently self-defeating because it craves an obstacle. And yet the unobtainable coquette is at the same time a model, whose desire the addict imitates. For the coquette desires *herself*: she appears not to need or want any man, but is happy and pleased with herself, and seems to possess a remarkable degree of independence and self-possession.

Although it is an illusion, the addict observes the coquette flaunting this "power," and he craves it. What he perceives as her desire for herself awakens his own desire for her. He is self-deceived, however, in convincing himself that he desires her because she is beautiful; his desire is an imitation, excited by the fascinated response of his neediness to an overwhelming obstacle that says to him, "You can't have me. I have myself, and have no need of you." He is scandalized.

This, then, is scandal, and it is a state of psychological and spiritual enslavement that is exaggerated in some, but which no human being escapes entirely. Everywhere people are pulled into relational orbit on the basis of a combination of the attraction of models and the repulsion of obstacles. This is as much as to say that everywhere rivalries, and potential rivalries, abound. And these relationships are essentially violent, whether the violence remains contained and hidden, or achieves expression.

This understanding of scandal lends poignancy to what Jesus had to say about scandalizing little children:

Whoever receives one such child in my name receives me; but whoever causes one of these little ones who believe in me to sin, it would be better for him to have a great millstone fastened round his neck and to be drowned in the depth of the sea. Woe to the world for temptations to sin! For it is necessary that temptations come, but woe to the man by whom the temptation comes! (Matt. 18:5-7)

It is most unfortunate that the RSV uses "sin" in its translation of this passage: "Whoever causes one of these little ones who believe in me to sin" and "temptations to sin," because the Greek text does not contain the word for sin. Some translations render the Greek as "stumble," which is better. Best of all, however, would be "scandalize" and "scandal." For what the Greek actually says is:

> Whoever receives one such child in my name receives me; but whoever *scandalizes* one of these little ones who believe in me, it would be better for him to have a great millstone fastened round his neck and to be drowned in the depth of the sea. Woe to the world because of *scandals*! For it is necessary that *scandals* come, but woe to the man by whom the *scandal* comes!

The reason modern versions do not translate the text this way is because translators have not grasped the fact that *scandalon* had its own special meaning for Jesus, being his way of speaking about the mimetic double-bind. Translators miss completely the meaning of this term, and thus resort to words like "sin" and "temptation" to render it, even though Greek has perfectly good words that could have been used here that mean precisely "sin" and "temptation," had that been the primary meaning the text wanted to convey.

That Girard has offered a cogent interpretation of scandal in this passage is confirmed by the broader context. Here is what comes immediately prior to Jesus' comment about scandalizing children:

At that time the disciples came to Jesus, saying, "Who is the greatest in the kingdom of heaven?" And calling to him a child, he put him in the midst of them, and said, "Truly, I say to you, unless you turn and become like children, you will never enter the kingdom of heaven. Whoever humbles himself like this child, he is the greatest in the kingdom of heaven." (Matt. 18:1-4 RSV)

The context is the theme of *rivalry.* Jesus' disciples are competing with one another for the position of greatest in the kingdom of heaven. This is the issue which Jesus is addressing when he calls before him a child and tells everyone that they must become like the child if they wish to enter the kingdom. The quality of the child to which Jesus draws attention is humility – quite appropriately so, since humility means not being not in rivalry with the other. Children wear their dependency on their sleeves. It is natural and becoming to them to do so, and they look ridiculous when they try to act like independent grownups. They learn everything by imitation, and they imitate their heroes and other models unashamedly and "innocently," up until the time when their hearts are inevitably broken – when they are "scandalized." They imitate trustingly and lovingly, and with a naivety regarding rivalry and its violence.

Jesus is enthusiastic about returning, in a sense, to this kind of non-rivalrous trust; but he is equally upset and disturbed when the trust of a child is destroyed by "scandal." This happens every time someone already initiated into the ways of the world offers him/herself to the child as a model, but at the same time does not want to be surpassed by the child, wants to keep the child down, enjoys wielding the power of influence over the child, profits from the child's admiration and uses the child as a secret means of validating his or her own desire. These are the operations of an enslavement which binds the child psychically to the model-obstacle dynamics that end in rivalry and violence. The one who mediates such desire to the child is a serpent indeed, injecting into the little one the most dangerous of venoms, and it calls forth Jesus' passionate declamation because he knows how it poisons the child's innocence. From the side of the model, scandal sneaks up upon the child unawares because the model is a hidden obstacle, stunting the child's growth into the full personhood that is *God's* desire for that child. And from the side of the obstacle, scandal takes possession of the child who is impressed and fascinated by the very power that smoothers, abuses, and stifles her. Either way, instead of growing into her own Self, the child becomes fixated on the model/obstacle, and grows up always measuring her Self against the model/obstacle, always wanting to be like the model/obstacle, craving to *be* the model/obstacle – all the while frustrated by the impossibility of such a wish, and forever the victim of covert or explicit violence, and the low self-esteem that the double-bind always generates.

Unless some major life-transforming shift occurs, the initial model-obstacle will generalize over the years into a self-perpetuating life-pattern, with many and various individuals playing the model-obstacle role throughout the child's life. These people are also scandalized. No one escapes this suffering, though some are poisoned more horribly than others. And some few do recover, becoming conscious of the double-bind and putting it "behind" them: "Get thee behind me, Satan!"

Jesus' disciples do not have this consciousness, but are stuck in scandal. They are scandals to each other. Each one of them wants to be the big guy, the greatest, the one who is the model that all the others will imitate and follow. In so asserting themselves they become obstacles to each other, rivals locked in a violence that surfaces in quarrels and jealousies, with which Jesus has to deal daily. Jesus is a realist: ""Woe to the world because of scandals! For it is necessary that scandals come…" He recognizes it and deals with it even among his closest associates.

But being common does not make it tolerable. In fact, to Jesus the state of scandal is utterly intolerable, whether one is the scandalizer or the scandalized (although, in point of fact, one cannot scandalize another without being a victim of scandal oneself). It is intolerable because it is the generator of the violence at the core of human relationships, yet no one wants to admit it is there. Admitting that one is scandalized feels like an insult to one's pride and independence – thus Jesus' brilliant move in holding up a naïve and humble child as the genuine model for a new humanity. So intolerable is scandal to Jesus that he resorts to extravagant metaphors in describing what one's reaction to it should be:

> *And if your hand or your foot scandalizes you, cut it off and throw it away; it is better for you to enter life maimed or lame than with two hands or two feet to be thrown into the eternal fire. And if your eye scandalizes you, pluck it out and throw it away; it is better for you to enter life with one eye than with two eyes to be thrown into the hell of fire.* (Matt. 18:8-9)

Not surprisingly, the RSV translates the above text as "if your hand or foot causes you to sin," giving the English reader no clue that the word used is actually *scandalize,* not sin. It is clear why Jesus is so adamant: the rivalrous relationship based on model/obstacle dynamics maims the whole person, including the "soul." Any length one must go to drain the poison will be worth it, ultimately. It will mean liberation from the hell of scandal, with its tormenting, fiery passions.

Scandal in Other Passages

This understanding of the term scandal helps us to understand many New Testament texts with deeper appreciation than the common translations allow. Take 1 John 2:9-10 (NAS) for example: "The one who says he is in the Light and yet hates his brother is in the darkness until now. The one who loves his brother abides in the Light and there is no cause for stumbling in him." In the Greek, the phrase translated "no cause for stumbling" is literally "there is no scandal in him." The imperative that we should go out of our way to avoid setting ourselves up as model/obstacle to the other, as well as to avoid succumbing to the seductive power of scandal ourselves, is key for the understanding of love that John is trying to elucidate. And, in fact, from the point of view of Girard's "interdividual psychology," which studies the mimetic dynamics of interpersonal relationships, the birth and development of scandal is indeed the primary corrupting factor in relationships, capable of destroying even the most intimate and loving unions. It was certainly the major operative factor that prevented Jesus' disciples from forming true community and entering into full communion with Jesus. The disciples were scandals to each other, each one wanting to thrust himself above the other as model/obstacle, constantly arguing and bickering over status and privilege.

Scandal epitomizes the crisis of the human condition as we find it expounded by Jesus, and constitutes the essence of a Girardian reading of "sin."[27] Given this understanding of the human condition, we can clearly see the relevance of Jesus' teachings. To demonstrate this we will limit ourselves, for reasons of space, mostly to examples from the Sermon on the Mount. There we read Jesus' exhortation to "love your enemies and pray for those who persecute you." (Matt. 5:44) This teaching, of course, characterized Jesus' entire ministry, and is a prescription for avoiding the snares of rivalry and its diabolic scandals. For rivalry cannot develop without mutual imitation. When the persecuted also persecutes, the parties become imitative doubles; but when the persecuted meets blows with prayers, reciprocal imitation is short-circuited, and scandal avoided. The entire passage is worth quoting:

> *You have heard that it was said, "An eye for an eye and a tooth for a tooth." But I say to you, Do not resist one who is evil. But if any one strikes you on the right cheek, turn to him the other also; and if any one would sue you and take your coat, let him have your cloak as well; and if any one forces you to go one mile, go with him two miles. Give to him who begs from you, and do not refuse him who would borrow from you. You have heard that it was said, "You shall love your neighbor and hate your enemy." But I say to you, Love your enemies and pray for those who persecute you, so that you may be sons of your Father who is in heaven; for he makes his sun rise on the evil and on the good, and sends rain on the just and on the unjust. For if you love those who love you, what reward have you? Do not even the tax collectors do the same? And if you salute only your brethren, what more are you doing than others? Do not even the Gentiles do the same? You, therefore, must be perfect, as your heavenly Father is perfect.* (5:38-48)

The *lex talionis* (literally, "law of retribution") which Jesus quotes – "an eye for an eye and a tooth for a tooth" – so central for one way of construing the meaning of justice, is really based upon imitation of the offender: you took out my eye, so I will take out yours. I must extract a pound of vengeance for your pound of crime: an equal exchange. The purpose of such laws was to limit the extent of vengeance, and prevent escalating vendettas; but Jesus wants to lead us out of the "economy of exchange" entirely, into an economy of mercy, generosity and grace. Only by returning evil with good can we avoid the implacable law of mimesis by which we become the mirror image of our enemy. Jesus' exhortation to "turn the other cheek" is a marvelous image for the surprising "Judo flip" he does with reciprocal violence. The natural imitative reaction is to return the blow exactly as it was delivered, copying the persecutor. Turning the other cheek is a deliberate, thoughtful act whose purpose is to interrupt the cycle of mimesis before it can escalate and ensnare both parties.

When Jesus was arrested, he had an opportunity to demonstrate what this meant in practice. Peter drew his sword and struck off the ear of the high priest's servant – which Jesus immediately healed – and this incident gave rise to Jesus' famous statement, "All who take the sword will perish by the sword," and his admonishment to Peter to put his sword back in its place. This, again, is the warning against the danger of reciprocal, imitative violence.

The Sermon on the Mount is full of allusions to people stuck in scandal and operating mimetically:

> *Beware of practicing your piety before men in order to be seen by them; for then you will have no reward from your Father who is in heaven. Thus, when you give alms, sound no trumpet before you, as the hypocrites do in the synagogues and in the streets, that they may be praised by men. Truly, I say to you, they have received their reward.* (Matt. 6:1-2)

The picture here is of those who set themselves up as models of religious piety for others to imitate. They want to be seen and admired by others. Yet they are wolves in sheep's clothing, because the moment they achieve their purpose and attract people's admiring gaze, they become obstacles to their admirers, blocking rather than assisting access to God:

> *But woe to you, scribes and Pharisees, hypocrites! because you shut the kingdom of heaven against men; for you neither enter yourselves, nor allow those who would enter to go in. Woe to you, scribes and Pharisees, hypocrites! for you traverse sea and land to make a single proselyte, and when he becomes a proselyte, you make him twice as much a child of hell as yourselves.* (Matt. 23:13-15)

As we saw in his dialogue with Peter, Jesus seems to reserve his strongest language for those who would tempt and lead others into scandalous mimetic relationships. In contradistinction to this, Jesus advises:

> *But when you give alms, do not let your left hand know what your right hand is doing, so that your alms may be in secret; and your Father who sees in secret will reward you. And when you pray, you must not be like the hypocrites; for they love to stand and pray in the synagogues and at the street corners, that they may be seen by men. Truly, I say to you, they have received their reward. But when you pray, go into your room and shut the door and pray to your Father who is in secret; and your Father who sees in secret will reward you. (Matt. 6:3-6)*

James Alison has done a marvelous job expounding this passage, and points out that the "room" to which Jesus refers (Greek: ταμειον), which is to be used as the place of prayer, is more accurately rendered "storeroom" or "pantry" – which in ancient near eastern homes was a completely enclosed room without windows, used to protect perishable food items from the extremes of heat and cold. Its relevance to prayer is that in such a room one could neither see others, nor be seen by them. The whole social world was shut out.

Alison paraphrases Jesus' meaning: "You are addicted to being who you are in the eyes of your adoring public, or your execrating public, it doesn't matter which, since crowd love and crowd hate give identity in just the same dangerous way. So, go into a place where you are forcibly in detox from the regard of those who give you identity so that your Father, who alone is not part of that give and take, can have a chance to call your identity into being."[28] The point of isolating oneself in the room is not simply, as I used to think, in order to block out noise and visual distractions as an aid to meditative concentration, but to phase out, temporarily at least, the mimetic social-other, allowing one's thoughts and feelings to be recentered upon One who models a different desire. That this is Jesus' real intent becomes clear when one realizes that the context of the passage is all about model/obstacle relations, and being ensnared by desire for approval from the human other.

As Alison makes clear, this desire shapes our very identity: "the trouble about seeking the approval of the social other, is that you will get it. You will act in such a way as to get that approval, and then become its puppet. And because of that you will be selling yourself short . . . Your 'self' will be a shadow of what you could be if you allowed the Creator to call you into being."[29] Commenting on those who do sell themselves short, Alison writes, "They get the approval, and with it they are given a 'self' that is the function of the group's desire. Belonging and approval go together. This means, incidentally, that someone is thereafter exceedingly unlikely to be self-critical in relationship to their group belonging. They will agree to cover up whatever in themselves and in other group members needs covering up in order for the group to maintain its unanimity, and for themselves to keep their reputation, which means their 'self.'[30]

It is not that Jesus thinks we can, or even should, completely shed the desire for approval. It is a matter, rather, of modeling our desire after what Alison calls "Another other" – that is, God. Jesus had a special name for his God: he called him "Abba." This is Aramaic for "daddy," a very intimate and childlike term that unashamedly expresses Jesus' dependence upon and intimacy with his Father. And the important point for our current discussion is that this Abba-God is not in rivalry with us. God's transcendence in this context means that he is "above" rivalry with human beings. We can go to God with our deepest needs – indeed, our deepest desires – and share with him fearing that it will come back to bite us, or stab us in the back. And then we learn to imitate this non-rivalrous way of being in our relationships with others – even our enemies!

One of Jesus' famous statements in the Sermon on the Mount is "Judge not, that you be not judged." Here is the entire passage:

> *Judge not, that you be not judged. For with the judgment you pronounce you will be judged, and the measure you give will be the measure you get. Why do you see the speck that is in your brother's eye, but do not notice the log that is in your own eye? Or how can you say to your brother, "Let me take the speck out of your eye," when there is the log in your own eye? You hypocrite, first take the log out of your own eye, and then you will see clearly to take the speck out of your brother's eye.* (Matt. 7:1-5)

Right away we see that Jesus is describing what I earlier called an "economy of exchange." When he says "the measure you give will be the measure you get," he is not talking about our relationship with God, but to what happens in human relationships of rivalry. When we judge others, they will judge us. The more we hate them, the more they will hate us. There is no spiritual law of "karma" operating here, but a sound insight into mimetic psychology. Rivals exchange equal measures of criticism and judgment, and are at the same time utterly blind to the fact that they are doubles – and thus rivalry inevitably contains an element of hypocrisy. Only when a rival wakes up to the fact that he is his rival's double can he be in a position to "see clearly" in order to remove the speck from the other's eye: because that "other" is in fact one's structural equivalent – one's "brother" (or sister). Jesus' prohibition against judging the other is meant to avoid being tightly bound in scandalous relationships, for the bond grows tighter as fascination with the rival increases. Judging the other is commonly a product of this kind of fascination, as I become continually preoccupied with my rival, my model/obstacle, wanting to critique her, debunk her, and show myself superior to her. Yet all the time I am at some level imitating her. The very time and attention I put into judging my rival betrays my level of fascination, and my inability to let go of her.

Exchange is something we take so much for granted that we

never meditate upon its strangeness, much less feel the need to critique it. But, as James G. Williams has written, "The fundamental anthropological question as I have heard Girard express it is, 'Why is reciprocity fundamental to human existence?' Why do we think and act in terms of tit for tat, giving and getting, always exchanging – and of course, perpetually imitating one another? 'What's in it for me?' 'One good turn deserves another.' 'One hand washes the other.' 'Give and you will receive.' All these expressions, which are part of our repertory of ordinary language, point to a fundamental principle of *retribution* that underlies much of human wisdom."[31]

Jesus' God is above the economy of exchange, based as it is upon imitation of the social other; "above" it, not in the sense of being an infinitely more powerful version of the same thing, but of existing in an entirely different mode, which comes to realization among us in the form of what Jesus calls the "kingdom of heaven." As we saw earlier, this was a concept the disciples utterly misunderstood, even to the point of bickering over who would be "greatest" in the kingdom of heaven! As though that kingdom were nothing more than an infinitely greater mirror image of the earthly kingdoms of mimetic exchange. When Jesus says in Matthew 5:20, "For I tell you, unless your righteousness exceeds that of the scribes and Pharisees, you will never enter the kingdom of heaven" – he is not talking about a more perfect achievement of the same kind of righteousness, but a righteousness of a completely different quality, not based upon the desire to be admired and the desire to judge (that is, to be the model and the obstacle), but upon transformation of the heart, which means the transformation of desire.

We saw in Genesis how human definitions of "good" and "evil" are the unavoidable fruit of mimetic rivalry, but Jesus' Abba has no share in such distinctions. He is a God who "...makes his sun rise on the evil and on the good, and sends rain on the just and on the unjust." (Matt. 5: 45) Jesus' God does not enter into arbitration of human disputes based upon rivalry.

> *One of the multitude said to him, "Teacher, bid my brother divide the inheritance with me." But he said to him, "Man, who made me a judge or divider over you?" And he said to them, "Take heed, and*

beware of all covetousness; for a man's life does not consist in the abundance of his possessions." (Luke 12:13-15)

Both brothers desire the same thing, the inheritance. No doubt each of them believes himself in the right and can argue his justifications, and no doubt casts aspersions upon the motives and character of the other. They are enemy twins, alike in their mutual imitation, despite the ideology that each of them erects to distinguish himself from the other. Modeling only his Abba, Jesus refuses to be made party to a dispute between mimetic doubles, and instead offers a warning about covetousness; that is, mimetic desire in its acquisitive form (I want to acquire what you have shown me is desirable by the fact of your possessing it.)

When he is approached by a Jewish ruler who asks, "Good teacher, what shall I do to inherit eternal life?" Jesus responds, "Why do you call me good? No one is good but God alone." (Luke 18:18-19) Some interpreters see this as Jesus' clever way of asserting his divinity, a way of saying, "If you are going to call me good, you must call me God." I see it, rather, as a straightforward declaration of God's transcendence with respect to the human values which are the outgrowth of mimetic rivalry. The man asking this question is a leader of the people. He is a man, as James Alison would put it, whose "self" has been completely formed by the desire for approval by the social-other. He tells Jesus that he has kept all the commandments since his youth. Jesus does not contradict this, but says that the man still lacks one thing: he should give away all his possessions and become his disciple. Mark, in his version, adds the note that Jesus looks upon him with love, or compassion: no doubt because he recognizes the man's bind. On the one hand, he has a desire for life; on the other hand, his whole self has been formed by imitation of the desire of the social-other, such that his "self" can barely even grow in this life – much less endure eternally. What is his achievement of great wealth except the fulfillment of a desire that, like all desire for wealth, boils down to a desire for "glory"; that is, to be the object of high regard, to achieve status through the admiring (or fearful) gaze of others, to be the obstacle and model for as many social-others as possible. The man, in other words, is caught in mimetic scandal, and his religious quest for eternal life is – can only be – a continuation of the same dynamics. He would add to his wealth the distinction of eternal life and a place in the kingdom of heaven (and a jolly great place, no doubt). Sincere though his desire for life may be, it knows only one kind of model: the economy of exchange. "What must I do to inherit eternal life?" he asks, as if the life Jesus offers can be purchased as a contractual transaction. And he wants to insure that his side of the bargain is balanced and complete.

When Jesus offers himself as a new model which sidesteps the old economy, he cannot wrap his mind or spirit around it; desire according to the old pattern proves way too deeply entrenched for the young ruler. Ironically, this man, who has been so earnestly questing for "life," now confronts it immanent possibility and feels as though Jesus were asking him to die – as indeed identity forged in the heat of scandal must begin to die when Jesus' invitation is accepted – for it is an invitation to the transformation of the very desire that has constituted the old self.

For hyper-mimetic individuals such as the ruler, puppets of scandal and desire, such an invitation is almost impossible to accept; thus Jesus' final comment, "How hard it is for those who have riches to enter the kingdom of God! For it is easier for a camel to go through the eye of a needle than for a rich man to enter the kingdom of God." (Luke 18:24-25) From the purely human point of view, our bondage to mimetic desire is such that we simply cannot liberate ourselves. Fortunately, the purely human is not the ultimate and final point of view, for Jesus follows up with the words, "What is impossible with men is possible with God." For God lives in the freedom beyond the mutual exchange of human regard.

Mimesis in the Gospel of John

The gospel of John has its own unique way of presenting Jesus' mimetic theme. John's Gospel is full of comments like, "I can do nothing on my own authority; as I hear, I judge; and my judgment is just, because I seek not my own will but the will of him who sent me." (John 5:30) Here we have a definition of a new kind of "justice" and "judgment," not based upon an economy of exchange. Jesus' judgment is "just" not because it conforms to the *lex talionis* of an eye for an eye, not because it is an impartial and balanced arbitration of the demands of warring parties, but because it is given from a point of view completely outside the realm of such balanced exchange. It is the manifestation of a desire totally conformed to the non-rivalrous God's, and thus completely free of scandal and any desire to play the model-obstacle game.

"I do not accept glory from human beings. . . . How can you believe when you accept glory from one another and do not seek the glory that comes from the one who alone is God?" (John 5:41, 44 NRS) For Jesus this constitutes the basis not only of justice and judgment, but truth itself: "He who speaks on his own authority seeks his own glory; but he who seeks the glory of him who sent him is true, and in him there is no falsehood." (7:18) "Seeking one's own glory" is the desire to be the admired model, and in being the admired model there is an implicit claim to authority. In mimetic theory, this comes down to the claim of anteriority for my desires over yours: mine is the original, yours the copy, therefore authority lies with me.But Jesus claims no originality for himself, and has no desire to be admired by others. Instead, he redefines the whole meaning of "authority," as well as "truth," making humble imitation of the Father's desire the source of both.

In the Gospel of John we see a massive subversion of all the important values of both Jewish and pagan religion: authority, truth, justice, judgment, glory, honor – all are redefined from a whole new point of departure: the imitation of God's desire (will). Eternal life itself has exactly the same source:

> *For I have not spoken on my own authority; the Father who sent me has himself given me commandment what to say and what to speak. And I know that his commandment is eternal life. What I say, therefore, I say as the Father has bidden me.* (John 12:49-50)

To obey the Father's commandment is eternal life, and the Father's commandment is the expression of His desire, which Jesus imitates – and in so doing receives life, resurrection. This is the only way out of the Satanic and diabolic bondage which results in death. To imitate Jesus is to imitate his own imitation of the Father, and nothing short of such a radical reorientation – which feels like death (because it *is* death, death of the self of scandal) – can liberate us from the perpetual cycles of violence into which our mimetic rivalries have plunged us. The human solution – murder of a scapegoat (to be examined in the next chapter) – creates only a faux liberation, and a temporary unity. Soon, the rivalrous impulse has our relationships by the jugular once again.

The Imitation of Christ

In a Girardian context, "imitation of Christ" means allowing Jesus to be one's model, and imitating Jesus' desires, attitudes, and acts. This, in turn, generates within the follower a desire that seeks to do the will of God, and seeks the good of the other rather than a covetous desire to acquire from the other. What is wonderful about this is that Jesus serves a God who is not in rivalry with human beings, and as an imitator of that God (his "Abba"), Jesus himself is not in rivalry with us, and has no desire to acquire or grasp from others. Nor does he covet or desire to wrest anything from God. On the contrary, Christ's is a spirit of generosity and self-giving love. As the famous text in Philippians puts it:

> *Cultivate this mind-set in your community, which is in fact a community in Christ Jesus, who, although being in the form of God, did not consider his equality with God as something to be exploited for his own advantage, but emptied himself, by taking the form of a slave; that is, by being born in the likeness of human beings. And being found in human form, he humbled himself by becoming obedient to death – even death on a cross.*[32]

Jesus' willingness to empty himself for the sake of loving us, and for the sake of "obedience" to God (another way of speaking about imitation), is held up here as the model for the entire community to imitate ("cultivate this mind-set in your community"). This relationship between Jesus and God becomes the mimetic foundation for a new community of disciples. It is new because, while mimetic, its mimesis is not acquisitive; it contains no rivalry, and thus no acquisitive desire, no covetousness, no scandal, no violence. When Jesus says, "Ask, and it will be given you; seek, and you will find; knock, and it will be opened to you. For everyone who asks receives, and he who seeks finds, and to him who knocks it will be opened." (Matt. 7:7-8) he is not proposing a *quid pro quo:* do this and God will give you that. He is indicating that God is not in rivalry with us, but wants to give to us, if only our entrapment in scandal did not prevent us from opening our mouths and asking. Prisoners of mimetic rivalry and scandal are always knocking at closed doors: the door of the fascinating model, where they will encounter ultimately nothing but an obstacle. But Jesus' "Abba" is the God of the open door, and in this God we find rest from the endless frustration typically produced by scandalous relationships.

> *Come to me, all who labor and are heavy laden, and I will give you rest. Take my yoke upon you, and learn from me; for I am gentle and lowly in heart, and you will find rest for your souls. For my yoke is easy, and my burden is light.* (Matt. 11:28-30)

The "yoke" to which Jesus refers was a common metaphor used by ancient Jewish Rabbis when accepting new pupils. Jesus was often called "Rabbi," by characters in the Gospels, and indeed he often acts like one. Rabbis were different in the way they interpreted Scripture and Torah, and when a student studied with a particular Rabbi, he was said to take that rabbi's "yoke" upon him. (The metaphor is one of training an ox to plow by yoking him to another, experienced ox. The yoke forces the new ox to imitate the experienced ox, and so it learns how to behave in the way the farmer desires.) When a student took a Rabbi's yoke upon himself, it meant that he left his home and his parents to devote his life to becoming like that Rabbi. This is what is in play when Jesus calls his disciples, asking them to follow him – and all of a sudden they up and leave their wives, homes, and livelihood, and take off with Jesus. This seems strange to us, but in the world of first century

Judaism, a parent would be proud if a son were accepted by a Rabbi to study, and would gladly give up the child to such a calling. But, as Rob Bell,[33] suggests, the radicalism of Jesus' move is that he calls students who would not have been considered talented enough or worthy of Rabbinical study, and are basically rejects. Jesus as a "Rabbi" with a band of followers like these yoked to him must have looked like some kind of circus act to the religious establishment of the day.

Jesus played the same basic game as the Rabbis, therefore, gathering students who would imitate him in everything, trying to become as much like him as they could. But Jesus' yoke was "easy" and the burden of carrying it was light. For he would put no obstacle in front of his students. He would not weight them down with the impressive heaviness of his own accomplishments, seeking their admiration, and looking to them as mirrors to reflect back his own glory. He did not want anything from them in an acquisitive sense. He did not want to be their scandal, leading them on to become like him, only to turn against them when they actually began to rival him.It is because Jesus is like this that imitating him is safe, and his way the real solution for the violent cycles of reciprocity within which the world operates. There is no risk of getting caught up in violent exchange with Jesus, for regardless of what we do to him, there will be no imitation coming back at us from his side of the field to enflame, validate, or feed the passion of rivalry. Through his nonviolent compassion, servanthood, humility, generosity, and love Jesus becomes the model for a new humanity.

The New Testament is full of this understanding of Jesus, and of the idea that being a Christian means imitating Jesus as model.[34] As 1 Peter tells us, "For to this you have been called, because Christ also suffered for you, leaving you an *example,* that you should *follow in his steps.*" (1 Pet. 2:21) If we ask the question what that example consists of, Peter immediately gives us the crux: "When he was abused, he did not return abuse; when he suffered, he did not threaten; but he entrusted himself to the one who judges justly." (2:23 NRS)

When the book of Hebrews tells its Christian readers to be "looking to Jesus, the pioneer and perfecter of our faith" (Heb.

12:2), it is talking about Jesus as the model to be imitated. In a way similar to Peter, the writer of Hebrews has in mind Jesus' non-retaliatory endurance of suffering from the hostility and persecution directed against him, even in crucifixion. (…who for the joy that was set before him endured the cross…" 12:2) Twice the writer even uses the specific word "imitate" (*mimeomai*), when he encourages his audience to become "…*imitators* of those who through faith and patience inherit the promises" (6:12), and again, when he tells them to "imitate" the faith of those who originally spoke the word of God to them (13:7). The imitation Hebrews envisions, then, is not only our direct imitation of Christ, but also of those who have shown by their way of life that they have effected a worthy imitation of Christ.

Imitation is key to the Christian life, spreading like a positive contagion throughout the network of churches. In 1 Thessalonians (probably the earliest text in the New Testament), the writer says: "For you, brethren, became *imitators* of the churches of God in Christ Jesus which are in Judea…" And again the emphasis of the imitation is on non-violent suffering: "…for you suffered the same things from your own countrymen as they did from the Jews…" (2:14) In other words, the Gentile Christians were experiencing the same kind of persecution from pagan Gentiles that Paul and other Jewish Christians were experiencing from the synagogues in Judea. They were to imitate the Judean churches in non-retaliation, just as the Judean churches were imitating Christ. We see this network of imitation also in 1 Thess. 1:6-7 (NRS), which says: "And you became *imitators* of us and of the Lord, for in spite of persecution you received the word with joy inspired by the Holy Spirit, so that you became an *example* to all the believers in Macedonia and in Achaia." The Thessalonian church, in other words, had imitated Paul and his cohorts, as well as the Lord, and in so doing became themselves a model for other Christian communities.

The network of imitation traces back to God, where the buck stops. For if churches were imitating other churches that were imitating the apostles, who were imitating Christ – Christ himself was imitating his Abba. Ultimately, through the path of nonrivalous human relationships, we are imitating God. Thus the author of Ephesians can say, "…be kind to one another, tenderhearted, forgiving one another, as God in Christ has forgiven you. Therefore be *imitators* of God, as beloved children, and walk in love, as Christ loved us and gave himself up for us…" (Eph. 4:32 – 5:2) The imitation encouraged here is directly of God, and is connected with qualities associated with self-giving.

Dozens of references could be cited from throughout the New Testament to illustrate the centrality of the idea of imitating the Christ-model as the paradigm of a new humanity and the mark of being a Christian, but the above will have to suffice for our purposes here.

Part II
THE SCAPEGOAT

Let him who is without sin cast the first stone.
(John 8:7)

Chapter Four
Sacrifice, Founding Murders, and the Scapegoat Mechanism

All religious rituals spring from the surrogate victim, and all the great institutions of mankind, both secular and religious, spring from ritual. Such is the case, as we have seen, with political power, legal institutions, medicine, the theater, philosophy and anthropology itself. It could hardly be otherwise, for the working basis of human thought, the process of "symbolization," is rooted in the surrogate victim.

René Girard, *Violence and the Sacred* [35]

‡‡

We have so far been examining in some depth the central idea of "mimetic theory," which is imitation, or mimesis. We have shown how human beings are essentially mimetic creatures, and how this impulse, deeply anchored in our very neurophysiology, leads to conflict. Inevitably, people's wants and desires are centered around acquiring something, whether it be gold or love; such desires spread contagiously (though not with mechanical inevitability) to others, and this leads to rivalry, which ends in hostility, conflict, and violence. We have seen how enmeshed in the web of such relationships human beings are; how, indeed, we are held captive in them because of the power of scandal to fascinate and fix attention. Dostoevsky's "underground man" may be an extreme caricature (but not, perhaps, as far from the mark as one might think), but everyone to some degree gets caught in the model-obstacle scandal, which left to its own devices only escalates in intensity. Only an uncommon spiritual education and maturity can empower a human being to escape from entrapment to this kind of relationality.

We have also seen the various ways in which Genesis, the Gospels, and the New Testament epistles reveal this complex of "sin," and, in the case of the New Testament, prescribe the imitation of Christ as the remedy. It is time now to move to another level of the Girardian discussion. In discussing sacrifice, founding murders, and the scapegoat mechanism, it is important to bear in mind that we are still discussing mimesis; but we are examining another aspect of it, another way in which mimesis plays out within human relationships. This will become clear as we proceed. Let us begin with sacrifice.

Sacrifice

Sacrifice is old. "Two constructions characterize the oldest Neolithic settlements and the earliest cities, the first forms of communal life that were able to achieve and retain stability for many generations: the granary and the place of sacrifice."[36] Discussing ancient sacrificial ritual in his book *Homo Necans*, Walter Burkert, one of the great scholars of ancient religion, writes, "The worshipper experiences the god most powerfully not just in pious conduct or in prayer, song, and dance, but in the deadly blow of the axe, the gush of blood, and the burning of thigh-pieces. The realm of the gods is sacred, but the 'sacred' act done at the 'sacred' place by the 'consecrating' actor consists of slaughtering sacrificial animals…"[37]

Let us think soberly about this for a moment, and face its implications squarely, for Burkert has made the profound statement that the most powerful experience of god for the typical ancient worshipper – the height of religious experience – was *an act of killing*. This is really quite amazing, and all the more so when one realizes that sacrifice was a universal human custom, entirely cross-cultural, and persisting from the humanity's earliest beginnings. Even a scholar of Burkert's stature is "astounded" by the similarity of sacrificial experience that obtains, despite local variation, from Athens to Babylon.[38] For ancient humans, to be religious was inseparable from the act of killing and the constant sight of blood. And this does not mean killing once or twice, or even several times. Sacrifice was enacted day after day, year after year. Only on the basis of such slaughter could an ancient feel it possible to draw near to the gods. Bloodshed and slaughter, says Burkert, is "the act of piety." Even if no temple or statue has been constructed, sacrifice marks the place where the god is present, and this place would be distinguished "by the heap of ashes left from 'sacred' offerings burnt there over long periods of time, or by the horns and skulls of slaughtered rams and bulls, or by the altar-stone where the blood must be sprinkled."[39]

We moderns, to whom the very idea of sacrifice appears alien, gape in amazement at the extent to which this institution controlled the life of ancient individuals and communities, its bizarre forms, and the zest with which it was pursued. Probably the most spectacular form was the *taurobolium* of Mithraic mystery religion. The person to be initiated crouched in a pit roofed with wooden beams. A bull stood upon the beams and was slaughtered, drenching the initiate in blood.[40] Regarding the zest for sacrifice, Croesus, king of Lydia, had 3,000 animals sacrificed at Delphi, and King Seleukos gave 1,000 sheep for a sacrifice at Didymos.[41]

When the Roman emperor Julian (known as Julian the Apostate) tried to revive paganism in the wake of his grandfather Constantine's Christian conversion, he slaughtered hecatombs of cattle, as had been common in Greek tradition.[42] A hecatomb was *one hundred* cattle! Of course, such extravagant piety was limited to those rich enough to indulge it, yet this pales in comparison to the numberless deaths and limitless oceans of blood spilled around the world throughout human history by legions of common folk (and priests on their behalf), beginning, probably, with *human* blood, and eventually replaced by animals. Sacrifice was the highlight not only of important seasonal celebrations, but underscored everything from initiations to life-transitions to treaty agreements and contracts. It was a ubiquitous practice.

Furthermore, the sacrificial practices of various peoples seem to be elaborated with a sense of anxiety, invested as they are with an almost obsessive concern for precision. This is very clear in the Hebrew Torah, for example, with its seemingly endless regulations governing proper sacrificial ritual. (For example, how burnt offerings are to be flayed and cut up, and the parts arranged on the altar, the entrails washed with water; what disqualifies a descendent of Aaron from offering sacrifice at the altar – such as having a mutilated face or a broken foot, or having scabs, etc.; precise ritual procedures for purifying leprosy and other diseases, and women after childbirth; and so on.) To cite a non-biblical example, John Hick writes about the ancient religion of India, "Vedic religion seems indeed to have been largely a matter of ritual sacrifice in which every detail was important and the slightest error or omission could cause the sacred spell to fail and chaos and calamity to ensue."[43]

All of this causes us to ask the question: how could it be that humanity, from its most remote origins, became enmeshed in a practice such as this? Before we give Girard's answer to that question, we must look a little more deeply into how he conceives the *function* of sacrifice in the ancient world. In *Violence and the Sacred,* Girard has shown in scrupulous detail how sacrifice served the sociological function of allowing a community to blow off violent energy in a channeled and controlled manner, so that mimetic rivalries, always present within a community, would not escalate to the point of anarchy and destroy the entire community. Ritually repeated sacrifice offered the community a chance to "kick the dog" rather than each other – the dog being the unfortunate sacrificial victim. Of course, societies gave all sorts of mythological and religious reasons for engaging in the act of sacrifice; but these are secondary justifications that (unconsciously) mask its real function.

The main point for us, seemingly obvious but often strangely overlooked in theological discussions, is that human and animal sacrifice was a *violent* institution. And, for Girard, sacrifice was an act of violence *before* it became anything else. Violence is the essence of the act, and no amount of poetic mythologizing, mystical philosophizing, or pious devotion can make it anything else. I believe this makes much more sense than the popular approach exemplified by Carl Jung and Joseph Campbell, which has humans first waxing philosophical about the nature of life and death, and expressing their insights poetically through mythology – and then acting it out ritually. In this scenario, the mind conceives the connection between death and life, that things die and are reborn, and then a human being is ritually killed in order to give concrete expression to this philosophical truth. But this completely fails to appreciate that when the act is stripped of the poetic and speculative mythology, we are talking about what is essentially an act of *murder*. We are talking about the murdering of countless human beings. (Most anthropologists agree that human sacrifice long predated animal sacrifice).

This objection might be countered with the accusation that it reads a Christian value judgment back into an ancient practice; but even apart from such a judgment, it seems that the deliberate, ritualized killing of a human being is not something people would be easily moved to do. It is certainly not something they would adopt casually as a way of giving expression to philosophical speculations about reality.

It seems to me that sacrifice's ubiquity and powerful grip upon all humanity for thousands of years is much better explained by Girard's theory, which explains it in terms of the profound social benefit it conferred upon ancient societies. In Girard's theory (and we will examine these points more deeply further on) it is murder of a victim that in the first instance founds the group itself, bringing the community into existence; and then its repetition as sacrifice keeps the group together by effectively discharging internal hostilities, thus helping to prevent their explosive accumulation. Human groups discover these benefits spontaneously and serendipitously, as we shall see, when they gang up on an innocent victim; but the benefits are so powerful that the act is repeated, and then repeated again and again until it becomes a formalized practice. It becomes, that is, a sacrificial ritual, an institution which becomes the very nerve center of the culture, and undergoes its own historical evolution.

The Problem of Violent Escalation

Really to grasp sacrifice as a solution, we must appreciate the problem. The number one fear for archaic and ancient communities was escalation of violence within the community, which was a constant threat. Flood, plague, earthquakes, famine – such disasters could be defended against, or at least mitigated, if the entire community pulled together in face of the challenge. Such disasters could even become the occasion for a divided community to revive a sense of camaraderie. But nothing can save a community if the threat is internal violence, the desire to destroy one another because of mutual rivalries. Ancient groups *had* to find some solution to this problem, and they weren't going to do it by reading Rousseau and having everyone sign a social contract. (Apologies to Rousseau for caricaturing his view here in order to make a point.) In his classic anthropological study of the Iatmul peoples of New Guinea, Gregory Batson stated how amazed he was that these people could live together in any kind of community at all, so violent were they, so proud and determined to avenge every slight. Batson records sorcery feuds in Iatmul culture that could result in up to fifteen deaths.[44]

In *Violence and the Sacred,* Girard discusses the example of the Kaingang Indians of Brazil.[45] These had been transferred to a reservation, where anthropologist Jules Henry was able to observe the self-destruction of their cultural existence. Henry attributed what he called the "social suicide" of these peoples to the cyclical vengeance of blood feuds even among close relatives. The community as a whole was splintered into small groups, hostile and suspicious toward each other. For a while, relations *within* each group exhibited a spirit of conciliation, and tolerance for offenses that would immediately be met with vengeance had they been perpetrated by an outsider. But eventually, even members of these small groups began to turn on each other, unable to maintain unity even against outside enemies. The problem was vengeance, and vengeance is so menacing because it operates *mimetically:* it is based upon reciprocal imitation. The desire to "get you back" is the desire to do to you what you did to me (or at least the equivalent, if I cannot do exactly the same). In vengeance, I copy your act. More profoundly, I copy the *desire* you displayed (or imagine you displayed) when you caused me harm: and now I desire to cause you harm as well.

There is a wonderful children's book by Dr. Seuss that perfectly illustrates the issue of escalation through mimesis, entitled *The Butter Battle Book.*[46] It is about the Yooks and the Zooks (even the names reflect mimesis), who live on opposite sides of a long and winding wall. One side eats their bread butter-side up while the other eats theirs butter-side down, and this bit of trivia is what starts an escalation of hostilities that is entirely mimetic, each side imitating the other's bid for power by developing larger and more insanely powerful weapons of destruction. Finally, each develops a tiny bomb with ultimate destructive capabilities. The only issue is which side will drop theirs first – a question left unresolved as generals on both sides of the wall stand confronting each other at the end, bombs in hand. Throughout the story, we get to see two rivals who seem to stand for exactly opposite "ideologies." Dr. Seuss deliberately made the ideological content trivial (buttering bread) in order to emphasize the fact that what motivates the rivals is not really the ideology, but the rivalry itself.

In archaic tribal groups and ancient communities, the issue of violent escalation was absolutely critical. Reciprocal, imitative violence could initiate cycles of vengeance that would quickly destroy the group. An example from the classics that comes immediately to mind is the story of the House of Atreus, memorialized especially by Aeschylus, the Greek tragedian, in his play-triology, the *Oresteia.* In quick review, Atreus had a violent quarrel with his brother, Thyestes. He killed Thyestes' sons, then invited him to a reconciliation banquet – at which he secretly fed Thyestes his own sons! Horrified when he discovers the trick, Thyestes begets another son, Aegisthus, specifically in order to have an avenger. When Atreus dies, the revenge stretches into the next generation, as Aegisthus proposes to take revenge upon Atreus' son, Agamemnon.

Meanwhile, Agamemnon is involved in his own vendetta. He has initiated the Trojan War in order to avenge his brother,

Menelaus, whose wife Helen was abducted by Paris, the Trojan prince. But his fleet's journey to Troy meets with difficulty right at the get-go, because Agamemnon has killed an animal sacred to the goddess Artemis, and she is taking revenge by blowing a contrary wind against his fleet, so that they cannot sail to Troy. (The gods were into the vengeance game, too.) To remedy the situation, Agamemnon has to sacrifice his daughter, Iphigeneia! Then they have smooth sailing to Troy. Ten years later, having defeated the Trojans, Agamemnon returns to Argos, but his wife, Clytaemnestra, is – to use the vernacular – pissed-off. She kills Agamemnon to avenge what he did to their daughter. And who helps her pull off this murderous plot? The man who had seduced her during Agamemnon's ten year absence, Aegisthus – who thus gets his revenge for the murder of his half-brothers by Agamemnon's father. It remains, then, for Orestes, son of Agamemnon, to avenge his father by murdering his mother (and Aegisthus)!

The first play in Aeschylus' *Oresteia* trilogy, the *Agamemnon,* shows clearly the fear and weariness which this kind of revenge-cycle could inspire within a society. The Chorus of old men are tired of all this slaughter, and they know that it is destroying the fabric of their society. Throughout the play they anticipate their king Agamemnon's fate, and fear for the future of their city. But there is nothing they can do about it. They are trapped.

From a different part of the ancient world, the theme of vengeance is paramount throughout the Hebrew Scriptures, constantly in play on individual, family, tribal, and national levels. An example of the individual level is Samson's revenge upon the Philistines, narrated in Judges 14. Samson married a Philistine woman, and promised to pay his Philistine companions a prize of thirty linen garments and thirty festal garments if they could guess the answer to a riddle within seven days of the marriage feast. When he discovered that they guessed the answer by intimidating his new bride into divulging it to them, he did indeed pay the prize: by going into a Philistine town, slaughtering thirty men, and taking their garments as spoil and giving them to those who guessed the riddle!

At the national level, after the reign of Solomon, Israel split into the southern kingdom of Judah and the northern kingdom of Israel, inaugurating a vicious rivalry which threatened to destroy both territories. Half of the book of 1 Kings, and the entire book of 2 Kings, is devoted to chronicling this rivalry, which ended only when Assyria destroyed Israel in 722 BCE. (Judah was destroyed about 150 years later by Babylon.)

Genesis 34 offers an excellent example of how quickly violence could escalate among groups populating the ancient near east, flaring up like wildfire. It tells the story of how the prince of the city of Shechem (whose name was also Shechem) raped Dinah, Jacob's daughter. Young prince Shechem was, however, genuinely taken with Dinah, and wanted her for his wife. Jacob was amenable to this, in part because it was a way to ameliorate some of the shame this deed had brought upon his daughter and his household, and in part because he wanted to live in the region of Shechem and needed to gain allies. Having the wealth and protection of the Shechemites as part of the family would certainly be helpful. There was only one problem: Hebrews were not allowed to marry Canaanite people. But this could be solved if the Shechemites were willing to undergo the painful rite of circumcision in order to make themselves part of the Hebrews. This they did; but on the third day, while the men were still sore from the rite, two of Jacob's sons, Simon and Levi, snuck into the city and murdered all the males! The text continues:

> *They killed Hamor and his son Shechem with the sword, and took Dinah out of Shechem's house, and went away. And the other sons of Jacob came upon the slain, and plundered the city, because their sister had been defiled. They took their flocks and their herds, their donkeys, and whatever was in the city and in the field. All their wealth, all their little ones and their wives, all that was in the houses, they captured and made their prey. Then Jacob said to Simon and Levi, "You have brought trouble on me by making me odious to the inhabitants of the land, the Canaanites and the Perizzites; my numbers are few, and if they gather themselves against me and attack me, I shall be destroyed, both I and my household." But they said, "Should our sister be treated like a whore?"* (Gen. 34:26-31 NRS)

Simon and Levi's comment reminds one of Lamech's, the boastful character mentioned in the early part of Genesis: *"I have slain a man for wounding me, a young man for striking me. If Cain is avenged sevenfold, truly Lamech seventy times seven."* Without meaning in the least to slight the seriousness of rape, I think it can fairly be said that the punishment inflicted by Simon and Levi was seventy-sevenfold beyond the extent of the crime.

The Bible shows us cultures that make the Hatfields and McCoys' famous feud look like a children's tussle. The cry for vengeance was especially endemic to honor/shame cultures, where the merest slight provoked not only retaliation, but the *obligation* to retaliate, or lose one's honor. The imitative quality here is obvious: they hurt us, so we shall hurt them. The escalation comes from the fact that even if the objective is to "even the score," retaliation is never actually mathematically equal to the harm or insult; on the contrary, it generally ups the ante, introducing more violent energy into the equation. The other side then imitates the new level of violence, while escalating it still more. No one in these cultures would have understood a Hamlet, convulsed with mental anguish as he resists and wrestles with the obligation tradition has laid upon him to avenge his father's death.

The story of the Shechemites illustrates how insanely committed to vengeance nomadic peoples like Jacob's tribe were. But reciprocal violence was a *universal* threat, because of human beings' hyper-mimetic sensitivity – our amazing capacity to imitate one another. There is an astonishing scene near the beginning of Mel Gibson's gruesome film, *Apocalypto,* which illustrates this wonderfully. A group of villagers is making its way through the jungle after the destruction of their village and the ravaging of their people by brutal Mayan warriors from the city. They have managed to kill a tapir, and are carrying the skinned carcass on poles, when they encounter hunters from the tribe that lives in the territory through which they are passing. The villagers ask permission to pass. The two lines of natives stand facing each other, in a situation reminiscent of a western showdown. There follows an intense minute of total silence, during which the two groups stand facing each other, motionless, breathlessly sizing each other up, trying to read each other's intentions and evaluate what the other side is going to do, and who is going to make the first move. Watching this scene, one can just imagine the mirror neurons blasting like fireworks, as everyone observes his potential opponent's slightest movement, and tries to read the other's intentions. Should one side detect in the other a movement towards violence – real or imagined doesn't matter – that movement will instantly be imitated, and escalation will ensue. This kind of sensitivity functioned *within* the group as well as toward strangers, which is why survival for such tribes hung upon gossamer threads, swiftly and easily broken by even the slightest hint of hostility, signaled by the flicker of an eyebrow or the twitch of a finger.

I am reminded of the intense close-ups in the film *The Good, The Bad, and The Ugly*, where, through the camera lens, we are allowed to experience the breathless suspension of time as three duelers scrutinize one another's faces, eyes, and hands, in a state of heightened readiness for the slightest sign of an intention to draw. Such scenes are intensely mimetic: the moment one of the duelers picks up the other's intention to draw, that intention is imitated, and the mimetic situation instantly escalates to the death of one of the parties. The opponents are mirror images. Despite the fact that we consider one of them "good" and the other "bad," *structurally* they are exactly the same. They imitate each other's desire to win, the desire to triumph over the rival, and they both imitate the prevailing notions of honor that make a man a "man." They also imitate each other's use of violence as a method to settle disputes. The "ugly" is the film's joke to reveal the superficiality and relativity of the other two categories, good and bad. The film pointedly makes it difficult to tell the difference – *structurally* they are identical, regardless of which side of the bread they butter.

The story of the Shechemites and the scene from *Apocalypto* deal with the issue of one tribe against another, but imagine the danger should this kind of reciprocal violence be unleashed within the community itself, so that the violence becomes a struggle of "us versus us" rather than "us versus them." This is what happened to the Kaingang. When mutual antagonisms born of mimetic rivalry fester, then break into an open fever within a community, the group faces a crisis of survival.

We see in Genesis, for example, a younger brother conning his fraternal twin out of his father's blessing and his inheritance rights as the firstborn. This is what Jacob did to Esau. We are not surprised to read that "Esau hated Jacob because of the blessing with which his father had blessed him, and Esau said to himself, 'The days of mourning for my father are approaching; then I will kill my brother Jacob.'" (Gen. 27:41) Because of this rivalry, the family did not survive as a unit – Jacob had to flee (although years later he became reconciled with Esau). Rivalries like this between members of families, or between families within the same tribe, or between various social groups within the community, seethe and churn and escalate over time. Due to the mimetic nature of rivalry, with each side demanding and seeking vengeance against the other, escalation is virtually unstoppable, unless some natural disaster or external enemy interrupts it, giving the community a reason to rally.

Unfortunately, groups could not rely upon natural disasters or enemies to show up conveniently at the precise moment one needed them in order to stop a precipitous escalation toward self-destruction. So the question for such groups was how to deal with internal rivalries in such a way that would facilitate a rallying for mutual survival. The answer was sacrifice. It is because this issue of internal violence was universal among world cultures that sacrifice was also a universal phenomenon. Sacrifice was a powerful antidote to the poison of internal rivalry and strife, because it offered groups a means of blowing off their violence by "ganging up" on a victim. In the scene from *Apocalypto,* the tension finally dissipates when the villagers throw the carcass of the tapir to the ground as an offering to the other tribe. Then they may safely continue their journey home. Although not technically a sacrificial ritual, the gesture is wonderfully symbolic as a portrayal of the reconciliation of hostile parties through the sacrifice of a victim.

Sacrifice was thus the lynchpin in efforts by which ancients attempted literally to maintain the world. For society, and the entire cosmos of human meaning it represented, was threatened by reciprocal violence, which therefore needed to be channeled out of the community. When such violence reached a point where the demise of unity was immanent, we see what Girard calls a *sacrificial crisis,* so named because at this point there is so much envy, mutual suspicion, and hostility built up among the members of the group that sacrificial rituals lose their sociological efficacy and are no longer capable of protecting the group from its own violence.

This kind of crisis may also develop as the result of a weakening of the group's belief in their sacrificial rituals and institutions. In order for sacrifice to serve the function we have been examining, people must believe completely and unwaveringly in the mythology that justifies it (for example, the increasing of fertility and prosperity, the guaranteeing of a covenant or contract, gaining favor of the gods to ensure victory in war, and so on). They must believe that the gods demand sacrifice, and that the system was instituted by the gods, and they must believe that the sacrificial victim is sacred. They must believe in the sacredness of the entire process. If these beliefs weaken, confidence in sacrifice will weaken; and when that happens, sacrifice can no longer effectively channel violence out from the community. Then the threatened community must somehow generate renewed sacrificial vigor and belief. This is what we see happening in *Apocalypto:* the Mayan rulers institute the building of more temples, and the offering of more human sacrifices, in order to generate prosperity and shore up their declining civilization. (I am not commenting here on the historical accuracy of the film, but simply using the plot as an illustration.)

Founding Murders and the Origin of Human Society and Religion

Earlier, we asked the question how it could be that humanity, from its most remote origins, became enmeshed in such a practice as sacrificial slaughter. Part of the answer, as we have just seen, is that sacrifice *worked.* It served as a bonding mechanism for members of a group who periodically found themselves at each other's throats, and thus prevented the escalation of mimetic rivalry. The principle was well understood by Dostoevsky.

Immediately after a small revolutionary group has murdered one of their own members and thrown his weighted body into a pond to sink, their leader, Pyotr Stephanovich, proclaims to them, "You are called upon to bring new life into the party which has grown decrepit and stinking with stagnation. Keep that always before your eyes to give you strength."[47] It is Stavrogin who understands the real power behind murder as a generator of vitality and strength for human groups. Referring to Pyotr's technique of designating team members with titles and rank as a way of motivating them, Stavrogin comments, "All that's just bureaucracy and sentimentality – all that's good glue, but there's something that's even better: put four members of a circle up to bumping off a fifth, on the pretext that he's going to inform, and the blood that's been spilled will immediately bind them together in a single knot. They will become your slaves, they won't dare to rebel or ask for an accounting. Ha ha ha!"[48]

Shakespeare also understood the principle of group cohesion through the murder of a victim. In *Julius Caesar,* after his wife Calphurnia has related a dream in which she saw Caesar's statue spouting blood like a fountain, and has begged Caesar not to attend the Senate that day, Decius tries to reassure Caesar (in order to lure him into the Senate for assassination) that the dream is actually a wonderful vision:

This dream is all amiss interpreted.
It was a vision fair and fortunate.
Your statue spouting blood in many pipes,
In which so many smiling Romans bathed,
Signifies that from you great Rome shall suck
Reviving blood, and that great men shall press
For tinctures, stains, relics, and cognizance.
This by Calphurnia's dream is signified.[49]

True it was that many cultures would suck reviving blood from their sacrificial victims; but, unfortunately, the "glue" was not permanently bonding. Sacrifice had to be repeated over and over again. For it was (and of course still is) tough for people to get along. Thanks to the genetic windfall of mirror neurons, *homo sapiens* had developed empathy through mutual imitation of the other's feeling states, which brought them together; but that same imitative capacity would set them against each other when copying the other's desire for possession of an object, and imitating the other's violent response (or perceived violent intentions). Sacrifice answers the question of how such creatures could ever have learned to live together in any kind of enduring society without destroying themselves through unrestrained cycles of reciprocal violence.

But this does not answer the question about how human beings became enmeshed in sacrificial practice in the first place. How, in other words, the mechanism was discovered. The answer to that question is of great importance for the Girardian perspective on the Bible. Humanity was religious, as far as we can tell, from its earliest beginnings; and from the beginning, humans' experience of the "sacred" was inseparable from the act of ritual killing. Burkert calls attention to the fact that the best parts of the animal were usually eaten by the worshippers as part of a feast, and wants to explain sacrifice as growing out of primitive hunting rituals that were followed by communal meals. Girard's explanation is quite different, and, I believe, more powerful, especially since it offers a more cogent explanation of the origin of *human* sacrifice. Girard's theory is that sacrifice began as the *repetition of a spontaneous murder*. This murder – in imitation of which the subsequent sacrificial murders sprang – he calls the *founding murder* because it actually founds or establishes a community and its civilization.

Founding murders happened throughout pre-Christian history (we will see later why it became increasingly difficult to effect a founding murder after the life and death of Jesus Christ, and the publication of the Gospels). In fact, founding murders go all the way back to the very beginning of human language and culture – to which such murders gave rise. We will now examine the dynamics at work in a prehistoric founding murder, in order to see clearly how sacrifice got started (and human culture along with it), and to appreciate the terror that haunted ancient cultures – the terror of falling back into the state of chaos that existed just prior to a founding murder. Of course, reconstructions of prehistorical scenarios are unprovable, and necessarily something of a caricature. But that doesn't mean Girard's reconstruction of the prehistorical founding murders is a pure, unsupported flight of fancy. On the contrary, it is a quite plausible scenario from a purely rational and scientific point of view, supported by many varieties of evidence, including neuroscience, paleontology, mythology, what we know about sacrificial cults from historical societies, and, as we shall see later, the Bible itself. Naturally, I am not going to attempt to marshal the evidence here, lest I end up with a book the size of *The Origin of Species*. My goal is to explain the ideas as clearly as I can.

We are about to embark upon the most theoretical part of this book. It presents material that is often given short summary treatment in books and articles about Girard's work that leaves readers more bewildered than enlightened. What follows is my own synthesis from a reading of many Girardian scholars, presented in a way that hopefully will give the reader a deeper understanding of the subject, yet without getting lost in the woods of pure theory. However, if what follows proves too abstract or dull for some readers, I suggest they skip to the last two paragraphs of this chapter, where I summarize the results. Then they may proceed to the next chapter, where their interest will hopefully be restimulated by direct engagement with the biblical text.

We concentrate now on the prehistoric era,[50] and focus on a group of hominids barely distinguishable from apes, often referred to as a "primal horde." Rivalries among apes and other higher primates are held in check and kept from violent escalation by the establishment of dominance patterns. A male chimp will make a periodic display of strength and courage that discourages competitors and keeps them subordinate, and a hierarchy fairly stabilizes relations. Early hominids, however, did not have such a built-in instinctual braking mechanism on reciprocal violence; or, perhaps more accurately, instinctual mechanisms were outstripped by the blessing of a superabundance of mirror neurons, giving us a hugely expanded capacity for imitation far beyond that possessed even by the apes. This was probably the reason for the increasing length of nursing period required for human infants. They needed much more care and attention because their survival was going to depend more upon learning than instinct – a shift attributable to the increased capacity for imitation. The abundance of mirror neurons, and the corresponding hyper-mimetic capacity, was also a curse, however, because it made it impossible to restrain acquisitive desires, even in the face of threats and dominance displays by alpha-males. The mimetic capacity of *homo sapiens* is at once an attractive and a repulsive force. Imitating the other's feelings and desires leads to empathy and closeness; but when the imitated desire is an acquisitive one, seeking to possess a particular object, imitation easily results in violent confrontation. Under the pressure of such an evolutionary leap, no doubt many groups did not need external threats or enemies in order to destroy themselves; their own competitiveness did the job quite nicely.

We must now imagine a situation in which early humans make cooperative attempts to hunt, gather, and do other work together, but end up skirmishing, clubbing each other to death, and so on. We are hypothesizing a time before society and culture existed. There is as yet no religion, no art, no politics – not even language. There is only the hyper-mimeticism that leads to bloody clashes that make everything alike. In order for culture to come into existence, there has to be "order," and order is based upon differences and distinctions. But in this reciprocal war of all-against-all there is nothing to distinguish one from another. Every creature is a mimetic mirror image of his/her neighbor, so that a kind of undifferentiated "sameness" prevails. So the question becomes: how will a basic distinction get introduced into this violently homogenous primal anarchy, so that human culture can even get started? How will they extract themselves from this violent blender in which they swirl, so as to introduce difference and order into the chaos?

Since the problem is produced by mimesis, the solution will also have to be mimetic – for there is no higher "control panel" to which this new creature might appeal. And mimesis will have to discover this solution all by itself, as it were, spontaneously, because there is as yet no language with which to reason out a solution. This, Girard believes, is exactly what did happen. The mimetic function itself happened upon a solution that nobody could have planned or predicted. It was a purely spontaneous discovery, made thousands of times by many hominid groups around the world, and it happened whenever a group (we cannot yet say "community") found itself mimetically aligning in unanimous accord to direct hatred and violence against a single victim. For this to happen, all it would take would be for some gesture – like the pointing of a finger at someone in hatred or fear – to be imitated by another. With two fingers pointing, it becomes easier to enlist a third. Then the process is on its way to possible mimetic escalation – what we have called a mimetic wave. This is a snowballing effect that can happen very quickly. As mimesis sweeps the group, the urge to attack the victim becomes more and more magnetic and irresistible. If a mimetic wave results, the entire group polarizes unanimously against the victim.

Experiencing this overwhelmingly powerful wave of mob violence against a victim, the group has stumbled upon a "glue" that generates a tremendous bonding effect. As mentioned earlier, the bond was not permanent; but it was effective enough to stabilize relationships for a while, and to give the group something like a self-conscious identity – the beginnings of community. What the group discovered when this mechanism was triggered is what Girard calls the "scapegoat mechanism." It is a *mimetic* mechanism because it is based upon all members of the group imitating each other; *not*, this time, imitating the other's desire for an object, but imitating the other's gesture of hatred for a single victim. Like iron filings reconfiguring under magnetic influence, the scapegoat mechanism mimetically realigns all members of the group, transforming the all-against-all chaos into a pattern of all-against-one. A collectivity forms as a result of unanimous polarization over-against the hated one, and the collective act of violence against the innocent scapegoat turns the group into a community (in seed only, of course – germination and growth will take time). Not only has violent energy been discharged, but the participants now feel a completely new and powerful kind of unity that must have felt quite miraculous, coming as it did so unexpectedly and serendipitously, right at the violent crescendo of an escalating crisis. A group of hominids experiencing this kind of cohesiveness for the very first time would hardly know what hit them. It would feel like a kind of miracle, for, suddenly, the group is pulled back from the brink of self-destruction, and they are saved, and more than saved: they are given a way to live and endure in each other's company. This mechanism, Girard believes, came to play the role for humanity that instinctual braking mechanisms play for animals. Instead of instinct, the mimetic mechanism of scapegoating prevented *homo sapiens* from self-destruction through mimetic rivalry.

Here then, is the first *difference,* the first meaningful *distinction,* created spontaneously through the scapegoat mechanism: the difference between the group and the expelled and murdered victim. Before, all was violent sameness. But now a distinction has been created that defines the group. Suddenly there is a sense of "in," which encompasses all the participants – *minus one;* for the "in" could only come into existence simultaneously with the creation of an "out." And that space of "out" is occupied by the single victim. On the basis of this first distinction – which is actually the distinction between the sacred and the profane (to be examined later) – more distinctions will be elaborated, and culture will arise. This is why Girard calls this event the *founding* murder.[51] The distinction between the group and its victim is the beginning of religion (and thus of culture itself): "religion" here referring to the experience of the sacred, and the offering of sacrifices. The victim is experienced as the embodiment of the sacred.

This will be developed more fully in a later chapter, but in anticipation I will say here that the "sacred" comes into being at the moment of the murder because the victim is perceived as larger-than-life, indeed, *transcendent,* thanks to the disproportion between cause and effect. The disproportion is that in the midst of a frightful war of all-against-all, the entire group becomes reconciled simply as a result of the elimination of one participant. The effect is enormous compared to the cause, making it seem miraculous. In addition, this effect is not something the participants were consciously attempting or even intending to achieve; thus it would feel like something that just "happened," something given to them, like a gift, making them feel awestruck and grateful. But grateful to whom? Certainly not to themselves, who were only the awestruck recipients of the miracle.

The only other option is the victim: the one who caused all the havoc must also be the one who caused this great healing. In these kinds of founding murders, therefore, we have the beginning of the "gods." After his or her death the victim is deified, in some cultures going on to become the celebrated "dying and resurrected god" that we read about hundreds of times in myths from all over the world. This, then, is the birth of the primitive sacred, and it becomes the very center of the newly formed community, giving rise, as mentioned earlier, to the religious cult – and hence to language, art, music, and all the other elements of human culture, developed originally as aspects of religion. (If this paragraph has seemed rather dense and fanciful, please bear in mind that it has been offered simply to "prime the pump," so to speak, in anticipation of fuller development later.) [52]

The founding murder, then, is essentially the moment of creation of the human world, and it will be remembered as such in creation myths, which so often in world mythology relate the creation of the world, or the creation of humanity, to the story of someone being killed. To anticipate a bit what we will cover in a later chapter, in creation myths it is always a matter of order brought forth from a state of formlessness and void – which is exactly the result of the founding murder. In expelling the victim, the participants expel chaos from amongst themselves, and by group psychological projection the victim becomes chaos' new embodiment. The newly created distinction between the group and the expelled "monster" is like the difference between light and murky darkness, or dry land and the roiling, chaotic sea. It is this distinction, felt in their very bones by the newly emerging community, that gives rise to the poetic interpretations we find in myths that recount the moment of creation. The myths' poetic expressions hide the truth of the grisly history that is the real genesis of the human cosmos.

The founding murder is the initial discovery of the scapegoat mechanism, and it becomes a precedent, a model for future imitation during those times when the achieved peace begins to unravel. Since the glue effected by the founding murder is only temporary, when violence once again threatens to undo unity and efface the old distinctions, we need not be surprised if the group "discovers" another person to blame – another victim. This time the process is not quite so spontaneous. Soon the group learns to look for victims whenever it feels threatened by its own violence (and, eventually, by any kind of external threat as well), until the process becomes formalized, and evolves over time into highly elaborate sacrificial rituals. A fully developed sacrificial cult has learned to use scapegoats as a kind of preventive medicine, as community insurance against its own mimetic rivalry. Group survival is too crucial for the "miracle" of cohesiveness to be left to chance: the immolation of scapegoats becomes an institution, a regular, ritualized practice that secures victims for deliberate destruction.

In coming to grips with understanding this process, we must realize that for archaic cultures everything was based upon imitation. Scholar Mircea Eliade gives us a feeling for the utter seriousness of imitation among archaic societies when he writes, "[T]he greater part of primitive man's actions were, so he thought, simply the repetition of a primeval action accomplished at the beginning of time by a divine being, or mythical figure. An act only had meaning in so far as it repeated a transcendent model, an archetype. . . . every action performed by the primitive supposes a transcendent model – his actions are effective only in so far as they are real, as they follow the pattern."[53]

We live today with an entirely different sense of time and history. History for us is linear, and moves toward an unknown future, with the present always in process of change. Not so for early humanity. On the contrary, to a typical modern person archaic cultures seem rigid, obsessively fixated on repetitive patterns. "History" was like riding a carousel – one went round and round, always returning to the same point from which one began, in an eternal recurrence decreed by the gods. Girard's point is that the reason for this fixation on the "repetition of a primeval action accomplished at the beginning of time" is that repetition protected the society, and did so because what was being repeated in sacrificial rituals was the founding murder; and what was being reaped as a result was the benefit of a well-ordered and "well-glued" society.

Glue is definitely the word to describe the communal religious experience of most of humankind prior to the Gospel. Speaking of the so-called "pre-axial" religions (i.e., prior to about 800 BCE, but also including much later religions which nevertheless perpetuate the old traditions), philosopher of religion John Hick says: "...the underlying concern is conservative, a defence against chaos, meaninglessness and the breakdown of social cohesion. Religious activity is concerned to keep fragile human life on an even keel..."[54] From the perspective of the founding murder, one can certainly understand why this should be so: groups knew, either from direct experience, or from ancestral memory, the chaos of mimetic violence. Anxious to preserve and develop the order that arose from the founding murder, they developed sacrificial rituals, and along with these an entire complex of religious imagery and practice – to the maintenance of which their central cultural concerns were dedicated.

These considerations give us a basis to understand in a more precise way the definition of *ritual* that Burkert gives in his book, *Creation of the Sacred.* He says that ritual entails "...***fixed behavioral patterns*** marked by ***exaggeration*** and ***repetition*** and often characterized by ***obsessive seriousness***... In principle, ritual reflects a preverbal state of communication, to be learned by ***imitation*** and to be understood by its ***function***."[55] (Emphasis mine) Burkert is not a Girardian (although he knows and has dialogued with Girard[56]), and yet the Girardian lens brings into focus every aspect of Burkert's definition, which I have highlighted. Sacrificial ritual is fixed, obsessive, and serious because it is imitating a founding murder. It has its genesis not from language, but from the preverbal mimetic fluctuation that results in unanimous violence against a victim. Once discovered, the scapegoat mechanism functions as a generator of order and cohesion. This function is "understood," not verbally, but in the very muscles, as it were, as they discharge their violent energy onto the victim, and reap the result of a cathartic peace. Learning this was a matter of imitating it over and over again, throughout the millennia during which sacrificial ritual held humanity in thrall. (And the imitation was often "exaggerated" because the artificiality of ritual requires exaggeration in order to stir up the violent emotions that will be discharged against the victim.)

Before moving on, it needs to be highlighted that despite the group's perception of an absolute difference between itself and the victim, the choice of the particular individual who will become the scapegoat is essentially *arbitrary*. Indeed, it can be nothing *but* arbitrary, since in the midst of violent anarchy there is no absolute difference among the participants, who are little more than mirror images of one another. But the group never realizes the arbitrary nature of the scapegoat; and it *must not realize it* if collective violence is going to issue in the creation of a unified community. Everyone must buy into the collective delusion that there is something hideously different about the victim, for only then will the group be able to align itself into mob solidarity, carry out the lynching, and experience the unity that comes from polarization against the scapegoat. The entire community might form a circle around the victim and stone her to death; or, in another favorite form of collective violence, form an arc opposite the victim, back her up against a cliff, and finally force her over the edge (the Roman Tarpeian Rock being the most famous ancient example). But regardless of the means of dispatch, participation must be unanimous in order for the illusion of difference to captivate the persecutors with the absoluteness necessary for the founding of community.

As sacrificial ritual developed after the founding murder, unanimous collective violence was discovered to hold an additional benefit: no one in particular could be singled out later as the party responsible for the victim's death. The entire village (or clan, or tribe, or whatever constituted the whole unit) participated in sacrifice, making it difficult for any potential vengeance-seekers to target an actual killer, since the "killer" was the entire community. The whole point of sacrificial ritual, after all, was to derail potential cycles of vengeance. It would have been counterproductive in the extreme to have the sacrificial victim become the occasion for a new vendetta.

It should be obvious that when I use the word "victim" I am speaking from our point of view, not from theirs. From *their* point of view, the "monster" is not a victim at all, and the violence against him or her appears as anything but arbitrary. To say that the victim is arbitrarily chosen, however, is *not* to say that there are no criteria involved in the choice. As a matter of fact, individuals chosen as scapegoats are often those who stand out by virtue of physical disabilities, or who have been marginalized in some way by the group. We will examine this in more detail later when we discuss the "marks" of a victim. But such accidental criteria do not change the fact that the choice of scapegoat is essentially arbitrary, in the sense that it is a role which, in principle, any one of the participants could fill (see the next subsection on "substitution").

To summarize our answer, then, to the initial question of how humanity – all peoples, all cultures, everywhere on the planet – became enmeshed in the continual, grisly slaughter of human beings and animals that we call sacrifice, the Girardian answer is that this violent practice began as a spontaneous discovery that was made by many (but not all) early hominid groups throughout the world. Those who discovered the efficacious benefits of scapegoating an innocent victim survived; those who didn't probably destroyed themselves through their own rivalrous violence (and/or were destroyed by other groups who cinched their own cohesiveness by scapegoating them).

Early humans' powerful mimetic capacity continually brought them to the brink of a crisis of self-extermination, by exacerbating the poisons of mimetic rivalry and reciprocal violence; but that *same mimetic capacity* also provided the remedy, as former rivals found themselves aligning as a mob against a victim, and so discovered a powerful new unity; and that *same mimetic capacity* also turned the spontaneous discovery into a precedent that was imitated, developing eventually into elaborate sacrificial cults.

The Sacrificial Crisis

Let us return, now, to societies in which a sacrificial cult has already been established, and a culture developed. Human cultures are based upon the distinguishing, separating, dividing, sorting, and ordering of differences. A society's ultimate fear is not difference; on the contrary, *the real fear is nondifference* or *nondifferentiation.* This seems counter-intuitive. Don't people in a society fear the one who appears different from them – a stranger, perhaps, or foreigner? Yes, but not because of difference *as such.* Difference is the life blood of civilization. Culture is all about distinction-making: creating and distinguishing roles, categories, hierarchies, rules of etiquette, job functions, language distinctions, and so on ad infinitum. We could cite a tremendous range of phenomena, all the way from how American government distinguishes between legislative, executive, and judicial branches, down to distinctions that govern the way we eat (the differences, for example, between fork and spoon, and the rules governing their usage). Most important are distinctions of hierarchy, such as the distinctions between laity and priest, priest and bishop, bishop and Pope. For a culture to retain its vitality such distinctions must be respected, honored, cherished, celebrated, affirmed, and they must make sense to those who participate in them. In the face of material destruction, even a small remnant of the people can reconstruct the culture. But when the carefully constructed system of differences that constitutes the culture itself erodes through loss of credibility, no remnant will be able, or even desire, to rebuild it.

The real fear, then, is not difference, but the *loss* of difference, the fear of collapse into nondifferentiated chaos. If we fear those who are different, it is because their difference from us is such that we can find no place for it within our own system of differentiations. Their difference thus threatens to expose the relative and essentially arbitrary nature of the system of differences that we hold sacred, thus undermining the system's authority and credibility, making it vulnerable to collapse. The earth has seen thousands of cultures, each one of which has tried its best to make its institutions sacred, to cement them in place and buttress them against external forces that differ in a "different kind of way," an absolute way that seems alien. Speaking of the Egyptians, John Hick writes, "Thus for the ancient Egyptians life existed in a tension between finite ordered existence and a limitless surrounding chaotic non-existence, which manifested itself in darkness, in the unbounded desert, in the annual flooding of the Nile, in states of sleep and in death."[57] *That* kind of difference, the difference that symbolizes or embodies non-difference itself, is the real fear, because we cannot understand it, we cannot fit it into our own system of relative differences. We fear it not *because* it is different, but because its absolute difference conjures up the fear of nondifferenitated meaninglessness.

Now, with regard to violence, when we think of a state of anarchy we tend to imagine it as a conflict of differences: every person or every group fighting for what *they* want, and coming to blows with others who want something different. At one level it does indeed appear that way; but Girard is looking at the situation *structurally*, where it is possible to perceive the fundamental reality of a generalized sameness which has been brought about by the *reciprocal* nature of the violence. As that violence intensifies, the various parties become more and more alike, because reciprocal violence is mimetic, and rivals are led inevitably to copy each other. The result is that the more violently they fight, the faster erodes the credibility of whatever cultural categories and labels had previously distinguished them.

As an example, take an aristocrat in a traditional society, who is distinguished from a peasant in a thousand ways, some quite visual and showy; but should the aristocrat be so unwise as to allow himself to be drawn into a shouting match with a peasant, the violence would quickly threaten to efface the distinction between them – which is why a nobleman must consider it beneath his dignity to have such an exchange with a person of lower station. He might indeed berate and shout at a peasant, but only as a form of heavy-handed abuse, *not* as an ongoing, argumentative exchange that would imply some kind of equality. Should he do that, their mutual imitation of each other's violence would produce a sameness that would make a mockery of the hierarchical distinction between them. Imagine, for example, the end result if the officer of Dostoevsky's *The Underground Man* adopted the same attitude towards the protagonist, as the protagonist displayed towards the officer, and started acting in the same way. Were this kind of thing to happen on a large scale within a society, it is obvious that the culture could not long survive.

When this kind of thing does happen, participants eventually sense at some level the insecurity of their cultural identity. An aristocrat, secure in his social ivory tower and bastioned behind a thousand etiquettes and ceremonies that elevate him above the peasant, should not even be giving the time of day to, much less obsessing about, his inferior. But should he allow such a thing to happen, and become locked into a reciprocal rivalry, he marshals more and more of his energies of thought and action towards the goal of defeating his opponent, not realizing that his obstacle has become his model, and that reciprocal conflict with the peasant is eroding from within the bedrock upon which his own claim to superiority is established.

This kind of reciprocal violence begins to happen more and more, and to accelerate in intensity, during a sacrificial crisis. Sacrificial crises are crises of violence, *reciprocal* violence which group members direct towards each other. As this kind of violence intensifies, it speeds up; that is, hostile exchanges between rivals happen with accelerating speed. One can observe a microcosmic version of this in any heated argument. The hotter the argument becomes, the faster the rivals talk and interject comments until finally neither of them can get a word in edgewise. Exchanges happen so fast that it can literally be dizzying trying to follow the exchanges. When an ancient culture was breaking down due to the spread of such hostile exchanges, it could lead to psychological disequilibrium. Exchanges of hostility volley back-and-forth so quickly that rivals lose their sense of identity; they "meld" into each other, so to speak, because their violence is reducing them to a structural sameness.

This situation is the height of sacrificial crisis, and it led ancient peoples' imaginations to conjure images of monsters that symbolically gave expression to the breakdown of cultural differentiation. During such times we see bizarre images appear in myth, literature, and art which represent blendings of elements that the culture traditionally defines as separate. Monsters are a mishmash of categories that should not combined, like the blending of a man and a bull to form the Minotaur. But in a sacrificial crisis a civilization is in eclipse, on the verge of self-destruction. Reciprocal violence is making a mockery of nicely drawn definitions as social hierarchies lose their authority, and rivals become enemy twins. In a sacrificial crisis the dreaded anarchy that the culture has worked so hard to suppress threatens to overtake the finely differentiated cultural structure like a tornado, leaving in its wake a jumble of forms. The specter of this nondifferentiation finds expression in mythological monsters – and the monstrosity is projected onto innocent victims.

We must remember once again that ancient societies did not have our modern, sophisticated judicial system. Waves of retaliation could only too easily become the general reality, and sacrificial crisis overwhelm a community. Every effort had to be made, therefore, to keep such violence at bay. This was achieved by strengthening hierarchical distinctions and institutions, giving them sacred status and buttressing them with taboos that promised horrible consequences to anyone foolish enough to buck them. How did this help keep reciprocal violence at bay? By keeping people confined within certain categories, thus making violent exchange between them unlikely. To use our aristocrat and peasant again as an example, as long as the distinction between them is sacred to both parties, a barrier of unquestionable authority, the only violence likely to occur is the "top-down" variety; i.e., aristocratic, "legitimate" abuse of the peasant. The "lateral" violence of reciprocal exchange, however, will seem unthinkable.

Notice that we are really talking here about using one form of violence to contain and control another. "Top-down" is still violence, but it is not the kind of violence that threatens the foundational differences of the culture. On the contrary, it helps to solidify them – until a sacrificial crisis is experienced, in which case such top-down differences can no longer effectively prevent reciprocal violence. Then the society slides ominously towards the dreaded nondifferentiation.

Why does Girard call what we have been discussing a *sacrificial* crisis? Because the outbreak and acceleration of reciprocal violence means that sacrifice is no longer channeling the hostility of rivals away from each other and onto the lightening rod of a single sacrificial victim. (For reasons we will examine shortly.) In ancient cultures sacrifice was the very heart and nerve center of everything else. Sacrifices not only reproduced what was believed to be the pattern from time immemorial, they also ensured the continuation of life itself, for both the individual and the community. The sacrificial cult was the sacred spiritual center of society, as the temple or place of sacrifice was the sacred geographical center. In ancient cultures, religion was not a compartmentalized institution, as in modern society, but suffused and upheld everything. Thus, if a society was being threatened with loss of its cultural differentiations, it could only be because the sacrificial cult was weakening. This would happen when people started questioning its authority, its sacredness, or stopped believing in its efficacy to deliver benefits such as renewed fertility to the soil. The sacrificial rituals would then become merely perfunctory. Attitudes of disrespect and acts of nonconformity at the rituals would increase. And these, too, would get copied by others and spread contagiously throughout the group. At that point, the rituals would be unable to perform their basic sociological function of providing an outlet for the pent up violence of mimetic rivalry. If people could not come together around the sacrificial altar, they couldn't come together at all. Then they would begin to direct their violence toward each other.

When this situation reached a climax, and internal violence had reduced the community to the brink of self-destruction, only one thing could save it: another founding murder. In the midst of the crisis of cultural collapse, the scapegoat mechanism could be triggered, and the in-fighting be entirely realigned from all-against-all to all-against-one, as we have seen. In this way, out of the ashes of the old culture, a new one could be born. And so we see that, in a way, the old mythologies had it right: for these ancient cultures, time was indeed circular, and humans did go through a kind of "eternal return," from creation to destruction, and back to creation or resurrection once again. But the historical reality behind the circle is not pretty like its poetic, mythological retelling.

Viewing sacrifice as the formal ritualization of a spontaneous founding murder explains why the sacrificial rituals of so many archaic groups began with the acting-out of a violently chaotic scenario before the climactic immolation of the victim. The community is acting-out the crisis of reciprocal violence that had threatened the group with self-destruction just prior to the moment of their "salvation" through the founding murder. The powerful memory of this crisis is retained in social memory through sacrificial rituals that imitate it in a stylized, but sometimes highly dangerous way. An example of such stylization would be when the natives of certain archaic cultures form lines and face-off against each other waving spears, shouting insults, and engaging in mock ritual battle. The line-against-line configuration – each line appearing as a mirror image of the other – is a stylistic way of displaying the lack of differentiation produced by reciprocal violence at the time of the original crisis. It shows the people's intuitive grasp of the real nature of the crisis: mimetic effacement of distinctions due to reciprocal rivalries.

The point of acting-out the original crisis is to stir up genuinely violent energy in order to discharge it at the climax of the ritual onto the victim. But this is a dangerous game. Acting out the hostility and chaos that prevailed at the time of the founding murder, stirring it up once again in ritually controlled ways, bringing it to a carefully orchestrated crescendo, and then dumping it onto a victim – this process must be strictly contained within proper ritual channels lest an accident occur, or an unintended insult give offense to a rival, or some other "spillage" of violence occur. The goal, after all, is to *expel* violence from the community, not inseminate the community with it. But one is conjuring here, after all, with *violence:* a power as volatile and raging as fire. Invoking it in order to control it is no simple matter, which is why sacrificial ritual is serious business. Sacrifice is an attempt to use "good" violence to cast out "bad" violence. The violence of reciprocal vengeance is to be cast out of the community through the violence done to a single victim. It is an ingenious system, made all the better by being so *inexpensive,* using a little bit of violence (the killing of a single human being or animal) to effect wholesale reconciliation for the entire community. Caiaphas, high priest of the Jerusalem temple during Jesus' ministry, understood these economics very well. Speaking to the council of the Sanhedrin, which had met in an effort to figure out what to do about Jesus' increasing popularity in Jerusalem during the Passover festival, Caiaphas said, "You know nothing at all; you do not understand that it is expedient for you that one man should die for the people, and that the whole nation should not perish." (John 11:49-50) He was teaching his fellow priests a basic lesson in sacrificial economics. But it is a process that uses violence to avert violence, and fighting fire with fire is always risky.

Substitution

Those of us who have become comfortable believing in an unconditionally loving God may wonder at the profoundly ineradicable human conviction that the gods (or God) demanded sacrifices. In *The Creation of the Sacred,* Walter Burkert discusses the fascinating example of finger sacrifice.[58] He tells the story of Aelius Aristeides, in the second century A.D., who was stricken with sickness and spent more than ten years of his life at the sanctuary of the healing god, Asclepius, seeking a cure. In his diary (which is preserved to us), Aristeides says that Asclepius appeared to him one night in a dream, telling him that he would die within three days. Fortunately for Aristeides, however, the god relented and revealed to him the way in which he could avoid this fate: it involved a series of sacrifices of animals to certain gods across the river, a random scattering of coins on the way back, and the sacrifice of a sheep in the temple of Asclepius. In addition, one more sacrifice was also required: Aristeides would have to "cut off a piece of his body for the sake of saving the whole." For Aristeides, as for untold thousands of people since the Paleolithic era, this sacrificed body part would have been the finger. But Aristeides is once again lucky: the god reconsiders, deeming the whole thing rather "laborious," and allows Aristeides to dedicate his finger ring instead.

This story nicely demonstrates how sacrifice is related to

substitution. Aristeides begins with sickness, which is interpreted as a threat from the sacred. The announcement of his impending death came directly from the god in a dream, and it is only the god who can implement a reversal of the fateful decree. In essence, the sacred is demanding his life. But, good news, the sacred will accept a substitute: animals must die, money must be offered, and a body part severed. The body part, the finger, is a substitute for the whole body threatened with death. But yet another phase in the series of substitutions in invoked when the finger ring is substituted for the finger. The series thus runs: Aristeides' own bodily life…a finger as substitute for the body…a ring as substitute for the finger.

What is this series of substitutions accomplishing? Essentially, it is pushing violence, and the threat of violence, farther and farther away from the worshipper. When sickness in the ancient world is understood as a manifestation of divine anger, or an attack by evil demons and demigods, we are moving in the realm of violence. The real threat is the god's violence, and just as we fight disease today by inoculation with the germ itself, so the poison of violence in the ancient world becomes also the remedy; namely, a violent act of sacrifice. Substitution comes into play, then, as a way to deflect the violence from oneself, or from the community. Each level of substituted "victim" involves a *lesser* violence than what was originally threatened. This is because sacrificial substitution works according to the principle of *pars pro toto* – the part for the whole. Thus, instead of the great violence of Aristeides' death, the lesser violence of a severed finger is substituted, the finger being a relatively expendable part that represents the whole body. Likewise, for the violence of a severed and bloody finger, the still lesser violence of being parted from one's ring is substituted. Instead of the whole finger, a mere "part" – the ring – suffices. In the end, instead of being wasted and slain by disease, one is merely robbed of one's ring.

Substitution notwithstanding, however, the threat of the ultimate violence was always there, hanging over one's head. Not everyone was lucky or clever enough to get off with an easy substitution. Burkert mentions how Orestes was pursued and driven mad by the Furies for killing his mother, Clytemnestra –

until he bit off one of his fingers. Then, says, Burkert, "the black Furies turned white, Orestes regained his senses, and he performed two types of sacrifice at the spot to both the black Furies and the white ones."[59] For Orestes, a mere ring would not do the trick – he had to sacrifice a complete finger. (But at least his life was spared.)

Let us look at another example, and see how the principle of sacrificial substitution can help us to understand a very strange text in Exodus. Moses is returning to Egypt after a forty year absence in Midian, at the behest of Yahweh, who wants to use him to free the Israelites from Egyptian domination. Moses brings with him his Midianite wife, Zipporah, and his sons. One night, while encamped in the desert, the following happens:

> *On the way, at a place where they spent the night, the LORD met him and tried to kill him. But Zipporah took a flint and cut off her son's foreskin, and touched Moses' feet with it, and said, "Truly you are a bridegroom of blood to me!" So he let him alone. It was then she said, "A bridegroom of blood by circumcision."* (4:24-26 NRS)

In this strange tale, Yahweh meets Moses and tries to kill him. It is significant that the encounter happens in the desert – traditional haunt of demons and monsters – and at night. Such conditions seem to invite the terrifying and destructive face of the sacred. We don't know why Yahweh sought to kill Moses. Perhaps he did something profane in Yahweh's presence, so that the sacred broke out against him, as it would do later against Nadab and Abihu, the priestly sons of Aaron who offered "unholy fire" before the Lord and were consumed. The crucial point is that Yahweh is demanding the life of Moses. What happens, however, is that Moses' wife interposes her son as ransom for the life of her husband. Yet the son's life, too, is spared, by substitution of the child's penis – producer of life. And yet the penis, too, is spared, by substitution of the foreskin for the entire organ. In other words, what is operating here is a chain of substitutions: foreskin for penis, penis for son, son for father. Circumcision is a substitutionary ransom from the death-threat of the sacred. [60]

It is clear that human beings all over the planet, from time immemorial, have known about this substitutionary principle. Burkert mentions that finger sacrifice is a common motif in folktales and fairytales, and comments, "Worldwide, it seems, in situations of distress and illness or even in anticipation of disaster, people would cut off a finger or part of a finger."[61] He goes on to say that the practice does not arise spontaneously, but is connected to established tradition which is learned and passed on; and yet the tradition is "surprisingly uniform, without direct cultural contacts." This is amazing. We are talking about a tradition that appears around the world, and yet, clearly in many cases this cannot be due to cultural borrowing. How did humanity learn about substitution?

From a Girardian point of view, it was learned from founding murders. For in the situation of a founding murder, everybody was reduced to a condition of mimetic sameness, allowing participants to vent their anger and rage on anyone they pleased to make the victim. It was really all the same who became the target: "Joe" would serve just as well as "Jack," because at this point in the crisis Joe was little more than a copy of Jack anyway. Thus, the choice of scapegoat was essentially arbitrary, a role which, in principle, anyone could fill. One scapegoat could act as a substitute for everyone's hated rival. Joe becomes a stand-in for any and all hated rivals sported by group members. Girard calls the victim of an original founding murder the "surrogate victim." He or she was a surrogate, a stand-in, drawing to himself or herself the animosity that each member of the group would otherwise be dumping on their own personal rivals. This was an amazing discovery for early hominids (albeit an unconscious one): that a single individual could be substituted for everybody's rival, and thus function as a substitute, in a sense, for the entire group. This discovery became the basic principle upon which the developing sacrificial cult was based, and it was eventually applied as a way to deal with all kinds of problems, such as sickness, which involved some kind of violence that could be diverted from oneself or the group through sacrificial substitution.

We must remember, however, what sacrificial substitution essentially is: a means of denying responsibility for one's own violence. Instead of taking responsibility for and dealing with their own mimetic rivalry, the participants made themselves believe in the hideousness and guilt of one unfortunate individual, transferring their mutual antagonisms onto that victim. It is also true, however, that this denial was unconscious – they *really believed* in the monstrosity and malevolence of the victim. That belief allowed them reconciliation with their rivals – but only temporarily. The blessing of peace had to be temporary, because it was based upon an *illusion* created by denial of their own violence. Eventually, their grudges and hostile feelings towards each other would be bound to surface once again. Then what worked before would be perpetrated again, and the illusion would continue to maintain its grip upon the community. This ensured that the true nature of the sacrificial act would remain hidden. While the sacrificial victim was ostensibly being offered to the gods to appease their wrath, or to solicit their help in war, or to ensure a bountiful harvest, and so on, the reality was that a grisly murder was being perpetrated, allowing everyone to dump their pent-up violence onto a substitute victim in a way completely legitimated by the society – legitimated, indeed, by *religion*.

It is important to understand that the substitutionary principle did not stop with the sacrificial victim. As we have seen, over time the principle was extended to encompass a series of further substitutions: something substitutes for the victim, and then something else substitutes for that substitute, and so on. This had the effect of distancing participants farther and farther from the violence of the sacrificial act. We took note of such a series in the bizarre tale of Yahweh's attempted murder of Moses, where the ritual of circumcision substitutes the foreskin for the penis, which substitutes for the boy, who substitutes for the man, Moses. In his book on the Gospel of Mark, scholar Robert Hamerton-Kelly discusses the series of substitutions involved in the sacrifices taking place in the Jerusalem temple of first century Judaism. First, the worshiper presented his own "profane" money to the temple money-changers, who exchanged it for the temple's own currency. This sacred money could then be used to purchase the animal for sacrifice that would represent the offerer before God. So the series looks like this. We begin with the sacred's demand for the life of the worshiper. In place of himself the worshiper substitutes his profane money, in place of which sacred money is substituted. Then, for the sacred money, an animal is substituted. This series of substitutions, Hamerton-Kelly says, "...enables the offerer to dissociate from the violence of the sacrifice while ensuring that the violence takes place and its benefits accrue." [62]

In order for substitution to operate effectively in sacrifice, the human or animal victim must bear some kind of similarity to the worshippers; but it must be just the right amount – not too much, and not too little. Too much similarity between the victim and his/her persecutors would run the risk of retaliation from relatives and friends of the victim. (This is exactly what happened when Agamemnon sacrificed his own daughter, Iphigenia. It enraged her mother, Clytaemnestra, who eventually avenged her daughter by murdering Agamemnon.) Therefore, human sacrificial victims were generally not chosen from among the accepted, "normal" members of the mainstream community.

Additionally, too much similarity between victim and group would make it difficult to deny the reality that the sacrifice is a murder. What is needed is some difference. While the choice of victim is essentially arbitrary, in the sense that there is no real difference between the victim and his or her sacrificers, the latter must find something to latch onto that will help them fantasize a difference. That difference may be something as trivial as a missing tooth, interpreted by the community as an ominous, monstrous sign. Or it may be that the victim limps, or is a stranger (more on these criteria later). But sacrificial ritual exists to help everyone deny that it is really one's fellows that one wishes to lynch. All that hostility needs to be displaced onto a scapegoat who appears monstrously different. Thus, if a potential victim bears too much similarity to the sacrificers, she must be made over, so to speak, so that she acquires a uniqueness that distances her. This is achieved in many ways in various cultures, as, for example, by forcing the victim to perform taboo-breaking acts prior to immolation, so as to imbue her with a sacred aura that separates her completely from her fellows, and establishes her guilt.

On the other hand, too little similarity will not work either. The group fantasizes a monstrous, sacred difference between itself and the sacrificial victim; but at the same time, if the substitutionary principle is to work, and the violence meant for others effectively displaced onto the victim, the group must maintain some unconscious sense that the victim is like them. I mentioned earlier the "kick the dog" syndrome, in which the worker comes home and delivers to an unfortunate dog the swift kick he really desires to give his boss. But kicking an animal when the real target of one's rage is a human boss will have only a tiny cathartic effect, because the victim is too dissimilar to the real target. One would probably achieve greater satisfaction by taking it out on the boss' secretary, or the human relations manager. For this reason, we find in some cultures all manner of creative effort spent on making animals destined for sacrifice human-like: talking to the animal as if it were human during the ritual (even apologizing to the animal for the harm about to be inflicted!), pampering the animal, dressing it up, and so on. In fact, Girard believes that the domestication of animals began as an effort to enhance the animals' substitutionary value as sacrificial victims. Raising and sheltering the animal within the community would increase its similarity to humans so that later, when slaughtered, it would produce a more effective cathartic release. Speaking of the Nuer people of the Upper Nile, Girard writes (citing the work of anthropologist E.E. Evans Pritchard):

> *The Nuer vocabulary is rich in words describing the ways of cattle.... This wealth of expression makes possible a precise and finely nuanced relationship between the cattle, on the one hand, and the human community on the other. The animals' color, the shape of their horns, their age, sex, and lineage are all duly noted and remembered, sometimes as far back as five generations. The cattle are thereby differentiated in such a way as to create a scale of values that approximates human distinctions and represents a virtual duplicate of human society. Among the names bestowed on each man is one that also belongs to the animal whose place in the herd is most similar to the place the man occupies in the tribe.*[63]

(I remind the reader again that none of this was done with conscious awareness of the true function of sacrifice. It was done in deference to the demands, taboos, and superstitions of the sacred.)

Since one's mimetic rivals were human, humans would obviously make the most effective sacrificial victims; and most anthropologists and archeologists agree that the earliest sacrifices were human. The substitution of animal for human victims was thus a major step forward in human history, and was probably not an easy one. It may have been motivated by sheer necessity; or by a powerful new ethical conviction, such as we find in the Hebrew Scriptures, which rail against human sacrifice (and, eventually, against all sacrifice). But this is a topic to be developed later in this book.

In the ongoing history of ancient societies, sacrificial substitution literally saved communities over and over again from their own reciprocal violence. I have stressed the unconscious nature of these proceedings. But it was part of the Bible's revelatory mission to enunciate it consciously and explicitly, as John does when he gives us Caiaphas' utterance, quoted earlier: "You know nothing at all; you do not understand that it is expedient for you that one man should die for the people, and that the whole nation should not perish." (John 11:49-50) Not only is the substitutionary principle here explicitly enunciated, but the Gospel shows it being consciously manipulated by the powers that be, who want to make Jesus a scapegoat to absorb the violence they fear will otherwise fall upon themselves.

Taboo and Myth

We have taken a luxurious amount of space to describe the founding murder, the scapegoat mechanism, and sacrificial ritual; but two other important concepts need to be addressed in order to complete the picture of the development of human society and culture: myth, and taboo (or prohibition). Girard understands mythology (particularly in its earliest forms) as imaginative reconstructions of founding murders *told from the point of view of the persecutors.* Mythology is a retelling that hides the innocence of the victim and disguises the arbitrariness of the choice, making the victim into a god or monster,[64] guilty of horrible crimes. Since a later chapter will be devoted entirely to mythology, I will not develop that topic here, but move to a brief explanation of Girard's understanding of taboo, or prohibition.

Three things lie at the heart of archaic and ancient cultures throughout the world: sacrifice, mythology, and prohibitions. We might call these the three "pillars" upon which those cultures were constructed. According to Girard, all of them grew out of founding murders. Prohibitions are taboos put in place in order to prevent the outbreak of another crisis similar to the one that led to the founding murder. Although much good was perceived to have resulted from that slaying, no one wanted a return to the violent days which preceded it. We must remember once again that we are dealing with societies, communities, tribes, and other groups that did not have our modern Western legal system as a check on the violence of vendettas, societies that lived every day on a fault line of violence that could easily shake the precarious balance that allowed them to live in relative harmony. The balance maintained by continual sacrifice needed to be supplemented by the observance of prohibitions covering every aspect of daily life likely to become a source of rivalry between people. Prohibitions were fundamentally intended to inhibit mimetic rivalry from erupting into actions that would spark reprisals and lead to violent escalation.

The repression of mimetic desire and rivalry was accomplished by the threat of terrible violence toward offenders, and a belief in horrendous consequences to the entire community should one of the rules be broken. Speaking of the ubiquitous "sky gods" of archaic cultures, and the sovereign gods of polytheistic civilizations, Mircea Eliade says that both types of gods "guarantee the order and the fertility of nature as long as the law is kept; rain ensures fertility, but any breaking of the law, any 'sin,' will endanger the normal functioning of the seasons, thus threatening the very life of society and nature. . . . a single infringement would be enough to endanger the balance of order at every cosmic level."[65] These sovereign gods were omnipotent and all-seeing (sometimes thousand-eyed!) punishers of the wicked – that is to say, the breakers of their rules. These gods were Big Brother on steroids. From the perspective of Girardian theory, the palpable fear behind belief in such gods is quite understandable: the breaking of a single taboo could threaten the entire cosmic order because, just as it only takes a spark to get a fire going, so one man grabbing another's wife or ox could be enough to unleash an epidemic of reciprocal violence within the community. The taboos had been put in place specifically to nail the lid on a Pandora's box that had previously been opened with devastating results.

Essentially, then, prohibition was one form of violence being used to control another. It was the heavy hand that proscribed certain behaviors, and threatened an ominous blow in the face of violation. "[T]he prohibitions of primitive peoples," writes Girard, "display a knowledge of violence and its ways that surpasses our modern comprehension." "The reason is clear," he continues – "the prohibitions were dictated by violence itself, by the violent manifestations of a previous crisis, and they are fixed in place as a bulwark against similar outbursts."[66] "Thus what motivates prohibition is the fear of violence."[67]

As an example of what has just been said about the function of prohibitions, we might consider the incest taboo, which is a universal anthropological phenomenon. Behind this taboo stands the fear of rivalrous competition between father and son for possession of the wife/mother. The father is, after all, a model to the son – and thus inevitably an obstacle as well, especially when it comes to relations with the mother. One need not invoke some instinctual, libidinal drive, as Freud did, to account for the son's violent urge to eliminate the old man. The son imitates what he perceives to be the father's desire for the mother, so the mother becomes sexually desirable to the son and the father becomes an obstacle. Since, by virtue of his power and dominance the father is inevitably an obstacle to the child, what the father desires and seems to reserve for himself will appear all the more precious to the child by virtue of its unattainability. Holding the nuclear family together under the potentially explosive pressure of such powerful mimetic dynamics could only be achieved by the pressure of a greater violence, always threatened, and occasionally enacted. The incest taboo is universal because the mimetic violence which it seeks to suppress is universal.

The only problem with something like the incest taboo is that it suppresses the symptom but does not address the real disease: acquisitive mimetic desire, the desire to possess what the model/obstacle possesses. In this regard the Bible shows a stunning level of awareness in its structuring of the Ten Commandments. The prohibitions against killing, adultery, stealing, and bearing false witness are all attempts to suppress acts of violence. But, as Girard points out, the tenth and final commandment prohibits, not an act, but *desire:* "You shall not covet your neighbor's house, you shall not covet your neighbor's wife, or his manservant, or his maidservant, or his ox, or his ass, or anything that is your neighbor's." (Exodus 20:17) The Hebrew word in this commandment usually translated "covet," means simply "desire," and it is prohibited because of the mimetic tendency of human beings to desire their neighbors' goods. In propounding this commandment, it is as if the writer had begun to list all the various goods that one neighbor might wish to wrest from another (house, wife, manservant, maidservant, ox, ass), then realized that this could get to be a *very* long list. Wanting to bring it to an end, he wrote, finally, "nor *anything* that is thy neighbor's." In other words, what is finally being prohibited is acquisitive mimetic desire itself, which the writer terms "covetousness." For that is really the underlying cause of the acts of violence listed in the previous commandments. In making this shift, says Girard, the tenth commandment sketches "a fundamental revolution in the understanding of desire."[68]

Prohibitions, however, had only limited effectiveness in suppressing violence, even among the Hebrews with their "revolutionary" understanding of the nature and danger of desire. No taboo could function as a complete solution apart from the scapegoat mechanism, sacrifice, and mythological propaganda. The problem, as the Apostle Paul saw very well, was that the very prohibitions meant to suppress desire could also stimulate it: "I would not have known what it is to covet if the law had not said, 'You shall not covet.' But sin, seizing an opportunity in the commandment, produced in me all kinds of covetousness." (Romans 7:8) The reason is simple. By erecting a prohibition as an obstacle, it soon becomes a model, suggesting the very thing it seeks to prohibit. As a powerful and violent obstacle it exerts a powerful fascination, which evokes and enflames the desire to perform the banned act. We saw this happen in the Garden of Eden. Prohibit the fruit and someone will surely want to eat it. The heavier the sanction for eating the fruit, the more desirable the fruit appears.

Prohibitions threaten violence in order to inhibit violence; but, as in all cases of using fire to fight fire, it can be difficult to tell where the good fire ends and bad fire begins. From a Girardian point of view, it would be better to steer clear of fire entirely; but the societies we have described were trapped in a violent cosmos from which there was no escape, for all attempts to escape the demon invariably invoked the demon. Sacrifice and prohibition, as ways to avert the violence of mimetic rivalry, were a devil's bargain that gave human beings no ultimate purchasing power, and provided no real ransom from their own violent cosmos. As temporary stop-gap measures they were roughly effective, and allowed civilization to proceed. But at the same time, they put human beings on a treadmill of eternal return that kept bringing them back to the place from which they had originally started, but still more deeply enslaved to violence.

The "Primitive" Sacred

To most people today the term "sacred" means holy, or consecrated to God; or, at the very least, possessing extreme and fundamental value. But Girard uses the term in the manner of academic anthropology, with reference to primitive (or "archaic") and ancient societies. Though anything or anyone can be sacred within these cultures, two qualities in particular always accompany manifestations of the sacred: it always exists over-against the rest of the "profane" world, and it has an ambivalent character: that is, it can be just as terrifying and destructive as it can be beneficent and beneficial. This is the biggest difference between the so-called "primitive" sacred, and modern usage of the term. For us, "sacred" is purely good and positive, while evil is displaced onto the devil, evil spirits, and so on. When the modern person fears God, the fear is usually of incurring the wrath of a God conceived as good and just. This is a far cry from the frightening wildness of the primitive sacred, which had no necessary alignment with concepts of justice or morality. The gods were capricious.

The sacred manifested itself through gods, rituals, myths, superstitions, nature – anything could become sacred. It transformed physical places and objects, turning dirt into "holy ground," stones into fetish objects, or a tree into the center of the universe. It was the power that flowed from venerated objects, sacred stones, totems, symbolic forms, ceremonial dances, sacrificial rites, and an uncountable number of other such channels. Anything that sacred power touched became sacred, and was marked as absolutely distinct from the rest of the profane world around it. The gods were sacred, and so were their temples and the furnishings within them, the ground upon which the temple stood, and the territory surrounding it, in diminishing potency as one traveled farther away from the sacred center. Time itself could be sacred, divided into sacred time and profane time; sacred time being, for example, the celebration of the New Year's festival, when the creation of the world was reenacted in order to renew and ensure the fertility of the soil.

As just mentioned, the most outstanding feature of the primitive sacred, found everywhere in world history and culture, was its ambivalence. The very Latin word, *sacer,* means both holy and accursed. (The equivalent Greek term, *hagios,* can mean both "pure" and "polluted.") Sacred power could be both a blessing and a curse. Nothing gives us a livelier picture of this ambivalence than the mythologies of the gods, who are utterly capricious, and who enter into relationships with human beings that result in the best of times one minute, the worst of times the next. Encounter with an ancient god was not exactly something one desired; and certainly not to be attempted without rigorous preparation to serve as protection. Otherwise, the result could be death. For the slightest misstep could provoke an attack from one's divine benefactor. (For example, expressing too much devotion to one god could provoke the jealousy of another). The sacred power could bless you, but at other times it could blast you. One was happy to have the sacred confined to a temple or sacrificial altar. This was not a power one wanted running loose throughout the community, for it was as likely to bring havoc as blessing.

Referring to the classical Homeric gods, for example, Oxford scholar Robin Lane Fox writes:

> *[I]ntimacy with a god was not easy. . . . men trembled in terror before the presence of their gods. The gods themselves knew their power: "The gods are not easy to cope with," remarked Hera, "when seen very clearly." . . . [I]n Homer's poems, no hero confessed to elation when a god revealed his presence. The hero did not court the gods or strive to meet them. He chanced upon them, and as the first terror left him, he might beg for practical, earthly favours. It took a very special hero, a child of one of the gods, to dare to protest to a god face to face. Other heroes were more restrained, and mere mortals, naturally, would observe the greatest restraint.*[69]

Writes Fox, "in gods and demigods, 'irreconcilable temper' was anticipated and widely feared."[70] Fear of the gods was not limited, of course, to Greece. In Akkadian, the language of ancient Babylon and Assyria, the basic concept associated with the gods was terror – *puluhtu*.[71] "To transmit religion is to transmit fear," says Burkert, who goes on to quote the first century Roman poet, Statius: "Fear, first of all, produced gods in the world." [72]

The darker side of the sacred is dramatically seen in the fact that certain persons were banned because contact with them was dangerous and defiling. Certain objects were prohibited because contact with them would cause one to become "polluted," as if catching a disease. The Hebrew Scriptures are full of examples. I will mention only the prohibition against contact with a human corpse, grave, or bones, which rendered one "unclean," or polluted, and required a certain lapse of time (usually seven days) and/or special sacred rites to make the violator clean again. Such taboos were expressions of the negative side of the sacred. The taboo object (or person) is set apart from the rest of the world in the same way as a positive manifestation would be; and just as positive sacred energy could flow, say, from a sacred healer into a sick body to bring wellness and healing, so negative sacred energy could flow from a grave, contaminating and polluting anyone coming into contact with it, whether deliberately or by accident.

The topic of the sacred in anthropology is vast, deep, and often perplexing. Some researchers have interpreted the seemingly arbitrary taboos of the sacred, and its capricious shifting between blessing and curse, as so many manifestations of an irrational and superstitious religious impulse. Other anthropologists consider the sacred impervious to any rational and universally applicable explanation. But Girard's theory claims to be able to provide just such an explanation, and it does so in terms of violence. Part of the power of Girard's analysis in *Violence and the Sacred* is the way in which it makes good sense of a plethora of culturally diverse, and often quite strange (to us), practices and beliefs. Yet everything can be boiled down to one commonly quoted sentence from *Violence and the Sacred:* "Violence is the heart and secret soul of the sacred."[73] What Girard means is that the sacred was both feared and venerated because it was really *human violence,* projected large upon a supernatural screen. From the very beginning of the human experience, because of its power both to destroy (during the sacrificial crisis) and to generate results (through a founding murder), *violence* was seen as both the number one problem *and* the number one solution. But human beings did not take responsibility for this violence, admitting it as their own; instead, they projected it as a transcendent reality, which they subsequently feared (as problem) and venerated (as solution). We have already examined the way in which this whole masquerade began, but the importance of understanding this process for our discussion of the sacred calls for a brief restatement.

Spontaneous discovery of the scapegoat mechanism by certain early hominid groups transformed a war of all-against-all into a war of all-against-one, which, thanks to the polarization of collective violence against the victim, laid the foundation for society. Through the scapegoat mechanism the people transferred blame onto the victim, who became the monstrous embodiment of the chaos and nondifferentiation which had characterized the group itself during its crisis of reciprocal violence. Thanks to this transfer of blame, the victim became an even greater source of fear after his death. For all of the violence, anger, fear, and guilt that was expelled from the community through its scapegoating maneuvers came to rest upon the head (or shall I say, dead body) of the victim. *And this was the projection, not of a single individual but of the entire group*, with everyone believing and acting the same way toward the victim. Thus the dead victim came to appear larger-than-life, taking on a transcendental quality. This process is not dissimilar to the way in which modern movie stars appear larger than life because they are the creation of a collective consciousness; but in the case of primitive cultures, where there was no external "reality check" whatsoever, we are talking about the creation of more than movie stars; we are talking about the creation of gods.

But the victim as a transcendental monstrosity is only half the equation. We must remember that immediately after the victim's death the group experiences a miraculous peace – a completely unexpected blessing for which they cannot but be grateful. Whom can the group hold responsible for this? (And, indeed, archaic peoples always asked "who," not "what," in face of puzzling or threatening events.) The participants certainly cannot think *themselves* responsible. They see themselves as the mere passive recipients of a "miracle," for none of their actions had been consciously deliberated. They have no way of understanding the true dynamics of the situation: that the mimetic energy previously flowing into reciprocal rivalries had realigned itself over against a single victim, and was discharged in the persecution of that victim, quelling the flames of group rivalry, and leading to a dramatic, newly constructed "peace." They are in complete denial, which always involves a certain passivity in which individuals see themselves as pawns of fate, or victims of the power of others. In this state of mind, nobody can be found able to be imagined powerful enough to create such a peace, except the one who had the power to create the war in the first place. Thus the inevitable conclusion begins to emerge, that the fearsome, larger-than-life monster they killed must also have a positive, benevolent side. And, more or less quickly, in addition to being feared, the victim comes to be *venerated*. Perhaps it had all been part of a plan, the plan of a dying and resurrected god who came among us to stir up trouble so that he could bring us blessing after his death. And tales begin to be told.

If what the victim is turning into here sounds a lot like what we know about ancient gods, that is no coincidence. Insight into the founding murder reveals that the gods were nothing other than imaginative representations of human beings who were originally the victims of collective violence. They were scapegoats, whose lynchings became the foundations of societies across the planet. Only a kind of god could wield as much power as the group attributed to the dead victim. Because that power was believed to have been used malevolently during the victim-god's lifetime to visit destruction upon the group, the god is feared: its carcass, its grave – everything associated with it – becomes a thing of dread. In terms of mimetic theory, the scapegoat became a supreme *Obstacle.*

But we discussed in a previous chapter the fascination that obstacles exercise upon mimetic human beings, and how easily they become models. This means that once the dead victim becomes an object of superstitious terror, it will also become an object of great fascination, and human beings will come to live in fascinated terror of the gods. And precisely for this reason it will then become a model to which they will look with a sense of veneration – for one stands in awe of great power. The "fear of the Lord" makes one bow down before the Lord's power. And veneration leads in turn to supplication: that is, requests directed to the power for help. Even if the god is felt basically as a menace, one always hopes that it won't be a menace to *oneself.* Thus one attempts to influence the terrifying power, perhaps even to manipulate it – through prayer, through ritual, through sacrifice, and so on.

We see, then, how it could have come about that the dead scapegoat, who had taken on an aura of god-like transcendence, became in time to be not only an object of fearful apprehension, but also of fascinated veneration and worship. The "god" is feared, placated, appeased, then venerated, entreated, worshipped, and loved for the benefits it generously bestows – all a product of group delusion based on the projection of the group's own violence onto a convenient target.[74] The benefit is that this newly created "Big Brother" in the sky keeps the people in line, along with the god's taboos and prohibitions that suppress rivalry, and gives them an ongoing outlet for their pent up anger and resentments in the form of the sacrificial slaughterings the Big Guy demands. This is the birth of religion. And, quite frankly, if it had not been discovered, homo sapiens would have extinguished themselves very early on thanks to their mimetic rivalries. To put it crudely but memorably, religion saved the human ass for tens of thousands of years. [75]

Once again, we must bear in mind that we are talking about *collective* violence. One individual killing another would not lead to this kind of result. The transfiguration of the victim occurs because the violence is collective, because the *entire community* made a single individual responsible for the evil and the good – all acting in concert, mimetically, to reinforce each other's belief and action. A modern comparison might help make this clear. One person hailing Hitler would be seen as a mere oddity; one hundred doing it would render it interesting; but a rally of thousands, all hailing Hitler in lock-step precision, invests Hitler with a kind of transcendental radiance that, even in the twentieth century, could not fail to produce awe.[76] Ancient victims became gods in somewhat similar fashion. But they did not need thousands to invest them with such power. For archaic and ancient groups, even a tribe of ten would be the world in which each individual existed, and the very definition of reality. And together, through group projection of responsibility, they would make the dead victim appear godlike.

If turning human victims into gods sounds like a far-fetched scenario, we should consider what still occasionally happens in India.[77] In September of 1987, an 18 year old Indian woman named Roop Kanwar committed *sati* in her village. "Sati" is a practice in which a widow immolates herself on her husband's funeral pyre. Roop had been married only eight months, but her husband (a 24 year old) had died of gastroenteritis the previous day. Whether Roop was forced into the flames or sacrificed herself voluntarily was never clearly decided. People associated with the event were arrested, but then acquitted. (The practice of sati was outlawed in India in 1829, but still occasionally occurs in remote villages.[78])

What is pertinent about this for our discussion is that "After her death, Roop Kanwar was hailed as a *sati mata* – a 'sati' mother, or pure mother."[79] Such immolated women are deified. Shrines are erected to them, and pilgrimages to the site of the pyre encouraged. The house of Charan Shah, for example, a 55 year old widow who immolated herself on her husband's pyre in 1999, "has become a shrine for the villagers, as they strongly believe that one who has become a sati is a deity; she is worshipped and endowed with gifts."[80] The term "sati" is derived from the name of the goddess Sati (*aka* Dakshayani) who immolated herself because she could not stand the way her father was humiliating her living husband. Working with the insight Girard brings to mythology (to be examined in a later chapter), it is not hard to discern in this myth the background of a real event in which an unfortunate female victim was burned alive, then glorified.

The controversies in modern India concerning whether widows perform sati voluntarily or are forced into it are interesting in light of the historical cover-up Girard discerns behind mythological tales that describe victims going willingly, sometimes even merrily, to their deaths. In sad truth, either the victim was forced and a myth was concocted that put a happy face on events, or the victim internalized the propaganda of the persecutors. (We will see something like this latter phenomenon in operation when we examine in detail the New Testament story of the Gerasene demoniac – a scapegoat who internalizes the scorn of the city populace, and acts out violence against himself.)

Returning to our discussion of the sacred, we remember that Girard traces the ambivalence of the sacred – its dual quality as both poison and remedy – back to the ambivalence surrounding the victim of a founding murder. For that unfortunate individual was initially perceived as the poison, the source of the group's degeneration into all-against-all violence; but, once eliminated, the victim turned out to be the remedy as well. This means that the victim is essentially *nondifferentiated*. The victim is both good *and* evil, poison *and* remedy. The victim, in other words, is sacred.

Indeed, this is how the sacred comes to birth within human experience. In an ordered cosmos, good and evil are clearly differentiated. There are "good guys" and "bad guys," good spirits and evil spirits, and, in a dualist system, a good god and an evil god who are clearly differentiated opponents. But the sacred is *both.* Its very being is nondifferentated.

Let us remember that this nondifferentiation was the very condition of the war of all-against-all, and the state into which all societies were terrified of lapsing. Just as the scapegoat mechanism did not do away with violence but simply transferred it into a "higher" register, neither did it do away with nondifferentiation – it simply expelled it from the group and resituated it in what one might call a quarantined space, the space of the victim, which became the space of the sacred. But what we disown and project comes back to haunt us. Ancient societies were thus continually haunted by the specter of a return of the nondifferentiation they had thrust so violently from their midst. The very "god" who brought order out of chaos and established the community, also threatened to strike the community and reduce it to nothingness.

We should also note that this sacred ambivalence was often matched by ambivalence on the part of the worshipers themselves. Especially in times of sacrificial crisis, when belief in the ritual process was waning, worshippers sometimes found it difficult to approach the sacrificial altar with a clear conscience. As examples, we can cite some strange aspects of ancient Greek ritual. The first century Greek historian, Plutarch, says that people in his day were very careful not to kill the animal until it shook its head in assent, because they were revolted and terrified by what they did. Greeks tried to get their animals to process to the altar voluntarily, and legends told of how animals would press forward toward the sacrifice on their own initiative, as though the people needed to feel innocent, and relieved of responsibility for the violence. [81]

Another strange thing is that Greek poets would wax eloquent during sacrificial rituals in such a way as to whip the participants into a frenzy of wailing and weeping – a custom that greatly upset Plato. Cesáreo Bandera has detailed the philosopher's reaction.[82] Plato thought that all this weeping and wailing around the act of sacrifice was totally out of place and sacrilegious, because it made it seem as though the sacrifice should be a sad occasion, as though the killing of the victim were something to be regretted and mourned. Plato did not want to get rid of sacrifice, or the sacred; on the contrary, he wanted to secure its power, because he understood how it stabilized society. He understood that the best way to make people obey the law was to make the law sacred in their eyes. He also understood that *sacredness came from unanimous belief,* and that any dissenting voices would undermine and weaken the sacred power.

In Plato's opinion that was precisely what the poets were doing with their participation in the rituals: they were introducing ambivalence into the people's feelings about the victim and the sacred act of its slaying. In order to eliminate that ambivalence Plato wanted to oust the poets from his Republic. In his Republic there would be no weeping, nor the slightest suggestion of a sense of guilt on the part of the killers when the victim was slaughtered. In this way Plato tried to use philosophy to make the Greek sacred rituals internally consistent, and thus stronger and more effective. Says Bandera, "[I]t is of the utmost importance not to look at the victim qua victim. One must avoid even the thought that the victim is being in any way victimized, as we would say today (had Plato had his way, the modern notion of "victimization" would have never existed)."[83]

The Greeks were not the only ones whose rituals betrayed this kind of ambivalence. One can hardly resist chuckling at the words uttered by certain Babylonian priests, according to a text (of which we have several copies spanning many centuries) that details the ritual procedure for sacrificing a bull. At one point after the slaying, the priest would bend down to the bull's severed head and say, "This deed was done by all the gods; I did not do it."(!)[84] Understanding sacrifice as the imitation and ritualization of an original founding murder – a *human* murder – explains the ambivalence, the mourning, and the pretence of innocence surrounding these ritual killings of animals. For they were, after all, as Bandera points out, only "half-veiled sign[s] of the implied human victim."[85]

In naming the sacred as a projection of human violence, we have named religion; for it is no exaggeration to say that until Christianity made its impact felt in the West, the religious experience of humanity was that of the sacred. Human groups prior to the advent of Christianity (but also for a long time thereafter, including within Christianity itself) experienced religion as the relation to a sacred power that was a mixture of malevolence and benevolence (or, expressed in moral categories, evil and good), with which the entire community attempted to establish good relations. Louis J. Martyn gives a succinct definition of religion, thus conceived, in his commentary on Galatians: *The various communal, cultic means – always involving the distinction of sacred from profane – by which human beings seek to know and to be happily related to the gods or God.* [86]

What Girard offers, then, is nothing less than an explanation of the genesis of religion itself, *and thus human culture itself,* because Girard believes, as do many anthropologists, that religion – that is, the sacred – was the first and fundamental human experience. Everything else grew and developed out of the necessities laid upon humanity by the sacred: language, money, the institution of kingship, domestication of animals, arts and crafts, and so on. There is no space in this book to detail how it is that the initial experience of the sacred through the founding murder gives rise to all the various aspects of human culture, but interested readers will do well to begin with chapters two and three of *Things Hidden.*

Earlier I hinted that it was the Judaeo-Christian tradition, and particularly the Christian Gospels, that impacted the West with a powerful "deconstruction" of sacred religion, bringing about the demise of sacrifice and mythology. Yet Christianity *as a religion* did not escape enmeshment with the sacred. Elements of the primitive sacred continued within Christendom's theology and practice in ways that we will examine later, especially with respect to the idea of a vengeful God, and the theology of atonement. The percolation of the Gospels and the preaching of Paul into pagan cultures brought about the demise of ancient religions, but would for a long time (right up to the present day!) continue to do battle with vestiges of the old sacred within Christianity itself.

The implications of what we have explored in this chapter are staggering. To state it baldly, Girard is saying that religion, and along with it human culture as such, began and developed from the murder of victims. He is saying that the first experience human beings had of working together as collective units in a way that produced a glue powerful enough to sustain community, happened when they discovered the power of the lynch mob. Only the powerfully cohesive force of the mimetic mob could overcome the powerfully repulsive force of mimetic rivals. In order to explain the switch from rivalry to reconciliation, Girard needs invoke no new mechanism: both the rivalry and the reconciliation owe their power to the same force: human beings' hyper-mimetic capacity. For all its benefits as empathy and goodwill, the mimetic capacity leads to overwhelming violence in two forms: the chaotic, head-on collisions of rivalry ("bad" violence), and the channeled, uniform collision of the mob against a scapegoat ("good" violence). And from this latter process, called the scapegoat mechanism, human religion and society are generated. From a Girardian point of view, therefore, violence is not some late add-on to the human condition; it has made us what we are from the very beginnings of emerging humanity.

Girard has offered us a strikingly original and, to me, convincing explanation for the ambivalent and mixed nature of the sacred, and the generation of human society. Yet Girard claims that these insights are not original with him. He got them from the Bible, both indirectly through Western novelists and playwrights who were influenced by the biblical tradition, and directly from the scriptures themselves. The information given in this chapter was presented in highly theoretical form; but it is time at last to turn to the Bible itself, and see how it all dovetails with the biblical revelation.

Chapter Five

Mimesis, Rivalry, and Founding Murder In Genesis 4

The story of Cain shows what the history of the twentieth century shows, namely, that if we dispense with the sacrificial structures upon which religion and culture for so long depended without at the same time renouncing the mimetic passions that made these structures necessary in the first place, then sooner or later we will become murderers.

Gil Bailie, *Violence Unveiled* [87]

‡‡

The mimetic understanding of envy and rivalry revealed in Genesis 2 and 3 continues in Genesis 4 with the story of Cain and Abel. In addition, the themes of sacrifice and the sacred are played out in Genesis 4, which alerts us to the beginning of humanity's religious culture founded upon the scapegoated victim. Let's take a look at these fascinating texts.

Now Adam knew Eve his wife, and she conceived and bore Cain, saying, "I have gotten a man with the help of the LORD." And again, she bore his brother Abel. Now Abel was a keeper of sheep, and Cain a tiller of the ground. In the course of time Cain brought to the LORD an offering of the fruit of the ground, and Abel brought of the firstlings of his flock and of their fat portions. And the LORD had regard for Abel and his offering, but for Cain and his offering he had no regard. So Cain was very angry, and his countenance fell. The LORD said to Cain, "Why are you angry, and why has your countenance fallen? If you do well, will you not be accepted? And if you do not do well, sin is couching at the door; its desire is for you, but you must master it."

Cain said to Abel his brother, "Let us go out to the field." And when they were in the field, Cain rose up against his brother Abel, and killed him. Then the LORD said to Cain, "Where is Abel your brother?" He said, "I do not know; am I my brother's keeper?" And the LORD said, "What have you done? The voice of your brother's blood is crying to me from the ground. And now you are cursed from the ground, which has opened its mouth to receive your brother's blood from your hand. When you till the ground, it shall no longer yield to you its strength; you shall be a fugitive and a wanderer on the earth."

Cain said to the LORD, "My punishment is greater than I can bear. Behold, thou hast driven me this day away from the ground; and from thy face I shall be hidden; and I shall be a fugitive and a wanderer on the earth, and whoever finds me will slay me." Then the LORD said to him, "Not so! If any one slays Cain, vengeance shall be taken on him sevenfold." And the LORD put a mark on Cain, lest any who came upon him should kill him.

Then Cain went away from the presence of the LORD, and dwelt in the land of Nod, east of Eden. Cain knew his wife, and she conceived and bore Enoch; and he built a city, and called the name of the city after the name of his son, Enoch. (Genesis 4:1-17)

Rivalry and Sacrifice

The text does not state explicitly the reason for God's acceptance of Abel's offering, and rejection of Cain's. Attempts to speculate about God's reasons often implicitly assume that the author was inept in omitting the most important piece of information we need in order to make sense of the story. In fact, the lack of a reason only highlights the real focus of the tale: the rivalry between the brothers. There is a rivalry between them, and the desired object is

God's acceptance. The story reveals what happens in cases of mimetic rivalry: obsession with one's rival eventually displaces the original object of desire, which can even be sacrificed, if necessary, for the sake of triumph over the enemy. That is exactly what Cain does. He becomes so obsessed with his rival Abel that he loses sight of what he had been originally competing for, God's acceptance. The result is that eventually his only concern, his only desire, becomes to triumph over Abel and destroy his rival – even if that means alienating God.

The story is therefore not about the vertical, God-relation, but the horizontal, human relation of envy and rivalry. The text does not state explicitly that Abel felt animosity towards Cain, but before we start using this story as a means of distinguishing two lines of humanity – the good line of Abel and the evil line of Cain (a view I adopted forty years ago upon reading Francis Schaeffer's *Genesis in Space and Time,* and held for quite a long time thereafter) – it is important to note that the story revolves around *sacrifice,* and it cannot be a coincidence that the one whose envy gets out of control, and who murders his brother, is the one whose sacrifice does not "work" (i.e., is not accepted by God and therefore does not procure blessing). To know why it doesn't work, we have only to compare the types of sacrifices offered by the two brothers. Abel sacrifices an *animal;* in fact not one but *several* animals (the firstlings of his flock and their fat portions). Abel's sacrificial ritual, in other words, involves lots of killing. He channels his violence into sacrificial slaughter, whereas Cain's offering is of the fruit of the ground, which allows him no outlet for violence.

It is possible to see in this story, then, something more than the simplistic notion of a good Abel versus an evil Cain. We can detect rivalry between two brothers who imitate each other's desire for the same thing – efficacious religion based on powerful sacrifices that procure the blessing of God – and compete for it. But one of them cannot control his mimetic rivalry because he lacks the violent sacrificial outlet. His violence therefore eventually erupts, and he kills his brother. As discussed previously, the prevention of such violence was precisely the function of sacrifice in ancient communities (notwithstanding their mythological and theological rationalizations). Sacrifice siphoned violence out of the community by expending it on a polarized "other," thus preventing brother from turning against brother.

Genesis 4:6-7 makes it clear that Cain is struggling with envious, mimetic desire. God says to him, "Why are you angry, and why has your countenance fallen? If you do well, will you not be accepted? And if you do not do well, sin is couching at the door; its desire is for you, but you must master it." For the sacrificial reason just mentioned, Cain is indeed unable to "master it," and kills his brother in the field.

Here, then, is the Bible's first example of the way in which the serpent of mimetic rivalry insinuates itself even between close blood relations, brother and brother, stirring up the poison of desire that leads to rivalry and violence. In Gen. 3:3 the Lord had said, "You shall not eat of the fruit of the tree which is in the midst of the garden, neither shall you touch it, lest you die." Abel's is the first recorded death following that narrative, and would thus appear to be the author's understanding of how the Lord's prediction was fulfilled. The fruit of mimetic rivalry will be death at the hands of one's own brother. (This is an insight not often recognized by theologians who interpret Gen. 3:3 in purely spiritual or metaphysical terms – "Death" as a kind of "Power" to which humanity becomes subject – and thus miss the text's anthropological realism.) In the Cain and Abel story, death is neither the power of the devil, nor a punishment from God, but a result of competitive rage between brothers. Genesis is concerned with *violence*, and this story is but the beginning: the subsequent narrative about Cain's descendants will lead to the boisterous and violent Lamech, followed immediately by the story of the flood, which is prefaced by the comment: "Now the earth was corrupt in God's sight, and the earth was filled with *violence*." (Gen. 6:11)

The Escalation of Violence

When Cain expresses his fear of being killed in reprisal for the murder of Abel ("Whoever finds me will slay me!"), God responds, *"Not so! If any one slays Cain, vengeance shall be taken on him sevenfold."* The text goes on to say that "the Lord put a mark on Cain, lest any who came upon him should kill him." This text is usually interpreted as the Lord threatening to execute his own sevenfold vengeance on any persecutors of Cain; and indeed this is a possible reading. The view of God in the Hebrew Scriptures is not completely shorn of violence.

On the other hand, it is clear that the whole point of the "mark of Cain" is the *prevention* of violence. The Lord puts a mark on Cain in order to save his life. But Cain is a murderer: why would the Lord desire to save the life of a murderer, while at the same time threatening a sevenfold worse fate to anyone who murders the murderer? We should note that the text does not say, "If any one slays Cain, *I* will take vengeance on him sevenfold." It says, rather, "vengeance shall be taken on him sevenfold." This allows the possibility of understanding the whole business about the mark of Cain rather differently. In this alternative reading, the mark upon Cain is a sign regarding the danger of escalating violence. The Lord hopes that by putting a warning sign on Cain, those who would seek vengeance against him will be dissuaded. God is saying, in effect, "Don't worry Cain, you will be safe, because I am going to mark you so that vengeance seekers will realize that if they kill you, there will be others who will come after them with an even fiercer, sevenfold vendetta." Seven is a symbolic number in the Bible which indicates completion or fullness. So the text is saying that once humans indulge their desire for vengeance, the escalation of violence will continue until it reaches apocalyptic fullness. On this reading, it is *human* violence which is really in view in this text, continuing the Cain and Abel narrative with its stress upon mimetic rivalry leading to violence between brothers.

Bearing this warning sign, Cain embarks upon his wanderings in the land of Nod, east of Eden, and builds a city. He has children, and they have children, and they have children, until eventually we arrive at Lamech – not insignificantly *seven* generations from Adam (the biblical number of completion). The implication here is that with Lamech the violence of humanity has reached its fullness. This escalation reaches a crescendo with Lamech's brag, recorded in 4:23-24: *"Adah and Zillah, hear my voice; you wives of Lamech, hearken to what I say: I have slain a man for wounding me, a young man for striking me. If Cain is avenged sevenfold, truly Lamech seventy times seven."* If God has warned of a sevenfold (that is, total) escalation of violence, Lamech despises this wisdom; not only will he deliberately seek vengeance nonetheless, he will raise it seventy times seven – and for a mere slap!

No wonder, then, that we do indeed eventually arrive at the apocalyptic situation described just prior to the flood: *Now the earth was corrupt in God's sight, and the earth was filled with violence.* (Gen. 6:11) The violence the text is referring to is particularly the violence of vendetta – the reciprocal violence which enemy brothers visit upon each other, and which is the result of eating the tree's fruit of the knowledge of good and evil. Surely Lamech thinks himself good and his violence justified; and he thinks the young man who slaps him nothing but a sassy cur worthy of annihilation.

The Founding Murder

Long before I read Girard, I was aware of what seemed to me a curious fact: that when the biblical narrative turns from the ahistorical symbolism of Eden to what it represents as real space-time human history, its first story narrates an act of murder. But why murder? Why not incest, perhaps, as the first act, showing the breaking of a universal taboo? After all, with only a mom, a dad, and two male children, incest seems a likely theme for the first sinful act east of Eden. Was murder given priority because it was considered a more serious crime? Perhaps, but I was left nonetheless with a vague sense that there was some reason why the story of a murder should also be the story of a beginning. Then I read what Girard had to say about the "founding murder," and it struck me with the force of a revelation.

The Bible's story of the first "historical" event involves murder because it is a story about the foundations of human civilization. No sooner does Cain kill Abel than he *builds a city* (Gen. 4:17). We have in the text, therefore, the conjunction of murder and the founding of community, and the narrative continues immediately to tell us how Cain's descendents became the inventors and developers of human culture. Genesis 4:20-22 tells us that Lamech, the arrogant boaster we met above, had a son named Jabel who became the father of those who dwell in tents and have cattle. So here we have the development of the nomadic way of life and culture. Lamech had another son, Jubal, "the father of all those who play the lyre and the pipe" – the development of music. Another son, Tubal-cain, became the "forger of all instruments of bronze and iron," indicating the invention and development of metallurgy, and the various techniques for forging tools and weapons. So we see that Cain's lineage is culturally creative and fertile, and responsible for the development of the various aesthetics and technologies of culture. All of this emanates from Cain's building a city, which happens in close association with the murder of an innocent victim. Girard would say that this story preserves the ancestral memory of a genuine historical truth: murder is generative of culture and civilization.[88]

The Innocence of the Victim

We have yet to discuss what is perhaps the most important theme in the story of Cain and Abel, and to appreciate it more deeply it will be helpful draw a comparison with another story about enemy brothers from the ancient world, Romulus and Remus – the brothers involved in the founding of Rome. Here is the story as told by the ancient Roman historian, Livy:

> *Romulus and Remus were seized with the desire of building a city… Alba and Lavinium would be small in comparison with the city which was to be founded. These pleasant anticipations were disturbed by the ancestral curse – ambition – which led to a deplorable quarrel over what was at first a trivial matter. As they were twins and no claim to precedence could be based on seniority, they decided to consult the tutelary deities of the place by means of augury, as to who was to give his name to the new city, and who was to rule it after it had been founded. Romulus accordingly selected the Palatine hill as his station for observation, Remus the Aventine hill.*

> *Remus is said to have been the first to receive an omen: six vultures appeared to him. The augury had just been announced to Romulus when double the number appeared to him. Each was saluted as king by his own party. The one side based their claim on the priority of the appearance, the other on the number of birds. Then followed an angry altercation; heated passions led to bloodshed; in the tumult Remus was killed. The more common report is that Remus contemptuously jumped over the newly raised walls and was forthwith killed by the enraged Romulus, who exclaimed, "So shall it be henceforth with everyone who leaps over my walls!" Romulus thus became sole ruler, and the city was called after him, its founder.*[89]

Livy tells this tale with enough realism that it is not difficult for us to grasp the underlying mimetic dynamics. Romulus and Remus are twins, which is already a clue regarding the mimetic nature of their relationship, twins being mirror reflections of one another. The twins were "seized with the desire of building a city." They both sported this desire; in fact, they were *seized* by it. Mimetic theory helps us understand that they were seized with desire precisely because they mirrored it to each other: it is a typical case of reciprocal imitation, each reinforcing the other's desire and spurring the other on towards intense rivalry. The rivalry between the brothers only magnifies their desire to build a grand city that will make other cities seem small by comparison. The grandiosity of the imagined city is a measure of the intensity of their rivalry.

The brothers are unaware of this, of course, at least consciously. They would no doubt deny that their desire to build the city is imitated from the other, a function of rivalry. Each wants to assert the precedence of his own desire, and so they argue over who has the right to have the city named after him. In order to settle the dispute, each brother selects a hill from which to observe birds according to the ancient divinatory practice of augury, and skyward omens soon appear. Remus sees only six vultures, but spots them first; Romulus sees twelve vultures, but spots them after Remus has already seen his. This leads to an argument over which is the genuine omen: seeing the most vultures, or seeing them first?

Ultimately, it doesn't matter because precedence is established by violence. Remus is killed, either in a group altercation, or when he defiantly jumps over the newly raised foundation of the city wall. His defiance is more than matched by his brother Romulus, however, who escalates it to the level of murder. He kills Remus, then yells, "So shall it be henceforth with everyone who leaps over my walls!" This arrogant boast reminds us of Cain's descendant Lamech, noted earlier, who announced that he would kill a young man merely for slapping him. And so Romulus wins, and today the Pope lives in Rome, not "Reme."

Tales about enemy brothers and twins appear with frequency in ancient mythological tales. As a matter of fact, the birth of twins caused anxiety in many ancient communities, and was considered a bad omen. For Girard, the explanation of this curious belief is that twins were an intuitively sensed symbol for the effacement of difference, since twins are identical. And as we discussed in the previous chapter, a cultural slide towards nondifferentiation was the great fear. In the ancient world, anything that seemed to presage such a calamity, such as the sameness of twins, could be interpreted as a bad omen. Sameness connoted violence, because violence produces the sameness of nondifferentiation. Thus, when twins or close brothers become a theme in mythology, the brothers are usually enemies; and in more sophisticated developments of the theme such as we see in the plays of the Greek tragedians, warring brothers are clearly used as a symbol for the tragic loss of differentiation, and the cultural threat brought about by mimetic rivalry.

In describing the sad relations between brothers Cain and Abel, then, the author of Genesis uses a common mythological theme – *but with a glaring difference* from the tale of Romulus and Remus, of which we must now take note. Rome was proud of its heritage, proud of Romulus, and proud of the attitude expressed in "So shall it be henceforth with everyone who leaps over my walls!" Quite so: few were bold enough to mess with Rome. Livy and his readers *accepted* the slaying of Remus as the settling of the dispute. Remus was no innocent victim; he foolishly defied the powerful spirit of imperial Rome, instantiated in the glorious Romulus, its noble founder. Genesis, on the other hand, has a quite different take on the theme of enemy brothers: *it tells the tale as one of murder, pure and simple.* Cain is guilty of innocent blood. It is true that from the standpoint of mimetic theory we can read between the lines and see that it is only because Abel possesses violent animal sacrifice that he is not the one to kill Cain; nevertheless, Abel is the victim of trickery and manslaughter, and Cain is clearly guilty. This is a complete deconstruction of the mythology we see operating in the Romulus/Remus story, which was told from the perspective of the victors, the Romans, thus making the murderer seem triumphant, noble, and justified.

In this way the Cain and Abel story sets the theme for the entire Hebrew Scriptures, as James Alison indicated when he titled one of his books *"Raising Abel."*[90] The cry of Abel stands at the very beginning of Genesis, and it is the cry of a victim. "What have you done? The voice of your brother's blood is crying to me from the ground," says the Lord. Similar cries will reverberate from Abel to Job to the souls of martyrs under the altar in Revelation 6:9-11, as Scripture constantly wrestles with the project of "rehabilitating" the victim: that is, establishing the victim's innocence in the face of persecution and mythological perspectives like that of Romulus and Remus, which cast a veil of illusion over the gruesome reality of murder. Quite against the universal fact of mythology, the Genesis story *gives voice to the victim,* letting it cry out from the very ground for justice. And being granted the opportunity to voice a complaint is the first step toward achieving that justice.

Chapter Six
The Primitive Sacred and the Hebrew Scriptures in Travail

In the biblical literature, the forces of myth and revelation contend with each other in the boldest and most explicit ways. . . . As an account of a people's origins and destiny, the Bible is the world's most striking example of a non-myth, not because those who produced these texts renounced the impulse to mythologize their violence, but because something operating in the consciousness of this people made them very clumsy myth-makers.

Gil Bailie, *Violence Unveiled* [91]

‡‡

In this chapter we will look at several types of biblical text, always with a single question in the back of our minds: *Is God really like this?* For we will encounter in many of these scriptures what Michael Hardin has referred to as the "Janus-faced God," Janus being the Roman god with two faces.[92] We will encounter a God of mercy but also of horrific vengeance, a God of multitudinous blessing, but also of curse. We want to know if God is really like this, and if he is not, how does one read such texts in a way that remains faithful to revelation?

Girard calls the Hebrew Scriptures a "text in travail." He means that these texts display competing notions about God: what God is like, what God desires, how God acts, and so on. Sometimes the Bible argues and debates with its own tradition on these issues. This does not mean that the scriptures are a mere mess of contradictions. In fact, there is a trajectory to revelation, a point towards which this internal scriptural struggle is striving; but it doesn't come to full fruition until we read certain sections of the New Testament and learn about God as wholly love. As scholar Raymond Schwager put it:

> *By themselves the Old Testament writings can therefore not be brought together under a common denominator. Different tendencies remain standing side by side. At most, a real center can be found only when all the writings are interpreted anew in the light of the fate of Jesus. Such a new interpretation is legitimate, since the Old Testament itself is a history of constant reinterpretation.* [93]

Despite this, the Hebrew Scriptures do reach amazing crescendos of spiritual revelation. At other points, however, that revelation is completely obscured.

I must stress that the categorizations I present are mine, not Girard's. The reader should take this chapter as an example of how one person uses Girardian ideas as a lens for reading the Hebrew Scriptures, and not as a straightforward reproduction of Girard's scriptural exegesis. I have categorized the biblical texts we will examine in this chapter under several labels, beginning with those I call "thick" texts, because they express an understanding of God completely imbued with the aura of the primitive sacred. Looking at such texts will help us form an even better idea of the connection between the sacred and violence. Then we look at what I call "thin" texts, because the element of the sacred, while present, is but a thin veil over the easily discernable reality of human violence, which is the real motive force within the narrative. Then we look at "challenge" texts, which seem to have been written with the express purpose of challenging prevailing notions of God as sacred violence. Some of these seem to be the result of later scribal editing, where traditional versions of stories were modified to reflect a more merciful and just view of God, leaving us with a text that evidences different points of view within the very same narrative. Finally, we look at "high watermark" texts in which the primitive sacred and its sacrificial mentality is either explicitly criticized, or largely eliminated in favor of an emphasis on love, mercy, and forgiveness.

Nuclear Power and "Thick" Sacred Texts

When discussing the centrality of vengeance in ancient cultures, we alluded briefly to the story of Samson's revenge upon the Philistines for pressuring his new bride into divulging the answer to his riddle. It was a revenge, the reader will recall, far out of proportion to the crime that triggered it. Samson went on a serial killing spree and murdered thirty men! We are reminded once again of Lamech's boast in Genesis: "I have killed a man for wounding me, a young man for striking me." But, of course, that is the whole point about vengeance: it is impossible to keep it under control or within equitable bounds. It is a force like wind, which, once loosed, quickly gathers speed and destructive power.

But there is something else to notice about the Samson story in our present context: his killing spree is attributed to Yahweh: "Then the spirit of the LORD rushed on him, and he went down to Ashkelon. He killed thirty men of the town, took their spoil, and gave the festal garments to those who had explained the riddle." (Judges 14:19) Samson manifests the power of the sacred, its indiscriminate violence and malevolent power of death. The sacred *kills*: it turns differentiated, living bodies into nondifferentiated, rotting animal matter. Interestingly, however, verse 19 contains a further sentence which I left out of the above quote: "In hot anger he went back to his father's house." Almost without realizing it, and evidently without meaning to do so, with this observation the text gives the game away, and points us toward the real cause of Samson's violent rampage: *human* anger. This is, nevertheless, what I would call a "thick" text, a text in which the idea of the God as primitive-sacred force is paramount.

The strange text in Exodus 4:24-26 about Yahweh's attempt to murder Moses, which we considered when discussing sacrificial substitution, is another example of a "thick" text. We can also point to I Samuel 16, which tells the story of how King Saul lost Yahweh's favor, so that Yahweh withdrew his spirit from Saul. But that is not all Yahweh does:

> *Now the spirit of the LORD departed from Saul, and an evil spirit from the LORD tormented him. And Saul's servants said to him, "Behold now, an evil spirit from God is tormenting you..."* (16:14-15)

Saul hears about David, son of Jesse, who is skillful at playing the lyre. David enters Saul's service, becomes his armor-bearer, and plays the lyre for the king. The story continues, "And whenever the evil spirit from God was upon Saul, David took the lyre and played it with his hand, so Saul was refreshed, and was well, and the evil spirit departed from him." (16:23) In this story Saul loses the benevolent side of the sacred (although not entirely – David is able to help ease his torment), and is plagued with the sacred's malevolent side. He loses the blessing and is hit with the curse. It is true that even in I Samuel there are ways in which this traditional sacred notion of the "double-faced" God is in process of being undermined. But my concern at the moment is just to point out examples of "thick" spots where traditional religion commandeers the text, and we see the sacred in full operation.

As we saw in the previous chapter, the double nature of the sacred inspired not only reverence and service, but also terror. To really get a feel for what the Hebrews (and other ancient peoples) were dealing with when they feared and worshiped the sacred, I am going to develop an extended analogy. In the motion picture thriller, *The China Syndrome,* news reporter Kimberly Wells (Jane Fonda), and cameraman Richard Adams (Michael Douglas), visit the Ventana nuclear power plant to film a news special. While observing activities in the control room, a geological tremor causes the plant to go into emergency shutdown, and the reporters get to witness Jack Godell (Jack Lemon) sweating plutonium as he tries to get the situation under control. It is a harrowing few minutes. At first they think it is a routine turbine trip, which means that the turbines have ceased to turn because the steam has been shut down – an automatic safety measure. But then a gauge seems to indicate way too much water in the core, so Godell makes the decision to open relief valves and dump the water, which, as his coworker strenuously informs him, is completely against the book. Nevertheless, Jack breaks the rules and dumps the water. Only then do they discover that the gauge was simply stuck, making the decision to dump the water as dangerous as it was unnecessary. Jack phones in an emergency situation and all plant workers scramble to evacuate. The water level continues to lower. In another bold and risky maneuver, Jack dumps pressure. The whole plant begins to quake. In dramatic, tight close-up Jack curses and prays in the same breath, begging God for a bailout. Eventually, the situation turns around and things get back to normal. Without realizing it, we have just witnessed a modern-day typology of the ancient (and biblical) experience of the sacred.

In the Bible, that which is sacred – Yahweh, the temple, the temple artifacts, and so on – is inextricably bound up with violence. This should come as no surprise to anyone who has read the Bible, especially the Old Testament; or, indeed, to anyone who holds beliefs about God as the ultimate punisher of the wicked. In this kind of theology, God's violent face is a given. Few readers, however, thoroughly explore the relationship between the sacred and violence in the Bible, and I think *The China Syndrome* is a good way to launch into it.

Even from outside, the Ventana nuclear power plant looks roughly like a temple, with its rectangular main building attached to a tall, silo-like tower. Before embarking upon their tour, Wells and Adams are introduced to a diagram which shows the process by which the nuclear plant produces electricity. It shows the reactor core, which contains 20 million uranium pellets, and around the core is water, used as a coolant. Inside the reactor assembly is a set of rods which controls the nuclear reaction. When the rods are lifted out of the core, a chain reaction begins that produces heat, which boils the water, which generates the steam that turns the turbine, which turns the generator, which produces electricity, which – I cannot resist saying – lights the house that Jack built. Thus oriented, the reporters begin their tour of the actual facility. One cannot fail to be impressed by the facility's sheer mass, and overwhelmed by the deafening noise of the turbine room. It is clear that what we have here is an attempt to contain, manipulate, channel, and control a wild, chaotic, and violent energy. Continuing down to the control room, into which they can only peer from a platform through bulletproof windows, we see several men seated before huge computers and controls which they operate and service. Clearly, running this plant and controlling this energy requires specialist technical knowledge and procedures so precise as to be ritualistic. One mistake, one bumbled procedure, and the results could be apocalyptic. The containment of this raw, undifferentiated power, its transmutation into manageable forms of energy which can be differentiated, parceled, and channeled out to meet the demands of human life, require round-the-clock supervision, constant surveillance, and the technical service provided by a team of 150 trained and dedicated professionals.

The reader has perhaps already begun to form the analogy with the Hebrew temple cult recorded in the Bible, and, in fact, the parallels are uncannily abundant. Like nuclear power plants, the temple contained an untamed, awesome power: the presence of God, revealed in the "Shekinah glory." The temple was God's dwelling, and just as nuclear power is generated from within the reactor core, so the presence of God was manifested from within the room called the "Holy of Holies." This was the inner heart or nerve center of the temple, the most sacred space where Yahweh dwelt. No one except the high priest was allowed access to the Holy of Holies, and even he only once a year on the Day of Atonement, when he performed certain "maintenance rituals" that cleansed the temple and its equipment. The temple complex was divided into several zones, the sacredness of each area decreasing in proportion to its distance from the Holy of Holies. At first remove there was the Court of the Priests where priests offered sacrifices; at second remove, and less sacred, was the courtyard for Jewish males; third remove was the court of the Gentiles, for non-Jews. This kind of sacred division was also applied to the geography of the entire world, with Jerusalem being the most holy city in Israel (because that's where the temple was), and Israel being the most holy land in the world. Beyond Israel stretched the Gentile lands, which were profane.[94] All of this sacred geography took its measure from the "nuclear core" which was the Holy of Holies in the Jerusalem temple. It was as though power emanated from that space and flowed outward, those in close proximity benefiting the most, and the power becoming less and less palpable as one moved farther and farther away.

Like nuclear power, the power of Yahweh and the sacredness that flowed from his presence was not merely beneficial – it was also threatening and violent. Those who benefited by proximity to the most sacred space were also the most threatened (as the people of Chernobyl and Okuma have also discovered). Those in most immediate danger were the ones whose job it was to service the temple cult: the priests and Levites – the technicians, as it were, who worked in the power plant itself. Their proximity to the sacred put them in great danger. There are texts in the Bible that are completely in the grip of this archaic-sacred understanding of God, where the mythology is piled on so thickly that it is virtually impossible to glimpse in them the true character of God. Consider the following story from the book of Leviticus, about the sons of Aaron, the high priest:

> *Now Nadab and Abihu, the sons of Aaron, each took his censer, and put fire in it, and laid incense on it, and offered unholy fire before the LORD, such as he had not commanded them. And fire came forth from the presence of the LORD and devoured them, and they died before the LORD.* (Lev. 10:1-2)

No one knows exactly what "unholy fire" means in this passage, or the precise nature of Nadab and Abihu's error. But it is clear that, like Jack Godell, they did something that was not "by the book," something Yahweh had not commanded. They "dumped the water," against specific instructions, and the result for Nadab and Abihu was something like a power leakage. They were both destroyed by the escaping radiation.

It is clear from the books of Leviticus and Numbers that the temple rituals had to be conducted with absolute precision. Hundreds of minute details had to be honored and precisely followed, or disaster would result. Nadab and Abihu were chief technicians, but they were assisted by hundreds of others: namely, priests (descendents of Aaron), who performed the rituals, and Levites (descendents of Levi), who took care of the equipment. And every one of these had to do his job with the rigor that the sacred demanded, or face the consequences.

In a nuclear power plant, where the awesome power of the atom is controlled by thousands of properly functioning technologies, there is no room for spontaneity. Everything is rigorously formalized. Technicians must operate according to a strict protocol. Nothing is left to chance, and workers are highly trained to do their specific jobs. So it was with the hundreds of rules and regulations we find in the Pentateuch (the first five books of the Bible) relating to the sacred: rules about the only proper way to offer sacrifices, the kinds of animals that qualify for sacrifices, rules about who is fit to be a priest and who must be disqualified (due, for example, to some physical defect), rules about how the temple and each of its fixtures must be constructed, how it is to be consecrated, and so on and on and on. When the temple is constructed and the glory of the Lord fills it, the humans had better do everything by the book, so as to control that energy and ensure that its effect for the community is beneficial, not disastrous. For Yahweh was a source of blessing, but also destruction.

In the book of Numbers, chapter 16, Moses and Aaron put down a rebellion staged by an Israelite named Korah. But the next day the people are upset because 250 Israelites died in the rebellion, and they blame Moses and Aaron. This is too much for Yahweh, who appears in a cloud of glory and says to Moses and Aaron, "Get away from the midst of this congregation, that I may consume them in a moment!" The text continues:

And they fell on their faces. And Moses said to Aaron, "Take your censer, and put fire in it from off the altar, and lay incense on it, and carry it quickly to the congregation, and make atonement for them; for wrath has gone forth from Yahweh, the plague has begun!" (16:45-46)

Yahweh's wrath has taken the form of a plague. It is as though radioactivity has begun leaking out into the community! One can almost picture Jack Lemon playing Aaron, breaking into a cold sweat.

> *So Aaron took it as Moses said, and ran into the midst of the assembly; and behold, the plague had already begun among the people; and he put on the incense, and made atonement for the people.* (16:47)

It's a race against time! Will Aaron be able to handle the incense properly, and perform the atonement ritual in time to save the people? Or will there be a massive meltdown, a "Yahweh-syndrome?"

> *And he stood between the dead and the living; and the plague was stopped. Now those who died by the plague were 14,700…* (16:48)

Like nuclear radiation, Yahweh's sacred plague is contaminating, and leaves destruction in its wake. This is a force you really don't want to let loose in your community! You want to keep it contained within the Holy of Holies because the sacred wears the malevolent face of sheer undifferentiated power that hits human communities with a devastating force capable of reducing everything to chaos.

Everything is blamed on some person or persons, whose guilt is considered responsible for the plague because it attracts the divine wrath. But how does a story like this develop? For Girard, the actual history behind a story like this was probably something like the following. If there was some kind of actual plague, people would have felt frightened, anxious, and helpless, confronting death day and night with no modern medical knowledge, and no effective techniques for dealing with disease – and all the while mourning their many losses. They would have been tired, demoralized, and frustrated. Many people would have started acting very selfishly, looking out to protect themselves and their families. Coping with such a disaster would have created new tensions in relationships, and exacerbated old ones. The same questions would have been asked that have been asked from time immemorial by human communities under siege: Why is this happening to us? What have we done wrong? But the question never remains on that level, of course, because people do not generally like to examine *themselves* about what *they* have done wrong. The question easily shifts to: *Who* has done something wrong? Which one of my neighbors is the guilty party? (A question that offers a marvelous opportunity to anyone wishing to make life difficult for a neighbor-rival, as we see happening over and over again in the witch trials of later history.) The very asking of such questions increases the tension within the community even more, introducing another level of fear and distrust of the neighbor. The tension becomes like boiling water in a pot that wants to let off steam. Then the search for a scapegoat begins. It is a pattern that by this time in history was already millennia old. Encoded now in traditional beliefs, institutions, and rituals, it operated automatically, like an instinct, and completely unconsciously. It was the default solution for pulling the community together.

It was really human violence, therefore, the physical and emotional violence of neighbor against neighbor, combined with the desire to deny responsibility, that fed the search for scapegoats under such conditions. Behind the ancient interpretation of plague as a transcendent, sacred scourge, a spectacular punishment by the divine power, we find the operation of something much more mundane: *human* violence.[95]

We have an easier time recognizing and understanding this process when it occurs in medieval Europe, or in the modern world, rather than in a passage of Scripture. The Black Death was commonly seen as a scourge from God in medieval times. Plague caused panic that led to violence against marginalized groups (especially the Jews), who were blamed for causing the crisis. In the medieval context it is easy for us to detect the scapegoating that underlay the theology, and we also realize that behind the scapegoating lay problems of human relations within the community itself, that were easier to deny than to face honestly. It is even easier to see this happening in the modern world. One easily detects the scapegoating behind comments like the one made by televangelist Pat Robertson, when he warned that if gay pride events were allowed in Disney World in Orlando, it could invite hurricanes to strike Florida, as well as terrorist bombs, earthquakes, tornados, and possibly a meteor![96]

Let us return to our analogy between the sacred in ancient Hebrew religion and nuclear power. For there are still more parallels. Just as nuclear technicians must wear special protective suits in order to enter the reactor containment area lest they be exposed to radioactive danger, so Israelite priests wore specially designed garments which followed the design specified in the Book, right down to the fringe on the bottom of their robes. Tons of regulations applied: priests had to be ritually purified through a seven day consecration ceremony before they could officiate; they were not permitted to come into contact with dead bodies, even of their closest relatives, lest they be contaminated and thus unable to officiate; they were not permitted to rend their garments or expose their hair as a sign of mourning. The following regulations are typical:

> *[A]ny of Aaron's descendants from generation to generation who have any bodily defect may not offer the sacrifices to God. If a man is blind, or has a broken nose or any extra fingers or toes, or has a broken foot or hand, or has a humped back, or is a dwarf, or has a defect in his eye, or has pimples or scabby skin, or has imperfect testicles – although he is a descendant of Aaron – he is not permitted to offer the fire sacrifices to the Lord because of his physical defect.* (Lev. 21:17-21 The Living Bible)

Leviticus records page after page of such instructions, regulating everything having to do with holiness and purity. To the modern person this concern about purity has an obsessive quality to it. It doth protest too much, and feels like something we might call obsessive-compulsive disorder. On the other hand, once we grasp the analogy to nuclear power it begins to seem reasonable, given the basic assumptions. Nuclear technicians are equally "obsessive," equally concerned with purity and contamination (filtration systems abound). An awesome power dwells in the heart of the plant, and it means both life and death. The power "dwells" there, but in truth it is isolated and *quarantined* there. Direct contact with it will result in death, so approach to this power must be mediated by a thousand techniques, while protecting oneself at all times against contamination.

By way of this extended nuclear analogy I have tried to give a sense of how it felt in the ancient world to deal with the sacred. The Hebrews were no different from other ancient peoples in experiencing the sacred as a terrifying and awesome supernatural power that was at once both creative and destructive; although, as we will see in a bit, that traditional religious inheritance was increasingly challenged and modified during the history of Israel. Nevertheless, even when certain Israelites, like some of the prophets, challenged this sacred notion of God (though never completely), and proclaimed a God who did not desire sacrifice, it was not until the Jew Jesus came along that the most dramatic step was taken on the road to the vision of God as love that we find in 1 John 4:7, "Beloved, let us love one another, because love is from God; everyone who loves is born of God and knows God. Whoever does not love does not know God, for God is love." Right up to the time of Jesus, Jewish religion was still coping with the presence of a devouring sacred in their midst, a God who, while righteous and just, was capable of inflicting devastating violence, perpetrating bloodbaths, annihilating enemies, destroying the world in a fiery conflagration, and who had a never-ending need for animal victims.

Gathering evidence from the Mishnah and first-century Jewish historian, Josephus, Robert Hamerton-Kelly sketches a dramatic picture of the Jerusalem temple in Jesus' day, its centrality and importance within the society, and its organized sacrificial procedures which made it what Hamerton-Kelly calls an abbatoir – that is, a slaughterhouse:

[The temple] overshadowed Jerusalem and dominated life in the

city. Eighty percent of employment in Jerusalem depended on the temple, not only on its day to day ritual needs but also on the periodic pilgrim festivals and the ongoing building project which it constituted. Nine thousand priests and Levites worked there, although not at the same time, operating what was in fact a giant abbatoir. The twice-daily official sacrifices on the vast ever-burning altar consumed thousands of animals and forests of wood. There were cattle pens on the north side and sometimes the water of the Kidron stream where the blood was flushed became so thick that it was sold to farmers as fertilizer. Over it all hung a pall of smoke from burning flesh, and when the great pilgrim festivals, like Passover, were in full swing the priests stood in blood sacrificing the victims of private offerings. Jews were expected to make the pilgrimage to the temple three times a year, twice in the spring – at Passover and Pentecost – and once in the fall, at Succoth. Therefore Jerusalem thrived on what today would be called the convention business.[97]

Nuclear power plant, indeed! Let us take a look at one more thick text to further clarify how the primitive sacred appears in the Hebrew Scriptures. King Saul has died, and David has been anointed king of Israel. He captures Jerusalem and turns it into the "City of David," and with his "mighty men" has many exploits and victories. 1 Chronicles 13 tells the story of David's move to consolidate the religious cult by gathering priests and Levites from throughout Israel to transport the famous ark of the covenant to Jerusalem from Kiriath-jearim, where it has been sitting neglected. The ark of the covenant was the chest containing Moses' tablets of the ten commandments, along with Aaron's rod. Two cherubim figurines with outstretched wings sat upon the lid of this chest, and it rested within the "Holy of Holies" of the tabernacle and, later, of the temple. It is here that Yahweh was enthroned, and it was upon the lid of this ark that blood was sprinkled for purification on the Day of Atonement. As Yahweh's throne, this was the most sacred spot in the cosmos. Here was the seat of power, the reactor core itself. No wonder David wanted it in his new capital of Jerusalem as part of his move to consolidate power. David, however, was in for a big lesson.

> *And David and all Israel went up to Ba'alah, that is, to Kir'iath-je'arim which belongs to Judah, to bring up from there the ark of God, which is called by the name of the LORD who sits enthroned above the cherubim. And they carried the ark of God upon a new cart, from the house of Abin'adab, and Uzzah and Ahi'o were driving the cart. And David and all Israel were making merry before God with all their might, with song and lyres and harps and tambourines and cymbals and trumpets.*
>
> *And when they came to the threshing floor of Chidon, Uzzah put out his hand to hold the ark, for the oxen stumbled. And the anger of the LORD was kindled against Uzzah; and he smote him because he put forth his hand to the ark; and he died there before God. And David was angry because the LORD had broken forth upon Uzzah; and that place is called Pe'rez-uz'za to this day.*
>
> *And David was afraid of God that day; and he said, "How can I bring the ark of God home to me?" So David did not take the ark home into the city of David, but took it aside to the house of O'bed-e'dom the Gittite. And the ark of God remained with the household of O'bed-e'dom in his house three months; and the LORD blessed the household of O'bed-e'dom and all that he had.* (1 Chron. 13:6-14)

Uzzah only wants to keep the ark from being jostled in the cart – but in dealings with the sacred, good intentions mean nothing. You do not mess with nuclear radioactivity, and you do not approach the sacred carelessly, naively, or casually. You must know exactly what you are doing. The power of the sacred breaks out against all those who do not know enough to take off their shoes like Moses when walking on sacred ground. On the other hand, with proper handling, as Obed-edom was evidently capable of providing, the sacred could bless. Like modern day people who want the benefits of nuclear power but are nervous about allowing the reactor to be built in *their* community, after this experience David recognizes the danger, and his lack of preparation. Before the city of David can become home to the ark, security measures have to be established, people trained, systems put in place. Thus we read in chapter 15:

> *David built houses for himself in the city of David; and he prepared a place for the ark of God, and pitched a tent for it. Then David said, "No one but the Levites may carry the ark of God, for the LORD chose them to carry the ark of the LORD and to minister to him for ever."*
>
> *And David assembled all Israel at Jerusalem, to bring up the ark of the LORD to its place, which he had prepared for it. And David gathered together the sons of Aaron and the Levites.... and said to them, "You are the heads of the fathers' houses of the Levites; sanctify yourselves, you and your brethren, so that you may bring up the ark of the LORD, the God of Israel, to the place that I have prepared for it. Because you did not carry it the first time, the LORD our God broke forth upon us, because we did not care for it in the way that is ordained."*
>
> *So the priests and the Levites sanctified themselves to bring up the ark of the LORD, the God of Israel. And the Levites carried the ark of God upon their shoulders with the poles, as Moses had commanded according to the word of the LORD.* (1 Chron. 15:1-4, 12-15)

So this time they did it "by the book." This time the technicians, the Levites, took over the handling of the sacred power. This time they carried it on poles, not in an ox cart. We read a bit further on that they sacrificed seven bulls and seven rams, and that David was clothed with a robe of fine linen, as were the Levites who were carrying the ark. After the ark was established in its new tent in Jerusalem, they offered burnt offerings, and "offerings of well-being," and David appointed certain Levites as ministers before the ark of Yahweh "to invoke, to thank, and to praise Yahweh, the God of Israel." The technology was now in place – by the book.

The big question that naturally forces itself upon religious readers of the Bible who encounter stories like these is: *Is this really the way God is?* The Hebrew Scriptures certainly talk as though it were. And many religious people today, perhaps even the majority, have no hesitation equating this version of the sacred with the God they worship. I do not believe that the power we see operating in such ancient stories is God; but if it is not God, then what is it? I will answer that question by posing another: Do we know of anything that is at one and the same time both creative and destructive, a poison as well as a remedy, that can become a generative force for culture as well as the potential demolisher of structure, form, order, and life itself? We do, and the answer of course is *violence.* Thousands of times every year the average person sees some form of violence portrayed in television and motion pictures as both the problem and the solution, the poison and the remedy, the curse and the blessing. It was the great insight of René Girard in *Violence and the Sacred* to grasp that the power ancient peoples worshiped in the sacred was really the power of their own violence, projected large into transcendental dimensions.

In the story of Numbers 16, quoted earlier, the wrath of Yahweh is perceived as a consuming plague. And indeed, violence itself is very much like a plague. Violence is *contagious* – it can be communicated and "caught." The more intense a debate becomes, for instance, the more people join in and take sides. This is what happens in the classic "barroom brawl." Also, like plague, violence causes suffering; and, like plague, violence can result in death. There are other images of Yahweh's wrath analogous to violence. The wrath of Yahweh often breaks out as fire, and violence is very much like fire. We often talk about the "heat of battle." Violence is capable of spreading like wild fire, consuming everything in its path and leaving devastation in its wake.

The other side of the coin – the other "face" of the sacred – is that Yahweh blesses his people and brings them prosperity. Violence, of course, exercises the same function. When the troublemaker is violently killed or expelled, peace and prosperity return to the community. When animals or humans are violently killed in sacrificial rituals, crops seem to grow. Just like Yahweh, violence both kills and gives life. To reference Girard's famous line once more: "Violence is the heart and secret soul of the sacred."

No wonder, then, that the ancient Hebrew temple cult looks so much like a nuclear facility: it is an instance of human beings trying to cope with their own violence, an incredible force which, once unleashed, will explode in chaos and destruction unless it is controlled and channeled, and made to flow as blessing. Insofar as they were a *religious* people, the Hebrews were no exception to the peoples of the rest of the world in their veneration of the primitive sacred. Hebrew history, however, is qualitatively different from that of other ancient peoples, because it was within the context of Hebrew religion that insight into the violent nature of the whole game was first realized (as a result of divine revelation, I believe, as does Girard). It was in the Hebrew Scriptures that the struggle against enslavement to violence-cum-religion was engaged and sustained for 2,000 years. We move on, then, from "thick" texts to "thin."

Thin Texts

I use the term "thin" because, while this type of text assumes a sacred violent concept of God, it is nevertheless extraordinarily easy to see through the game and discern what is really motivating the action – *human* violence. In some of these texts it is even possible to discern the scapegoat mechanism itself quite clearly. Such texts give the game away even in their attempt to hide it. As an example we can examine the story narrated in 2 Samuel 21, about the revenge of the Gibeonites. These people had originally been part of the Canaanite population marked for total destruction by Joshua and his armies. They escaped that fate, however, by deceiving Joshua about their identity, claiming to be refugees from a land far from Canaan. Joshua believes them, and enters into a treaty pledging Israel not to harm them. He does this, so the story goes, without consulting the Lord in this matter, and it turns out he has been duped. But it is too late – he has already made a binding oath to these people.

So the Gibeonites were not massacred along with the rest of the Canaanite population. Instead, they became part of Israel – but only as second-class citizens, if not slaves, chopping wood, carrying water, and attending to the care of the tabernacle. Thus, centuries later, when Saul became the first king of Israel, the Gibeonites made easy targets as scapegoats, and he persecuted them. But sometime after the death of Saul, and during the reign of David, the Gibeonites once again came to occupy center stage.

Now there was a famine in the days of David for three years, year after year; and David sought the face of the LORD. And the LORD said, "There is bloodguilt on Saul and on his house, because he put the Gib'eonites to death." So the king called the Gib'eonites. Now the Gib'eonites were not of the people of Israel, but of the remnant of the Amorites; although the people of Israel had sworn to spare them, Saul had sought to slay them in his zeal for the people of Israel and Judah.

And David said to the Gib'eonites, "What shall I do for you? And how shall I make expiation, that you may bless the heritage of the LORD?" The Gib'eonites said to him, "It is not a matter of silver or gold between us and Saul or his house; neither is it for us to put any man to death in Israel." And he said, "What do you say that I shall do for you?" They said to the king, "The man who consumed us and planned to destroy us, so that we should have no place in all the territory of Israel, let seven of his sons be given to us, so that we may hang them up before the LORD at Gibeon on the mountain of the LORD." And the king said, "I will give them." But the king spared Mephib'osheth, the son of Saul's son Jonathan, because of the oath of the LORD which was between them, between David and Jonathan the son of Saul.

The king took the two sons of Rizpah the daughter of Ai'ah, whom she bore to Saul, Armo'ni and Mephib'osheth; and the five sons of Merab the daughter of Saul, whom she bore to A'dri-el the son of Barzil'lai the Meho'lathite; and he gave them into the hands of the Gib'eonites, and they hanged them on the mountain before the LORD, and the seven of them perished together. They were put to death in the first days of harvest, at the beginning of barley harvest. Then Rizpah the daughter of Ai'ah took sackcloth, and spread it for herself on the rock, from the beginning of harvest until rain fell upon them from the heavens; and she did not allow the birds of the air to come upon them by day, or the beasts of the field by night.

When David was told what Rizpah the daughter of Ai'ah, the concubine of Saul, had done, David went and took the bones of Saul and the bones of his son Jonathan from the men of Jabesh-gilead, who had stolen them from the public square of Beth-shan, where the Philistines had hanged them, on the day the Philistines killed Saul on Gilbo'a; and he brought up from there the bones of Saul and the bones of his son Jonathan; and they gathered the bones of those who were hanged. And they buried the bones of Saul and his son Jonathan in the land of Benjamin in Zela, in the tomb of Kish his father; and they did all that the king commanded. And after that God heeded supplications for the land. (2 Sam. 21:1-14)

The first thing we must notice about this story is how little a role the Lord (Yahweh) plays in it. He comes in briefly at the beginning, when David consults the Lord; and God (Elohim) is mentioned at the end as heeding supplications for the land; meaning, presumably, that he stops the famine. But although the Lord comes into the story only briefly, his appearance certainly packs a wallop. He has been wiping out thousands with a famine that has lasted for several years. David's inquiring of the Lord to discover guilty parties was a typical move, not just for Israelites but for all ancient peoples (cf. the book of Jonah where the sailors encounter a violent storm at sea and immediately surmise that some individual must be responsible). People expected and sought a *personal* cause for such disasters: someone must have done something wrong, and the famine is God's punishment, which will continue until the guilty party is singled out and punished. David received the answer that the guilty party was Saul, who had murdered Gibeonites.[98] We see, then, that the God operating here is the archaic-sacred God, not the just God of Abraham, and certainly not the nonviolent and loving "Abba" of Jesus. The famine represents a typical outbreak of sacred violence as the divine wrathful response to an individual's wrongdoing, and the story tells us that once appropriate victims were sacrificed, the sacred was appeased and the famine ceased.

All of this, as I said, is "business as usual" for ancient peoples – searching out personal causes for impersonal disasters, and seeking someone upon whom to fix the guilt. What is extraordinary about the biblical story, however, is how easily we are able to see through to what is really going on, despite the layer of sacred theology that thinly veils it (which is why I call this kind of text "thin"). Almost in spite of itself, the text reveals what it seeks to hide. I can think of no better analogy for this phenomenon than Jesus' parable that the kingdom of heaven is like new wine being poured into old wineskins. This creates a problem for the skins, because as the new wine ferments, it expands, and eventually it will break the skins that confine it. The Hebrew Scriptures strain towards a revelation of human violence and the scapegoat mechanism, and in a text like the one from 2 Samuel we see that revelation very close to the surface, as though trying to break through from its confinement within the old wineskins of an archaic sacred concept of God. We sense this, for instance, in 2 Sam. 24:14 when David, unable to choose between three options the Lord has offered him as punishment for taking a census of Israel, says to the prophet Gad, "I am in great distress; let us fall into the hand of the LORD, for his mercy is great; *but let me not fall into the hand of man.*"

Disasters like famines could put a huge strain on human relationships, obviously, and on the entire structure of society, creating a crisis that threatened the integrity of the hierarchical distinctions that defined the culture. Before things got to the point of total breakdown, however, we have seen how ancient peoples started looking for scapegoats. They didn't consciously know that is what they were doing. *We* know what they were doing, because the revelation of the scapegoat mechanism has been made available to us in Scripture; but in ancient times the mechanism was entirely unconscious – as it had to be in order for it to work.

Now, Saul was guilty of killing Gibeonites, but he was not guilty of causing a famine by killing them. But David faces a delicate situation. Ever since his assumption of the kingship he has faced problem after problem. In addition to his wars with foreigners (the Philistines, Moabites, Edomites, Ammonites, Syrians, and others), 2 Sam. 3:1 tells us that there was "a long war" between David and the house of Saul. David's own house was internally rived by the conspiracy and rebellion of his son Absalom, who led an uprising against David, causing David to flee Jerusalem. David also had continual trouble with the captain of his army, Joab, who, against the king's orders, killed first Abner (Saul's military leader, but who had made peace with David), then Absalom, then Amasa, the man David intended to make captain in place of Joab. Even after Absalom's rebellion is put down, David has to deal with continuing unrest in Israel. And through all this he is trying to consolidate his kingship, set up shop in Jerusalem, establish the religious cult there (thus his bringing of the ark to Jerusalem), and deal with internal problems that pose an even greater threat than foreign enemies. And now, here comes a famine wreaking pain and death, week after hungry week, month after month, year after year, for three whole years! Something must be done, but there is no technological solution available, and no foreign aid. There is only the obvious and time-honored expedient of finding someone on whom to cast blame.

The text of 2 Samuel itself makes it easy to discern the truth. Since the time of Joshua, the Gibeonites had been living quite tenuously in Israel, occupying a marginalized social position. At times they were accepted, at times barely tolerated, and sometimes persecuted. Saul also had a highly troubled reign, and one can see how the Gibeonites would have made an easy target for scapegoating. But now, with the Davidic regime change, Saul becomes the scapegoat. The way for David to consolidate his power is clear: scapegoat Saul and destroy his lineage. The famine offers a highly convenient opportunity: blame it on Saul for breaking Joshua's oath never to harm the Gibeonites. Take the side of the Gibeonite underdog, and scapegoat Saul as a murderer whose bloody deeds have brought famine upon Israel. How convenient that it is Saul's sons who will have to be handed over to the Gibeonites, the very ones who could pose a future threat to David's power.

The text of 2 Samuel does not present the story this way, of course, imbued as it is with the spirit of archaic sacred violence. My point, however, once again, is that *we* can read the story this way without too much difficulty. One need not look far to discern the real machinations going on behind the scenes, the human violence that is at work there. Ostensibly, the story is about appeasing the wrath of a sacred divinity; but it is easy to see that the real wrath which needs to be appeased in this story belongs to the Gibeonites (conveniently enough for David). Despite its appeal to an archaic-sacred idea of God, the story is not told mythologically, but with grim realism.

And this brings us to a key point: one of the reasons the Hebrew Scriptures are so violent is that they are engaged in a process of pulling back the mythological veil that for millennia had hidden from humanity the full realism of its own violence. The Hebrew tradition is so steeped in this realism that there are times (as in 2 Samuel) when the truth about human scapegoating shines through despite the theological framework of divine sacred-violence. It is as though the author just cannot keep from looking human violence in the face. His sacred theology prevents his seeing with complete clarity; but at the same time he is no longer completely under its spell, and cannot convincingly transfer all the violence onto God. Rarely does one find this kind of realism in texts elsewhere in the ancient world (Greek tragedy being one exception, but without pushing the envelope as far as the Hebrew Scriptures[99]).

Not only is the curtain that covers the scapegoat mechanism partially lifted in 2 Samuel, but we also get to witness the disgusting and pathetic aftermath, including the terrifying grief of the mother, Rizpah, who had been Saul's concubine. Two of the seven victims lynched were her sons. All the way from April to autumn she attended the hanging corpses, fending off the vultures. The full dimensions of her deed are aptly expressed by Alfred Edershim:

> *From the commencement of the barely harvest in April, until the early rains of autumn evidence the removal of the curse from the land, hung those lifeless, putrescent bodies, which a fierce Syrian sun shriveled and dried; and beneath them, ceaseless, restless, was the weird form of Saul's concubine. When she lay down at night it was on the coarse hair-cloth of mourners, which she spread upon the rock; but day and night was she on her wild, terrible watch to chase from the mangled bodies the birds of prey that, with hoarse*

croaking, swooped around them, and the jackals whose hungry howls woke the echoes of the night.[100]

It is this realism that turns many people away from the Bible; yet it is to this very realism that we owe our ability to place responsibility for violence where it belongs: *let me not fall into the hand of man.* This is the beginning of the possibility of conceiving God as love.

Challenge Texts

We now move to a third type of scriptural text, which I call "challenge" texts. Sometimes the whole story seems to have been written with a challenge to sacred violence in mind; other times, an older narrative seems to have been edited by later scribes who were reticent about the way in which the divine character was represented in the stories, but who nevertheless had too much respect for tradition to alter the original completely. They therefore dropped some elements and added others, but left traces of the original, leaving us with texts that sometimes appear contradictory or enigmatic. A prime example is the famous story of Abraham's sacrifice of his son Isaac.

> *After these things Elohim tested Abraham, and said to him, "Abraham!" And he said, "Here am I." He said, "Take your son, your only son Isaac, whom you love, and go to the land of Mori'ah, and offer him there as a burnt offering upon one of the mountains of which I shall tell you." So Abraham rose early in the morning, saddled his ass, and took two of his young men with him, and his son Isaac; and he cut the wood for the burnt offering, and arose and went to the place of which Elohim had told him.*
>
> *On the third day Abraham lifted up his eyes and saw the place afar off. Then Abraham said to his young men, "Stay here with the ass; I and the lad will go yonder and worship, and come again to you." And Abraham took the wood of the burnt offering, and laid it on Isaac his son; and he took in his hand the fire and the knife. So they went both of them together. And Isaac said to his father Abraham, "My father!" And he said, "Here am I, my son." He said,*

"Behold, the fire and the wood; but where is the lamb for a burnt offering?" Abraham said, "Elohim will provide himself the lamb for a burnt offering, my son." So they went both of them together.

When they came to the place of which Elohim had told him, Abraham built an altar there, and laid the wood in order, and bound Isaac his son, and laid him on the altar, upon the wood. Then Abraham put forth his hand, and took the knife to slay his son. But the angel of the LORD called to him from heaven, and said, "Abraham, Abraham!" And he said, "Here am I." He said, "Do not lay your hand on the lad or do anything to him; for now I know that you fear Elohim, seeing you have not withheld your son, your only son, from me." And Abraham lifted up his eyes and looked, and behold, behind him was a ram, caught in a thicket by his horns; and Abraham went and took the ram, and offered it up as a burnt offering instead of his son.

So Abraham called the name of that place The LORD will provide; as it is said to this day, "On the mount of the LORD it shall be provided." And the angel of the LORD called to Abraham a second time from heaven, and said, "By myself I have sworn, says the LORD, because you have done this, and have not withheld your son, your only son, I will indeed bless you, and I will multiply your descendants as the stars of heaven and as the sand which is on the seashore. And your descendants shall possess the gate of their enemies, and by your descendants shall all the nations of the earth bless themselves, because you have obeyed my voice." So Abraham returned to his young men, and they arose and went together to Beer-sheba; and Abraham dwelt at Beer-sheba. (Genesis 22:1-19)

This story has caused no end of perplexity to interpreters, and is a downright scandal to some. How could God demand of Abraham the sacrifice of his living child? Even if God pops up in the end with something like, "Surprise! You don't have to do it – I was just testing you!" – how could God pull such a stunt? What kind of test of faith is it, the passing grade of which is one's willingness to murder one's child? What kind of God would demand such a test, and use the willingness to kill a child as a gauge of one's love for God, or faith in God? Would any human parent in their right mind say to their spouse, "Honey, I want to make sure you love me more than anything else in the world. To prove it, I want you to kill our child." The answer is obvious. (I remember as a teenager watching

God Was Wrong, a Nicholas Ray film. It starred James Mason as a psychotic who believed that he had received a direct command from God to sacrifice his son. It was such a compelling and terrifying drama that I never forgot it, though I saw the film only once.)

The enigma posed by this amazing story can be resolved if one understands it as the result of later modifications made to an original narrative in which God really does command Abraham to sacrifice Isaac, and Abraham really does. I have cited the RSV translation of this text, with one exception: where the RSV reads "God," I have substituted the actual word from the original Hebrew, *Elohim.* Doing this will help to make it clear for the reader that in this story, it is *Elohim* who commands Abraham to go to a mountain in the land of Moriah and sacrifice Isaac. However, it is the *angel of the LORD* who stops him. ("LORD" with all capital letters in the RSV represents the Hebrew *Yahweh.*) It is the LORD, Yahweh, who provides the ram as a substitute for Isaac, and Abraham therefore names the place, "The LORD will provide." And it is the angel of the LORD who blesses Abraham with the promises. It is possible, then, that the story which now appears in Scripture had a previous version in which Abraham really did sacrifice his son at the command of *Elohim,* who then remarked, "...now I know that you fear *Elohim,* seeing you have not withheld your son, your only son, from me."

Further confirmation of this reading is the startling fact that in the scriptural version Abraham returns to his men, *but there is no mention of Isaac returning with him.* Since the entire drama has turned around whether or not Isaac will be saved, it seems quite a stunning omission not to show him coming back down the mountain safe and sound at his father's side. But this omission is easily explained if one assumes the existence of a more archaic version of the story in which Isaac really was immolated on the altar of Elohim. Later, more enlightened scribes were uncomfortable with the story, but they also revered the tradition; so they retained much of it, including the command to sacrifice Isaac and the praise of Abraham for not withholding his son. However, the new version praises Abraham only for his *willingness* to do it, not the literal act.

In this later, "spiritualizing" interpretation, willingness alone is all that is needed to betoken absolute surrender to and trust of the LORD. The literal murder was prevented by Yahweh, who, in the editor's opinion, would never command such a thing.

Girard understands this story as one of the great watersheds in human history, because it evidences the Hebrew Scriptures' great victory over millennia of human sacrifice. To be sure, it is not the shining anti-sacrificial message that we will get later from the prophets; but the shift from human to animal sacrifice is one giant step forward for humanity nonetheless. The text as we have it represents a fundamental rejection of the validity of human sacrifice, and associates this move with the worship of Yahweh.

Another example of a challenge text is the story of Noah's ark and the flood. Amazingly, at the end of the story, after the long and dramatic narration of God's use of violence to destroy humanity, the text says that God *repented* of what he had done! The rainbow becomes the symbol of God's covenant with humanity that he shall never again resort to such total destruction. It is hard to resist reading this as an interpretive addition to the story by an editor or group of scribes who were uncomfortable with the notion of God's violent destruction of the world. As is well known, the story of the flood was ubiquitous in the ancient world, and we find different versions of the story among peoples the world over. We have three versions of the story from the Babylonians alone, and a version from the Sumerians dating from the third millennium BCE; and these have lots of similarities to the version in Genesis. But the Hebrew version shows God repenting of his act, a move which implies a strong critique of the violent-sacred view of God that we find in the Babylonian and Sumerian versions, and in the Genesis narrative itself; for, again, the scribes have too much reverence for the tradition simply to chuck it out; instead, they look for a way to reinterpret what they have received, and they are not afraid to do that by showing God capable of repenting for his violence.

While the previous examples require the hypothesis of scribal editors who introduced their own view of God into a preexisting text, there are other texts which seem to have been composed initially with the express purpose of challenging sacred violence –

at least in the sense of desiring to scale it back, even if not eliminating it completely. Such texts attempt to push the interpretive envelope in the direction of mercy and the moral character of God and God's justice. An example would be the book of Jonah, which seems to have been written for the purpose of criticizing a theology that represents God as a lover of vengeance. The book makes it clear that the real source of a desire for vengeance is *human*. It is Jonah who craves the destruction of Ninevah, not God. He is downright disappointed that God wants to show mercy to those horrible Ninevites. True, the God represented in the book of Jonah is indeed capable of destroying Nineveh, and will do so if they refuse to repent; so the book does not totally abandon a violent-sacred conception of God. But the emphasis – indeed, the real point – of the book, is the idea that God greatly prefers mercy, even with respect to a people as vicious as the Assyrians. In fact, it is hard to avoid the impression that the whole business about the Lord threatening to destroy Nineveh unless they repent is little more than a pretext for teaching Jonah about mercy and compassion.

We should note in this connection that the Gentile sailors onboard the boat with Jonah showed more compassion towards Jonah than he showed towards himself. It was Jonah who told the sailors to throw him into the sea so that the storm would stop: a typically sacrificial solution. But, the text says, "Nevertheless the men rowed hard to bring the ship back to land…" The sailors were able to recognize that Jonah had done no wrong towards them that would make him worthy of death, and they actually rejected the sacrificial solution (!) – until the storm became so bad that, in order to save their own lives, they had no choice. Nevertheless, the story shows a stunning reversal, in which Gentiles evince more of the Lord's compassion than his own prophet. Even if their "compassion" was ten parts fear and desire for self-preservation, and one part mercy, it is nevertheless astounding that they should recognize Jonah's innocence, and work hard in an attempt to reject sacrificial victimization.

I sometimes wonder if the violent-sacred that remains part of the conception of God in the book of Jonah is to be taken seriously at all. Is the author just trying to push the envelope a bit, wanting his readers to privilege God's mercy and compassion over and above wrath and vengeance, while yet continuing to believe in these latter qualities? Or is the author subtly moving his readership to abandon the idea of a wrathful God entirely? After all, it is difficult to take the idea of wrath in Jonah quite seriously, since the book is hilarious from start to finish: it is a comedy, if not a farce, the story of a prophet who runs away from the Lord when the Lord calls him, gets on a boat thinking he can escape, only to be overtaken by a mighty storm and sacrificed by sailors – then swallowed by a giant fish and vomited up three days later! Then he gives in and goes to Ninevah, grudgingly, and preaches: and the Assyrians repent! The king, and with him the entire city, cover themselves and their animals with sackcloth and ashes, and turn from their violence (2:8). Then Jonah pouts, saying that he would just as soon die!

As if hoping that the Lord will change his mind and destroy those blood-suckers, Jonah positions himself outside the city to watch, "waiting to see what would become of the city." (4:5) He shelters from the terrible heat under the shade of a bush that God has made grow to protect him. But the next day God "appoints a worm" to attack the bush, which withers, and Jonah is exposed to the fury of the sun and hot east wind, which God hurls at him, as God hurled the sea wind earlier in the story, in pursuit of the fleeing prophet. Jonah is so angry about the loss of his shade that, once again, he cries out "It is better for me to die than to live!" (4:8)

"Is it right for you to be angry about the bush?" God asks. Jonah responds, "Yes, angry enough to die!"(4:9) Then comes the lesson of the story, when the Lord gently suggests that Jonah's reaction might just be a bit over the top: Jonah is concerned, after all, about a *plant* – that grew and withered within twenty-four hours! – yet angry with God for being concerned about a great city of 120,000 people… and their cattle.

Were this story to be made into a motion picture today, who would we cast in such a role? Jim Carrey comes to mind. Because, in truth, the story is just that zany. With a story like this, can we really take Yahweh's wrath seriously? If the author himself takes it seriously, he certainly doesn't feel the need to walk on literary eggshells around the idea. This is definitely not a heavy-handed treatment of God's wrath. It is presented in a light, comedic vein, all with a view towards a lesson about mercy and compassion. If sacrifice is ultimately vindicated in this story because it works (Yahweh does indeed stop the storm and save the sailors as a result of the sacrifice), it is nonetheless something the sailors try hard to avoid, recognizing, as they do, that they would incur guilt should they kill Jonah, since he had done no wrong towards them. And we should remember that the story does not in fact demonstrate any efficacy of sacrifice, since Jonah cast overboard doesn't die. Or, if he does, he is almost immediately resurrected in the most ridiculous, hilarious way: swallowed by a giant fish, then vomited up! Is this not a comedic way of undermining the whole idea of sacrifice by making it ridiculous?

I may be wrong in my estimation of the book of Jonah and its author's intention. But there can be no doubt that, at the very least, we have in this piece of Hebrew literature an attempt to highlight God's love, mercy, and compassion, over against violent-sacred notions of vengeance. The heart and soul of the story is Jonah's flight from God – *not* because he was afraid of the Assyrians, but because he was afraid that God would forgive his hated enemies, and he didn't want to be the channel for that. Jonah could not help but prepare the way for an eventual undermining of the entire sacred-violent concept of God, as the incompatibility between opposing notions of the character of God made itself felt more and more consciously in the history of Israel.

The story of Abraham's bargaining with the Lord for the lives of the people of Sodom in Genesis 18:22-33 is another example of a text written with the express purpose of placing God beyond the violent sacred. Abraham is the perfect foil for the comedic Jonah, being everything that Jonah is not. If the book of Jonah critiques the attitude of those who glory in anticipation of "the Day of the Lord," eagerly awaiting God's violent recompense of the wicked, this story of Abraham show us the contrasting, positive virtue of those who are more concerned with the salvation of the innocent than with the destruction of the wicked. In this extraordinary story, Abraham is disturbed by what he perceives to be the Lord's intention to "destroy the righteous with the wicked." *This is exactly what the archaic sacred would do,* like a nuclear blast, or the plague that indiscriminately destroyed almost fifteen thousand people.

Abraham dares to question this, asking, "Suppose there are fifty righteous in the city; wilt thou then destroy the place and not spare it for the fifty righteous who are in it? Far be it from thee to do such a thing, to slay the righteous with the wicked, so that the righteous fare as the wicked! Far be that from thee! Shall not the Judge of all the earth do right?" Notice the passion of these sentences, the welling-up of deep ethical conviction that flies directly in the face of the conception of God's wrath that we saw operating in "thick" texts of sacred violence. Abraham simply would not be happy with a God who would send a plague to destroy, willy-nilly, 14,700 people.

Having dared to pose the question, Abraham is not even satisfied with the Lord's generous response: "If I find at Sodom fifty righteous in the city, I will spare the whole place for their sake." Abraham decides to push the matter further: "Suppose five of the fifty righteous are lacking? Wilt thou destroy the whole city for lack of five?" One has to chuckle over Abraham's cleverness in bargaining. Instead of asking God to spare the city for the sake of forty-five people, he phrases his request negatively – "Suppose five of the fifty righteous are lacking? – because five, after all, is such a tiny number, and could hardly be supposed to make much difference. The Lord agrees. Then Abraham, with all politeness and obsequiousness, pushes it to forty righteous, then thirty, then twenty…. then gets the Lord down to a mere ten! *And the Lord agrees*! He will not destroy Sodom if a mere ten righteous people are found.

And here the bargaining stops. In fact, ten righteous people are *not* found in Sodom, and everyone is destroyed, except for Lot and his family, whom the angel of the Lord snatches out of the city just in the nick of time. In this story, then, we do not have a nonviolent God – but neither do we have the God of the primitive sacred. On the contrary, we have an ethical God, a judge. More than that, we have a judge who is full of mercy, who does not even insist upon the justice he represents but is willing to spare the many evil for the sake of a few righteous – a mere ten! And the text leaves the question open whether Abraham could have gone even further in his bargaining.

This story also represents a subtle critique and subversion of sacrifice. The sacrificial paradigm is: kill one to spare the many. But the paradigm of this story is: spare the many because of the righteous *life* of the few. It is not the death of a victim that will persuade Yahweh to be merciful, but the merit of righteous lives. And in the story Yahweh makes it a point to save those who would become innocent victims: Lot, his wife, and his two daughters. "When morning dawned, the angels urged Lot, saying, 'Arise, take your wife and your two daughters who are here, lest you be consumed in the punishment of the city.' But he lingered; so the men seized him and his wife and his two daughters by the hand, the LORD being merciful to him, and they brought him forth and set him outside the city." (19:15-16) Notice the emphasis on the angels' intention to show mercy: when Lot lingers, the "men" (i.e., angels) *seize* everyone by the hand and lead them out of the city, "the LORD being merciful to him."

Of course, a few verses later the sacred reasserts itself: Lot's wife is famously turned into a pillar of stone because she disobeys the angels' command not to look back during their flight from the doomed city. This is not even what we would consider an act of just judgment, much less mercy. The point I am making is not that such stories offer a view of God completely exorcised of sacred violence. Obviously, the story of the destruction of Sodom and Gomorrah and the crystallization of Lot's wife is a long way from Jesus' vision of God as love. But we are interested in the interpretive trajectory within which a story like this is situated, how it attempts to push the envelope of its received tradition about God. The amazing thing is that in this story the debate about the nature of God comes consciously and clearly to the fore.

Modern Fundamentalists and Evangelicals would find this way of understanding Scripture as containing differing points of view completely unacceptable (to say the least). To them, there can be no contradictions within Scripture, and every chapter, every paragraph, every word, is given the same interpretive weight, and considered to be the direct and unchallengeable Word of God.[101] Yet, within this story, we see Abraham portrayed as unafraid to challenge God's word to him. He is not afraid to question God's intention, and attempt to hold God accountable to his own opinion of what God should be like.

The ancient Jewish rabbis, and the scribes before them, possessed a similar attitude towards Scripture. It might be the "Word of God," but that didn't mean it couldn't be challenged. They respected Scripture, even venerated it, just as Abraham venerated and bowed down before the angel of the Lord, displaying all manner of proper oriental obsequiousness. But this did not prevent Abraham from challenging the Lord's word. The point is that Abraham's attitude in the story is very much a reflection of the scribal attitude towards the scriptures themselves. This is why we find various theologies in the Bible, and not all of them agree. *The Bible argues with itself*: what we are interested in following is how the chaff of the violent sacred becomes separated (and eventually discarded) from the kernel of love. It was neither a short nor an easy process.

High Watermark Texts

The fourth kind of text is what I call "high watermark." In such texts, sacrifice and sacrificial ways of thinking come under major censure, the innocence of victims is forthrightly proclaimed over against mythological illusions, and mercy and forgiveness are portrayed as superior practices reflecting the will of God, in contrast with vengeance. This does not mean that the Hebrew Scriptures rise to the stunning clarity of the New Testament's revelation of God as love; but it is with texts like these that the road to that revelation was being paved. We begin with the famous text found in 1 Kings 3:16-28, often referred to as "The Judgment of Solomon." This text offers a stunning critique of sacrificial thinking that often flies right over the heads of interpreters, which is why I want to call attention to it here. (I am using the NRSV translation.)

> *Later, two women who were prostitutes came to the king and stood before him. The one woman said, "Please, my lord, this woman and I live in the same house; and I gave birth while she was in the house. Then on the third day after I gave birth, this woman also gave birth. We were together; there was no one else with us in the house, only the two of us were in the house. Then this woman's son died in the night, because she lay on him. She got up in the middle of the night and took my son from beside me while your servant slept. She laid him at her breast, and laid her dead son at my breast. When I rose in the morning to nurse my son, I saw that he was dead; but when I looked at him closely in the morning, clearly it was not the son I had borne." But the other woman said, "No, the living son is mine, and the dead son is yours." The first said, "No, the dead son is yours, and the living son is mine." So they argued before the king.*

Before getting to Solomon's solution to the women's quarrel, we pause to note the narrative's spectacular representation of mimetic rivalry between doubles. It is the same theme we met before in the stories of Cain and Abel, and Romulus and Remus. The two women are not literally sisters, but the text makes every effort to highlight the fact that, structurally, they are "twins." Notice how the women are mirror images of each other: both are prostitutes, both live in the same house, sleep in the same room, bear infants at the same time, and argue the same way and over the identical object of desire. The reciprocal, mimetic quality of their struggle is highlighted by the way in which the author represents their argumentation, with the one merely reversing what the other says – a literal mirror image:

> "No, the living son is mine, and the dead son is yours."
> "No, the dead son is yours, and the living son is mine."

We are brought back once again to the theme we saw in Genesis 2 – the knowledge of good and evil. These women have been bitten deeply by the serpent of mimetic rivalry that has corrupted their relationship and turned them into bitter rivals. As a result, their eyes are "opened," and each one perceives herself and her cause as good, and the other as an enemy. They have indeed become "like gods." But the laugh is on the serpent, for there really is no distinction between the two women, as the story makes absolutely clear. Reciprocal violence, whether physical or, as with these women, merely verbal, produces lack of distinction. It turns participants into mimetic doubles who can act no more creatively than to shout back the reverse of each other's claims. Since the image is reversed (the women arguing opposite points of view), we are duped into thinking that there is a substantive distinction between them. But the parallel dialogue demonstrates the absolute structural symmetry.

The lack of differentiation between the two women, so glaringly presented in this story, represents in microcosm the great fear of ancient societies which we have already examined – the nondifferentiation so quickly produced by reciprocal violence. As we have seen, ancient communities short-circuited the escalation of such violence by triggering the scapegoat mechanism, which led to a reconciliation of the combatants. This gave rise to the essential structure of sacrifice, which became the community's method for avoiding violent escalation. Sacrifice became the quintessentially imitated institution in the ancient world for reconciling enemy neighbors – which brings us back to the story of 2 Kings.

Both women have the same desire: to possess the living baby. Each woman perceives the other as an obstacle, and thus as model also, stimulating the reciprocal imitation which has reduced them to mirror images of one another by the time they seek the judgment of the king. The fact that one of them has to be the real mother of the child is not the point. For although real motherhood certainly is a substantive distinction, the whole point of the story is that the reciprocal violence between the two women has blurred the distinction to the point that no one is able to judge between them. In this condition they appear before Solomon, and we wonder: will the king be able to distinguish between them? The answer is no. In his opening comment, Solomon can only reiterate the "mirror-dialogue" of the two women, repeating first what "the one says" and then what "the other says," thereby highlighting the collapse of substantial difference between them.

> *Then the king said, "The one says, 'This is my son that is alive, and your son is dead'; while the other says, 'Not so! Your son is dead, and my son is the living one.'"*

Therefore, instead of attempting to distinguish between them, Solomon resorts to the ancient solution that we examined earlier. With the differences between the parties irrevocably effaced, Solomon proposes to create a *new* difference: the difference between two reconciled women, and a sacrificed baby. Thus he proposes a solution which owes its efficacy to time-honored sacrificial thinking:

> *So the king said, "Bring me a sword," and they brought a sword before the king. The king said, "Divide the living boy in two; then give half to the one, and half to the other."*

Sacrifice was more than a practice; it was also a way of thinking which had developed based upon ritual practice. For millennia, human thoughts had flown like a great river through the channel cut by sacrificial practice, and had come to constitute an entire worldview. Solomon's proposal to settle the dispute by killing the infant is a wonderful example of the way in which someone steeped in sacrificial practice would have thought. While not truly guilty, the infant could nonetheless be considered the "cause" of the dispute, in a manner analogous to that which makes Jonah the "cause" of the storm, or Saul the "cause" of Israel's famine. In times of trouble sacrificial thinking always looked to find the person responsible for the crisis, then kill or expel them from the community. In this way the scapegoat mechanism could direct the violence of the parties towards the victim, and achieve reconciliation among the parties. This is how Solomon is proposing to reconcile the rival women. It is not simply a matter of reconciliation through balanced division of equity; for in this case, to effect settlement *a human being has to die.*

Something completely unexpected emerges in the biblical story, however, which astonished the people and spread the story throughout Israel.

> *But the woman whose son was alive said to the king – because compassion for her son burned within her – "Please, my lord, give her the living boy; certainly do not kill him!" The other said, "It shall be neither mine nor yours; divide it." Then the king responded: "Give the first woman the living boy; do not kill him. She is his mother." All Israel heard of the judgment that the king had rendered; and they stood in awe of the king, because they perceived that the wisdom of God was in him, to execute justice.*

Possibly Solomon himself did not expect this reaction from one of the women. If so, his wisdom was that he recognized immediately its significance and meaning, and gave a wise and appropriate response. It is also possible that Solomon had anticipated everything, and that with stunning originality and depth of psychological and spiritual insight he had proposed a sacrificial solution precisely in order to find out which of the women would reject it. And *this* would be the way of distinguishing between the two women. In the ancient world, only one way of achieving differentiation (order) in a situation of nondifferentiation (chaos) was known: establish a first, basic difference between reconciled rivals and a scapegoated victim. But the judgment of Solomon dramatically reveals another alternative, radically different and radically creative, and exactly the opposite of the scapegoat mechanism: total, nonviolent, self-giving love. *The choice to reject violence and the sacrificial solution becomes itself a point of differentiation between the two women, and a way of distinguishing the true mother.* (And, in the larger anthropological picture, a new way of creating reconciliation among warring parties, a new way of generating community in the midst of chaos.)

It does not matter if the woman reckoned in this way to be the true mother was in fact the actual biological progenitor of the child; in fact, she may not have been. There is no way of knowing from the story. We assume that she is, but the real point of the story is not about biological motherhood, but about renouncing the desire to possess the highly coveted object, the willingness to give up one's own claim upon desire in order to save life. *The true mother is the one who cares for the life of the child more than she cares about her rivalry with the other*. One of the women is so invested in mimetic antagonism with her double that she would rather the child be killed than see her rival triumph. This illustrates precisely what Girard has said many times about the nature of mimetic rivalry, that as the rivalry intensifies, the object of desire drops out of the picture entirely. The war is no longer about "Helen" (Greek propaganda notwithstanding), but about achieving triumph over those horrible Trojans (or, vice-versa, those horrible Greeks). The woman who prefers victory over her opponent to the life of the child is not fit to be the child's mother, even if she does happen to be its biological parent; and, of course, the converse is also true. The real mother is the one who *loves* the child and wants it to live. Love and life triumph in this story over the sacrificial power of murder and death.

Before moving to our next example of a high-watermark text, I do not want to overlook the fact that the story ends with the claim that in his judgment Solomon executed *justice*. This story certainly lays claim to being the Hebrew Scripture's *locus classicus* for the theme of justice, so prevalent in the rest of Scripture. But we see here an understanding of justice that is radically different from many other presentations of the theme in the Hebrew Scriptures. "The Judgment of Solomon" is a high-watermark text which should not be uncritically assimilated to other passages using the word "justice" or expressing a concept of it, for many if not most such passages are really talking about reciprocal violence: an eye for an eye and a tooth for a tooth. That kind of justice imitates the other's violence as a means of producing reconciliation based upon a balanced exchange. In contrast, Solomon's justice *breaks* the pattern of imitation that exists between the antagonists. It is not interested in balanced exchange, or "pay-back," or punishment, or equity. Only the "not-mother" would be interested in that kind of justice, for whom dividing the infant seems a balanced, equitable solution. But love does not stand upon the demand for such justice. For the sake of a life it is willing to relinquish all claims and demands, and by so doing breaks the pattern of reciprocal imitation, allowing something startlingly new to emerge.

This high-watermark text has incendiary power in relation to the sacrificial structures upon which the sacred relies, and it is telling that nowhere does the story have resort to typical sacred functions or themes. Solomon does not "inquire of the Lord" in this story. He casts no lots. He does not invoke the primitive sacred in any of its manifestations. Nor does the text say that the Lord smote the lying woman, or that a prophet of Yahweh pronounced a word of condemnation and the woman died. Instead, Solomon relies upon the power of a mother's love to rise above an intense mimetic rivalry and reject a proffered sacrificial solution. *Human* violence, which is the real secret of the sacred, is thereby renounced.

All of this anticipates the critique of sacrifice that will become completely explicit some time later in the prophets: *"For I desire steadfast love and not sacrifice, the knowledge of God rather than burnt offerings."* (Hosea 6:6) Among the prophets we find high-watermark passages of stunning anti-sacrificial clarity, such as Amos 5:21-22, 24:

> *I hate, I despise your feasts, and take no delight in your solemn assemblies. Even though you offer me your burnt offerings and cereal offerings, I will not accept them, and the peace offerings of your fatted beasts I will not look upon.... But let justice roll down like waters, and righteousness like an ever-flowing stream.*

James Alison has pointed to the demand laid out in Exodus that all Hebrew firstborn sons be sacrificed to the Lord, and the prophet Jeremiah's subsequent challenge to that idea.[102] Jeremiah proclaims that it never even entered the Lord's mind to command such a horrible thing. Here are the texts, beginning with Exodus:

> *You shall not delay to offer from the fulness of your harvest and from the outflow of your presses. The first-born of your sons you shall give to me. You shall do likewise with your oxen and with your sheep: seven days it shall be with its dam; on the eighth day you shall give it to me.* (Ex. 22:29-30)

> *Because the people have forsaken me, and have profaned this place by burning incense in it to other gods whom neither they nor their*

fathers nor the kings of Judah have known; and because they have filled this place with the blood of innocents, and have built the high places of Ba'al to burn their sons in the fire as burnt offerings to Ba'al, which I did not command or decree, nor did it come into my mind; therefore, behold, days are coming, says the LORD, when this place shall no more be called Topheth, or the valley of the son of Hinnom, but the valley of Slaughter. (Jeremiah 19:4-7)

The "give me the firstborn of your sons" in the Exodus passage is often interpreted spiritually, as though Yahweh is not asking for the literal sacrifice of Hebrew children. But this interpretation overlooks the fact that the text says, "you must do the same with your flocks and herds" – and these animals were, of course, literally killed. True, the Hebrews found a way to ransom their firstborn so they could escape that sacrificial fate; but the demand itself seems to have been real enough at a certain stage in Hebrew religion. Child sacrifice was indulged by Israel's neighbors, after all, and many times in its history the Israelites took it up themselves. In Jeremiah's time, Israelites were sacrificing their children in the fire to the god Ba'al. When Yahweh speaks through Jeremiah and says, "...to burn their children in the fire as burnt offerings to Ba'al, which I did not command or decree, nor did it enter my mind," what never entered Yahweh's mind was the very idea of sacrificing children, whether to Ba'al, or to himself. But this directly challenges the Exodus passage, showing us once again how the Hebrew Scriptures contain varying points of view, amounting to an ongoing debate about the sacred, sacrifice, and the nature of God.

Other high-watermark texts in the scriptures are those that explicitly reveal the scapegoat mechanism and the collective violence which upon it relies. Psalm 22 is a good example:

Many bulls surround me, strong bulls of Bashan encircle me; Roaring lions that tear their prey open their mouths wide against me. (12-13 NIV)

Dogs surround me; a pack of villains encircles me; they pierce my hands and my feet. All my bones are on display; people stare and gloat over me. (16-17 NIV)

The Psalms are full of passages like this one, which show us a victim surrounded by persecutors. Psalm 31:33 says, "Yea, I hear the whispering of many – terror on every side! – They scheme together against me, as they plot to take my life."

The representation of collective violence in the Hebrew Scriptures takes many different forms: the kings of the nations unite against the Lord's anointed; the wicked gang up on the innocent or just man; all the people, led by false priests and prophets, turn against the one true prophet; all the nations threaten the one holy city, Jerusalem; and so on. That we are dealing with hyperbole in many of these texts is beside the point. The point is that such scriptures are revealing the very thing that mythology hid: collective violence against an innocent victim. Sometimes this is done in conjunction with an explicit claim of innocence, or a statement about the essentially arbitrary nature of the persecution, which is "without cause."

> *More in number than the hairs of my head are those who hate me without cause; many are those who would destroy me, my enemies who accuse me falsely. What I did not steal must I now restore?* (Psalm 69:4 NRSV)

We saw how the Bible advocated for the victim as early as the Cain and Abel story, giving voice to Abel's blood which cried out from the ground, in stark contrast to the mythological representation of Romulus' murder of Remus, of which Rome boasted. In the Genesis text God says that Abel's blood is crying out to him from the ground. Is it crying for vengeance? It would seem so. Indeed, we hear the chilling cry for vengeance many times in the Bible, especially in Psalms, as victims call down curses upon their adversaries, sometimes in the most excruciatingly vicious language: "Pour out your indignation upon them, and let your burning anger overtake them. May their camp be a desolation; let no one live in their tents... add guilt to their guilt; may they have no acquittal from you. Let them be blotted out of the book of the living." (Psalm

69:24-25, 27-28)

Many readers of the Bible have been offended by imprecatory cries like these, and the authors of such psalms have been called paranoid, and have been said to be suffering from hallucinations, believing themselves to be the target of group persecutions. But such interpreters miss the point, the significance of which cannot be overestimated: in these texts *the victim is being revealed and given voice for the first time in human history.* The anger and pain of the victim is becoming visible because Israel refuses (even if not consistently) to indulge in the mythological cover-up. There can be no question of arriving at Jesus' turning of the other cheek to the enemy, or his forgiveness of the violent mob, until the hardened lie of mythology has been cracked open and the victim allowed to emerge into history. And can we expect that emergence sound pretty? We cannot expect to hear, in the first instance, "Father forgive them…" First it must be acknowledged that there really is a victim, then we must hear the voice of outrage and pain. Winning through to a higher revelation will require long historical preparation.

The amazing thing is that the writers of Scripture inclined their ears toward victims, whose words of pain and rage the writers thought worthy of being recorded – and this in an era when writing was the prerogative of rich and educationally privileged groups, and was used mainly in the service of empire (to record the victories of kings, or facilitate business transactions), or religion (which was itself in the service of empire). That the cries of victims should have been deemed to have religious significance, and be written down, and passed on for posterity, is simply extraordinary.

Collective violence against an innocent victim is an explicit theme in the story of Joseph, who is persecuted by his brothers. The narrative makes his innocence very clear. Despite their treatment of him (selling him into slavery), Joseph is ultimately vindicated by God, and rises to the position of Pharaoh's right-hand-man. Nevertheless, Joseph refuses to take vengeance upon his brothers. He forgives them, and obtains a place for them in Egypt where they can live and thrive. (We will examine the story of Joseph in greater detail in the chapter on mythology, where we will compare it to the story of Oedipus in order to make clear the contrast between scriptural revelation and mythological obfuscation.)

Another high watermark text that reveals collective violence against an innocent victim is given to us by the prophet Isaiah (In the section scholars call "Second Isaiah." I will be using the NRSV translation for the texts that follow.) Isaiah paints a picture of someone called the "servant" of the Lord, commonly referred to in biblical scholarship as the "suffering servant." Whoever this nameless one is, his career begins when the Lord makes his mouth like a sharp sword (49:2) to speak to the people of Israel who are exiled in Babylon.

The section most relevant for our purposes is the so-called "Fourth Servant Song" of Isaiah 52:13 – 53:12. Here we see, as Girard points out,[103] that the servant possessed all the marks of someone who would be singled out for victimization. He was ugly even as a youth: *he had no form or majesty that we should look at him, nothing in his appearance that we should desire him.* (52:2b) In fact, his appearance was so marred that people were astonished at him: *Just as there were many who were astonished at him – so marred was his appearance, beyond human semblance, and his form beyond that of mortals…* (52:14) He is a kind of persona non grata from whom the people hide their faces: *He was despised and rejected by others; a man of suffering and acquainted with infirmity; and as one from whom others hide their faces he was despised, and we held him of no account.* (3) This person was thus predisposed, as Girard says, "to the role of a veritable human scapegoat."[104] He suffers the collective violence of the mob: he is wounded, crushed, punished, oppressed, afflicted, stricken, cut off from the land of the living, and buried with the wicked. All this is inflicted by the "we," the collective mob who speaks in 53:1-10.[105]

Following the typical pattern of laying blame and guilt on the scapegoat, the people think that God is striking him down: *…yet we accounted him stricken, struck down by God, and afflicted.* (4b) Amazingly, however, the people come to recognize their *own* guilt: *All we like sheep have gone astray; we have all turned to our own way.* (6a) They also come to recognize the innocence of the victim: *By a perversion of justice he was taken away.* (8a) *…although he had done no* *violence, and there was no deceit in his mouth.* (9b) They also recognize the victim's totally nonviolent response: *He was oppressed, and he was afflicted, yet he did not open his mouth; like a lamb that is led to the slaughter, and like a sheep that before its shearers is silent, so he did not open his mouth.* (7)

All of this sounds like a typical scapegoat scenario: while abusing him, the people believe completely in the victim's guilt: he is ugly, and he is a community pariah, making it obvious that God has cursed him. But this time their assumptions are completely upset when they come to realize that he is actually suffering *for their own sakes*: "he was wounded for our transgressions." And this, Isaiah perceives, was part of God's plan. It is why God opened the servant's ears to teach and train him every morning, so that he could become the vehicle for the revelation of a new aspect of God. Notice that in 50:4-6 it is *God* who opens the servant's ears every morning. He is not a puppet, in other words, of the mimetic "crowd," but is taught *directly* by God, to whom he listens. And the immediate result of God's teaching is that the servant learns *nonviolence:*

> *Morning by morning he wakens – wakens my ear to listen as those who are taught. The Lord God has opened my ear, and I was not rebellious, I did not turn backward. I gave my back to those who struck me, and my cheeks to those who pulled out the beard; I did not hide my face from insult and spitting.*

This remarkable description of nonviolent behavior, directed by the Lord's teaching, is a new vision contributed by Isaiah and not found in any other biblical prophetic tradition. Unlike the prophet Jeremiah, for example, in the Second Isaiah texts there are no prayers for revenge upon the enemy. This nonviolent turning of the back and offering of the cheek is how God's revelation becomes visible through the servant. Furthermore, as Raymond Schwager points out, the servant's mission is not for himself alone; it is not even for the nation of Israel alone: he is fulfilling a mission that concerns *all* nations, to which he will become a light.

It is too light a thing that you should be my servant to raise up the tribes of Jacob and to restore the survivors of Israel; I will give you as a light to the nations, that my salvation may reach to the ends of the earth. (49:6)

Schwager comments, "If one reflects on how widespread the notion of vengeance was in the Old Testament, it becomes doubly clear that with the nonviolent behavior of the servant of Yahweh something new is indeed happening."[106] Schwager points out that even the text itself recognizes its own newness in 43:18-19: *Do not remember the former things, or consider the things of old. I am about to do a new thing; now it springs forth, do you not perceive it?*

Whether the suffering servant is an actual, historically lynched individual, or a figure for the nation of Israel itself (as some commentators believe), does not matter for our purposes. A mob united against one individual, or a mob of nations united against Israel – structurally we are dealing with the same thing either way. The point is how clearly the passage reveals the scapegoat mechanism.[107] And the clarity of that revelation, it can be said, is directly due to the servant's nonviolence. For any attempt to retaliate against the mob – even just verbally – would immediately have caused the servant to lose his distinctiveness from the mob, thus obscuring the revelation of the scapegoat mechanism. The servant's refusal to imitate the mob's violence allows his real innocence, and the essential arbitrariness and wrongness of his persecution, to stand out in high relief. Because the Spirit of the Lord was upon him, working through him, the servant was able to surrender even the hateful gaze, or defiant and haughty attitude, with which an unarmed victim can still throw a spirit of violence back at his persecutors. But whenever a victim does this, it serves only to confirm for the persecutors the rightness of their actions. It was the servant's completely nonviolent response (including, possibly, forgiveness of the persecutors even during the lynching) that forced the people to see themselves in a new way, and brought them to the conclusions we noted earlier: *All we like sheep have gone astray; we have all turned to our own way; By a perversion of justice he was taken away….*

In spite of Second Isaiah's astonishing breakthrough to a new level of revelatory clarity, Schwager tells us that "...later Old Testament authors did not ascribe a special place to this prophet... the statements found in the fourth song of the servant about universal and vicarious suffering were left for centuries 'lying there, misunderstood, like an eccentric addition.' Not a single biblical author or Jewish writer referred to them explicitly."[108] This is absolutely astonishing. But that would change once the early Christian community saw in these suffering servant passages prophecies of Christ and his passion. In the early church, the seeds of this new vision found receptive soil in which to germinate, and these Isaiah passages were among the Christians' most frequently quoted texts from the Hebrew Scriptures. The servant passages helped early Christians grasp the meaning and significance of Christ's passion as a work of God for the sake of the world. The seeds Isaiah planted blossomed in the New Testament into a full and transparent revelation of the scapegoat mechanism; they also helped the early Christians (and probably even Jesus himself) to realize, in both understanding and action, the only possible response to human violence which will not turn the victim into a mirror image of the victimizer: the nonviolent response of love and forgiveness, generated from some field completely outside the closed circle of reciprocal imitation.

Chapter Seven
Mythology

"I could tell you many things if I wanted to,
but in this city an ox stands on my tongue."

(From the Watchman's speech in the opening of Aeschylus' *Agamemnon*)

‡‡

Before jumping into mythology proper, let us begin as Girard does in *The Scapegoat,* by talking about what he calls "persecution texts." As one might assume from the name, these are texts written by persecutors. Not, however, by repentant persecutors conscious of their aggression and abuse of innocent victims, but persecutors who fully believe in the rightness of their actions and the guilt of the victim. And that attitude is fully reflected in their written texts. We are all familiar with such texts; for example, documents written to prosecute innocent victims in Salem, Massachusetts, which purport to give accurate accounts of horrible crimes committed by the devil's cohorts; or, again, texts from medieval Europe, or Hitler's regime, detailing the crimes of the Jews. From whatever time or place such documents come, we are able to recognize them as the products of persecutors.

But stop to think a moment: how is it that we are able to make such an identification? Since such a text is entirely molded by the delusions of its writer, and proffers itself as a story of genuine historical merit, how is it that we can read it and immediately sense not only that the events did not happen the way they are being reported, but also have a sense of what really was going on behind the scenes? We do not credit the text, but neither do we regard it simply as pure fantasy and discount the whole thing. Rather, we are able to sense that the text is *based upon something real, but which it distorts.* And we possess the competence – which neither the author himself nor his community possessed – to decipher what that reality actually was: the persecution of victims.

We are able to decipher such texts today because we have an understanding of how collective violence, bigotry, and persecution work, and the kinds of distortions these things produce in the minds of those who practice them. And one doesn't have to be a social scientist or expert to do this: it is an ability we all have, almost instinctively. We take this for granted, but we should not. Most human beings throughout history were far more credulous than we are when it came to believing all manner of evil about their neighbors. Today, not only are we more conscious of the scapegoating game, we are downright allergic to it.[109] We are highly sensitive to victimization, to the point that we are able to detect its slightest traces, even when the perpetrators have skillfully covered their tracks. How this skill was historically achieved is a question we will pursue later. For our purposes now we need only recognize that we have it, and understand that it works because we are alert to certain characteristic "signs" in texts that allow us to identify them as *persecution* texts. What are these signs? What are the traces that alert us to the fact that we are dealing with a text written from the point of view of persecutors?

The Four "C's"

Conveniently, these signs all begin with the letter "C": crisis, criteria, crimes, and collective violence. Girard does not call them "The Four C's" – that is my own designation, but I find it helpful. We will examine each "C" briefly, beginning with ***crisis***. Usually, one does not have to read very far in a typical persecution text before coming upon some indication, some "sign," that points to a crisis within the group or society of the persecutors. This crisis may be explicitly referenced in the text, or it may only be implied. But it is this crisis that creates the conditions of social unrest that set people to looking for scapegoats to blame. The crisis may be a matter of internal affairs (political battles, economic disturbances, religious conflicts, and so on), or external matters such as plague, drought, flood, famine, war, and the like. One often finds references to such crises in persecution texts, as the author points out the terrible things that are happening in his tribe, town, village, city, or country. *But* (and here is the main point), the text does not address the issue of natural causes for these problems. Instead, it seeks someone to blame. After all, any crisis – a plague, an economic downturn, a Viking invasion – will place an additional weight of suffering, frustration, and fear upon those affected, which easily exacerbates preexisting tensions and rivalries, and multiplies new ones. This is why any such crisis ultimately becomes a *social* crisis. Human relations suffer and disintegrate along with the culture. But nobody wants to admit that they might have any responsibility in this. Thus the search for scapegoats to blame: a process of which the writers of persecution texts remain completely oblivious.

Which leads to the second "C": ***Crimes.*** Victims in persecution texts are often accused of the worst possible crimes. This is because the individual is being made responsible for the ills of the entire community – thus her crime (or crimes) must be big enough to call down the wrath of God upon the entire community. It is not surprising, therefore, to find that the same types of crimes are mentioned over and over again in persecution texts, crimes of great horror that corrupt the very foundations of the culture: incest, patricide, matricide, rape, beastiality, and so on.

What these crimes have in common is that they transgress certain sacred boundaries and efface sacred cultural differences. They are a cause of fear and horror because they dare to mix categories which the society sanctifies as separate. Incest destroys the distinction between mother/son or father/daughter; beastiality destroys the distinction between human and animal; patricide transgresses the hierarchical distinction between father and son; and so on. As mentioned earlier, these distinctions were the supporting pillars of archaic and ancient societies, put in place originally as a means of suppressing the violence of mimetic rivalry. The incest taboo dissuaded the son from sexual relations with his mother, which would unleash violence between father and son. A jealous son was also dissuaded from giving expression to competitive rage against his father by virtue of the hierarchical taboo that we term "patriarchy." Signs of disrespect towards the father in some societies was punishable by death. Prohibitions were like an iron fence standing between certain classes of individuals, making violent reciprocity nearly impossible. When someone was so rash as actually to violate a taboo, the act was perceived as a threat to the entire society, because it attacked one of society's foundational distinctions, thus raising the old, nasty specter of nondifferentiation – that state of all-against-all from which the society had emerged in the first place. The deed must therefore be punished with swift vengeance in order to dissuade others, and the taboo distinctions must be maintained with a sense of sacred awe, and people's belief in them never be allowed to weaken. (Should a weakening occur, the people would have a sacrificial crisis on their hands.) We can understand, then, why someone who actually commits such a crime would easily become the target of collective violence, in the same way that a cancer becomes the focus of the body's efforts to attack and destroy, before it reduces the body's finely systematized differences to a globular, undifferentiated mass.

The most spectacular foundational crimes are few in number, so they are used again and again throughout history as accusations against scapegoats, whether she be an old woman in Salem accused of wanton intercourse with the devil, or a Jewess in medieval France accused of beastiality and giving birth to pigs. The point is that when we read a text in which such accusations appear, we are sure of two things: first, that the accusations are generally false; and, second, that we need not for that reason discard the entire text as historically worthless and untrustworthy. We know how to interpret the evidence of which the delusionary writers leave traces in their texts. We believe that we can see through to the real history going on behind the textual scene. And our sense of certainty increases dramatically when stereotypical accusations are accompanied by indications of a social crisis in the background (giving the writer a reason for desperately wanting to blame someone). Our certainty increases even more when, in the same text, we see that the person being blamed carries the typical marks of a victim – which is our third "C" – ***criteria***.

To say that the unfortunate individual upon whom the group unloads its anger is an essentially arbitrary target, means that even if the person *did* commit the crime of which he or she happens to be accused, that is not the *real* reason for the lynching; it is only the pretext. *Anyone* could become the victim. However, because scapegoating will not work unless everyone wholeheartedly believes the individual to be some kind of de-humanized monster, there is a tendency to pick someone against whom it will be easy to rally unanimous hostility. And this is easily achieved if the individual possesses some quality that already marginalizes him, or marks him as strange, or different. This is why victims of collective violence are likely to fulfill certain characteristic criteria. Physical criteria are perhaps the most obvious: deformities, congenital diseases, speech impediments, and so on. But there are also social abnormalities: individuals who are eccentric, odd, mad, or simply nonconformists. There are also the outsiders: strangers, aliens, prisoners of war. Also at risk of being victimized are "marginal insiders." The poor fall into this category, but the rich and powerful as well. Bill Gates, precisely by virtue of his money and power, is a marginalized figure in our society, and in times of social upheaval, kings, princes, wealthy industrialists, and so on, can become targets for scapegoating.

Anything in a society that stands out as extreme exists on the margin of the culture and is thus liable to victimization. Extreme ugliness or extreme beauty; extreme poverty or extreme wealth; extreme failure or success; weakness (the elderly, children, women) or strength; degradation (moral degenerates, prodigal sons, prostitutes, criminals) or virtue (saints, heroes). Naturally, the weak and poor are easier to persecute, and so receive the lion's share of the scapegoating; but under certain conditions the rich and powerful can be substituted as victims.

The fourth and final "C" is ***collective violence***. When a text gives hints or states explicitly that the accusations against an individual or minority group are unanimous, being affirmed by the entire group, or that everyone participated in the violence, we may suspect that we are in the presence of a persecution text. When collective violence is mentioned in such a text, naturally it will not be placed in a negative light, but portrayed positively, even as virtuous. A medieval text may tell us, for instance, that the entire community rose up "with one voice" to accuse the Jew; or we may read that the entire courtroom burst into unanimous condemnation of the witch; or that a criminal was torn apart by the mob. Because it is a persecution text, written from the point of view of the persecutors, the author will not be aware of his scapegoating, and will present the mob's acts as entirely justified. The mob's rightness is simply obvious to him, needing no justification, because he is himself completely a victim of the collective delusion. Therefore, quite naively, he does not bother to disguise the fact of collective violence. He has no clue that readers such as ourselves would understand such references as evidence of persecution. He doesn't realize that he is leaving tracks whereby we, enlightened as we are regarding scapegoating dynamics, will be able to find our way to the actual historical truth behind the veil of group delusion.

Girard says that when some of these four C's are visible in texts, we know that we are dealing with persecutions. All four are not always present together in the same text; but the presence of even a couple such signs make it likely that we are dealing with distortions characteristic of the persecutor mentality. We should realize that there is nothing particularly controversial about Girard's claim here. He is simply making explicit the way modern historians generally operate when dealing with texts of this nature. We do not buy into the perspective of such texts, even when they purport to be real history. We do not believe the accusations made against the "witches" in Salem; but we certainly do believe in the reality of persecutions of helpless women, because we understand the ***crisis*** New England society was facing at that time, and we can detect the ***criteria*** by which typical victims were chosen (women, the weak, the old and feeble, the mad, those without connections that could provide strong advocacy, and so on). We see the exaggerated and stereotypical ***crimes*** of which they are accused (intercourse with the devil, and so on). And we see the ***collective*** paranoia. The four C's enable us to know what kind of text we are dealing with; and even if on rare occasion we recognize that some of the victims may in fact be guilty of certain of the crimes of which they are accused, we understand how the accusations are nonetheless being used as pretext for scapegoating, and do not share the credulity of the narrator.

Most important for our discussion of mythology is to realize that while we are skeptical of a persecution text's perspective, we do not make the absurd claim that the text contains no real history whatsoever, that it is all simply fiction, and no witch hunting and burning ever took place. Obviously, we know that it did, especially since we have other kinds of evidence which provide further confirmation.

We come at last, then, to the significant point to which the preceding discussion has been leading: *Girard's key move is to apply exactly the same interpretative method that we use for persecution texts from the historical era, to ancient and archaic mythologies*. That is to say, when a myth contains some or all of the four C's, we should treat it as a text of persecution no different from a medieval account of Jews who maliciously poisoned all the town's wells and streams. This quite original idea of Girard's rubs abrasively against the grain of modern academic and popular estimates of the nature of mythology, which is venerated as a treasure house of poetic, philosophical, psychological, and spiritual insight. Girard challenges this attitude, which he sees as not only naïve, but as throwing a veil of protection around mythology that only perpetuates the illusion that blinded those who first spun the tales. (An illusion that the Bible was already in process of deconstructing thousands of years ago.) A myth, therefore, according to Girard, is *a tale told from the perspective of persecutors.*

If a human culture was founded as the result of the murder of a victim, and maintained in good order by the ritual imitation of that murder, the imagination of the persecutors also told the story of that murder in an endless variety of ways. And yet not so various as we may think. Because when we take a hard sober look at them, we discover that huge numbers of mythologies from every corner of the planet *all share the characteristics of historical persecution texts, revealing all of the four C's* (although not always within the same myth, as is true also of historical persecution texts). But that sober look is seldom taken in academia or pop culture. We refuse to see the history behind these myths, even though a similar refusal to acknowledge the historical persecution of women behind bigoted and slanted stories of witch trials would strike us as outrageous.

Let us look at a few examples of how the four C's show up in myth. Regarding the ***criteria*** that mark out victims, world mythology fairly teems with references to heroes, gods, goddesses, and other beings who are lame, blind, or crippled, while some appear among the people as foreigners, newcomers, or strangers. The gods of myth are commonly accused of committing terrible ***crimes*** (Zeus' rape of Leda, Europa, and other women, for example). Some gods become victims of ***collective violence***. Dionysus, for example, was ripped apart by the Titans. (His followers, the Maenads, which means "raving ones," are portrayed as whipping themselves into wild frenzies, then tearing apart and devouring animals, men, and children.) And myths often allude to some ***crisis*** that is ravishing the community (plague, famine, and so on). Sometimes the reference is direct, while at other times the crisis is portrayed symbolically.

The best way to gain an understanding of Girard's approach to myth is by analyzing one. I will use one of his own favorite examples, which, fortunately, is a story most people are somewhat familiar with (thanks to Freud) – the myth of Oedipus. We know of this myth thanks to Sophocles' trilogy of plays involving Oedipus, but Sophocles was using a myth that had long been in circulation among the Greeks (Homer's Odyssey also contains an account of the tale). In short sum, because of a prophecy that their son would eventually murder his father and marry his mother, Oedipus' father Laius, king of Thebes, orders his wife Jocasta to kill the infant; but she cannot bring herself to do it, and orders a servant to take the baby to a mountain and abandon it there to die of exposure. Fortunately, baby Oedipus is rescued by a shepherd, who takes him to Corinth where he is adopted and raised by the king. Later, as a young man, when Oedipus is informed by the Delphic oracle that he is fated to kill his father and mate with his mother, he flees Corinth in order to spare the king and queen – whom he thinks are his real parents. Ironically, he travels to Thebes, his true birthplace, and during the journey he meets and kills his *real* father, Laius, in a dispute over right-of-way passage at a crossroads. Meanwhile, the city of Thebes has been enslaved by a Sphinx, whom Oedipus encounters and defeats by solving the Sphinx's riddle. As a result, he is made king of Thebes, and marries Lauis' widow, Jocasta – his mother!

Sophocles' play, *Oedipus the King,* begins after all of these events have already happened, and Thebes is now suffering from a plague epidemic; and in good ancient fashion, the Thebans conclude that the gods must be angry at the city for some reason. It turns out they are angry because the murderer of Thebes' former king, Laius, was never caught – so Oedipus vows to find the criminal. During the course of the play the truth gradually emerges that Oedipus himself is the murderer, that he has killed his own father and married his own mother in fulfillment of the very prophecy he tried to escape. The truth revealed, Jocasta hangs herself, Oedipus blinds himself, and has himself exiled from Thebes.

The Oedipus myth is an excellent example of the kind of story that would easily be recognized as a persecution text had it come down to us not as a Greek myth, but as a narrative, say, from thirteenth century Christian Europe about Oedipus the Jew. In that case, we would easily read between the lines and conclude that the story reflects a genuinely historical scapegoating of a real victim. But because the Oedipus tale comes to us in the form of hallowed mythological tradition, we never consider the possibility that it might be the imaginative retelling of a real persecution. Consider the four C's characteristic of persecution texts – we find *all four* in the Oedipus myth. The story portrays a *crisis*: a plague is ravaging the Theban community. Oedipus possesses several characteristics that constitute *criteria* marking out a person as a potential victim: he is a total stranger to the Thebans when he first arrives (a "social outsider"); he limps (the very name "Oedipus" means *swollen foot,* and this may be the real reason he was abandoned as an infant); and he is the son of a king, and later a king himself (a "marginal insider"). Any of these criteria alone, much less summed together, would have had the power to draw the attention of a crowd looking for someone to blame. And Oedipus is, of course, blamed. It is the king himself who has brought the plague upon Thebes, because of his *crimes* – the third "C". And these are not petty crimes, but precisely the stereotypical, monstrous crimes that victims of collective violence are often accused of: Swollen Foot has committed patricide and incest! And, of course, the myth shows us the unanimous tide of opinion against Oedipus – the whole city agrees to his expulsion. In fact, so powerful is the collective movement against Oedipus that he himself agrees that he is guilty as charged! Thus the final "C" of *collective violence* is clearly evidenced in the tale.

Once one stops looking at the Oedipus myth as hallowed ground and examines it with the same saavy with which we approach historical persecution texts, it does not take much imagination to reconstruct a historical background involving a lame individual with a swollen foot, being taunted with the name "Swollen Foot," perhaps arriving as a stranger in a new city, finding himself the object of blame for an incident of plague, and becoming the victim of collective expulsion. Any detailed historical reconstruction is impossible, of course; but with all four C's evidenced in this tale we can be quite certain of the fact that behind the original myth, and far behind Sophocles' eloquent and poetic piece of theater, lay a real, historical victim of collective persecution and expulsion. Only a kind of sacred reverence for mythology prevents us from applying the same canons of interpretation to this text that we commonly apply to historical persecution texts.

We come now once again to the heart of the matter: myths are tales told from the perspective of persecutors who have murdered or expelled a victim. Admittedly, not all myths lend themselves as easily as Oedipus to this kind of analysis. Some myths are less suggestive of persecution because they have far more imaginatively transfigured the original events, which are sometimes represented in highly stylized ways. Nevertheless, it remains possible to discern at least some of the "C's" even in many of these. For example, many myths reflect the *crisis* in highly symbolic fashion, telling of a time when day and night became confused, or the sun and moon became twins (and thus indistinguishable), leading to catastrophic results.

Such symbols represent a crisis of nondifferentiation, and the tale involves the resolution of that crisis, which results in the founding or reestablishing of order. Obviously, there was no literal, original crisis of the moon and sun becoming twins; but the image serves as an imaginative, symbolic way of representing the real, historical terror of reciprocal violence which reduces all players to enemy twins, and threatens the culture with nondifferentiation.

If the crisis is presented symbolically in some myths, other myths distort the *crimes*. The crimes of which the original scapegoat had been accused in order to justify his or her persecution are sometimes presented as mere pranks played by a capricious god. It is easy to see through this guise, however, once we become aware of how persecution texts are structured, and realize that what a myth portrays as an "accident," or a "prank," or a "game," could have originally been a serious accusation. Such transformation from crime to accident or prank might happen because of a desire to rehabilitate the reputation of a certain god. At certain times and places the crimes of the gods came to seem morally revolting, and there arose a desire to cast certain gods in a better light. Then such stories were modified, and the offending gods cast as mere tricksters, or an accident prone fools, or something akin to tragic figures subject to an unkind fate, victims of necessity.

Some myths lack any indication at all of *collective violence*. Others substitute for collective action the deed of a single being, perhaps in an effort to exonerate the community from all responsibility. Girard shows that in some cases one can discern a deliberate effort to efface *all* signs of violence – collective and individual – because of a developing moral conscience (such as we see, for example, among some of the Greek and Roman philosophers who expressed disgust at the violence common in their cultures' myths). This whole area of study – the historical transformation of myths so as to eliminate traces of violence – is a fascinating topic which I do not have the space to pursue in more detail here. Interested readers should refer to the relevant chapters in *The Scapegoat*.

Obviously, arguments of the type just made cannot in and of themselves provide proof that such transformations actually occurred; although there are cases, cited by Girard in *The Scapegoat*, in which we happen to possess both earlier and later versions of the same myth, and can actually see such transformations taking place. Minus the luxury of such comparative data, however, one can only form stronger or weaker inferences, which grow in strength to the degree that there are other C's unambiguously represented in the text. If, for example, we see the typical marks of a victim (Oedipus' limp, for instance), and there is a representation of collective violence, as well as indications of a cultural crisis – but no mention of any crimes or accusations – we can draw the strong inference that for some reason the expected accusations have been erased from the story (or never included from the beginning). And this argument would be strengthened even more if we could cite a historical reason that would provide a motive for the omission.

One great difference between myths and historical persecution texts written after the decline of mythology in Western civilization, is that while the latter demonize the victims and hold them responsible for evil, mythology not only demonizes, it *deifies* the victim. To help the reader recall that process, so alien to our modern experience, I will summarize it again very briefly: The creation or restoration of social order after the death of the victim was a truly powerful experience, for which ancient peoples could not but feel grateful. But how were they to explain it? To whom could they attribute this great good? Certainly they could not attribute it to their *own* initiative: all they did was kill or expel the cause of the evil that had been besetting them. The subsequent positive social outcome was a complete surprise, having (seemingly) nothing to do with their own agency. Therefore, it came to be seen as the work of a god, part of a divine plan. Thus the gods have two faces: one is feared, while one is venerated, thanked, and worshiped. This is why the sacred was perceived as an ambivalent power, combining both good and evil, capable of bestowing both death and life, destruction and creation.

Girard's interpretation of myth is thus the opposite of positions like that of the late Joseph Campbell, who understood myths about the death and resurrection of the god to be modeled after the processes of nature observed by ancient peoples. They saw all around them plant life dying, and new life sprouting from the humus. From this, they extrapolated to create poetic stories of a spiritual nature, about death and resurrection. And these themes were eventually acted-out in the form of rituals. For Girard, however, myths about dying and resurrected gods were not spun as poetic-philosophical ruminations on nature and the meaning of life and death, then subsequently acted-out in ritual form. Rather, the *act* comes first: the slaying of a victim, which creates community and order. That concrete experience then becomes a kind of template, not only for the sacrificial rituals that will be based upon it, but for a whole way of understanding and apprehending reality, including nature. It becomes a way of thinking and solving problems, with applicability far beyond the realm of the strictly religious. It becomes the "sacrificial thinking" mentioned earlier. In other words, people did not imagine the process of life coming out of death, create tales to celebrate it, and then kill someone to demonstrate it or magically promote life; first they killed someone, discovering the sacred in the process, and then told tales about it – tales which show us both the terror and evil, and the new life and order that emerged from the killing.

Positions like Campbell's, which put thought before action, cannot reasonably explain why an entire group would willingly unite around the ritualized murder of another human being. Girard's scapegoat mechanism seems to me a much more likely explanation. It all began with murder, as the Bible itself hints (Cain and Abel), which then became an entrenched practice (one might almost say *addictive* practice), because it worked so well in procuring survival benefits for the group – and this in turn gave rise to myths about creation, death and resurrection.

Before moving on to a comparison of mythology with the Bible, it might be helpful to look at another example of how Girard would read a myth with a view towards the four C's, so the pattern is clear to the reader. Now that we have been through the process with Swollen Foot, we can move more quickly. Girard offers many examples, scattered throughout his many books and articles, including one about how the Ojibwa people originated when six supernatural beings emerged from the ocean and started mingling with human beings. One of them was to keep his eyes covered and not look at the people; but, overcome with curiosity, he lifted his veil slightly, and his glance fell upon a person who was immediately struck dead. As a result, his five companions caused him to return to the "bosom of the great water." The five Ojibwa clans are said to have descended from the five remaining beings.

To a Girardian reader, sacrificial thinking and collective violence fairly leap from the text of this myth. One recognizes immediately that it is a story of unanimity minus one; that is, five beings expel a sixth, and go on to father the people and culture of the Ojibwas. This is a representation of *collective violence* against a single victim. All five of his companions send the "guilty" one back into the ocean. He is expelled unanimously. Despite its stylized brevity, in this myth we can see quite clearly the theme of cultural generation springing from an act of collective expulsion: the Ojibwa clans claim descent from a group of beings who collectively expelled one of their members.

Short as it is, the Ojibwa myth actually contains all four C's. In addition to collective violence, the *crisis* is represented symbolically by the ominous occurrence of supernatural beings coming up out of the sea. The sea is typically an image of chaos, and in the mingling of these sea-beings with humans, we have a representation of the threat of nondifferentiation. (We find a similar representation in Genesis 6:1, when we read about how the "sons of God" made wives of the "daughters of men.") Things are getting mixed up that should remain separate, and the results are threatening and disastrous. The myth uses these images as a way of expressing the society's fear of nondifferentiation – the state that originally existed before the "community" came into being, and the state toward which human relations tend whenever cultural differences begin to lose their authority under the pressure of a mimetic crisis.

In the midst of such a crisis groups look for a scapegoat, and we have already said that while the choice of scapegoat-victims is essentially arbitrary, there are certain marks of victimage, certain criteria, that make one a likely target. Is there any suggestion of a scapegoat in this short Ojibwa tale, any marks of a victim? We find a possible subtle trace in the supernatural being who is veiled, the one who must not look at the people. This is not a lot to go on, but we might have here a quick glimpse of an historical scapegoat, someone like a prisoner of war, or captive criminal, or anyone whose subservience demands the propriety of maintaining downcast eyes.

The third "C" is *crimes,* and in this myth the crime is murder. The one with the veiled eyes kills a human being. His doing so with a mere glance is highly suggestive of the "evil eye" – a common accusation against victims in many cultures. In the medieval and ancient worlds, those who were accused of possessing the "evil eye" had better, for their own protection, keep those eyes downcast. (This is why Jesus, in the famous story of the woman caught in adultery, refuses to look the lynch mob in the face, but, instead, crouches down to write or doodle in the sand while conversing with them. To have looked them in the eye would have been to invite the misinterpretation of defiance, and trigger the scapegoat mechanism against himself. See John 8:1-11.[110])

We see, then, how a myth about the origin of the Ojibwa clans yields clues that lead us to suspect the myth is a fanciful reconstruction of an original event, in which order and group identity arose from the collective murder of a victim. It may sound to some as though this analysis stretches matters and reads a preconceived theory into the myth. Yet it must be admitted rather remarkable that in a short tale like this we can find allusions to all four C's. The pattern of collective violence against a single victim is especially clear, even if we have only a possible trace of the stereotypical marks of a victim. It must also be remembered that huge quantities of myths can be produced that are amenable to this kind of analysis. We are not dealing with a mere handful of stories, nor are we limiting ourselves to a handful of peoples and cultures. The phenomenon is worldwide, cross-cultural, and trans-historical. Myths from all over the world, and from all periods of history, fit the pattern. It is true that not all myths contain all four C's, but, as indicated above, Girard has shown how myths have their own historical development, which is often characterized by a desire to suppress violence. As myths are retold, things distasteful to later generations sometimes get reframed, and originally graphic violence can become more highly stylized, or may be eliminated from the story completely.

Genesis and the Babylonian Creation Myth

Based on what we know about founding murders, it should not surprise us to discover that hundreds of what anthropologists call "foundation myths" from around the world connect the beginnings of a tribe, a nation, humanity, or the cosmos itself, with a violent killing. The most famous example is probably the Babylonian creation myth, *Enuma Elish.* In this myth, Tiamat, primeval god of watery chaos, is mother to all the gods. The younger gods, however, are proving noisy and disruptive, greatly disturbing Tiamat and her husband Apsu. Tiamat is unable to bring herself to do away with them, but Apsu plans to slaughter his children so he can get some rest. Unfortunately for him, one of his children, the god Ea, murders him first. Then Tiamat, along with strange and fierce creatures of destruction that she has created for the purpose, goes out to avenge her husband's death. The gods are terrified. A couple of challengers are unable to stop Tiamat's onslaught, until Marduk challenges her to single combat. He entangles her in a net and sends a hurricane blast of wind into her face. When Tiamat opens her mouth to suck Marduk down, the wind rages into her belly and inflates it. Marduk swiftly splits open her belly with an arrow, flings her down, and straddles the carcass. He smashes her skull, severs her arteries, and blood streams down the north wind "to the unknown ends of the world."

All the gods offer Marduk thanks and send him gifts, and Marduk rests, pondering what he might create from the dead carcass. He splits it apart and with the upper half constructs the arc of the sky, Tiamat's belly button forming the zenith, then sets the constellations in place. From the rest of her he creates the earth, and lays the foundation for his own city which he plans to build – Babylon. The gods go wild with adulation and make Marduk their king. A bit later, Marduk calls all the gods together and declares, "Whosoever started the war, and incited Tiamat, and gathered an army, let the one who started the war be given up to me, and he shall bear the penalty for his crime, that you may dwell in peace."

The gods answer that the instigator was Qingu, Tiamat's consort, whereupon "they bound him and held him in front of Ea, imposed the penalty on him and cut off his blood. He created mankind from his blood."[111]

Having the Girardian analysis at our disposal, it is not difficult to discern that this myth deals with a *crisis,* the essence of which we can recognize once again as nondifferentiation, symbolized by Tiamat as watery chaos. (Water is a great symbol for nondifferentiation because it holds no permanent patterns, everything slips and melds and blends in a continual dance of chaotic liquid forms.) Notice, however, that behind this symbolism of nondifferentiation we glimpse traces of social unrest and rivalry: Apsu is about to take vengeance upon the younger gods because of their inconsiderate and noisy partying; but he is preempted by Ea, who murders him; then Tiamat seeks vengeance against the gods; Marduk slays Tiamat, then seeks further vengeance against Qingu, her consort and organizer. What do we see playing itself out in this story about the relations among gods, if not rivalry and vengeance – which, as has been said several times already, is always the great, underlying problem, and the primary threat of nondifferentiation in ancient cultures. Tiamat as watery chaos is a symbolic way of speaking about the nondifferentiation of deteriorating social relations.

There is not much indication in this myth of the *criteria* of a victim, unless we see a trace of it in the fact that Tiamat is a woman. We do, however, see accusations and *crimes.* Humanity itself is created from the blood of the murdered Qingu, who is charged with instigating war against the young gods who stand entirely justified ("he shall bear the penalty for his crime"). *Collective violence* is indicated in the participation of all the gods, who rally in complete unity behind their hero, Marduk; and, later, they all participate in binding Qingu so Ea can slay him.

In *Enuma Elish* we see the slaying of watery chaos, which results in a new order: Marduk is now supreme king of all the gods. He creates the cosmos, gives the command to build Babylon, establishes its temple and religious/sacrificial cult, and apportions shrines for all the other gods. In her introduction to *Enuma Elish,* translator Stephanie Dalley, writes, "the forces of evil and chaos are overcome, whereupon the present order of the universe can be established, with its religious centres, its divisions of time, its celestial bodies moving according to proper rules, and with mankind invented to serve the gods. The gods themselves behave in an orderly fashion: they assemble, discuss, agree, and elect their leaders in a gathering of males . . . "[112] Marduk's slaying of Tiamat is portrayed in highly poetic and imaginative images as a supernatural battle between single combatants; but in the execution of Qingu the truth emerges more clearly. Here we see the stark reality of collective, mob violence against a single victim. Qingu is bound and murdered in the presence of the gods – *and this is pictured as the genesis of humanity.*

Marduk is the great hero-god of Babylon, and in this tale we hear the bombast, the pride, and the self-justification of an empire, in a way similar to Rome's myth about Romulus' slaying of Remus. And just as that myth posed a dramatic contrast to the Bible's tale of Cain and Abel, owing especially to the way in which the victim was portrayed, so too does *Enuma Elish* contrast with the creation narrative of Genesis.[113] In contrast to the common mythological motif in which a slaying lays the groundwork for the creation of the cosmos, the opening words of the Bible present us with a magisterial account of the calm and peaceful Spirit, creating *without violence*:

> *In the beginning God created the heavens and the earth. Then earth was without form and void, and darkness was upon the face of the deep; and the Spirit of God was moving over the face of the waters.*

In Genesis we once again confront the watery chaos of nondifferentiation, out of which God will bring forth an entire ordered cosmos, built upon a system of stable and enduring differences. This is achieved by the Spirit of God, who moves over the face of the waters. In Hebrew the word translated as spirit also means *wind* – perhaps a deliberate allusion to the wind by which Marduk slew Tiamat. But the Spirit's wind is nothing like Marduk's hurricane, which he blasted into his victim's belly in order to inflate it, then split it open. The God of Genesis 1 is pointedly nonviolent, and creates through the eloquent agency of simple commands: "And God said, 'Let there be light"; and there was light." God introduces difference into the homogeneous void, not by violently severing a carcass, but by serenely willing and speaking: "And God saw that the light was good; and God *separated* the light from the darkness. God called the light Day, and the darkness he called Night. And there was evening, and there was morning, one day." The "tohu wa vohu" (without form and void) of Genesis' primal waters pose no more challenge to Yahweh than clay does to a potter – less, in fact, for the Spirit shapes it through the agency of speech alone. We must also notice that the God of Genesis 1 is not in rivalry with anybody or anything. We read of no quarrels, no bumptious exchanges between rivals, no wars, no murders. And at the end of the process we read:

> *Thus the heavens and the earth were finished, and all the host of them. And on the seventh day God finished his work which he had done, and he rested on the seventh day from all his work which he had done.*

One cannot help but chuckle at the mention of Yahweh *resting* after his work – his "work" being the effortless utterance of a few words! But the reference is illuminated (and rendered, perhaps, even funnier) by way of contrast with *Enuma Elish,* which describes Marduk as taking a much needed rest after his grisly battle with Tiamat.

Of course, the creation of humans in Genesis is equally nonviolent, requiring no blood, no mob lynching of a rouge "instigator." (We might also add that in *Enuma Elish,* the purpose for the creation of humanity is simply to give the gods relief from their work: the humans will now shoulder the burden. Genesis, in contrast, gives human beings a privileged position of honor and authority over creation, and stresses humanity's creation in the image of God.) Obviously, then, the Genesis account contains a self-conscious rejection of the mythological creation through violence that was so much a part of the cultural experience of Israel's neighbors. *Enuma Elish* was recited as part of the Babylonian New Year festival, when the idol of their patron God Marduk was paraded down "Main Street" and into the temple. Yet Genesis' critique of such mythology was more than a protest against idolatry, for Genesis (along with the Bible as a whole) begins the process of unveiling the victim, the real, honest-to-goodness victim who lies dead and forever silenced in the world of myth. It rehabilitates the accused victim by giving voice to his or her innocence. The veiled being in the Ojibwa myth, expelled from the group because he kills with his eyes, is actually the victim, mythologically transfigured, his voice of protest and petition forever lost to history, hidden behind a veil of poetic stylization and mythological justification. The Bible lifts this veil.

Oedipus and Joseph

We have already examined Girard's analysis of the Oedipus myth. But Girard has pointed out that Genesis has its own version of the Oedipus tale, and we will find the contrast between Genesis' version and the Greek version even more marked than the contrast between the creation narratives. Genesis' version of the Oedipus myth is actually the story of Joseph and his brothers. This is not to imply that author of the Joseph story consciously used Oedipus as a model in order to critique the myth (as may indeed have been the case with Genesis 1 and *Enuma Elish*). The point is not that the author of Genesis knew the Oedipus myth (although of course he might have), and deliberately used it to construct a contrasting tale; the point is rather to show how differently Genesis approaches the same *kind* of story. For the fact is that the tales of Oedipus and Joseph display an amazing structural similarity, which Girard analyzes in *I See Satan Fall Like Lightning,* and with still more elegance and depth in *Oedipus Unbound.*[114]

What does Girard mean when he says that the two stories are "structurally" the same? In general, they are both stories about an expelled outcast who rises to great heights thanks to an ability to remedy a crisis. However, there is much more in the specifics, and we shall look at them through the lens of the four C's.

First, *crisis.* The story of Oedipus begins with a family crisis. Laius and his wife Jocasta hear a terrible prophecy about their son, that he will eventually kill his father and marry his mother. In order to eliminate this potential rival for his throne and his wife, Laius issues a command for the infant Oedipus' death by exposure. Joseph's family is also in crisis. His brothers are full of envy, coveting the special attention and affection that their father shows Joseph, and offended by Joseph's dream in which he sees his brothers bowing down to him. They are so maddened that they come to the point of plotting his murder. In both stories, therefore, the real nature of the crisis is rivalry. Later in the lives of both protagonists, crisis appears again: while Oedipus is king Thebes is stricken with plague; and while Joseph is Pharaoh's right hand man Egypt is stricken with famine. As we have seen, both plague and famine are common ways in which myths represent the threat of nondifferentiation that results from rampant mimetic rivalry within a society.

Second, the *criteria* of a victim. Oedipus has a physical deformity and limps. He becomes king of Thebes when he liberates the city from enslavement to the Sphinx, but he arrived there as a foreigner from Corinth, a stranger – another victimary criterion. And even though Joseph becomes the head of Potiphar's household, and later the virtual head of the entire nation, like Oedipus he arrived in Egypt as a stranger, while also bearing the additional victim-mark of slavery (his brothers sold him as a slave to Midianites, who took him to Egypt). Both men solve some kind of mystery or riddle – Oedipus solves the Sphinx's riddle, and Joseph interprets the mystery of Pharaoh's dream – which catapults them to positions of great power within societies of which they are not natives, making them easy targets for blame when things go wrong. Both protagonists therefore possess characteristics that mark them out as potential scapegoats.

Third, *crimes.* Oedipus is accused of incest and patricide, blamed for the plague wracking Thebes, and expelled from the land. Joseph eventually triumphs as ruler of Egypt, but as the head of Potiphar's household his elevated status set him up for Potiphar's wife's accusation of rape, as a result of which he landed in prison. Because

Potiphar had come to love and trust him like a son, the accusation of rape in this case approximates incest. Patricide and incest were taboos because they destroyed distinctions crucial to the stable functioning of society, making an absurdity of the sacred differences between father, mother, and son. In addition, Joseph's dream of his brothers bowing down to him seems to make a mockery of the hierarchical pecking-order of sibling births, so important to the tribal societies of the ancient near east. Both Oedipus and Joseph, therefore, as accused confusers and destroyers of sacred order, embody the chaos of nondifferentiation that ancients so desperately sought to expel from their communities.

Finally, *collective violence.* Oedipus is expelled by the society of Thebes, and Joseph by his brothers. In each case the expulsion is unanimous – everyone agrees to it. (Judah dissents in order to save Joseph's life, but agrees with his expulsion into slavery.) In fact, both protagonists are expelled *twice*. Oedipus is expelled first by his parents, and later by Thebes; Joseph is expelled first by his brothers, and later by Potiphar and his wife.

We see, then, how these stories, though different in content, are *structurally* equivalent. It is not important for our purposes which story came first, or whether there is a direct dependence of one upon the other, and similar questions. What is significant is that we allow the structural equivalence of the two stories to highlight the crucial difference between them, which is that *the two stories are told from completely different perspectives.* Oedipus is told from the perspective of the persecutors. It blames Oedipus for horrendous crimes. It even has Oedipus admitting to them himself, gouging out his eyes and accepting expulsion. Oedipus is therefore a quintessentially "mythical" story, for this is precisely what myth does, according to Girard: justify (albeit unconsciously) the scapegoating murders and expulsions that form the basis of community solidarity. The Bible, on the other hand, portrays Joseph as innocent. Joseph is decidedly *not* guilty of the crimes of which he is accused by Potiphar's wife, and he is as unjustly expelled from Potiphar's household as he was from his own.

With the story of Joseph Genesis brings to a grand climax the rehabilitation of the victim. But the truly stunning thing is that the story goes far beyond simple vindication. Not only is the victim given voice and shown innocent, but Joseph forgives his persecutors! In the beginning of Genesis, the dead Abel's voice cried out to God from the ground, not only for vindication, but for vengeance; but at the end of Genesis, the living Joseph is raised to a position of penultimate worldly power, perfectly positioned to wreak vengeance against his brothers, yet foregoes that opportunity and forgives them. They have been forced by a famine in Palestine to seek help from Egypt, and they do not recognize the great ruler as their little brother whom they scapegoated so many years earlier. But instead of using this as an opportunity to repay them in kind, Joseph forgives his brothers, creating not only one of the most moving scenes in world literature, but a stunning reversal of what all ancient societies would have considered the completely just, appropriate, even *sane* action to take in such a situation.

It is precisely Joseph's refusal to avenge himself that allows the scapegoat mechanism to be exposed. Because Joseph is nonviolent from beginning to end, his innocence is all the more powerfully confirmed, and the mechanism that illicitly accuses him is all the more effectively revealed as the lie it is. This story is therefore one of the Hebrew Scriptures' greatest triumphs over mythology and its power of illusion over all ancient peoples.

Chapter Eight
The Gospel Revelation of Myth and Murder

People do not wish to know that the whole of human culture is based on the mythic process of conjuring away man's violence by endlessly projecting it upon new victims. All cultures and religions[115] are built on this foundation, which they then conceal, just as the tomb is built around the dead body that it conceals.

René Girard, *Things Hidden* [116]

‡‡

A Murderer and Liar From the Beginning

In the eighth chapter of the gospel of John, Jesus has an extraordinary exchange with a group of Jewish followers in the temple. These Jews have believed in Jesus, yet they try to stone him. What does Jesus say to provoke such a reaction? He tells them that if they continue in his word they will know the truth, and it will set them free. This offends their dignity, because as descendants of Abraham they do not consider themselves to be slaves in need of liberation. But Jesus is speaking of slavery to "sin," of which they are completely unconscious. What slavery to sin actually means becomes evident within the context of the debate, and its most immediate meaning is connected to homicide. Jesus answers them, "I know that you are descendants of Abraham; yet you look for an opportunity to kill me, because there is no place in you for my word. I declare what I have seen in the Father's presence; as for you, you do what you have heard from your father." (8:37-38)[117] The debate continues:

> *They answered him, "Abraham is our father." Jesus said to them, "If you were Abraham's children, you would do what Abraham did, but now you seek to kill me, a man who has told you the truth which I heard from God; this is not what Abraham did. You do what your father did." They said to him, "We were not born of fornication; we have one Father, even God." Jesus said to them, "If God were your Father, you would love me, for I proceeded and came forth from God; I came not of my own accord, but he sent me. Why do you not understand what I say? It is because you cannot bear to hear my word. You are of your father the devil, and your will is to do your father's desires. He was a murderer from the beginning, and has nothing to do with the truth, because there is no truth in him. When he lies, he speaks according to his own nature, for he is a liar and the father of lies. But, because I tell the truth, you do not believe me.* (John 8:39-45)

In this amazing exchange, we have two parties: Jesus, and a group of his Jewish followers who do not really understand, it turns out, what following Jesus means. We should notice right away that Jesus is not confronted here by a single individual, but by a crowd. The text represents the situation of the scapegoat: a single victim surrounded by a group unanimously bent upon "lynching" him. And, indeed, the debate ends with the crowd attempting to stone Jesus, but he escapes.

Each party has a different "father." Jesus' father is God, and the group's father is the "devil." Jesus declares what he has seen in the Father's presence, and he "keeps his word" (8:55). In other words, Jesus imitates his Father. The crowd, on the other hand, does what they have heard from their father – they imitate a quite different model. Let us recall that the real significance of mimetic theory is the light it sheds upon the nature of *desire,* showing how human beings imitate one another's desires. Just so, Jesus says of the crowd that their will is to do their father's desires. They imitate a model whose desires are utterly opposed to those of Jesus' Father. The text is indicating two opposed mimetic patterns, two alternative models for imitation. *The crowd imitates a model that desires the killing of a victim.* ("but now you seek to kill me . . . You do what your father did.") Jesus names the crowd's father-model the devil. "You are of your father the devil . . ." And he has two very important things to say about this devil: "He was a murderer from the beginning, and has nothing to do with the truth because there is no truth in him. When he lies, he speaks according to his own nature, for he is a liar and the father of lies." The devil that the crowd imitates is both a murderer and a liar. Before my study of Girard's work, I always took Jesus' comment as a reference to the story of the "fall," where the devil, in the form of the serpent, lies to Eve about the consequences of eating the forbidden fruit; and if one stretches the matter, the serpent could also be seen as a kind of "murderer," since human beings come to experience death as a result of their disobedience. Jesus does say, after all, that the devil has been a liar and murderer "from the beginning."

But Girard has provided a much more cogent interpretation of Jesus' words, understood as a reference to Cain. "From the beginning" does not refer to the pre-historical story of the garden and the serpent, but to the beginning of human history as we know it. When Adam and Eve are expelled from the garden into the land "east of Eden," the Bible moves us into what it takes to be the beginnings of human history as such, and the first event it narrates within that history – the *beginning* of that history – is the murder of Abel by his brother Cain. And in that story, not only is Cain a murderer, he is also a liar in that he lures his brother into the field (presumably under some false pretext), so that he can kill him away from the eyes of witnesses.

We have already seen how the story of Cain and Abel implies that Cain's murder was a "founding" event, by juxtaposing it with the narrative of Cain's building a city, and the subsequent development of culture through succeeding generations. If Jesus is thinking of Cain's deed when he says that the devil has been a liar and murderer from the beginning, is he also thinking of this as a kind of "foundation" upon which human beings have erected their culture? Jesus seems to be thinking precisely that, for he often plays upon the idea, sometimes ironically: "unless a grain of wheat falls into the earth and dies, it remains alone; but if it dies, it bears much fruit." (John 12:24) Jesus says this in John 12 at the very moment when he realizes that it is time for him to be murdered. He is not spouting some generalized philosophy concerning the cycles of nature, nor is he making a theological comment about the atonement. He is talking about his murder, his lynching, which he now realizes is immanent: "The hour has come for the Son of Man to be glorified . . . Now is my soul troubled. And what shall I say? 'Father, save me from this hour'? No, for this purpose I have come to this hour." (8:23, 27)

In speaking about the seed that dies and bears much fruit, Jesus is commenting on the *generative* power of the scapegoat mechanism – but with a twist. He knows that his lynching will be foundational – it will bear "much fruit" – just as did the lynchings of untold other victims; but Jesus' murder will become foundational not because it conforms to the age-old illusion that dominates all scapegoating crowds, but because it *exposes it.* Jesus' death exposes that illusion because it is *structurally* identical to the old pattern – a victim murdered by unanimous, collective violence becomes the foundation of a new human order – but, while the structure is identical, the *meaning* is entirely different. As a result of Jesus' death, the structure, "unanimity-minus-one" will come to signify an entirely different meaning; it will signify that the victim is *innocent*, and that the crowd is guilty, composed of murderers and liars (who, however, "know not what they do," and whom Jesus forgives). Jesus' death will throw all cultural institutions into question, because all institutions – religious, legal, political, economic – combined unanimously to condemn Jesus.

The Foundation of the [Human] World

Speaking of the group that will eventually shout for his crucifixion, Jesus comments:

"Therefore also the Wisdom of God said, 'I will send them prophets

> *and apostles, some of whom they will kill and persecute,' that the blood of all the prophets,* ***shed from the foundation of the world,*** *may be required of this generation, from the blood of Abel to the blood of Zechari'ah, who perished between the altar and the sanctuary. Yes, I tell you, it shall be required of this generation."* (Luke 11:49-51)

"This generation" means Jesus' contemporaries, who murdered him. What does he mean when he refers to the blood of all the prophets shed "from the foundation of the world?" Does he mean from the moment of creation of the world? Obviously not, since there were no prophets then. The prophets were a historical phenomenon that arose within the history of Israel. In fact, Jesus explains what he means by "the blood of all the prophets shed from the foundation of the world" by explicating it in the phrase that follows: "from the blood of Abel to the blood of Zechariah[118] ..." This makes it clear that by "foundation of the world" Jesus does not mean the creation of earth, but the establishment of the *human* world, the human cultural order. The blood of Abel became the foundation for the human world, as Genesis itself implies. Jesus is referring to the founding murder, and all the repetitions of that murder throughout history. He is referring to the pattern of persecution of innocent victims by collective violence, which, with his own death, he intends finally to expose for the grim lynching that it really is, lifting the "mythological veil" that from time immemorial had blinded people's eyes to the truth.

What does Jesus mean when he says that all the blood shed from Abel to Zechariah "shall be required of this generation"? Thanks to his presence among them, Jesus' contemporaries have the opportunity to recognize their own violence in both its forms: the reciprocal violence of mimetic rivalry (the "poison"), and the collective violence of the scapegoat mechanism (the "remedy"). Because they are the first human generation to have these phenomena presented to them with complete clarity, they are also the first generation to bear complete responsibility for its rejection. The truth has been revealed to them with an authority higher than that of violence. Jesus' authority has its source in the fact that, in the language of John, he comes from God his "Father," and desires only the Father's desires. That means he is not ensnared in the mimetic entanglements and scandals that inevitably climax in scapegoating violence. He has no "log" in his own eye, so he is able to see clearly to remove the "speck" from his brothers' (and sisters') eyes. The "light" that is in him is really *light,* not darkness, and therefore gives illumination to all who are in the house, and everything taking place within it.

Jesus exposes human violence wherever he goes. Indeed, his mere presence seems almost to draw it forth from people. And this puts his contemporaries in a crisis position that does not allow them to sit on the fence. If they come down on the right side of that fence, they have an unprecedented opportunity to learn from Jesus. He will teach them the meaning of their own history – all the way from Abel to the prophet Zechariah; and if they will not learn this, they will be doomed to repeat it. But if they do that, their repetition of the scapegoat mechanism – enacted against Jesus himself – will bear much more responsibility than all previous repetitions, precisely because it will have been carried out in the face of Jesus' complete exposure of the game. Previously, mythological lies hid the truth; but now that Jesus has brought everything into the light, the question becomes – does his generation *want* to know the truth? (We should also bear in mind that Jesus' contemporaries play a *representative* role for the entire human race. The Gospels do not lead us to imagine Jesus being offered a more welcome reception from *any* generation among whom he might have appeared.)

This passage in Luke 11 is important because it shows how Jesus is thinking about history, how he connects history's very foundations with the murder of Abel, and how he sees the same murderous foundation being repeated over and over again throughout history. When, therefore, Jesus says in Matthew 13:35, "I will proclaim what has been hidden from the foundation of the world," he is not talking about proclaiming some kind of theological mystery hidden in the mind of God when God created the world; he is talking about exposing the dirty little secret about the origin and foundation of the human world order. He intends to make plain what human beings have been hiding from the very beginning, from the moment Cain lied to his brother and killed him, then denied all responsibility for the deed and went out and built a city, while no doubt creating myths to vilify Abel.

The Lies That Cover the Murder

In John 8:44 Jesus says, "When he [the devil] lies, he speaks according to his own nature, for he is a liar and the father of lies…" The *father* of lies. Let us not allow this little phrase to pass by too quickly. To be a "father" is to be generative of something. The devil is not simply a liar, but the *generator* of lies. And in the context of John 8, the lies being spoken of are connected with murder, for Jesus says the devil is a liar and a murderer. The scapegoat mechanism begins with the illusion of the need to kill the monster, and ends with the propagation of myths. Once the deed is done, the crowd is certainly in no position to admit that they bear any guilt; they are not going to fall suddenly to their knees and repent. They will seek, rather, to justify the deed – particularly since the resulting reconciliation of rivals is a benefit the community can maintain only so long as the myth of the victim's guilt is perpetuated. The whole thing is a shared, *group* delusion – no one individual is in a position to declare the truth to the others. Rather, everyone mutually (mimetically) reinforces group belief.

We must not read back into archaic and ancient cultures the modern Western sensitivity, formed after two millennia of Christian influence, wherein "whistle-blowing" and investigative journalism are common and laudable phenomena. If civilization itself was based upon collective persecution, and if everything grew and developed from that foundation, then people lived within a closed system. The truth was too threatening, for it could topple the foundations of social life itself. When, for whatever reason, people did become suspicious and doubtful of the old lies (that is to say, when a "sacrificial crisis" developed), a new founding murder would generate a new or revised order, and a reinvigorated set of myths.

To say, then, that the devil is a liar and the father of lies, is to indicate that the devil is that which generates the lie of mythology in conjunction with the collective murder of a victim. *This is the very situation in which Jesus finds himself at the moment he makes this statement.* He is confronted by a mob, violently polarizing against him, a mob that transforms before his very eyes from followers into persecutors (the "mimetic wave" in action) who now see Jesus as deserving to be stoned. This is a mob, therefore, that is imitating its father the devil in desiring to kill a victim, under the influence of a lie concerning the victim's guilt. The devil is its "father" because the devil represents the mimetic force that generates the mob, binding it together through the power of accusation and the desire to kill. Thus the devil *generates* the mob.[119]

Jesus says elsewhere in John: "I do not receive glory from men. But I know that you have not the love of God within you. ... How can you believe, who receive glory from one another and do not seek the glory that comes from the only God?" (5:41-42, 44) In other words, the human crowd is constituted by the mutual giving and receiving of glory (approval) among its members. Their profound imitation of one another in this game pushes out the love of God, as they copy each other's desire to cast blame upon and murder a scapegoat.

Jesus, on the other hand, does not "receive glory from men" – does not, in other words, participate in the game of exchange of approval, which builds camaraderie by agreeing with (i.e., imitating) the other's desire. He will have no part in the "devil." Jesus is not captive to the group's denial, which runs so deep that people cannot see their own violence even when they are doing the very same thing of which they accuse others. Matthew 23:29-36 records some famously harsh words by Jesus concerning the Jewish scribes and Pharisees:

> *"Woe to you, scribes and Pharisees, hypocrites! For you build the tombs of the prophets and adorn the monuments of the righteous, saying, 'If we had lived in the days of our fathers, we would not have taken part with them in shedding the blood of the prophets.' Thus you witness against yourselves, that you are sons of those who murdered the prophets."*

Like the crowd in John 8, these scribes and Pharisees are possessed of a lying and murderous spirit of violence, and Jesus does not hesitate to confront their denial of this fact head-on. He calls them hypocrites because they deny being like their forefathers, who killed the prophets. In fact, they even build and decorate tombs of martyred prophets, declaring all the while that they would never have murdered such righteous and innocent men the way their forefathers did. But what were their forefathers doing when they murdered the prophets? They were scapegoating innocent victims, believing themselves just while calling the prophets criminal. And what are the scribes and Pharisees doing when they say that they would never have taken part with their forefathers in such heinous undertakings? They are scapegoating their forefathers, portraying them as criminal while justifying themselves. Thus, without meaning to do so, they give the game away by showing that they are repeating (imitating) the exact same pattern of scapegoating violence that possessed their forefathers. We see in this text how the *denial* of scapegoating makes possible the *perpetuation* of scapegoating. The crowd that scapegoats is in thrall to the power of the communal delusion, and the only one who knows the truth – the scapegoated victim – is not exactly in a position to demand a hearing. The victim is silenced. And subsequent mythological tales, told from the perspective of the persecutors, attempt to ensure that the victim's voice will remain silent forever.

Jesus' Exposure of the Scapegoat Mechanism

It was not by his teaching alone that Jesus intended to expose the scapegoat mechanism, but by the way he lived his life, and, in fact, by the very *giving* of his life. In John 10, Jesus tells his disciples, "I am the good shepherd. The good shepherd lays down his life for the sheep." And he goes on to say, "For this reason the Father loves me, because I lay down my life, that I may take it again. No one takes it from me, but *I lay it down of my own accord.* I have power to lay it down, and I have power to take it again; this charge I have received from my Father." Jesus is drawing a very important distinction here. His victimization will be different than all those from Abel to Zechariah, for they had their lives taken from them, but Jesus will *give* his life. He will give it in order to expose the violence in human hearts, and the scapegoat mechanism itself. This will involve not only exposing the mythic illusion that keeps humanity in ignorant denial of its own violence, but also challenging the spiritual arrogance that lives in self-justification and refuses to hear the truth even when it is proclaimed. Jesus knows that challenging such arrogance will provoke a violent response, and he is ready for it – he has *come* for this purpose. Nobody takes his life; he gives it in the service of this revelation. It is his Father's desire that humanity should be set free from the demonic spirit of murder and myth, and Jesus imitates his Father's desire, making it his own. In the service of this desire he intends to walk right into the trap, and allow himself to be scapegoated.

Luke shows Jesus doing this very thing right at the beginning of his public ministry. In chapter 4 we read how Jesus stands up to read Torah in his hometown synagogue in Nazareth, and reads from Isaiah the prophet, *"The Spirit of the Lord is upon me, because he has anointed me to preach good news to the poor. He has sent me to proclaim release to the captives and recovering of sight to the blind, to set at liberty those who are oppressed, to proclaim the acceptable year of the Lord."* The congregation's initial reaction seems positive, but that quickly changes when Jesus says, *"Today this scripture has been fulfilled in your hearing."* The crowd wonders how Jesus, a local carpenter's son, can fulfill a Messianic prophecy. Sensing their skepticism, Jesus retorts that no prophet is acceptable in his own county, among his own people. Then he compares their disbelief in him to Israel's disbelief in the ancient prophets Elijah and Elisha. These prophets actually had to journey *outside* of Israel, into Phoenician and Syrian Gentile territory, in order to find individuals receptive to the spirit of God for whom they could do miracles. Of course, the congregation is highly offended by this comparison, and what happens next forms a paradigm that previsions the meaning and shape of Jesus' entire subsequent ministry:

> *When they heard this, all in the synagogue were filled with wrath. And they rose up and put him out of the city, and led him to the brow of the hill on which their city was built, that they might throw him down headlong. But passing through the midst of them he went away.* (Luke 4:28-30)

Luke frames the story of Jesus' life by placing this story at the beginning and the crucifixion at the end; and in both cases we are dealing with unanimous collective violence against an innocent victim. But the Nazareth story makes it quite clear that Jesus walked deliberately into the trap, and it would appear that he did so in order to expose the scapegoat mechanism. And why would he want to do that? To liberate the participants who believe wholeheartedly in the righteousness of what they are doing. If Jesus can display his innocence in a way that is absolutely undeniable, then his persecutors would either have to acknowledge the truth and repent, or become demonically entrenched in their violence and lies. "You shall know the truth, and the truth shall set you free." This was Jesus' hope; but it could backfire. The crowd could know the truth, and refuse it. "And the last state of that man becomes worse than the first. So it shall be also with this evil generation." (Matt. 12:45)

One more gospel text will help us cinch the idea that it was Jesus' deliberate intention to expose the scapegoat mechanism. In Matthew 21:33-43, Jesus tells the following parable:

> *"Hear another parable. There was a householder who planted a vineyard, and set a hedge around it, and dug a wine press in it, and built a tower, and let it out to tenants, and went into another country. When the season of fruit drew near, he sent his servants to the tenants, to get his fruit; and the tenants took his servants and beat one, killed another, and stoned another. Again he sent other servants, more than the first; and they did the same to them. Afterward he sent his son to them, saying, `They will respect my son.' But when the tenants saw the son, they said to themselves, `This is the heir; come, let us kill him and have his inheritance.' And they took him and cast him out of the vineyard, and killed him.*

When therefore the owner of the vineyard comes, what will he do to those tenants?"

They said to him, "He will put those wretches to a miserable death, and let out the vineyard to other tenants who will give him the fruits in their seasons."

Jesus said to them, "Have you never read in the scriptures: `The very stone which the builders rejected has become the head of the corner; this was the Lord's doing, and it is marvelous in our eyes'?"

This is a parable about collective violence against innocent victims, some of whom are expelled, while others are murdered. And the same thing happens to the son. The "son," of course, is Jesus, and the parable indicates that Jesus is only the latest in a long line of persecuted victims ("from Abel to Zechariah"). Notice that although he is the son, there is no difference between his death and the death of those who preceded him, in terms of pattern or structure. For the tenants, murdering the son is just "business as usual," and they do nothing different to him than what they had done numerous times before to others. If Jesus' death is different, it is not because he suffered more than other martyrs, either physically or spiritually, nor because his death was lonelier, or more humiliating, or more gruesome (despite Mel Gibson's heroic attempt to render it so). This common idea is quite mistaken. Such considerations are not what make Jesus' death unique. The uniqueness of his death is found in its *meaning* – which became clear to the disciples only after the resurrection, once the Holy Spirit had opened their eyes to understand what had been hidden since the foundation of the (human) world: the scapegoat mechanism, and the human violence that invented and perpetuated it.

Of great interest is Jesus' commentary on this parable about the vineyard, which he gives when he finishes telling the story. He says, "Have you never read in the scriptures: 'The very stone which the builders rejected has become the head of the corner; this was the Lord's doing, and it is marvelous in our eyes'?" This is a quote from the Hebrew Scriptures, and Jesus uses it to explicate the meaning of the parable. The quote became quite popular among Jesus' disciples after the resurrection, and we find it quoted by Peter in the Book of Acts, as well as elsewhere in the New Testament. It is nothing less than a succinct statement of the scapegoat mechanism, ironically turned on its head. It tells of builders (collective violence) who reject a stone (single victim). That stone is rejected, and thus becomes the *cornerstone* in an elaborated structure. This is exactly what we have been saying about the role of the victim, first in the founding murder, and then in the sustaining function of sacrifice. Everything is built and maintained upon the foundation of the victim.

But the scripture says "...this was the Lord's doing, and it is marvelous in our eyes." How can this be? How can the idea of a rejected victim becoming the foundation for human community be "marvelous," and "the Lord's doing"? Because the same mechanism that killed and silenced so many previous messengers will have the *reverse effect* when used upon the son, Jesus. Like victims of previous founding murders, the son is rejected; and, like them, the son will become a cornerstone, a foundation. But *this* victim will become foundational through the exposure of the victimage mechanism itself, thus founding a society that for the first time in human history will be built upon conscious rejection of victimization. This will be possible only because the Lord will *raise this victim from the dead* in order to vindicate him. He will rise from the dead still bearing the scars of martyrdom in his hands, feet, and side: he will rise, but *as victim.*

In his use of the scripture about the rejected stone that becomes the cornerstone, Jesus reveals his understanding of his own mission: to become a scapegoat who will turn the foundation of human community on its head. The *victim* will be revealed. And out of this affirmation of the victim will come all of the Christian values that affirm the infinite value of every lowly soul, including the poorest of the poor – the kind of ethic we see embodied in a St. Francis of Assisi, or a Mother Teresa, the kind of values that Frederick Nietzsche so despised because he thought they represented nothing more than the resentment of slaves trying to guilt-trip the powerful and wealthy.

Before ending the discussion of this parable, I offer a quick note about the comment that specifies the fate deserved by the tenants, which might be perplexing to some readers: "He will put those wretches to a miserable death, and let out the vineyard to other tenants who will give him the fruits in their seasons." If God is understood to be the owner of the vineyard, doesn't this attribute sacred-violence to God? It would seem so. It is not clear, however, that Jesus means his parable to be interpreted in such a strictly allegorical way. Because the human owner of the vineyard would naturally act this way does not mean God would. Jesus is telling a story that unfolds within the human realm of violent reciprocal exchange, and he wants to point out the collective violence of the scapegoat mechanism, and highlight the victim, the rejected stone, not make a theological statement about the character of God.

However, even if we assume that the owner of the vineyard *is* God, we should note that in Matthew's Gospel it is the *crowd* who makes this assertion, not Jesus. His response to their angry imprecation is, "Have you never read in the scriptures: `The very stone which the builders rejected has become the head of the corner; this was the Lord's doing, and it is marvelous in our eyes'?" It is as if Jesus says to them, "What are you saying? Don't you know your own scriptures? Don't you know that it's not about God wreaking vengeance on his enemies, it's not about sacred-violence? Instead, it's about seeing the victim underlying that violence, the stone which the builders rejected. That's why I told you this story, and if you had read your own scriptures properly you would have understood this."

(The fact that Luke has Jesus making the violent statement while the crowd reacts with shock, while Matthew has the crowd making the statement, and Mark leaves it ambiguous, shows that the early church itself had an issue with this part of the parable.)

The Four C's and the Lynching of Jesus

We have shown that Jesus intended to expose the scapegoating violence that constitutes the foundation of human cultural order. And we indicated that he did this not only through his teaching, but especially by his manner of death. But it is time to take a closer look at how powerful the revelation of the scapegoat mechanism really is in the New Testament Gospels, which leads us back to a consideration of the four C's, this time in the context of Jesus' lynching. As a quick review, these four C's show up in myths as stereotypical representations (although one does not always find all four together in the same myth). Tthe reader will recall that the scapegoat mechanism is the triggering of *unanimous, collective violence* against a victim, who is usually marked out by certain *criteria* that suggest easy victimization, and who will be accused of terrible *crimes;* and in the background is always some kind of societal *crisis* which exacerbates the problem of human relations within the community, leading to an increase of reciprocal violence.

In his wonderful book, *Saved From Sacrifice,* Mark Heim has done an excellent job of laying out the many ways in which the four C's are factors in the passion of Christ, and I will rely heavily upon his extended treatment for my more concise summary here.[120] It is important to realize that the presence of these factors in the story of Jesus' passion cannot be an accident; on the contrary, it is obvious that the Gospel writers knew exactly what they were doing, and that the Gospels are structured quite deliberately to emphasize – indeed, to *expose* – the scapegoat mechanism.

First, *crisis.* There is a general scholarly consensus today that first century Judaism was not monolithic, meaning that the religion was not dominated by one single theological outlook. On the contrary, Judaism was highly splintered into many competing groups – many "Cain and Abels," we might say, competing for God's favor and convinced that they were the truly righteous who knew and did God's will. The divisions ran deep, with some groups going so far as to reject worship in the Jerusalem temple itself, railing against what they believed to be a corrupt priesthood. Some divisions involved theological interpretation and/or religious practice. Other divisions grew primarily from Israel's political situation under Roman domination and the attitudes taken by various groups towards Rome (although in those days politics and religion were not distinguished the way they are in the modern world). Should they cooperate with Rome, or rebel? Should they wait for the Messiah to overthrow the Romans, or take matters into their own hands? Pharisees, Sadducees, lawyers and scribes, Essenes, the Dead Sea community, Samaritans, Zealots – such groups were only the most conspicuous. There were also various apocalyptic groups expecting an immanent end of the world, and various factions led by individuals claiming to be the Messiah. The Jewish historian Josephus tells us about several of these operating just before, during, and after Jesus' lifetime.

Jesus, then, as a first century Jew, was born into a religious society torn by rivalry. But we must now look at the specific circumstances that surrounded his lynching. The Gospels portray it as happening in Jerusalem during Passover Week – the Jews' greatest religious celebration. Imagine the situation during this week. We have a people whose country is occupied by a hated, idol-worshipping, foreign power, whose soldiers populate the streets, whose governor uses repressive actions against rebels and Jewish patriots, and whose coffers are enriched by Jewish taxes. The Jews have their own king, Herod, but he is only half-Jewish, a tyrant, and a Roman puppet – and he cannot get along with the Roman governor, Pontius Pilate. The Jewish people themselves cannot get along with Pilate, or with Herod, or with each other, being splintered, as mentioned above, into many competing factions.

All of these tensions are most concentrated in the city of Jerusalem, and now Holy Week brings thousands pouring into Jerusalem from around the world, both Jews and curious pagans. Tensions are exacerbated simply by the physical crowding within the city; but on top of that this is *Jerusalem,* the most sacred city for the majority of Jews; and this is *Passover,* the most sacred festival that celebrates – of all things! – the Jews' exodus from foreign oppression in Egypt. There has been trouble before during Passover, including rioting followed by massacre. And now yet another charismatic preacher, whom many are calling "Messiah," comes into the city with his ragamuffin band of mostly peasant followers – and Pilate's forces are on full military alert. As Heim points out, under such circumstances the smallest incident could become like spark to tinder, and torch the entire community.

We see then that first century Judaism was going through

exactly the kind of crisis that precipitates the triggering of the scapegoat mechanism. Even if the crisis is later represented mythically as something external like a foreign invader or a natural disaster, the real trigger for scapegoating is the accumulation of *internal* animosities and rivalries, which have worsened to the point of requiring the morale boost which aggression against a victim provides. The Gospels show us just such a society in just such a crisis. Furthermore, the Gospels make it clear that Jesus walks deliberately into this tinderbox of passionate conflict: he "sets his face" towards Jerusalem; he predicts his suffering and death to his disciples; he refuses to allow himself to be dissuaded from his chosen course, even when Peter, one of his special intimates, tempts him. The Gospels also show how conflict follows Jesus like a magnet throughout his short time in the city, as he is approached by representatives of various factions who want to question and debate him, hoping either to get him on their side, or to debunk him. But the Gospels show that no one of these factions alone are able to claim victory over Jesus in debate; instead, they will all have to gang up on him.

Second, *criteria*. We recall that victims who become the dumping ground for collective violence are usually chosen (albeit unconsciously) on the basis of certain criteria. They bear certain "marks" of a victim: physical defects, marginalized social status, foreigner or stranger, odd behavior, and so on. It is easy to see how Jesus could be targeted in just such a way. He was from a marginalized lower class family, and might have been labeled with the stigma of being a *mamzer* – a Hebrew term meaning "bastard." Bruce Chilton writes, "Such men and women lived in a caste apart, unable to marry within the established bloodlines of Israel, and so were often excluded from the mainstream of religious life."[121] Also, he arrived in Jerusalem as a stranger from Galilee, a region without close ties to the Jerusalem temple cult, and populated by lots of Gentiles, so that Galileans were regarded with some suspicion in Jerusalem. Furthermore, Jesus was extremely charismatic and attracted much attention, and would easily have been perceived as a threat by both political and religious authorities. We have seen how someone who embodies any extreme can draw the attention of persecutors.

Third, *crimes.* Scapegoats are usually accused of the most terrible crimes, and Jesus was no exception. He was accused of the worst possible crime against Roman authority – sedition. In Luke 23:2 we read, "We found this man perverting our nation, forbidding us to pay taxes to the emperor, and saying that he himself is the Messiah, a king." As if that were not enough, Jesus was also accused of the worst possible religious crime: blasphemy. "Then the high priest tore his robes and said, 'He has uttered blasphemy! Why do we still need witnesses? You have now heard his blasphemy. What is your judgment?' They answered: 'He deserves death.'" (Matt. 26:65-66) Just like Oedipus and thousands of others before him, Jesus was reckoned guilty of horrendous crimes against God and state. He was both heretic and traitor.

Fourth, *collective violence.* Here is where we see what the Gospels are really up to in their presentation of Jesus' Passion. The four Gospels go out of their way to make it clear that *everyone* stands against Jesus, whether actively or passively. We are told that the crowd yells "with one voice" for Jesus' crucifixion. The shouting against Jesus even crosses factional and class lines within Judaism. Even inveterate enemies like the Roman and Jewish authorities agree together that Jesus deserves death. Those few who raise sympathetic voices in the Sanhedrin during Jesus' trial are overwhelmed by protest and quickly reduced to silence. Pilate's personal doubts (based on his wife's disturbing dream and her warning not to become involved in the affair of "that innocent man") are ineffective in the face of pressure from the crowd to which he yields. Even more dramatically, Jesus' own disciples abandon him. Judas betrays him, and Peter denies ever having known him. Instead of raising their voices in protest, the disciples' fearful silence becomes part of the irresistible collective movement against Jesus the scapegoat. Only his mother and a few crying women remain loyal to Jesus: but their impotent voices can be raised only in lamentation. They are essentially silenced, along with the victim. The Gospels thus show Jesus smothered by a great tide of collective violence.

The Gospels' Exposure of the Scapegoat Mechanism

What this brief examination of the four C's in the Gospel narratives show us is how similar – indeed, structurally identical – Jesus' lynching was to countless others before it, as Jesus himself indicated in his parable of the vineyard. Once upon a time I used to believe that there had to be something about Jesus' death that made it quantitatively worse than other martyrdoms: worse physical suffering, perhaps (but that was easily disproved), or more profound spiritual suffering. But I was looking for uniqueness in the wrong place. The Gospel narratives offer a masterfully drawn portrait of a quite typical, even mundane, if you will, scapegoating incident; but they also offer something extra: a kind of "backstage" view of events, that changes the way we see and understand what is going on. Instead of being caught up in the collective delusion, shouting for the death of the blasphemer and traitor, we are allowed to see Jesus as a victim, allowed to see that from start to finish he was entirely innocent.

We see this backstage view, for instance, through the eyes of the centurion who speaks from the foot of the cross in Luke 23:47, "Certainly this man was innocent." We get the same view from Judas' perspective when he laments, "I have sinned in betraying innocent blood." (Matt. 27:4) We get it from the view of the thief crucified next to Jesus, who says, "We are receiving the due reward of our deeds; but this man has done nothing wrong." (Luke 23:41) We get it from Mark when he tells us in his Gospel that "...many bore false witness against him, and their witnesses did not agree." (14:56) We even get it from Jesus himself when he quotes Psalm 35:10, "They hated me without a cause." (John 15:25)

This, then, is how the Gospels expose the illusionary power of the scapegoat mechanism: by vouching for the innocence of the victim, telling the story of the lynching from the victim's perspective rather than the persecutors', and showing us behind-the-scene details about how Jesus was set-up and done-in. Showing us, for example, Judas' dissatisfaction, leading to his betrayal of Jesus; showing how people standing in the crowd before Pilate were bribed with money to shout for Jesus' crucifixion in order to ensure unanimity; showing false witnesses and the lack of agreement among them; showing Pilate's concern to pacify the mob, and his savvy understanding that a single victim like Jesus would help to deflect tensions during the dangerous week of Passover. And building up to all of this, the Gospels have given us a narrative of Jesus' life in which we get to hear his preaching, and witness his miracles, so that by the time we reach the climactic scene in Jerusalem, we completely believe in his total innocence.

It might help to grasp the uniqueness of the Gospels' presentation of Jesus' life and Passion by comparing it briefly with another text, which in many ways might be considered quite similar. In his dialogue, *Phaedo,* Plato narrates the death of Socrates, whom he shows as totally innocent of the trumped-up charges against him. In addition, Socrates is depicted as a victim of the more or less collective violence of the Athenian community against him. But Plato's perspective on the death of Socrates, however touching it may be, and whatever impact it has had since on sympathetic readers, is quite different from the Gospel's exposure of the scapegoat mechanism.

First of all, though Socrates is condemned by a majority vote, we do not see anything like the monolithic unanimity the Gospels' show operating against Jesus. Nor do Socrates' disciples and closest friends abandon him; on the contrary, they do everything they can to save him. Furthermore, the *Phaedo* gives us an account of how, on his last day of life, Socrates sits with friends who are visiting him in prison, and philosophizes eloquently about the immortality of the soul. The scene is a far cry from the pathetic moaning of Jesus on the cross, and his few, barely uttered sound bites – not to mention the grisly, fleshy reality of crucifixion itself. We cannot speak of the "Passion" of Socrates. And if the scapegoat mechanism is to be revealed, it must certainly be through a passionate appeal to the heart. Moreover, Plato shows us a Socrates who *accepts the judgment against him.* Even though his friends offer him a means of escape, he nobly accepts the sentence of death. In one sense, this makes him like Jesus, who "set his face" towards Jerusalem; but Socrates accepts the sentence not in order to expose his victimization and the scapegoat mechanism, but because of his conviction that the State is supreme over the individual, and that since he has enjoyed the benefits of Athenian citizenship all his life, he is also obligated to accept Athenian judgment and obey Athenian law, even if, in his judgment, it moves unfairly to condemn him. One should honor the collective of which one is a member and from which one has benefited, even when it is in the wrong. It is clear, then, that Plato does not grasp – and his texts certainly do not give us a powerful exposure of – the scapegoat mechanism.

That the Gospels understand their narrative as an exposure of the scapegoat mechanism is clear from many passages. Consider, for example, the following passage from the Gospel of Luke:

> *And when he* [Pilate] *learned that he* [Jesus] *belonged to Herod's jurisdiction, he sent him over to Herod, who was himself in Jerusalem at that time. When Herod saw Jesus, he was very glad, for he had long desired to see him, because he had heard about him, and he was hoping to see some sign done by him. So he questioned him at some length; but he made no answer. The chief priests and the scribes stood by, vehemently accusing him. And Herod with his soldiers treated him with contempt and mocked him; then, arraying him in gorgeous apparel, he sent him back to Pilate. And Herod and Pilate became friends with each other that very day, for before this they had been at enmity with each other.* (Luke 23:7-12)

Here we have a vivid picture of Jesus being shuttled back and forth between Pilate and Herod. Not only do we get to see how the abuse and mocking of Jesus creates camaraderie among Herod's soldiers, but *it even makes friends of Herod and Pilate!* Luke seems quite aware of how Jesus fulfills the basic scapegoat function, drawing to himself the violence that would otherwise be exchanged between mimetic rivals, and thus uniting them. It is quite ironic that there has been so much talk in the post-Enlightenment West about "demythologizing" the Bible, a term popularized by Rudolph Bultmann, who saw Jesus' miracles as mythological material with no basis in actual history. The irony is that in point of fact it is the Gospels that do the demythologizing – of myth itself. They are the most potent power deconstructive of mythic illusion ever unleashed within human culture. We can understand this once we realize what mythology actually is, and see how the Gospels resolutely refuse the mythological mindset, relating the story of Jesus' lynching with unprecedented historical realism. (The "realism" I am talking about here has nothing to do with the accuracy of particular historical details. The Bible does not have to be one hundred percent accurate in its journalistic reporting in order to capture the truth that matters.)

The achievement of this realism in the Gospels is, frankly, a miracle, because the scapegoat mechanism as the founding power of human civilization, was a totalizing force of illusion. It was a movement of *all* against one (and once it did its work, that "one" was no longer around to contradict the illusion). The Gospels are so committed to representing the overwhelming force of the collective illusion that they do not shy even from portraying Jesus' own disciples as cowards and betrayers – men who would appear as heroes if rendered mythologically. The first miracle is the frankness and honesty with which the Gospels portray these people.

The second miracle is the fact that, despite his abandonment by even his closest friends, the voice of Jesus was *not* ultimately silenced. For, surely, by all rights it should have been. The disciples' hopes and dreams were shattered, everything they had lived and dreamed for three amazing years had been destroyed. Later they gathered in terrified hiding from the authorities. Their voice, and their view of events, should have been snuffed from the pages of history. But this time, as we say, the devil overplayed his hand. This time some of the witnesses had a miraculous change of mood and attitude, and became recipients of a radically reconfigured understanding of the events they had witnessed. And they wrote documents structured on the basis of that new understanding. The Gospels were written by those who had come to understand the scapegoat mechanism and the heinousness of the crime perpetrated by the crowd against the victim, and those manuscripts were copied and circulated throughout the entire known world. And people *responded* to them! Something in those documents moved people deeply, converted them, and ultimately toppled the entire mythologically-based ancient world. The Hebrew Scriptures had prepared the way with criticisms and parodies of pagan myths, the prophets' critique of sacrifice, and giving voice to the victim. But they never broke *completely* free of the very thing they were criticizing, being themselves too invested in the violent-sacred view of God. In order for that freedom to be achieved, we needed Jesus' vision of a God so loving that he does not create new victims by avenging old ones, but instead forgives his enemies.

"But I say to you, Love your enemies and pray for those who persecute you, so that you may be sons of your Father who is in heaven . . ." (Matt.5:44) Only in this way could the Gosepls' demythologizing power become a potent force in history. Had Jesus fought back, had he summoned angels, or even slapped the other's cheek, the revelation of the scapegoat mechanism would have been impossible. Jesus would immediately have become involved in mimetic exchange with his enemies, imitating their violence, and they his. This would only have facilitated the enemy's legitimization of his own violence. A persecutor expects a slap back, and when he receives it he feels all the more justified in delivering a still more devastating blow. But by turning the other cheek, by uttering "Father forgive them for they know not what they do," Jesus made it impossible for his persecutors to engage in the kind of imitative escalation that only reinforces each party's sense of righteous indignation and creates enemy twins. Instead, persecutors are forced either to look at themselves and examine their actions in the light of a dawning conscience, or divert themselves with other victims more willing to engage in exchange of hostilities.

Jesus and the Sacred

Girard has shown that discharge of mimetic rivalry through the scapegoat mechanism led to the creation of the so-called "primitive sacred," with its dual character as poison and remedy, good and evil. The sacred was essentially violence, *human* violence, writ large upon a transcendent screen. Human beings lived in an ambivalent relationship with the sacred, therefore, just as they did with their own violence, at once in terror of its destructive power, and worshipping it for its blessings. Now, the life and death of Jesus revealed the violence of the human heart, exposing both of its faces: mimetic rivalry, and the scapegoat mechanism. But if Jesus was savvy to this hidden reality, if it was his purpose to expose it and call human beings to a responsible accounting for it, did he also understand the connection between these forms of violence and the sacred? And if so, did he also expose the sacred?

We used *The China Syndrome* as a powerful and suggestive analogy to launch our investigation of the sacred in the Hebrew Scriptures, and as we take up the issue of the sacred once again, this time in relation to Jesus, another film comes to mind that perfectly illustrates the point I wish to make. In *The Wizard of Oz*, Dorothy, her dog Toto, the Scarecrow, the Tin Man, and the Cowardly Lion travel to Oz to ask the Wizard, "The Great and Powerful Oz," to grant them their wishes. Their initial encounter with the Wizard is terrifying. Speaking with an angry, booming voice, Oz appears as a giant green face, floating menacingly above explosions of flame and smoke. The lion completely loses his nerve, turns tail, and runs, while the others shake and their knees knock. The Wizard will grant their requests, he says, but only if they first achieve a seemingly impossible task: kill the Wicked Witch of the West.

This they do, but when they return to encounter the Wizard once more, he is no more amicable than before, and not particularly disposed to grant their wishes. He tells them to go away and come back tomorrow. This is rather too much for Dorothy, who screws up her courage to step forward and confront the Wizard. While this exchange is going on, however, little Toto runs to the side of the room where a curtain hangs, cordoning off a little cubicle. Toto grabs the curtain and pulls it open, and there, standing at a large control panel, manipulating knobs and levers and speaking into a microphone, is a man.

"Pay no attention to that man behind the curtain!" the Wizard yells. "The great Oz has spoken!" But it is too late. The game is up. When Dorothy asks the man who he is, he has to admit that he is the "Great and Powerful" Wizard of Oz.

Matthew tells us that at the moment Jesus died, "the curtain of the temple was torn in two, from top to bottom." (Matt. 27:51) The curtain Matthew is referring to was the veil that separated the Holy of Holies – the most sacred enclosure within the temple – from the rest of the temple. Nobody passed beyond that veil into the Holy of Holies except the high priest; and he only once a year, on the Day of Atonement. As mentioned earlier in this book, that room housed the nuclear core of the temple power plant. It was the very place where Yahweh manifested his presence on earth, the most sacred square footage in the universe. To lift this veil and peer behind the curtain was unthinkable, except for one human being, one time a year – and then only after he had been properly prepared for the experience. It was as unthinkable for a human being casually to part that curtain as it would be for someone today to stroll unprepared into an area highly contaminated with nuclear waste. Even more unthinkable, because it was no physical and natural danger that lurked behind that curtain – *Yahweh* dwelt there, and Yahweh was God and Spirit, and to fall into his punishing hands would be unimaginable terror.

And yet, at the moment Jesus died, that curtain was torn in two, Matthew tells us, from top to bottom. Whether it actually happened historically is irrelevant for our purposes; but the momentousness of such an event for Matthew's Gospel cannot be overstated. And we can hardly overestimate Matthew's radical effrontery even to suggest such a thing. But what was discovered when the curtain of the Holy of Holies was torn? Well, nothing. Matthew says nothing about it. He does not say that the Shekinah Glory came pouring forth, devouring everyone in its path, or that the angel of the LORD was standing there with a blazing sword. No, it seems that for all intents and purposes it was just… a room. Which is exactly what Jesus had more or less said it was. For when he was leaving the temple one day with his disciples, they started ogling and admiring the buildings of the temple complex. It was, after all, the temple restored by that great ancient builder, Herod, and was one of the marvels of the ancient world. Its sacredness was emphasized by the splendor of its immensity and beauty. But Jesus' reaction was, "You see all these, do you not? Truly I say to you, there will not be left here one stone upon another, that will not be thrown down." (Matt. 24:2)

To Jesus, the temple was simply architecture, a building complex of stone – and it would be destroyed. And the destruction was begun at the moment of Jesus' death, when the veil was ripped. Jesus was Toto, opening the curtain, allowing humanity to gaze, unafraid and unashamed, upon the pathetic truth about the "Great and Powerful Wizard." What we learned is that behind all that fire and brimstone rained upon Sodom and Gomorrah, behind Samson's murderous rampages at the behest of the "spirit of Yahweh," behind Joshua's mandate from the Most High God to invade and slaughter all the men, women, and children in Caanan, behind the plague that consumed 14,700 Israelites in the desert, behind Elijah's slaughter of the 450 prophets of Baal and 400 prophets of Asherah, behind all such outbreaks of sacred violence, so manifold in their modalities, so imaginative in their spirited evocation of cruelty and horror – behind all of this, as its very source and font, was *human* violence, operating levers and switches and speaking into a microphone to boost its voice to terrifying decibels. It was violence which produced the sacred in the first place, and continued to maintain it through millennia of religious myth and ritual.

But, one might wonder, didn't Jesus *defend* the temple? Didn't he cast out the money-changers who were profaning the temple court, upsetting their tables and loosing the animals they were selling for sacrifice, saying that they had turned "my Father's house" into a den of thieves? Yes, he did all these acts: but not in defense of the temple. Or, at least, not in defense of the sacrificial function of the temple – which function was the real nerve center of the entire complex.

What I am saying here might sound strange to those who are used to thinking of this episode as Jesus "cleansing" the temple (as it is often called), and who have been taught that what upset Jesus was not sacrifice as such, but the exorbitant rates being charged by the money-changers and sellers of sacrificial animals. But a closer look at the story in the various Gospels casts doubt upon this interpretation. Listen, for example, to John's account:

In the temple he found those who were selling oxen and sheep and pigeons, and the money-changers at their business. And making a whip of cords, he drove them all, with the sheep and oxen, out of the temple; and he poured out the coins of the money-changers and overturned their tables. And he told those who sold the pigeons, "Take these things away; you shall not make my Father's house a house of trade." His disciples remembered that it was written, "Zeal for thy house will consume me." (2:14-17)

John shows Jesus driving all the sacrificial sheep and oxen out of the temple, and telling the pigeon-sellers to get their birds out of the temple as well. He also overturns the tables of the money-changers. These were the men who exchanged common, profane coinage for the sacred temple currency that was needed in order to purchase an animal for sacrifice. Now, with the sacred currency scattered all over the floor (!), and the birds and animals themselves removed from the temple, it seems pretty clear that Jesus' intention was not to "cleanse" the temple in the sense of reforming the greedy economic practices that made it difficult for poor people to purchase sacrificial animals. On the contrary, Jesus' actions were an attack upon the entire institution of sacrifice, with the goal of making it impossible to conduct the business of sacrifice at all. True, in John's account Jesus seems to make an economic statement: "you shall not make my Father's house a house of trade." But without this trade, there could be no sacrifice; and sacrifice was the temple's heart and soul, its primary reason for being. Jesus was trying to bring to a halt the entire sacrificial operation of the temple.

In his Gospel, Mark gives us the extra "little" detail that Jesus "would not allow anyone to carry anything through the temple." (11:16) What would people be carrying through the temple? Primarily, their animals for sacrifice. Blocking people from carrying these through the temple would be an attempt to shut down the sacrificial operation entirely. Clearly, Jesus was attempting to disrupt and completely halt the temple's religious *raison d'etre* – sacrifice.

John tells us that, later, the disciples remembered a verse from the Hebrew Scriptures which they thought applicable to the incident: "Zeal for thy house will consume me." So they understood Jesus' act as an expression of "zeal" for "his Father's house." This would seem to indicate a positive regard for the temple; but how can that be consistent with the interpretation given above? It is the other Gospel writers who provide the answer. Luke 19:46, Matthew 21:13, and Mark 11:17 all show Jesus making the following comment: "It is written, 'My house shall be a house of prayer'; but you have made it a den of robbers." Jesus can accept the temple as his "Father's house," but only by virtue of a radical reinterpretation of the meaning and purpose of "temple," which he bases upon a text from the Hebrew Scriptures – "My house shall be a house of prayer." *Not,* that is to say, a house of sacrifice, which Jesus just made it impossible to conduct. Mark 11:17 gives us a slightly different version of Jesus' comment, which is still more radical:

> *And he taught, and said to them, "Is it not written, 'My house shall be called a house of prayer for all the nations'? But you have made it a den of robbers."*

A house of prayer *for all nations!* This means that the official Hebrew sacrificial cultus that excluded Gentiles from participation (who could not even move farther into the temple than the Court of the Gentiles) – is itself excluded by Jesus. In other words, the only thing Jesus wants to exclude is exclusion itself, and sacrificial cults are built upon exclusion, beginning with exclusion of the victim, and extending from there to exclude any person, place, or thing that inhabits the so-called realm of the profane. If there is to be a temple that he can call his "Father's house," it must be a universally welcoming place of prayer, not a place of exclusive, cultic sacrificial rites.

But the temple from which Jesus sought to exclude sacrifice was obviously *not* that temple of prayer Jesus desired. And his driving out of the moneychangers who made the sacrificial operation possible, as well as the animals themselves, was of course only a temporary interruption, more a symbolic, prophetic gesture than a serious attempt to co-opt and transform the temple. This is why we need not take the "whip of cords" (mentioned only by John) seriously as an instrument of violence, nor, indeed, the entire episode as an unleashing of violence by Jesus. Forceful and assertive it no doubt was, and effective because of its shock value, and Jesus' uncanny charisma and authority. But we have no reason to read violence into the incident. The whip would have been used to move the animals, not slash the backs of men. The whip need never have grazed even the skin of any animal in order to get them moving. The incident was primarily symbolic, the kind of thing the ancient Hebrew prophets used to do in order to get attention and deliver God's message to the people – a kind of "religious performance art," if you will.

It becomes clear right after this incident that Jesus has a vision of "temple" that completely subverts the stone structure in Jerusalem, which, for him, was anything but sacred. Immediately following his "cleansing" of the temple, John shows Jesus confronted by Jews who ask him "What sign have you to show us for doing this?" And his answer is, "Destroy this temple and in three days I will raise it up." The Jews answer, ""It has taken forty-six years to build this temple, and will you raise it up in three days?" "But," John writes, "he spoke of the temple of his body." Furthermore, it is not long after this, according to the other Gospel writers, that Jesus responds to his disciples' admiring comments about the temple buildings, with the comment quoted earlier: "You see all these, do you not? Truly I say to you, there will not be left here one stone upon another that will not be thrown down." (Matt. 24:2)

Jesus finds nothing sacred about the Jerusalem temple and its daily countless rituals of violent bloodletting. His prophetic attack against the sacrificial operation of the temple was an attack upon the sacred itself, the *violent* sacred (for there was no other kind). The whole history of Israel had been bound up with this violent sacred, as had the history of all other peoples. But it was Israel's uniqueness to hear another call, which in her long history came through at times only ambiguously, but at other times with astonishing clarity. Jesus stands in the tradition of this prophetic call away from entanglement with the sacred, and gives it its final, pure, and unambiguous declaration.

The Resurrected Lamb

To return, then, to where we began this section: in exposing the mimetic desire that animates the human heart and leads to the violence of rivalry, and in exposing the violence of the scapegoat mechanism by making himself its living target, Jesus revealed human violence as the essence of the sacred. That is why the sacred structures reacted so strongly to condemn him, persecuting the one who dared expose the truth, dared to blaspheme against the Jewish and Roman sacred structures. Thus the end for Jesus was not so happy as for Toto and Dorothy.

And yet, in the end, the sacred did not triumph. The sacred had been humanity's age-old way of maintaining peace, but Jesus inaugurated a startlingly new path: "*My* peace I leave with you; *my* peace I give you; not as the world gives do I give to you." (John 14:27a) This saying does not refer to some mystical peace within the individual. Jesus is speaking to a group here, and in Greek all the "you's" are plural. He is referring to a new peace in interdividual relationships, a peace within human community that Jesus himself establishes in an entirely new, nonviolent way. It is *his* way, and *his* peace; not the peace that follows in the wake of a founding murder or a sacrificial ritual.

One can reasonably ask the question, however, why the life and death of Jesus of Nazareth did not become simply another one-paragraph curiosity in Josephus' history of the Jewish people, along with would-be Messiahs like the shepherd Athronges, or Simon of Peraea, Herod's rebellious slave. Crucified along with thieves, his closest followers disbanded, disheartened, and terrified of reprisals, how is it that the peasant Jesus of Nazareth is even *known* to us today? This, of course, is part of the huge question concerning the origins of Christianity and its amazing rise from an obscure ripple on the Sea of Galilee to a tidal wave engulfing the entire Roman Empire.

An entirely reasonable answer – some think the only possible rational answer – is the resurrection. Jesus rose from the dead. It was this event that turned everything around, inspired and motivated the disciples, and caused them to gather their thoughts and memories, now deepened with the advantage of enlightened hindsight, and record them in written form. It was the resurrection that demonstrated to the disciples that Jesus really was who he said he was, and, further, unveiled for them the meaning of his victimization. For it was not Rome that had the last say regarding the meaning of Jesus' death. Rome could only bury Jesus, just as it had buried a million other pathetic victims upon whose bodies an empire had been raised and sustained. But only God could raise Jesus from the dead. And the crucial point for the Girardian understanding of the Bible that is God raised him *as victim.* He was resurrected *with the scars and wounds of his victimization still visible in his resurrected flesh*. In the book of Revelation it is the "lamb who was slain" who is given the authority to open the seals of history and pronounce judgment upon it. This means that God reads history from the perspective of the expelled and murdered victim, and that the final evaluation and judgment of our history has to do with where we stand vis-à-vis the victim.

It was not enough that founding murders and the scapegoat mechanism be exposed; after all, when Toto opened the curtain, allowing a privileged few to glimpse the truth, it could just as quickly have been pulled shut again. Had Jesus simply died, this would no doubt have been the case. Exposure was not enough; the scapegoat mechanism had to be *triumphed over.* "In the world you have tribulation; but be of good cheer, I have overcome the world." (John 16:33b) But such a triumph would have been impossible had Jesus used violence. Fighting fire with fire would only have led to being mimetically assimilated to the very thing he wished to defeat. Rather, he overcame the world *precisely as victim,* and *as victim* God raised him from the dead.

But we would not know any of this if the Gospels had never been composed. Those scriptures were not written simply to be informative history books, or biographies; they were written first and foremost as witnesses to the resurrection. And, indeed, it is only the resurrection that can adequately account for the progression from terrified and devastated disciples, hiding from the authorities, to the composition of scriptures encoding a radical new vision of God, the world, and human being. For this new vision could only come from personal transformation. As James Alison aptly points out in his wonderful little book, *Knowing Jesus,* the apostles not only bear witness *to* the resurrection as a sheer fact – the way, for example, we might witness a traffic accident – but they bear witness also *from* the resurrection. "That is to say, it was a happening which profoundly changed them, not only turning pusillanimous fisherfolk into international heroes and martyrs, but causing them to rethink the whole of their lives, their relationship to their homeland, their culture, its values, and radically altering their understanding of who God is."[122] That radical alteration in understanding would soon profoundly change entire civilizations.

Part III
COMPASSION OR APOCALYPSE

"Lord, how often shall my brother sin against me, and I forgive him? As many as seven times?"

Jesus said to him, "I do not say to you seven times, but seventy times seven." (Matt. 18:21-22)

Chapter Nine
The Gerasene Demoniac

Possession is not an individual phenomenon; it is the result of aggravated mimeticism. There are always at least two beings who possess each other reciprocally, each is the other's scandal, his model-obstacle. Each is the other's demon….

René Girard, *The Scapegoat* [123]

‡‡

It seems clear from the Gospels that as concerns Jesus himself, changing the world beyond Israel was to be a matter for his followers after his death and resurrection. The way the Gospels present it, Jesus knew that his time was short, and that Jerusalem was the central goal of his activity. It was there that he would score his ultimate triumph over the power of Satan, and this would need to be accomplished before any serious mission to the Gentiles could be mounted.

Jesus, himself a Jew, made Jews his primary audience, for they were the inheritors of a millennial-old scriptural tradition that had already seen through the lies of mythology and proclaimed the innocence of the victim, even if these astounding insights were still "in travail" with the primitive sacred. Despite their desire to imitate Gentile culture (about which they were warned many times in the Hebrew Scriptures), Jewish culture possessed a core of uniqueness in the ancient world. In particular, it possessed that knowledge of the victim which was to become the basis for Jesus' own self-understanding, and which he passed on to his disciples (although it did not truly begin to come into focus until after the risen victim, on the road to Emmaus, had demonstrated the new perspective from which to read the scriptures).

To better grasp the radical nature of that revelation, we examine in this chapter the story of the Gerasene demoniac. This is a story which at first sight appears to be nothing but one more exorcism account, albeit the most spectacular recorded in the Gospels. I read this story for years with no sense that it contained any message other than that Jesus was superior to demons (mingled, perhaps, with a tinge of anti-Roman innuendo, visible in the name of the demon: "legion"). Thus, for me, as for many others, Girard's penetrating analysis of this text in *The Scapegoat* was a stunning eye-opener, demonstrating the sense in which Gospel texts are structured by the revelation of the scapegoat mechanism and the victim, *even when these are not explicitly mentioned in the text.* The writers of the Gospels were in possession of a new way of viewing the world, and that new perspective could not help but inform the way they told their stories, even when they were not consciously aware of it. The following story is a prime example:

> *They came to the other side of the sea, to the country of the Ger'asenes. And when he had come out of the boat, there met him out of the tombs a man with an unclean spirit, who lived among the tombs; and no one could bind him any more, even with a chain; for he had often been bound with fetters and chains, but the chains he wrenched apart, and the fetters he broke in pieces; and no one had the strength to subdue him. Night and day among the tombs and on the mountains he was always crying out, and bruising himself with stones.*
>
> *And when he saw Jesus from afar, he ran and worshiped him; and crying out with a loud voice, he said, "What have you to do with me, Jesus, Son of the Most High God? I adjure you by God, do not torment me." For he had said to him, "Come out of the man, you unclean spirit!" And Jesus asked him, "What is your name?" He replied, "My name is Legion; for we are many." And he begged him eagerly not to send them out of the country. Now a great herd of swine was feeding there on the hillside; and they begged him, "Send us to the swine, let us enter them." So he gave them leave. And the unclean spirits came out, and entered the swine; and the*

herd, numbering about two thousand, rushed down the steep bank into the sea, and were drowned in the sea. The herdsmen fled, and told it in the city and in the country.

And people came to see what it was that had happened. And they came to Jesus, and saw the demoniac sitting there, clothed and in his right mind, the man who had had the legion; and they were afraid. And those who had seen it told what had happened to the demoniac and to the swine. And they began to beg Jesus to depart from their neighborhood. And as he was getting into the boat, the man who had been possessed with demons begged him that he might be with him. But he refused, and said to him, "Go home to your friends, and tell them how much the Lord has done for you, and how he has had mercy on you." And he went away and began to proclaim in the Decap'olis how much Jesus had done for him; and all men marveled. (Mark 5:1-20; see also Luke 8:26 ff; Matt. 8:28 ff. – Matthew uses the term "Gaderene" rather than Mark and Luke's "Gerasene.")

The Gerasenes and Their Scapegoat

Here we have a story in which Jesus takes his disciples to the land of the Gerasenes, a non-Jewish community (as we can tell by the fact that they raise pigs). It is strange that Jesus takes his disciples across the Lake of Galilee into this territory, for it is clear from other Gospel texts that Jesus understood his mission to be limited to the "children of Israel" (though he was not without compassion and the willingness to recognize and acknowledge faith when he encountered it among Gentiles). The story of Jesus' visit there turns out to be a profound anticipation of what is in store for Gentile societies that will sooner or later be penetrated by the gospel. Girard's foundational insight is his recognition of the social aspect of the story; specifically, the recognition of the demoniac as a *scapegoat*. The demoniac has had a tortured yet intimate relationship with the people of the town. They have bound him many times, and in every instance he has broken free and escaped. They have tied him down, ostensibly in order to restrain him from harming others and himself. But he always escapes, and they always go chase him down; or perhaps he sometimes wanders back into town, where they capture and bind him once again. And yet again he escapes. This cycle has evidently been repeating itself for a long time.

Rather than take this strange, cyclical pattern for granted, we need to ask what is really going on here in the relationship between the individual demoniac and the townspeople of Gerasa. It is as important to notice what the text lacks, as what it contains. On first reading, we might take this primarily as a story about one man's deliverance from demon possession, rather like the plot of the film, *The Exorcist.* But there is a huge difference. The biblical story doesn't read like "Hollywood." It lacks the spectacular "CGI," the special effects that we have come to expect and thrill to in films like *The Exorcist.* The Gerasene demoniac does not levitate, his head does not spin 360 degrees, he does not cause objects to fly telekinetically through the air, nor does he possess a supernatural strength with which he might smash barehanded through the doors or walls of prisons. Marks tells us only that "... the chains he wrenched apart, and the fetters he broke in pieces; and no one had the strength to subdue him." Luke says simply that the demoniac had been "...kept under guard, and bound with chains and fetters, but he broke the bonds and was driven by the demon into the desert." And Matthew's highly abbreviated version of the story has no mention of chains and fetters at all.

So before we start visualizing the Geresene demoniac as the Incredible Hulk, we should consider whether the text really warrants such theatricality. Clearly, it doesn't. All of the descriptions of the unfortunate man's actions – wrenching his chains apart, lacerating himself with stones, crying out – sound remarkably natural. Given time, cleverness, and reasonable strength, old chains and fetters can be defeated. The man was no doubt strengthened by wild, adrenalized urges, but the text gives no justification for imagining deeds of supernatural strength that would require Hollywood special effects to recreate.

Having come to this understanding, the question emerges: why then did no one have the strength to subdue him? A group of men can subdue even the wildest maniac. Once bound, he may escape once – but over and over again? Is it reasonable to assume that the

Geresene townsfolk could find no way whatsoever to keep this guy down? Unless their ineffectiveness was not so much a matter of lack of strength and ability, as lack of *will.* But why? From Girard's point of view the answer is obvious: the man was a scapegoat. He was something like the infamous town drunk that small towns mocked and despised in the era before Alcoholics Anonymous began to rehabilitate the image of the alcoholic.

James Alison draws this comparison in a talk given in 2004 at the National Cathedral in Washington, D.C.[124] As Alison points out, although the drunk is maligned by the community, he or she also subtly serves the community's interests by enabling the citizens to feel good about themselves. They are able to occupy the high ground of conscience because they have a scapegoat to blame, to mock, to gossip about, to cast aspersion upon – and at times even attempt to help, or at least restrain. Without their scapegoat the people would be deprived of a bonding mechanism. If the drunk actually recovered, the townspeople would likely feel uncomfortable: guilty, perhaps, for having lacked the moral imagination to see this person as a human being, and uncomfortable because without a scapegoat conveniently at hand on which to dump their frustrations, without that dog to kick, they are left feeling stuck with themselves. Something like this seems to have happened with the Gerasenes. They are certainly less than overjoyed to see their demoniac healed.

Girard has illuminated the tug-of-war that exists between the demoniac and the townspeople, showing how the back-and-forth of bondage and escape, bondage and escape, has a reciprocal quality that alerts us to the presence of rivalry, and indicates a kind of mutual dependence. The demoniac and the townsfolk rely upon each other for their identities, which are formed "over-against" each other. For the townsfolk, the demoniac is the "not-us" that allows them to cement their own identity as a people (and they probably have other scapegoats as well). The existence of the demoniac allows them to draw a line in the sand which indicates the boundaries of cultural identity, defining what is "inside" and what is "outside" of their community. There must be someone like the demoniac in order for that boundary and the identity constructed upon it to exist. The demoniac was *necessary* to the Gerasenes. They did not want to lose their demoniac, their "town drunk." They must have him around as the hapless recipient of their own projected violence. They must be able to see the devil clearly *out there, in him.* That is what makes "in here" feel safe, good, and just. The Gerasenes, of course, were no more conscious of what they were doing than were any of the other societies throughout history that did the same thing. And because of that we might say that the Gerasenes were themselves "possessed," blindly controlled by the scapegoat mechanism and relying upon it for their survival. The important point is that the relationship between town and demoniac is mutual, with the Gerasenes needing their scapegoat as much as the scapegoat needed them. The reciprocal nature of the relationship is what has always been missed by commentators and exegetes.

The Scapegoat and His Gerasenes

But if the Gerasenes needed their scapegoat, in what sense did the demoniac need the Gerasenes? The demon that speaks to Jesus names itself "Legion," and in accordance with the name, a multitude of demons are being driven out of the man. But Mark's version makes it clear that this legion is no mere aggregation, but constitutes a *collective* – a population of many, which is at the same time a single entity answering Jesus with one voice: "My name is Legion." In Mark 5:9 there is an amazing transition from singular to plural within the very same sentence: "*My* name is Legion, for *we* are many." The man is thus possessed by many and one; or, we might say, many-as-one.

Now, Luke tells us specifically that the man was "from the city," and the reference is more than incidental, for the Gerasene city in its relation to the demoniac was also many operating as one. Matthew's version stresses that after the miracle, when the people came out to investigate what had happened, *all the city* came, and *with one mind and purpose* they begged Jesus to leave their land. *The demon "Legion" is therefore a mirror image of the city itself in its capacity as a collectivity, the city operating as many-as-one.* This explains

Legion's strange request that Jesus not send them "out of the country." (5:10) Why does Legion make this strange request? The answer has nothing to do with patriotism. Legion cannot bear to leave the country because it *is* the country in its capacity as violent unanimity-minus-one. Legion is the satanic principle of the scapegoat mechanism, which is the very structuring principle of Gerasene society.

To be kicked out of Gerasene country is a very unusual thing for demon to fear. In traditional demonology, a demon lusts for a body to possess, and if kicked out of one body it can easily take up residence in another – even a pig's. Ancient exorcists often cast out demons by sending them into some other nearby body; and they also required the demon to manifest some sign in the immediate vicinity (like knocking something over), so the exorcist could be certain they really had left the possessed victim. But all this was local. When they came out they always remained within the local vicinity. But when Legion meets Jesus, it is afraid of being kicked out from its *country*, and this it cannot tolerate. This is what it fears the most, and Legion *anticipates* that Jesus will command this. Why? Because it knows that Jesus knows – that Legion and the Gerasene country are mirror images of the same satanic reality.

> *The demons are in the image of the human group; they are the imago of this group because they are its imitation. Like the society of the Gerasenes at the end of our text, the society of demons at the beginning possesses a structure, a kind of organization; it is the unity of the multiple: "My name is Legion; for there are many of us." Just as one voice is raised at the end to speak in the name of all the Gerasenes, one voice is raised at the beginning to speak in the name of all the demons. These two voices say the same thing. Since all coexistence between Jesus and the demons is impossible, to beg him not to chase away the demons, when one is a demon, is the same as begging him to depart, if one is from Gerasa.*[125]

To be cast outside its country would therefore be equivalent to disintegration and deconstruction, an abyss of non-being. (Thus, in Luke's version, rather than asking not to be sent out of the country,

Legion asks that Jesus not send them "into the abyss.") This is what Jesus knows, and Legion knows that he knows – which makes Jesus far more insightful and powerful than the typical local exorcists who operated *within* the total system that Jesus threatens to disrupt.

Legion's is the oneness that exists over-against scapegoats who have been sacrificed in one way or another for the sake of the collective. This is what possesses the demoniac. He has internalized the collective abuse; in fact, he imitates it. Marks says, "Night and day among the tombs and on the mountains he was always crying out, and bruising himself with stones." What is going on here? It is an imitation of the ever present threat hanging over this man, the threat of stoning. Victims of collective violence in ancient near eastern societies were often stoned to death. The Gerasenes wanted their scapegoat alive, but the threat of stoning was no doubt an ever present sanction. Possessed by the town's attitude towards him, and the violent abusive voices he has heard, he pathologically bruises himself with stones, doing unto himself before others can do unto him. To mitigate the pain of group ostracism and expulsion, he agrees with his tormentors' opinion of him, symbolically acting out their violence through self-infliction of wounds. The demoniac has formed his identity in relation to the city, and thus, in a sense, he needs the city just as much as the city needs him. For he knows no other way to live, no other way to think about himself, no other way to act. He truly is possessed.

The Crowd

But the Gospel writers give us the story of his liberation, the consideration of which will bring us to the main reason for our examining this story. Because of the reciprocal relation between the demoniac and the Gerasene community, the demoniac's liberation will have implications for the Gerasenes. If the scapegoat is the source of their unity, what will be the result of the scapegoat's liberation, except dissolution of that unity? This is exactly what we see happening when Legion leaves the man: the demonic unity is dissolved into a multiplicity of chaotic, violent elements, which enter the pigs and charge down the hill into the sea – a biblical symbol for chaos. Without the scapegoat mechanism to generate its unity, Legion is simply untamed and violent anarchy. It is no longer the organized society, or even the mob aligned against the scapegoat: it is simply the "crowd," loose and rampaging, and driven by fear.

Jesus himself used the image of a herd of pigs as a metaphor for human crowds. "Cast not your pearls before swine," he said, referring to the futility of offering spiritual wisdom to masses caught up in mimetic waves, "lest they trample them under foot and turn to attack you." Crowds are all around Jesus in the Gospels, and the story of the demoniac is sandwiched between episodes in which the crowd looms large. Jesus took his disciples to Gerasa in the first place to escape the press of crowds in Galilee, and immediately after the miracle Mark tells us that "[W]hen Jesus had crossed again in the boat to the other side, a great crowd gathered around him; and he was beside the sea." (5:21) In the herd of pigs, Legion has "unraveled," become the crowd in its irrationally mimetic state, without organization and purpose because it can no longer organize itself against the scapegoat.

I mentioned stoning as a typical form of collective violence in the ancient world, but there was another very common method of execution typical of towns situated (as many were) on hillsides with steep cliffs (Rome's Tarpeian rock being one of the most infamous examples). The community would form a partial circle around the victim to block any escape, while throwing stones and backing the victim up to the edge of the cliff, until finally the victim plummeted to his or her death. Jesus himself was almost a victim of this venerable form of collective violence in his own home town of Nazareth, as recorded in Luke 4.[126] The fate that Jesus avoids in Nazareth is suffered by the pigs in Gerasa. Some translations have the swine rushing down a steep embankment into the sea, but Girard has shown that the meaning of the miracle is better revealed by those translations that take the Greek word κρημνος to mean a "cliff" rather than a slope. (The accompanying Greek preposition κατα would then mean "down and over.") Translating the text this way reveals the picture of a herd of pigs charging over a cliff and falling into the sea – the same thing that had happened countless times in the ancient world to countless victims of mob violence. The real excitement of Jesus' miracle, therefore, is that *for the first time in history it is the crowd, the mob, that is cast over the cliff, while the scapegoat goes free!* Rather than the scapegoat being cast out of the city, the city is cast out of the scapegoat, who now sits there "clothed and in his right mind." And as if to make sure that we get the point, Mark's text emphasizes one more time that all of this happened to the demoniac who was "sitting there, clothed and in his right mind, *the man who had had the legion…*" Yes, the man who had had the legion, who had been the victim of the crowd, is restored and healed, while the mob has unraveled, becoming a trampling chaos that undid itself by the force of its own violence. (The miracle at Gerasa thus bears a family resemblance to the famous story of the woman taken in adultery in John 8. There, Jesus defused the sacred violence agitating her accusers, dispersed the mob, and sent the woman freely on her way.)

This is the deeper reason for the Gerasenes' fear of Jesus. It is not, as I used to think (and as most commentators assume) that they fear Jesus as an economic threat, since he has just lost them a hefty chunk of pork real estate. Jesus poses a threat to their society far more fundamental than economics. Their victim has been rehabilitated. They see him now "clothed and in his right mind," and can no longer function as their scapegoat. The best thing for them now would be for the man simply to leave the country so they can forget all about him, and get back to the business of marginalizing other scapegoats. And this is exactly what the healed man wishes to do. But when he asks permission to join the disciples in following Jesus, the answer is no. Jesus wants him to "Go home to your friends, and tell them how much the Lord has done for you, and how he has had mercy on you." This will make things a bit more difficult for Gerasenes society, as we will now see.

The Fate of Gentile Civilization

We arrive now at the import of this story for world history. For Jesus' directive to the man, his preference that the man not accompany him but return to his own people and share with them the great things God has done for him, is an anticipatory view of the fate that awaits Western civilization, and eventually the world. Jesus knows full well how unsettling his miracle has been for the people: so much so that "with one voice" they rejected him out of hand, and begged him to leave their country. He knows, therefore, that if he sends the restored man back to his own people, that man's presence will continue to unsettle them. He knows that as the man, now fully clothed and in his right mind, shares his newfound sanity and joyous gratitude with his fellows, he will provoke new and unwelcomed self-doubt; for they will be forced to confront their victim whom they had marginalized, now speaking eloquently and emotively about God's wonderful mercy and grace towards him!

No doubt it will be but a moment before another case of possession pops up within the community, and Gerasene life will return to business as usual. But the voice of the healed demoniac will continue to act like a thorn in Gerasene flesh, a herald of things to come, a vanguard force for the power of the gospel that just a few years hence will wash a flood of good news over this land, changing it irrevocably. Then, new kinds of communities will be seen springing up in the Decapolis region called *ecclesia,* churches. They too will be based on the blood of a victim: but they will be raising Abel, not murdering him, because they will be worshipping the risen victim. They will be proclaiming the good news about a new way of being human, which understands life from the perspective of the victim, not the persecutor.[127]

In *The Scapegoat* Girard seems to take Jesus' exorcism as a definitive expulsion of the demons, leading to their destruction. Girard feels that Jesus granted Legion's request not to be sent out of the country because he knew it would make no ultimate difference: the drowning pigs consign the demons to destruction in the abyss anyway. This may be true in reference to the possession of the demoniac: *his* legion is utterly destroyed, for he is no longer possessed by his role as city scapegoat. In a larger sense, however, the exorcism had the value of a *sign,* and was not the permanent destruction of the satanic power that lived within the structure of Gerasene society. This is demonstrated clearly enough by the fact that the community "with one voice" urgently requests that Jesus leave their land; which, as Girard pointed out in the above quote, is only the reverse image of Legion asking Jesus not to send him out of the country. So the Gerasene legion is still alive and well, albeit feeling quite threatened, and soon to experience the subtle and continuous discomfort of a healed demoniac in its midst.

Jesus' concern at this point was not with the utter destruction of the demons, which would have had its corollary in the destruction of Gerasa itself. He had compassion on the demoniac, and freed him, exposing the truth about the mimetic crowd; but the demons were not utterly destroyed, or expelled from Gerasa. The pigs drowned, but the Gerasenes no doubt quickly found themselves another demoniac scapegoat to take the place of the one they had lost.

What we have in the Gerasene story is a triumphant glimpse – yet still only a glimpse – of things to come. Legion fully realizes that Jesus has the power to destroy him completely, and is so terrified by the prospect that he/they are willing to settle for the bodies of pigs rather than the "abyss" of separation from the Gerasenes. That more complete dissolution will come only in the wake of Paul and other missionaries of the early church, of whom Jesus himself said that they would do greater things than he had done. Gospel penetration of the Gentile world will spell the eventual collapse of civilizations like Gerasa's. Their structures of myth and sacrificial ritual will not be able to withstand the onslaught of the liberating Good News. Everywhere the gospel is preached, the ancient ways will be stripped of their efficacy. Not because the gospel is primarily a negative, destructive force, but because sacred violence could not tolerate the exposure of its deepest structural secrets.

In the meantime, Jesus' task was to lay the foundation which would facilitate that dramatic transformation of culture, and his mission lay in the direction of Jerusalem, not Gerasa. Until Jesus could say to his Father on the cross, "It is accomplished," there would be no hope for people like the Gerasenes, enslaved to myth, sacrificial ritual, and prohibition; just as possessed, in their own way, as the demoniac himself. But in the light and hope of that future accomplishment Jesus sends the demoniac, clothed and in his right mind, back to his own people to be a kind of proto-missionary in anticipation of greater voices like that of Paul's to come. Based on the rebuff given to his Master, the restored man could no doubt expect to encounter similar resistance from his town fellows. He was going back into a closed system that did not want to be disrupted. This encounter of gospel and pagan culture would occur over and over again in the years after Jesus' death and resurrection. And, just like the Gerasenes, cultures would kick against it, sometimes ferociously, yet without succeeding in ridding themselves of their uninvited guest. The gospel would undermine their sacred structures. Where there was classical balance and stability, the gospel would provoke doubt, pangs of conscience, and unexpected eruptions of the most extravagant charity based on a new conception – indeed, a new *experience* – of what it means to be human.

For James Alison, the story of the Gerasene demoniac is the story of "...what it looks like when the living God, the utterly vivacious Creator out of nothing, draws near to the ersatz god of group being and belonging, and by gently taking the weakest member of the group, begins to collapse the group's belonging, humanizing the 'bad guy' and thus initiating the possibility of a quite different sort of social formation."[128] Alison succinctly states what we might call the internal logic of Jesus' miracle at Gerasa, commenting that the exorcism of the demoniac was "...nothing less than the humanizing and domestication of the man in question, even at the expense of the stability of the social group of which he has been such an important part. This is not the logic of 'it is better that one man should be cast out than that the whole nation should be disturbed.' This is the logic of 'it is good that one man should be made human and that the whole nation should learn to live differently', the logic which prefers the one lost sheep to the ninety-nine which never strayed..."[129] And doesn't that logic sound just like Jesus, who was always concerned about the poor rejected souls who served the thankless function of being weird so the rest could feel normal, being evil so the rest could be good? This is Jesus' logic of the kingdom of God, where there is more joy in heaven over the recovery of one lost sinner than over the ninety-nine righteous.

Before closing this discussion, it might be well to remind the reader of what I said at the beginning of this chapter: "Gospel texts are structured by the revelation of the scapegoat mechanism and the victim, *even when these are not explicitly mentioned in the text.* The writers of the Gospels were in possession of a new way of viewing the world, and that new perspective could not help but inform the way they told their stories, even when they were not consciously aware of it." The claim, therefore, is not that everything just expounded is explicitly stated in the Gospel text. Nowhere, for example, does the text explicitly mention that the demoniac was the community's scapegoat. And for some, that might be reason enough to discredit Girard's interpretation right from the start.

But it is important to understand that Girard is drawing out what he believes are the implications of the text. The truth that informs the Gospels structures not just the words on the surface, but the deeper "grammar" of the text as well. That truth is a way of seeing that runs so deep even the writers themselves cannot spell it out completely, yet it informs the whole way in which they tell the story. This is why an exposition like the one Girard gives is able to draw out and make so much meaningful sense out of the various features of the story. When one understands that what one is looking at is not just a piece of floating ice but the tip of an iceberg, and when one understands something of the shape of that iceberg, one is able to recognize and understand the meaning and function of surface features in a far more profound way.

Chapter Ten
The Apostle Paul

The death of Christ was for Paul an epiphany of sacred violence.

Robert G. Hamerton-Kelly
Sacred Violence: Paul's Hermeneutic of the Cross [130]

Therefore, if anyone is in Christ, the new creation has come: the old has gone, the new is here! (2 Cor. 5:17 NIV)

‡‡

The Conversion of Paul

Even if the Gerasenes had welcomed Jesus, he would have had no time to linger in Gentile territory, travelling about effecting cures on behalf of other Gentile scapegoats. For, as mentioned earlier, the Gospels present Jesus as fully cognizant that his primary mission was to Israel and would score its triumphant climax in Jerusalem. His goal was to open wide the minds of those already prepared by the Hebrew Scriptures and Jewish religion, so that they could grasp the full depth of distinction between the violence of humanity and the God of love. Jesus had first to effect the full revelation of the scapegoat mechanism and the innocent victim in order for someone like the apostle Paul to be transformed into a dauntless messenger, passionately proclaiming a new paradigm for humanity throughout Gentile territory. Where Jesus did not venture to go, his companions did – and far beyond Gerasa.

One man whose understanding of God was altered most radically by his encounter with the risen Christ was Saul of Tarsus, later known as Paul the apostle. He was the ideal person to spearhead the missionary force of the gospel. He had received a rigorous religious training in Judaism, and excelled his contemporaries in knowledge and passion for his religious tradition. This was, on the one hand, a major stumbling block that led him to persecute followers of Jesus; on the other hand it was a major asset, because it prepared Paul to grasp with incredible depth the significance of Christ's revelation. What Paul needed was the "gestalt switch" that Christ provided; he needed the "key," a new interpretive perspective from which to read the Hebrew Scriptures in order to unlock their truly divine meaning. He was given this key, or at least the fundamental elements of it, on his way to Damascus.

The story of Paul's conversion is recorded more than once in Acts, and I will quote the best known version, from Acts 9. It is a story soaked in violence. Paul (at the time named "Saul") was "breathing threats and murder against the disciples of the Lord." He had been present during the stoning of Stephen, the first recorded martyr among Jesus' early followers, and shortly thereafter he headed north to Damascus to round up other followers of "The Way" that lived there, and bring them bound back to Jerusalem. The Acts 9 account continues:

> *Now as he was going along and approaching Damascus, suddenly a light from heaven flashed around him. He fell to the ground and heard a voice saying to him, "Saul, Saul, why do you persecute me?" He asked, "Who are you, Lord?" The reply came, "I am Jesus, whom you are persecuting. But get up and enter the city, and you will be told what you are to do." The men who were traveling with him stood speechless because they heard the voice but saw no one. Saul got up from the ground, and though his eyes were open, he could see nothing; so they led him by the hand and brought him into Damascus. For three days he was without sight, and neither ate nor drank.* (Acts 9:3-9 NRSV)

Those who think of Christian conversion as primarily a spiritual matter involving the salvation of the soul overlook the concrete nature of Saul's conversion, the essence of which was *his recognition of himself as a violent persecutor of innocent victims.* Of course, Saul was not persecuting Jesus in any direct, literal sense; but Jesus had identified himself with his followers, and in fact with all victims ("for I was hungry and you gave me food, I was thirsty and you gave me drink, I was a stranger and you welcomed me, I was naked and you clothed me, I was sick and you visited me, I was in prison and you came to me." Matt. 25:35-36).

In his persecution of innocent victims, therefore, Saul was persecuting Jesus. And he was convinced of the righteousness of his cause, and saw himself as carrying out God's will. He was following in the footsteps of Phinehas, of whom it is recorded in the book of Numbers that in his zealousness for Yahweh he thrust a spear through a Hebrew man and his unlawfully taken Gentile wife. For an enthusiast like Saul, Phinehas would have been a religious hero, a model of how one shows dedication to God. When giving the Galatians an account of his pre-Christian religious experience, Paul wrote: "You have heard, no doubt, of my earlier life in Judaism. I was violently persecuting the church of God and was trying to destroy it. I advanced in Judaism beyond many among my people of the same age, for I was far more zealous for the traditions of my ancestors." (Gal. 1:13-14) "Zealousness" was an admired trait in the religious circles within which Saul moved. What it really connotes is sacred violence. First century Judaism was a multifaceted religion, and we must not generalize from Paul's own religiosity to the entirety of the religion. But sacred violence was definitely an aspect, as Paul's own experience testifies. The Hebrew Scriptures, as we have seen, contain high-watermark texts that reveal a God who rejects sacrifice and demands love for marginalized victims. But Saul had read those Scriptures with violent eyes, as did many others, using them to misinterpret his own violence as zealousness for God's honor and truth.

One can appreciate, therefore, the blinding shock it must have been to be struck suddenly with the epiphany that exactly the reverse was true: that he was actually a *persecutor,* that he was persecuting innocent victims, and that his zealous spirit was actually *against* God rather than defending God! This epiphany took the form of a vision of the innocent victim: "Saul, Saul, why do you persecute me?" Saul responded, "Who are you, Lord?" The reply came, "I am Jesus, whom you are persecuting."

Perhaps the climactic moment of his conversion came a bit later, after he had sat blinded for three days in Damascus. A Christian disciple named Ananias had a vision in which Jesus told him to go find Saul and lay his hands upon him so that he might regain his sight. Understandably, Ananias was terrified. Why, after all, should he seek out the very man who had come with the intent and power to arrest him? But the Lord explained that Saul was going to be his chosen instrument, and Ananias went. The text says, "So Ananias went and entered the house. He laid his hands on Saul and said, 'Brother Saul, the Lord Jesus, who appeared to you on your way here, has sent me so that you may regain your sight and be filled with the Holy Spirit.' And immediately something like scales fell from his eyes, and his sight was restored." (Acts 9:17-18 NRSV) Here, then, is Ananias imitating his Lord Jesus by forgiving and ministering to his enemy, whom he calls *brother!*

This has to be one of the most extraordinary moments in history. Jesus modeled a new way of being human that involved forgiving and loving *even one's enemies* – an unheard of absurdity in the ancient world (and absurd to many, of course, even today). Ananias faithfully imitated that model, and the impact on Saul was titanic. It literally transformed him. He spent the next three years in Damascus studying the Hebrew Scriptures, now from an entirely different perspective – that of the *victim,* the point of view of Jesus. The scriptures came alive to him in a new way, for Christ had given him the key to understanding them. This so fired him up that Saul, now called Paul, spent the remaining years of his life traveling on missionary journeys, attempting to announce to the entire world the message with which he had been entrusted. He had "good news" to spread.

Paul and the Law

It is important to grasp that Paul's entire understanding of the gospel was anchored in his conversion experience; but – and this is crucial – not because it was a "visionary" spiritual experience, but because of the transformed perspective it produced in Paul's mind and heart. "Do not conform any longer to the pattern of this world," Paul wrote, "but be transformed by the renewing of your mind. Then you will be able to test and approve what God's will is – his good, pleasing and perfect will." (Rom. 12:2 NIV) Paul's instruction to the Roman congregation comes directly out of his own experience: his stunning realization on the road to Damascus that what he had thought to be pleasing to God was in fact ungodly violence, nothing more than conformity to the sacred power structures of this world. Essentially, Paul's transformative experience was "an epiphany of sacred violence," as Robert Hamerton-Kelly, the foremost Girardian scholar of Paul, calls it.[131]

What this means is that Paul suddenly understood that his zealous religiosity on God's behalf was nothing but violence dressed up in sacred garb. He realized that the Mosaic Law he had strained to keep and fulfill with such rigor was itself part of the system of sacred violence, even if its fundamental intentions were good. Like all primitive sacred prohibitions and taboos, The Mosaic Law cursed as well as blessed. It blessed the Hebrews if they lived up to it and cursed them if they didn't. Perceptive readers of the high-watermark texts of the Hebrew Scriptures could find their way towards a more generous vision, but as a structure of prohibitions, conformity with which was sanctioned by violent punishment, the Mosaic Law was full of God's cursing power. The problem for Paul was his realization that it had cursed Jesus. *The very one who had been revealed to him as Lord and innocent victim, had been cursed by the Mosaic Law!* In Galatians 3:13 Paul says:

> *Christ redeemed us from the curse of the law by becoming a curse for us, for it is written, "Cursed is everyone who hangs on a tree"…* (NRSV)

Paul is citing a text from the Mosaic Law (Deuteronomy 12:23) which says that anyone who is hanged or crucified is cursed by God. He is not citing the Law here in order to agree with it, as if he believed that *God* cursed Christ. He is saying that Christ redeemed us from the law by allowing himself to be cursed by it, so that we could recognize the violence that masquerades as God's will. Christ *redeems* us: the metaphor of redeeming in the Roman world meant paying a certain price to obtain the freedom of a slave. Living within the system of sacred violence meant being enslaved, and it was to rescue humanity from that bondage that Jesus "paid the price" of being born "under the law" (Gal. 4:4) and becoming a victim of sacred violence. He "became a curse" not because God, his Abba, cursed him, but because the Mosaic Law and its zealous enforcers cursed him as he hung from the cross.

No wonder the cross becomes Paul's central symbol. It was the locus of revelation concerning the true nature of the Law. No wonder, too, that Paul says in Galatians: *Through the law I died to the law so that I might live to God.* (2:19 NRSV) He died to the law *through the law itself.* In other words, in the very midst of carrying out its provisions with dedication and zeal the nature of the law itself had been revealed to him, making it clear that he would have to defect from the law if he wanted to live for God. He realized that the Law was an instrument of sacred violence. "As a result of the vision Paul identified his persecuting violence as the work of the Mosaic Law in his life. The Law had created a way of life founded on sacred violence and the crucifixion of Christ is the logical outcome of such a way of life. Once Paul realized this, he could only 'die to the Law in order that I might live for God.'"[132]

This understanding would continue to deepen throughout Paul's subsequent years as he himself became a victim of violence as he carried his radical message into Asia Minor, and on to Rome. It makes sense, therefore, that Paul would refer to the process of becoming a Christian as being "crucified with Christ." For it involves sharing the space of the victim, taking the victim's suffering upon oneself in imitation of Christ. With ironic appropriateness, much of the persecution that Paul suffered was inflicted – as Jesus himself predicted for his followers (John 16:2) –

by those convinced that they were doing the will of God; just as Paul himself had been when, as Saul, he zealously prosecuted those law of Moses breaking Jesus-followers. No wonder, then, that Paul says in Galatians 3:19 9 (NRSV):

> *Why then the law? It was added because of transgressions.... and it was ordained through angels by a mediator.*

In other words, Paul understood the function of the law in the same way Girard has explained the function of primitive prohibitions and taboos: they were established in order to suppress the mimetic desire that leads to violence ("transgressions"). They are able to suppress violence because they carry the sanction of the threat of punishment – i.e., greater violence – if they are broken. They are a form of violence – *sacred* violence, to be precise, since they are deemed divine in origin and a direct expression of the will of God. But, says Paul, the law was not given directly by God but by angels, and through a mediator, Moses.

Paul and Sacrifice

Prohibition, as explained in an earlier chapter, represents only one of the three pillars of the primitive sacred, the other two being mythology and sacrifice. Without the sacrificial rituals, prohibitions alone would hardly suffice to keep "transgressions" (the violent passions of mimetic desire) at bay. As might be expected, then, another result of Paul's epiphany was that he no longer took animals into sacred space for slaughter. In the churches Paul founded there was no sacrifice. Paul does not attack the concept of temple; on the contrary, he retains his enthusiasm for the idea; but the place of worship is no longer the old, physical temple complex, but the body of believers interacting in faith, hope, and love. Referring to his work establishing the Corinthian church, Paul wrote "[L]ike a skilled master builder I laid a foundation." (1 Cor.3:15) A few verses later it becomes clear that the foundation to which he is referring is not one of stone, but is Jesus Christ himself, and the believers in Christ constitute the structure erected upon that foundation.

In a sense, then, Paul subverts the idea of temple even as he continues to use it. For Paul's new temple, the *real* temple, is threatening to the old order temples of antiquity, including the Jerusalem temple. Those physical structures had for their foundations a hidden reality: the murdered victim. Paul's true temple, on the other hand, has as its foundation Jesus Christ – who is also a murdered victim; but in Paul's new temple of believers (and here lies the whole difference) the victim is revealed and proclaimed, not hidden. This temple reveals what the old temples hid. The difference is indeed foundational, and utterly subversive.

The same is true for sacrifice. Paul sometimes makes use of the word sacrifice, as for example in Romans 12:1-2: "I appeal to you therefore, brethren, by the mercies of God, to present your bodies as a living sacrifice, holy and acceptable to God, which is your spiritual worship." Then he goes on to talk about not being conformed to "this world/age," but being renewed in mind in order to do the proper will of God. Here again we see how in the very process of using the image of sacrifice, Paul is subverting it. For sacrifice traditionally meant saving the communal life by murdering (sacrificing) a victim, which is the whole violent pattern of thought and practice from which Paul is urging his congregants to liberate themselves. Paul retains the idea of sacrifice, just as he retains the idea of temple; but he makes of it a metaphor for the voluntary giving up of one's ego (mimetic desire and rivalry) for the sake of the other, in imitation of Jesus. One can call this "sacrifice," but the old and new realities are in fact diametrically incompatible, and situating the old terminology within a framework of thought erected upon the foundation of the revealed victim, could not but subvert the old order, even as it sought to use its imagery.

This incompatibility often surfaces directly in Paul's letters. The foundation upon which he builds, Jesus Christ, is anti-sacrificial, and thus not at all "conformed to this world." And so we should not be surprised to see Paul's thinking at times exploding the old sacrificial order. I will cite two of the many examples offered by Hamerton-Kelly.[133] In 2 Cor. 5:14-15 Paul writes:

For the love of Christ urges us on, because we are convinced that one has died for all; therefore all have died. And he died for all, so that those who live might live no longer for themselves, but for him who died and was raised for them. (NRSV)

This passage turns the old sacrificial form completely on its head. The old order mandated that one should die so that all might live. What we have here, however, is Christ dying for all – *and therefore all die!* ("...one has died for all; therefore all have died.")This is a complete short-circuiting of sacrificial thinking. It transforms the polarized victim-dies-instead-of-the-group mentality into a situation where the entire group identifies itself *with* the victim, dying *with* him. And as Christ died, not because his life was taken, but because he *gave* his life for the sake of our liberation, so Christ's compassionate self-giving becomes a model for believers who identify themselves with him. They no longer live selfishly "for themselves," sacrificing others in order to insure their own continued existence. Instead, they too "die" in identification with Christ, in that they give themselves for the sake of the other. All of this happens in love, not fear. There are no gods to be afraid of or placate with bloody offerings. In his dying Christ was raised; and in Paul's thinking, through identification with Christ we shall all likewise be raised. Life comes from the compassionate giving we model after Christ, as opposed to the old model's self-centered system of death which for millennia had kept cowering humanity in thrall. We can see, then, how utterly alien is the structure of Paul's thought here to the institution of temple sacrifice.

This passage is a good example of how readily we read into Paul (and other New Testament texts) the sacrificial concepts that to this day continue to plague Christianity (see the section on "Sacrificial Christianity"). As soon as we see something like "Christ died for us," the majority of Bible readers immediately default to the idea of sacrifice. Even a text like 2 Cor. 5:14-15, quoted above, where Paul spells out his anti-sacrificial understanding of the phrase, is likely to pass right by interpreters because of their ingrained sacrificial programming. This is not surprising, since sacrifice and the kind of thinking it generates is as old as humankind, deeply ingrained in our DNA. But just a couple of verses later in 2 Cor. 5:17 Paul goes on to say, "So if anyone is in Christ, there is a new creation: everything old has passed away; see, everything has become new!" How in the world could that be true if the core of Paul's proclamation was the been-there-done-that-for-a-few-millennia idea of sacrifice?

The other example from Hamerton-Kelly is Paul's comment in Galatians 4:4-5:

> *But when the time had fully come, God <u>sent forth</u> his Son, born of woman, born under the law, to redeem those who were under the law, so that we might receive adoption as sons.*

The deep "grammar" of Paul's thinking here is a reversal of the sacrificial rituals described in Leviticus that would have been near and dear to his heart in his earlier zealous life as "Saul." Leviticus 14 describes a ritual in which impurities from disease are transferred onto a living bird which is then released: "he [the priest] shall let the living bird go out of the city into the open field." (14:53) English translations render this as "letting the bird go" or "releasing the bird" – but the Hebrew verb is the same one used in Leviticus 16 where a goat is "sent forth." Leviticus 16 describes the famous "scapegoat" ritual performed by the high priest on the Day of Atonement, in which the priest lays hands on a goat while the people of Israel confess their sins. The sins are transferred onto the goat, which is then sent away into the wilderness, carrying the people's sins with it. In both the bird and goat rituals, the basic movement is that the victim/scapegoat is "sent forth," away from the realm of the sacred ceremony into the profane, thus removing sin or impurity from the sacred precinct. In both texts, the Septuagint (the ancient Greek translation of the Hebrew Scriptures) translates the Hebrew verb meaning "send forth" with the Greek word εξαποστελλω – *which is the same word Paul uses when he talks about God <u>sending forth</u> his Son to be born under the law*. This is the only place where Paul uses this term, and Leviticus 14 and 16 are the only places where the Septuagint uses the term in connection with the purpose of redeeming. It is very likely, therefore, that Paul has these rituals specifically in mind and is using them to explicate the meaning of Christ's work: *but as a reverse movement*. The sacrificial movement of the Mosaic texts – sending forth the bird and goat *away* from the sacred precinct – is reversed in Paul; instead, God "sends forth" Christ *into* the realm of the sacred ("born under the law," the sacred Law of Moses). Rather than sanctifying the sacred by removing sin from its midst, as in the Levitical rituals, Christ is born/sent into the sacred with the express purpose of rescuing from it all those who have been condemned there as "sinners," all those who, in Hamerton-Kelly's words: "…have been imprisoned under the powers of violence there."[134]

The above exegesis may seem a stretch to the modern reader, since it largely hangs upon Paul's use of the Greek word εξαποστελλω. But one must realize that Paul approached the Hebrew Scriptures with the training of the ancient rabbis, who memorized texts and strung texts together based on word similarities.[135] Paul is indeed thinking of Christ in terms of Mosaic rituals; but he is indicating, ironically, that the scapegoat who saves the community is one God sent forth into *our* violent-sacred realm. And why? To become our scapegoat in order to expose the religious illusion of sacred violence and set us free.

I went into the above exegesis in order to show how deeply structures which are subversive to sacrificial thinking run in Pauline thought. They are present even when not overtly expressed, because they form the matrix within which his entire understanding of Christ was formed. Paul's conversion epiphany had revealed to him that the entire sacrificial system was an expression of sacred violence.

Paul and Myth

Prohibition and sacrifice, two of the pillars of sacred violence, were under deconstruction in Paul's interpretation of the gospel. What about mythology? In the ancient world the gods of the myths were often thought to appear to mortals in the form of human beings; and in the Greek city of Lystra, Paul and his companion Barnabas were proclaimed gods after healing a cripple. In the face of an adoring crowd, they protested, "Friends, why are you doing this? We are mortals just like you, and we bring you good news, that you should turn from these worthless things to the living God..." (Acts 14:15a) They would have been safer to accept the public's attribution of divinity than to challenge the notion of "gods," for the crowd turned on them, stoning Paul and dragging him out of town, thinking him dead. In another city, Ephesus, a silversmith named Demetrius who made and sold silver statuettes of the goddess Artemis (whose temple in Ephesus was one of the seven wonders of the ancient world), grew concerned because "this Paul has persuaded and drawn away a considerable number of people by saying that gods made with hands are not gods." (Acts 19:26) Demetrius incited a riot, and two of Paul's cohorts were grabbed and dragged into the city amphitheater, where for two hours the crowd shouted them down with cries of "Great is Artemis of the Ephesians!" until finally the town clerk quieted them down and defused the riot. (These texts in Acts are representative of the New Testament's suspicion of crowds, and its ability to portray sacred collective violence as a mere lynch mob.)

In his debunking of the gods of mythology, Paul was of course following old Jewish tradition modeled on the Hebrew Scriptures, which had for centuries been debunking Gentile myths. But he was doing so with a depth of insight the Jewish tradition had not attained. For classic Jewish polemics against Gentile idol worship had not emancipated itself from its own version of sacred violence, being, on the contrary, often completely animated by a spirit of violent mimetic rivalry with "idol worshippers." But Paul's debunking of the gods did not proceed from sacred partisan polemics. That is something that would have interested "Saul," but not the Paul to whom Jesus had said, "Saul, Saul, why are you persecuting me?" Paul was not interested in spouting violent Jewish apologetics while damning Gentile idol worshipers.[136] For as Paul himself wrote to the Galatians, "There is neither Jew nor Greek . . . for you are all one in Christ Jesus." (Gal. 3:28) It was no longer about one sacred religion attacking and destroying another; it was about the end of sacred religion altogether, and the emergence of a new humanity.

Paul and the Deconstruction of Sacred Divisions

This is the final thing I will say about Paul here, and it is crucial for much of what follows later. One of the first things that Paul seems to have understood after his conversion is that the sacred violence that crucified Christ was one and the same with the Mosaic violence that divided Jews from Gentiles. From very early in his ministry, the issue of relations between Jewish and Gentile believers in Christ was right in Paul's face. He had to confront positions different from his own even in Peter and James. That the Christian revelation would result in the collapse of sacred divisions and hierarchies was not immediately apparent in its full radical dimensions even to Jesus' own disciples. For Peter and James a major sticking point was the Jew-Gentile distinction. Regardless of their liberality and charity in other areas, they struggled with the idea that God and his Messiah would enter into relationship with Gentiles without first requiring them to keep the law God gave through Moses. Surely they should be circumcised; and of course God would want them to keep the kosher laws, and fulfill other important requirements of Torah as well.

In Galatians 2 Paul tells the story of his confrontation with Peter in Antioch, when Peter came to visit. All went well until emissaries showed up who had been sent from Jerusalem by James. It seems that Peter had been eating with Gentiles in Antioch – a big "no-no" for keepers of Mosaic Law – no doubt with Paul's encouragement. James had sent some men to see what was going on, because it was not clear to James, as it was to Paul, that being a follower of Messiah Jesus excused one from the obligations imposed upon every law-abiding Jew, such as the prohibition against eating with Gentiles. When James' henchmen showed up, fearing their judgment Peter started segregating himself from the Gentiles at mealtime; and, mimetic waves being what they are, all the other Jewish Christians followed Peter's example (even Paul's close associate Barnabas), segregating themselves as well. In 2:14 Paul says that they were "not acting consistently with the truth of the gospel." The "Good News" (gospel) that Paul was spreading meant that boundaries and divisions previously considered sacred, such as the Jew-Gentile distinction, had to be dismantled, because he realized that they were expressions of the same sacred violence that crucified Christ. Jesus Christ had made himself victim of that violence in order to redeem us from enslavement to the sacred system. And in imitation of Christ, Paul goes on to say in 2:20 that "I have been crucified with Christ…" As a follower of the Crucified he can no longer advocate and support hierarchies that divide the world into "sacred" and "profane," and create victims by erecting walls of division between people. Such walls are maintained by the expulsion of what is considered impure, sinful, monstrous, unholy, or evil. "In Christ," Paul sees the essentially arbitrary nature of such distinctions and the violence motivating them, even though they be all "gussied-up" in sacred dress.

Paul's understanding of the gospel as the end of sacred divisions was quickly expanded beyond the Jew-Gentile distinction. As he writes in Galatians 3:28: "There is no longer Jew or Greek, there is no longer slave or free, there is no longer male and female; for all of you are one in Christ Jesus." This proclamation was destined to dismantle empires. Paul's churches were to represent a new humanity which did not play the game of sacred hierarchies (although we shall see further on that this did not remain the case for very long, unfortunately). It is not easy to grasp the full radical import of Paul's statement, for it is not meant as a simple revolution: that is, a mere reversal of hierarchy. It is not meant as a declaration that those who were previously victims are now "the new boss." It is far more radical than that. It leaps beyond the entire realm of violent dialectic into a breakthrough realm of human existence where identity is constituted by imitation of Christ. This does not mean what it has so often been taken to mean, however: a religious identity complete with sacred dogma and hierarchies, existing over against a profane realm of nonbelievers. Such a move simply recreates the very thing Paul is dismantling. The church for Paul does not exist "over against" anything. It does not need scapegoats in order to constitute its own identity.

In this regard, Paul's instructions to his Corinthian congregation are revealing (1 Cor. 8). One of the hot-button issues he had to deal with in that church was whether or not meat that had been sacrificed by pagans to idols was acceptable for Christian consumption. We see here, incidentally, how far beyond sacrifice these Christians were: not only had they given up sacrifice when they became Christians, some of them were scandalized by the very thought of eating the flesh of any animal that had been sacrificed to the gods by their pagan neighbors. What Paul says in response to their concerns is, essentially: "Get over it – it's just food. Eat, enjoy, and be grateful." Since idols are nothing, meat offered to them is mere food and one need not be afraid to eat it.

But Paul goes beyond even this, and here is the crucial move. If eating such meat really is nothing, then it should be just as easy *not* to eat it as to eat it. Although he agrees with those who feel free to eat such meat, Paul advises that if eating is going to wound a "weaker" brother or sister's conscience and cause them to "stumble,"[137] one should abstain from eating it for their sake. Such abstinence demonstrates the freedom of love, in contradistinction to the entrenched slavery of rivalry. It is self-giving in imitation of Christ: giving up a privilege that one has a genuine right to, for the sake of the other. Although we often use the expression "self-sacrifice" to denote this kind of thing, that is an unfortunate terminology; for this is not about sacrificing oneself to appease a god or anyone else. It is about participating "in Christ," as Paul likes to put it: imitating Christ in surrendering all rivalry, even when one really does hold the high ground, for love of the other. That is true freedom, and the manifestation of a new humanity, and there is nothing sacrificial about it.

We see then how Paul thinks outside the box from a perspective that soars beyond debates arising from distinctions between sacred and profane. Such distinctions and the rivalries they generate (along with victims!) are passé. For Paul it is all about being "renewed in the spirit of your minds" (Eph. 5:23). When he instructs his congregations to "clothe yourselves with the new self, created according to the likeness of God in true righteousness and holiness" (Eph. 5:24), it is easy for interpreters to read into words like "righteousness" and "holiness" the typical conceptual trappings of the old sacred. But the "new" self is new precisely because such terms indicate something other than the old sacred.

For Paul the holiness of God has become what we see in *Jesus*, and previous perceptions of Yahweh are now altered almost beyond recognition. Holiness no longer has anything to do with the old distinction between sacred and profane. On the contrary, it means its abolition. For this reason, Paul's "holy" communities were ones in which differences were defined by the various gifts the Spirit bestowed upon each member, not by violent hierarchies and structures of exclusion. He compared the church to a human body with many parts, all of which are crucial to the healthy functioning of the organism, and none of which are privileged above the others.

(Ah, yes, one might object, it is all well and good to talk about the dismantling of exclusionary practices *within* the church itself, but what about the distinction between Paul's churches and the pagan world itself? "In Christ" there is no division between male and female, slave and free; but what about the division: "in Christ" versus "not in Christ?" Doesn't Paul still allow that division? In a sense, yes; but there is a big difference between a fellowship that establishes its core identity by excluding the evil other, and one that exists for the purpose of exposing that very device. If we must talk in terms of exclusion, then we might say that Paul's purpose was to exclude sacred exclusion; which, in an ironic way, is exclusionary – of exclusion itself.

Of course, there is a fine line to walk here. Once the principle of sacred exclusion is out in the open and understood, one can use it to scapegoat the scapegoaters. And it is true that Paul's churches very quickly fell short of the true spirit of Christ that had formed their communities in the first place, and at times operated in the old sacred mode – which led to all kinds of problems in the relations between pagans and Christians. But this would not have made Paul happy.)

It became Paul's privilege to carry this message and ministry into parts of the world where Jesus had neither time nor mandate to travel. What was merely hinted at in Jesus' token venture into Gerasa was now more fully realized in Paul's missionary excursions into Asia Minor, Greece, and Rome, where he constantly confronted various forms of sacred religion upheld by the three pillars of sacrifice, myth, and prohibition. Like Jesus in Gerasa, wherever Paul went he encountered "demoniacs" in need of humanization; and, like Jesus, he encountered major resistance from Jews and Gentiles alike. His own account of his sufferings in 2 Corinthians mentions: "...imprisonments, with countless floggings, and often near death. Five times I have received from the Jews the forty lashes minus one. Three times I was beaten with rods. Once I received a stoning." (11:23b-25a NRSV) He goes on to tell how "Three times I was shipwrecked; for a night and a day I was adrift at sea; on frequent journeys, in danger from rivers, danger from bandits, danger from my own people, danger from Gentiles, danger in the city, danger in the wilderness, danger at sea, danger from false brothers and sisters; in toil and hardship, through many a sleepless night, hungry and thirsty, often without food, cold and naked." (2 Cor. 11:25b-27 NRSV) But none of that mattered to Paul. He was on fire to reveal to the world what had been revealed to him. It flew directly in the face of the pillars of sacred religion, and it would eventually pull them down.

What pulled those pillars down was not some spiritual, abstract Savior, but Christ *crucified.* Christ's victory was accomplished precisely *as victim*. Thus Paul could write: "For Jews demand signs and Greeks seek wisdom, but we preach Christ crucified, a stumbling block to Jews and folly to Gentiles, but to those who are called, both Jews and Greeks, Christ the power of God and the wisdom of God." (1 Cor. 1:22-24) The "power" and "wisdom" of Christ consisted precisely in Christ's status as *crucified victim.* Paul says that it was the apparent absurdity of attributing wisdom and power to a crucified, cursed victim that made following Jesus an offense to Jews and a joke to Greeks. Yet this was the very heart of Paul's message. It was the innocent victim revealed to Paul, now raised by God and made Lord, which gave him his epiphany of the violent nature of the sacred, and empowered him to see and oppose the violent expulsion of the other. The church was to be the outpost of a new humanity in which differences were not constructed by scapegoating, but varieties of contribution to the general good. The only thing expelled was to be expulsion itself.

Christ the risen victim had become like a virus in the ancient software of the sacred, wreaking havoc with its meticulously excluding distinctions. And for a few wild and turbulent years, Paul was the main carrier of that virus. Eventually, computers would start to crash. Ancient civilization, especially in the West, was about to undergo a monumental transformation.

Chapter Eleven
Paradigm for a New Humanity

The Christians, O king, . . . do not do to others what they would not wish to be done to themselves. They comfort those who wrong them and make friends of them: they labour to do good to their enemies. . . . He that has gives freely to him who has not. If they see a stranger, they bring him under their roof and rejoice over him as if over their own brother: they call themselves brethren, not after the flesh but after the Sprit and in God.

Aristides, *Apology*, 15 (to the Emperor Hadrian, c. 130 A.D.)

Wherever texts speaking of a new form of humanity that refuses to seek vengeance, of those who love their enemies, of those who serve the Christ in the form of the needy brother or sister – wherever these texts are preserved, examined, heard, acted upon, then whatever the intentions of those who hold to narrow definitions of religion and culture, the texts will have their way; they will work in history.

James G. Williams, *The Bible, Violence, and the Sacred* [138]

‡‡

Historical Transformation

We are building toward Girard's understanding of our contemporary situation and its relation to apocalypse. In order to appreciate it more fully, however, it is helpful to understand how we arrived at the current crisis via the monumental transformation mentioned in the previous paragraph. That transformation occurred (and is occurring) for Girard at the level of what we might call "cultural leavening," a metaphor used by Paul (Gal. 5:9, 1 Cor. 5:6), who in turn was probably referencing Jesus' parable about the bit of leaven that leavens the whole loaf (Matt. 13:33, Luke 13:20-21). Whatever Girard might believe about eternal life and other theological dogmas, he is not himself a theologian. He works at the level of anthropology and is interested in how God works through the concretely human; and thus history becomes crucial. At a particular time and place there really was a person whose life really did impact the world in a way that changed everything, by revealing something that had never been revealed before, and doing something that had never been done before. We might think here of the mutation of one specific gene at a certain time and place, which over time gives rise to momentous historical consequences.

This is not to say that for Girard God is identical with human history as such; that history arose from founding murders and developed as a closed-system. God has to come in some sense from "outside" humanity, or from some undecideable abyss within it (as Anthony Bartlett would put it[139]), from some unfathomable depth that is beyond and utterly "other" than human history as it was known until Christ. God erupts, revelation "happens," in order to make us aware of that to which we are blind. Blind because, in a sense, our very eyes were formed by it.

This section, then, seeks to give a quick flavor of the transformation Jesus effected at the historical level. What he brought into the world was a joyous, positive thing; but it also destabilized the world in a way that could prove to be terminal, as we shall see, if we continue to play the Gerasenes in rejecting the miracle. But before we get there, let us take a brief look at the beginnings of the transformation of Western civilization. (The reader should note that in most of what follows in this section on the "New Humanity," I am not drawing directly upon Girard; I am, however, basing myself to the best of my knowledge on Girardian presuppositions.)

Paul, as shown above, was in the vanguard of those carrying the Good News. As we saw, his work began to deconstruct sacred divisions and hierarchies among people on the basis of his love for his crucified Lord. Others worked with him, and more were to follow. Peter himself was pushed, rather against his will, to recognize the full inclusiveness that being in Christ entailed. I wish everyone could read James Alison's wonderful exposition of the incident recorded in Acts 10, which tells the story of Peter's baptism of the Roman centurion Cornelius and his family. Alison calls that occasion "perhaps the most significant date in the history of the world outside Judaism."[140] Cornelius, a God-fearing Gentile, has a vision in which an angel tells him to send men to find and bring Peter to his house. Meanwhile, Peter has a vision in which in God commands him to kill and eat reptiles, birds, and animals that the Mosaic Law considers unclean – anathema! Peter, a faithful follower of Jesus, but still also of the Mosaic Law, responds, "Surely not, Lord! I have never eaten anything impure or unclean!" But the voice in the vision says to him "Do not call anything impure that God has made clean." The voice further tells him that men are about to arrive looking for him, and that he should go with them. Peter is obviously quite perplexed by this experience. The story continues:

> *The following day they came to Caesarea. Cornelius was expecting them and had called together his relatives and close friends. On Peter's arrival Cornelius met him, and falling at his feet, worshiped him. But Peter made him get up, saying, "Stand up; I am only a mortal." And as he talked with him, he went in and found that many had assembled; and he said to them, "You yourselves know that it is unlawful for a Jew to associate with or to visit a Gentile; but God has shown me that I should not call anyone profane or unclean. So when I was sent for, I came without objection. Now may I ask why you sent for me?"* (Acts 10: 24-29 NRSV)

The centurion relates the experience of his vision, and ends by saying, "Now we are all here in the presence of God to listen to everything the Lord has commanded you to tell us." As Alison points out, up until this point Peter had naturally assumed that the Jesus-story was essentially a Jewish story, for the benefit of Israel and those who converted to Judaism. Suddenly, he is as it were "pushed" into preaching the story of Jesus to unclean Gentiles into whose home he had believed it sacrilegious even to enter. These are people who live without the benefit of "nuclear power," who are not hooked up to the sacred power grid that emanates from the temple. They are profane. Yet as Peter relates to them the story of Jesus and the proclamation of forgiveness in his name, "the Holy Spirit came on all who heard the message. The circumcised believers who had come with Peter were astonished that the gift of the Holy Spirit had been poured out even on the Gentiles. For they heard them speaking in tongues and praising God. Then Peter said, 'Can anyone keep these people from being baptized with water? They have received the Holy Spirit just as we have.' So he ordered that they be baptized in the name of Jesus Christ. Then they asked Peter to stay with them for a few days." At this point Alison comments:

> *Peter hasn't even finished telling the story when already "The Holy Spirit fell on all who heard the word." This is the maximum moment of being disconcerted. That a holy story should be told to a group of the impure as something confrontational, something to make them feel bad about themselves so that they might purify themselves, maybe even going so far as to seek circumcision, is perfectly comprehensible. Yet, as you watch the story being told you notice that, rather than being confronted and downcast, the listeners all find themselves overwhelmed from within with a sense of delight, seeing the story as good news for themselves. That is seriously weird.*[141]

Seriously weird indeed, by all the standards of sacred holiness. It means that the story Peter tells is *not* holy at all; not, at least, in terms of a sacred understanding. Quite the contrary. As Peter is learning, the story of Jesus is the beginning of the end of the sacred and the divisions it erects to exclude the other. Alison calls this moment "a cultural earthquake of immeasurably great proportions." It is a moment in which Peter himself is learning the significance of his own message, and learning it from people his sacred religiosity had deemed profane. Cornelius and his family, meanwhile, have just gone from excluded, second-class outsiders to cozy insiders. "[W]e see the dawning realization that God likes the impure people, that God wants them to be on the inside of God's story just as they are. God is not confronting them to get them to repent, or even inviting them to become something else. God is possessing them with delight, and they are delighting in being possessed."[142] It is not, Alison says, that these previously impure Gentiles are seeking the approval of the authorities in order to be included: "They just find themselves on the inside of the story, starting to work out what it means. The 'authority' on the 'pure' side finds his world being deconstructed in what must have been a very muddling and painful way before recognizing that that deconstruction and that pain was a good thing, come from God, and not a loss of face, or of argument, or of principle."[143]

As we saw in the case of Paul, the proclamation of Jesus' death and resurrection destabilized more than the Jew-Gentile distinction. It birthed – at first in only a few hearts – a new sense of the "human" as such, and a completely new experience of community. And thus it began to destabilize the old civilizations. Jesus knew that his legacy would be a powerful leaven, destined to permeate and affect the entire human loaf. Call it leaven, call it a virus, call it a mustard seed that grows into a towering tree, call it fermenting wine that eventually explodes the old wineskins, call it the Holy Spirit – call it what you will, it entered the bloodstream of Western civilization as a first step toward changing the entire world's experience of being human.

The ways in which the "leaven" (to stick with one of Jesus' own metaphors) was transmitted through the human dough are so numerous that libraries of volumes have been written about the subject. The gospel spread by word of mouth, by written documents, by iconography, by incredibly daring missionary ventures into territories of tribes and clans as wild as those of the Celts, the Picts, the Franks, and the Saxons. It was also spread by kings and popes whose primary aim was simply to extend their dominions. Much of what these people transmitted was not the gospel, the really "Good News" that Jesus had come to deliver; quite the contrary, for *sacred religion* began to accumulate around the gospel almost from the beginning, like barnacles attaching themselves to a sunken treasure, sometimes obscuring it almost entirely. But not entirely. No matter how violent the Church became, it could not help but bear witness to the victim – through its own language and teachings – whose death and resurrection put the lie to its own violence. After all, it had in its hands the New Testament, which contained language that Rome had not been able to extinguish even when it opposed it directly. And when Rome finally stopped trying, and under Constantine did something far more damaging – made Christianity the empire's official religion, gathering together Christian elders from across the empire to elaborate an official orthodoxy – even then, burdened under layers and layers of sacred encrustation, the gospel could not be entirely tamed. The words were there.

Even in the medieval ages when illiteracy prevailed in the West, those words were at least preached, and often quite effectively. Medieval sermons display some of the highest quality of rhetoric ever produced in western civilization. But, even when words failed, the iconography of the crucifixion alone was capable of reaping a harvest of hearts. The sick held the crucifix in their hands and took courage. Illiterate peasants identified with it and were comforted, believing that God understood their suffering. The image of the Crucified became part of the culture, inescapably there for all to see, so that even those who felt no spiritual connection with it had nevertheless to look often upon the crucified victim, if only as part of a perfunctory religious ceremony, or as aesthetic contemplation of art. Yet no onlooker could ever be quite safe from gentle invasion by the image's proper meaning. One never knew when even the most impenitent of sinners would have a sudden change of heart, erupting with unexpected compassion. Such things could and did happen beyond the purview of official Christendom, spontaneously, and without fanfare, with results that can never be measured because only the spectacular results – the St. Francises, for example – are visible to the eyes of written history. The millions of small acts of charity, kindness, and forgiveness inspired by the Crucified have gone unrecorded.

The outstretched arms of Christ, who in the midst of his agony opens his arms to embrace even his enemies from the very cross to which they nailed him, evoked a response of imitation, opening the hearts of onlookers who began to feel differently about others, and found new vistas of compassion opening up for exploration quite as new and surprising as the "New World" was to Columbus.

Despite all the horrible things the Church did in the name of the cross, including emblazoning it upon the flags and shields of crusading knights, it was hard to turn Jesus into a warrior, and hard to turn the crucifix (as opposed to the bare cross) into a military symbol. Artemis and Diana had their bows, used for murdering humans as well as hunting animals, and Thor wielded his hammer; but the fact is that no matter how violent Christendom became it never dared create an image of Jesus wielding a halberd, or a mace, or a crossbow. It would have been patently absurd to everyone. There were limits in this regard that even popes could not cross. Even at its hypocritical worst, it was simply not possible for Christendom to turn Jesus into Thor.

True, the crucifix could be neutered of its significance as a sign of the victim. Jesus' torn body was cleaned up, abstracted, adorned in silver and gold, and used to justify a religion that gradually became steeped in the old sacred, more pagan than Christian. The crucifix was transformed into an aesthetic object and became a tool of sacred religion. Then Protestants glorified the naked cross, empty of the body, which made it even easier to forget Jesus' very real, grisly murder, and facilitated interpretations of the death of Christ as a purely spiritual transaction between Jesus and his Father.

Nevertheless, despite all of this the victim continued to speak to many hearts throughout the history of Christendom. And the West was never the same. One recalls Swinburne's famous line, "Thou hast conquered, O pale Galilean . . ." Swinburne did not mean this as a compliment. But it was certainly true enough. After Jesus, we have not been able to hide the innocent victim. Not entirely, not forever, not without difficulty. The more Jesus we have in our midst, the harder it is to hide the victim. The Church was stuck with a crucified, victim-God, even when it tried to dress him up as Christ Pantocrator, the stern and All-Powerful Judge.

Through many modalities, including the New Testament

documents, creeds, sermons, liturgies, monastic movements, lives and deeds of saints, and so on, a transformed understanding of what it means to be human was being carried into the world, sometimes haltingly, and sometimes for the worst of motives; but also sometimes from a deep wellspring of compassion and a transformed vision of the world. I say this contra the kind of presentation of history that we find in an eminent historian like Ramsey MacMullen,[144] who believes that early Christianity spread so quickly largely for accidental reasons (often political) that had nothing to do with the content of Christian belief or the impact of Christian behavior, which he claims was really nothing new. I believe that, on the contrary, Christianity birthed a profoundly new way of being human which had a deep impact upon ancient peoples. One does not have to be a believer to recognize this. Hubert Dreyfus, professor emeritus of philosophy at Berkeley, and Sean Dorrance Kelly, chairman of Yale's philosophy department, have this to say in their recent book, *All Things Shining:*

> *As he is described in the Gospels, Jesus totally transforms people's understanding of what it is to be a human being. This is a superhuman thing to do. Like a god the biblical Jesus reveals a new Christian World. … The central movements of the next nearly two thousands years of history in the West can be understood as attempts to spell out Jesus' understanding of human existence.*[145]

Dreyfus and Kelly recognize this even though they are advocating a return to pagan polytheism. (We will be taking a closer look at *All Things Shining* later.) Theologian David Bentley Hart notes that "even pagan critics of the church were aware of the astonishing range of Christians' exertions on behalf of others."[146] To be sure, Hart says, there had been in pagan culture a certain "theatrical lavishness" which had been part of the "patrician cultural code of honor," and rich men who desired a good reputation were expected to provide gifts and "grand displays of public largesse" on festal days; and occasionally emperors such as Nerva and Trajan would make attempts to improve the lot of the poor (hoping to halt population decline in order to keep the Roman armies well stocked). But, says Hart, "one finds nothing in pagan society remotely comparable in magnitude to the Christian willingness to provide continuously for persons in need, male and female, young and old, free and bound alike."[147] And this was because the compassion of Christ established a radically new valuation of human persons – *all* persons.

Hart considers that "the most radical novelty" of the Christian community in the first three centuries was that "it transcended and so, in an ultimate sense, annulled 'natural' human divisions."[148] He is talking about traditionally sacred hierarchies and their social categories of exclusion (male over female, free men over slaves, adults over children, and so on), which we saw Paul triumphantly, and Peter somewhat reluctantly, dismantling. In this they were imitating their Master. We have seen how Christ's life and teaching always sided with the victim; how, indeed, he put himself in the very place of the victim surrounded by mob violence and excluded from society, and maintained this position all the way to his final cry: "My God, my God, why have you forsaken me?" How then could imitating Christ not lead to spectacular attempts to accept, heal, and humanize the rejected and the marginalized, as Christ did for the Gerasene demoniac? Here we see possibly the most spectacular result of Christ's exposure of the scapegoat mechanism. When Jesus was resurrected *with the scars of his victimization still showing on his hands and side,* a new humanity arose with him. That humanity would be built, stone by stone, upon the foundation of the Jesus-stone, the stone which the builders rejected. If the old humanity was founded on victims, the new would be also – victims liberated, accepted, and welcomed!

Although the outpost and vanguard of that new humanity was the church, because of the blending of church and state in the history of Western civilization "the stone that the builders rejected" became intimately interwoven into the architecture of Western culture. Hart turns a wonderful phrase when he says that "…we are the heirs of a culture that, in a sense, sprang from Peter's tears."[149] He is referring to the famous story of Peter's emotional breakdown at the crowing of the cock, when he is forced to confront his betrayal of Jesus. The claim that our culture springs from Peter's tears refers to the fact that we are the inheritors of an ancient history of Christian values, which formed a truly radical break with the immemorial human past. The values associated with the crucified and risen Jesus gave a whole new valorization to individual human beings. It is worth quoting Hart's fine expression of the difference between this new Christian and old pagan view of the human individual:

> *To the literate classes of late antiquity . . . this tale of Peter weeping would more likely have seemed an aesthetic mistake; for Peter, as a rustic, could not possibly have been a worthy object of a well-bred man's sympathy, nor could his grief possibly have possessed the sort of tragic dignity necessary to make it worthy of anyone's notice. At most, the grief of a man of Peter's class might have had a place in comic literature: the querulous complaints of an indolent slave, the self-pitying expostulations of a witless peon, the anguished laments of a cuckolded taverner, and so on. Of course, in a tragic or epic setting a servant's tears might have been played as accompaniment to his master's sorrows, rather like the sympathetic whining of a devoted dog. But, when one compares this scene from the Gospels to the sort of emotional portraiture one finds in great Roman writers, comic or serious, one discovers – as the great literary critic Erich Auerbach noted half a century ago – that it is only in Peter that one sees "the image of a man in the highest and deepest and most tragic sense." Yet Peter remains, for all that, a Galilaean peasant. This is not merely a violation of good taste; it is an act of rebellion.*
>
> *This is not, obviously, a claim regarding the explicit intent of any of the evangelists. But even Christianity's most implacable modern critics should be willing to acknowledge that, in these texts and others like them, we see something beginning to emerge from darkness into full visibility, arguably for the first time in our history: the human person as such, invested with an intrinsic and inviolable dignity, and possessed of an infinite value. It would not even be implausible to argue that our very ability to speak of "persons" as we do is a consequence of the revolution in moral sensibility that Christianity brought about."*[150]

The new attitudes and values generated by the Christian community and the New Testament texts were truly subversive. "[I]t is all but impossible," says Hart, "for us to recover any real sense of the scandal that many pagans naturally felt at the bizarre prodigality with which the early Christians were willing to grant full humanity to persons of every class and condition, and of either sex."[151] A whole series of books could obviously be written in illustration of this, but perhaps I could cite just a couple of examples to give the flavor of the phenomenon. Jerome cites the example of a wealthy Roman named Fabiola, a fourth-century Christian woman who utterly changed her lifestyle as an expression of her repentance. "We are told that she sold off her considerable property holdings in order to found a hospital, to which she admitted the suffering sick and poor whom she gathered from the streets."[152] But this is the least of it. Jerome says:

> *Should I now recount the various calamities of human beings, the mutilated noses, eyes dug out, feet half burnt, ghastly hands, distended bellies, emaciated thighs, swollen legs, and maggots raging in eaten-away and rotting flesh? Did she [not] often wash the pus-filled discharge from wounds, which another person would not dare to look at? She would provide food to her patients with her own hand, and a barely-breathing corpse would be moistened with sips of liquid.*

Jerome did not expect every Christian to be able to do what Fabiola did. But he did hold her up as an example to be imitated by all Christians:

> *I know that many wealthy and devout persons, due to a weak stomach, perform compassion of this sort through the ministry of others and are merciful with [their] money, not with [their own] hand. I certainly do not blame them and would never construe their faintness of soul as a lack of faith. But while I pardon a squeamish stomach, I praise to heaven the zeal of a mind that is perfected.*[153]

My argument here is not that these values were ideally realized by the church as a whole; but we fail to realize what a miracle it is that these values existed at all, and that people became free to imagine such things – and, yes, at times actually *do* them, as in the case of Fabiola. In the ancient world, human beings had no intrinsic worth. To be at or near the bottom of the hierarchy was a horror. Of course situations varied by culture and time period, but usually it meant guaranteed suffering of physical and emotional abuse, while always walking the edge of becoming the day's convenient scapegoat. And the whole system had for millennia been upheld by the gods.

The motive force behind deeds such as Fabiola's that broke down the walls of separation that marginalized the poor, the shamed, the sick, and the ugly, was the understanding that *Christ was synonymous with the poor and marginalized.* ("Truly, I say to you, as you did it to one of the least of these my brethren, you did it to me." Matt. 25:40) And this led to the realization, stated by Jerome, that "The man whom we despise, whom we are unable to look at, even a glance at whom makes us vomit, is similar to us, is made of the same clay as we are, is formed out of the same elements." When Jesus redefined God as utterly nonviolent in contradistinction to all the gods ever conceived, he also radically revalued the individual as a beloved child of God. In imitation of him, human beings could now embark upon a path of liberation from the sacred violence of oppressive social structures, and from the panoply of violent divine overlords who, in exchange for helping control the community's mimetic passions, demanded a constant holocaust of human and animal victims.

Sacrificial Christianity and Atonement Theology

But if what has been said so far is true, one might ask why the subsequent history of the church is replete with the horror of violence, hatred, and bigotry? Why does a violent God seem to dominate so much of the action, and the sacred zealousness of Saul continue under the banner of Christ's church? Despite his praise of Fabiola, was not Jerome himself a participant in a hierarchical structure that was in no small measure violently patriarchal and oppressive? Certainly he was. But the failings of the church do not require one to participate in the modern intellectual frenzy of making Christianity a whipping boy, and refusing to acknowledge the astonishing freedom and infinite worth it brought to human beings. When the gospel was shining through it, the church produced a quality of charity and fellowship which was a radical departure from anything previously seen on the planet.

Once we have said that, however, we must admit and examine the phenomenon that Girard refers to as "sacrificial Christianity,"[154] by which he means Christianity mingled with sacred violence. "Modern intellectuals," writes Girard, "tend to confuse the deep meaning of the Gospel with the history of Christianity, which is fundamentally *the slow process of coping with the heritage of the sacred mentality and with our mimetic behavior.* Men could not possibly do away with the sacred altogether, dismissing at once the mentality they had lived with for thousands and thousands of years."[155] After all that has been said in this book, the term "sacrificial Christianity" may sound like something of an oxymoron: how can there be a sacrificial Christianity? How can sacrifice and Christianity be combined? Is not one of Girard's main theses that Christ brought a revelation that crippled, and eventually overthrew, sacrifice?

Indeed it is. But, as Girard points out in the above quote, the gospel had its work cut out for it. The sacred did not die easily (in fact, it continues to live on to this day in muted tones). The church had indeed made a clean break from both the Gentile and Hebrew past by ceasing to offer of sacrifices. The Christian communities Paul established throughout the western world formed their sense of community through an entirely new sensibility that did not involve rallying around sacrificial rituals. Nevertheless, sacrifice was a hard nut to crack. In some areas converted to Christianity sacrifice proved impossible to defeat. Walter Burkert cites an old German expression, "decked out like an ox at Pentecost," originally referring to an ox slaughtered during the Christian festival of Pentecost. He also says that the slaughter of a sheep in front of the church is still a feature of regular Sunday service in Soviet Armenia. (Burkert's book was published in 1972; I do not know if the practice still continues.) Then he gives us the following amazing account:

> *Isolated Greek communities in Cappadocia celebrated the ancient sacrificial ritual well into the twentieth century: opposite the conventional altar in the chapel of the saint would be a sacrificial altarstone, upon which incense was burned when candles were lit; during prayers, it would be decked with wreaths. The sacrificer would bring the animal – a goat or a sheep – into the chapel, leading it three times around the sacrificial stone while children threw grass and flowers onto it. As the priest stood at the altar, the keeper of the animal would make a sign of the cross with his knife three times and then slaughter the animal while praying. The blood was supposed to sprinkle the stone. After this, outside the chapel, the animal would be carved up and the feast prepared. The priest, like his ancient counterpart, received the animal's thigh and skin, as well as its head and feet.*[156]

Burkert goes on to say that "Christianity is here no more than a transparent cover for the ancient form that underlies it: that is to say, for the sacred act of blood-sacrifice." Indeed.

The persistence of actual sacrificial ritual within Christian churches, however, was an extremely rare phenomenon. Christianity virtually wiped it out. Sacrificial ways of *thinking,* on the other hand, were much more difficult to eradicate. Even after cessation of the rituals, the sacrificial *mentality* lived on within the church and asserted itself at various times and places as a way of solving problems, structuring hierarchies, creating theological doctrines, and more. When critics attack the Christian church for the violent aspects of its history, it is usually sacrificial Christianity they are attacking.

Jesus himself would have been the last one to be surprised by the infiltration of sacred violence into the church's theology and practice. Girard remarks:

> *The most extraordinary thing is that Jesus knew this from the beginning. If you read the Gospel, everything is already there. Jesus appoints Peter as the founding father of the Church. Peter is the most mimetic of his disciples, the apostle who denied Christ not once, but three times. In the Gethsemane episode, when a group of*

armed men come to arrest Jesus, Peter takes his sword and strikes the servant of the high priest, cutting off his ear. "Put your sword back in its place," Jesus says to him, "for all who draw the sword will die by the sword" (Matthew 26:52). Again, this is a warning against the mimetic reciprocity of violence. Man has a tendency to relapse into the sacred, prompting violence to defend any idea or principle seen simply as sacred. Christ is aware of this and strongly opposes it.[157]

Jesus was quite aware that his followers were imbued with sacred religion. And judging from his parable of the dough that must undergo a process of leavening, and his prayers for Peter that his faith might not fail him when Satan "sifts him like wheat" (Luke 22:31), Jesus seems to have anticipated a long struggle. As Girard indicates, "It took centuries for the Western world to acquire a Christian sensibility."[158] Girard seems to talk at times as though the inevitability of this process exonerated the church of full responsibility, and in this he has been taken to task by at least one Girardian scholar.[159] Putting the issue of responsibility to one side, however, the development of a sacrificial Christianity is certainly not surprising.

Undergirding, justifying, and in some cases motivating violent thought and practice within the church was (and is) what Girard calls the "sacrificial reading" of the New Testament: "I believe it is possible to demonstrate that historical Christianity took on a persecutory character as a result of the sacrificial reading of the Passion and Redemption."[160] A sacrificial reading of the Passion and Redemption means an interpretation of Jesus' death that validates the concept of sacrifice (e.g., Jesus died because God the Father required his death as a sacrifice for sin), thus imputing violence to God. In propounding this kind of theology, the church was imitating the sacred violence it inherited from the pagan world, and preparing the way for Christian militancy – and eventually the Crusades.

Girard has made it clear that he is not a theologian. In *Things Hidden* he critiqued sacrificial atonement theology, but the analysis has been performed with much greater depth by Protestant

Girardian scholars like Anthony Bartlett and Michael Hardin who, in addition to their books addressing the topic, have websites and offer seminars called "The Nonviolent Atonement." (It was at one of these seminars that I first met both men.) Interested readers should pursue their work.[161]

Now, it must be admitted that sacrifice appears as a way of interpreting the meaning of Christ's death in the New Testament itself. The author of the book of Hebrews, for instance, laid out a scheme in which Christ's death functioned as the final, climactic sacrifice in the long history of the Hebrew sacrificial cult. Since Christ was without blemish, the perfect Son of God, he could be the true and final sacrifice in contrast to the untold thousands of animals whose blood was not valuable enough to do anything more than temporarily defer the punishing wrath of God. According to Hebrews, it was the blood of God's own perfect Son, not animals, which secured for us eternal life and vitiated the need for any more sacrificial offerings.

It is important to realize, however, the irony of this perspective in the book of Hebrews. While the book endorses the concept of sacrifice, its real purpose is to declare it a defunct institution. Yes, the author is still thinking sacrificially. That is, he wants to continue using sacrificial concepts as a way of comprehending the death of Christ; *but his real purpose is anti-sacrificial.* He wants to tell us about a sacrifice that *ends all sacrifice,* and he is doing so using the sacrificial images and concepts with which he is intimately familiar. Could the author have lived a few more decades and broadened his Christian horizons beyond their narrowly Jewish contours, he would probably have looked back on his Hebrews treatise as an "early work." He would have recognized it as a deconstructive work that cut the sacrificial branch out from under itself. In this respect I agree with Stephan Finlan rather than Michael Hardin, that the author of Hebrews is not rejecting sacrificial logic altogether. Rather, as Finlan states, "This does seem to be a case where a writer's discourse leads to conclusions that go beyond his own awareness. Hebrews goes so far as to say that the new covenant 'has made the first one obsolete' (8:13), and now 'the time comes to set things right' (9:10). The new not only fulfills the old; it replaces it. This is a discourse of supersession (replacement). Hebrews is aware of this but does not seem to realize that real supersession, a real "setting things right," would mean going beyond sacrificial thinking altogether." [162]

Unfortunately, there is a very thin line between the deconstructive sacrificial thinking we find in the book of Hebrews – which is essentially anti-sacrificial in nature – and sacrificial thinking generative of sacred violence. This latter is the direction in which certain violent minds took theology of atonement. We need to remember that the interpretation of Jesus' death as a sacrifice demanded by God in exchange for forgiveness of sins (the so-called "satisfaction" and "penal substitution" theories of atonement being the main versions), was only one way in which the early church tried to understand the meaning of Jesus' crucifixion. Some theologians of the early church understood Jesus' death primarily as the means by which Christ overthrew the devil (an interpretation known as "Christus Victor"). Others understood it as an exemplary demonstration God's love meant to change human hearts (classically known as the "moral influence" theory of the atonement).

For many centuries these views, along with other variants, were all fluidly on the table for consideration and edification. It was not until just after the end of the first millennium that the satisfaction theory of atonement began to grab the attention of elite medieval theologians in such a way as to become the dominant explanation for Christ's death.[163] To this day neither the Roman Catholic Church nor the mainline Protestant denominations have made any particular atonement theory authoritatively binding on theologians; however, some variety of penal substitution theory has become the hands-down *de facto* winner among orthodox Catholics and Protestant Fundamentalists and Evangelicals. Especially these Protestant groups hardly recognize a believer as Christian unless he or she confesses that Jesus died as a sacrifice to appease the wrath of God the Father for the forgiveness of sins.

Living with this view of Jesus' death has never been easy for the church, as evidenced by the ongoing attempts over the years to mitigate the divine violence inherent within such atonement theologies. Most popular is the attempt to explain it in terms of divine justice: even though God is love, he is also just, and must balance love's compassion with justice's demands. By dumping the punishment for our sin onto Jesus, God both satisfies the demands of his justice (sin gets punished) and allows his loving kindness to flow freely to those who ask forgiveness. This takes care of the problem for those who have no issue with violence so long as it is administered in the name of "justice." But in fact it brings us right back to what Michael Hardin calls the "Janus-faced God," the schizoid God who is on the one hand a loving, forgiving, and merciful Christ figure, and on the other a terrifying, wrathful, violent figure capable of eternally torturing those who refuse to accept his gift of grace. (And this is supposed to satisfy his "justice!")

The Janus-faced God slipping into Christian theology opened the door for all kinds of church perpetrated violence. After all, once the unalloyed message of 1 John that "God is love" is blended with the notion of a violent God, whether that violence is conceived as wrath, anger, vengeance, punishment, or "bringing to justice," it cannot be long before the followers of that God begin to think and act violently: in the name of God expressing their own wrath, anger, vengeance, and punishment, keen on bringing evildoers to justice, and using theology to justify an urge to violence that they never completely surrendered in the act of conversion. The nonviolent Jesus can always be ignored or rationalized away, trumped by the ever-popular idea of a God who doesn't forgive one's damned enemies, but pounds them, gives them their comeuppance, and "brings them to justice." This kind of god is a Siamese twin: one head is named Jesus, and the other Clint Eastwood.

Because atonement is a "hot issue" today, and because Girard's perspective (and that of other Girardian scholars) is so valuable, it is worth exploring this in a little more depth before pressing on to Girard's take on the contemporary world. Doing so will help us better understand how Christianity gave its modern enemies so much fodder to blast it with; and a Girardian perspective on atonement may be a welcomed change for readers who have grappled with traditional violent atonement theology.

The popularity of satisfaction atonement theology began with the publication of an erudite and eloquent treatise, *Cur Deus Homo* ("Why God Man?"), written by Anselm, Benedictine monk and Archbishop of Canterbury (*c.*1033–1109). As the title implies, in *Cur Deus Homo* Anselm tried to explain why God became human in Jesus Christ. The treatise grabbed the attention of theological thinkers immediately, and became a medieval "best seller." It became the classic statement of the satisfaction theory of atonement, leading to the *de facto* dominance of that theory within the Roman church for the next thousand years.

Five hundred years after Anselm, Luther put a legal spin on matters, developing the penal substitution theory, variations of which became dominant within Protestant churches. (We need not go deeply into the differences between "satisfaction" and "penal substitution" theories here. In one case what is required is satisfaction for effacing God's honor; in the other case it is a matter of incurring a legal debt by breaking God's law. The important thing is that they both posit a debt owed to God by humanity, which incurs God's wrath, and which humanity cannot pay. The wrath ends up falling not upon the deserving culprits, but upon God himself in the person of the Son, Jesus Christ. Both varieties envision violence within the very heart of the divine nature.)

In his excellent book on the history of atonement doctrine, *Cross-Purposes: The Violent Grammar of Christian Atonement,* Anthony Bartlett relates an incident which helps us grasp the interrelationship between violence and Anselm's atonement theology.[164] In 1098, having left England and living at the time near Rome, Anselm was in the process of finishing *Cur Deus Homo* when he was invited by a Norman knight named Roger of Apulia to witness a nearby siege he was conducting. Pope Urban II also attended. (This was the Pope who two years previously had initiated the First Crusade as a holy war against Muslims to liberate Jerusalem.) Roger set up special tents for Anselm and Urban, safely removed from the battleground, from which they could comfortably observe the slaughter. Invoking this scene, Bartlett comments on the picture of "two eminent churchmen so much at ease with a warrior aristocracy and assisting at a cruel act of war almost as entertainment."[165] Bartlett goes on to argue, persuasively I believe, for a cultural "organic context" within which the satisfaction atonement theory Anselm laid out in *Cur Deus Homo* made sense, a context involving the militarization of the church and the transformation of local chiefs and their armed gangs into Christian knights.

A truly pivotal shift had occurred not long before the events of the First Crusade when Gregory VII had propounded the idea of *penitential warfare,* which promised that knights fighting on the Pope's behalf against the Holy Roman Emperor would receive an eternal reward. A few years later, Pope Urban II, who observed Roger of Apulia's battle siege alongside Anselm, would make participation in the First Crusade a means for warriors to obtain forgiveness of all their sins. It is a simple logic of exchange, a *quid pro quo*: give God your suffering, endurance, and strength (and possibly your life) during the journey to Jerusalem and the battle against the Muslims, and God will grant forgiveness for all your sins. "...the warrior holds an irrescusable claim on divine forgiveness, because his whole life has been thrown into the bargain, over an extended period involving extreme hardship and danger."[166] Bartlett asks:

> *Anselm had contact with the court of the Norman kings of England, both indirectly and directly during the 1080s onward, as well as being abbot of an important monastery that would certainly have experienced a trickle-down of news and attitudes working through Christendom. Would an intelligence as sharp and sensitive as Anselm's have missed the emergence of a pivotal idea like meritorious violence? Or, perhaps we should say that out of the permeating warrior ethos of the time Anselm distilled his own version, parallel to that of the pope?*

The essential idea operating in Anselm's approach to atonement – that Christ lays down his life to restore God's honor, obtaining satisfaction for the injury done by humanity's sins – is "...the theological sophistication of a thought that was coalescing at that very moment in the preparation of the First Crusade."[167] The warrior suffers, risks death, and possibly dies in order to restore God's honor in the Holy Land, and obtain forgiveness of his sins. The model that Anselm imitates when developing his atonement theology was the warrior ethos of his culture. As Anthony Bartlett says in *Virtually Christian*, "It is unfathomably ironic that the icon of human non-retaliation, Jesus' cross, gets turned in the tradition into a supreme piece of vengeance – God's 'just' punishment of Jesus in our place."[168]

A contemporary of Anselm's named Peter Abelard looked at things in a vastly different way than Anselm. His understanding of the atonement has come to be called the "moral influence" theory, and although we have no space to go into it, it is worth noting its compatibility with the Girardian perspective. Abelard saw it as God's will that Jesus undergo suffering and death, not because God needed it to satisfy his injured honor, but because *we* needed it. God poured himself out for us in order to show us how much love he has for us, and to move our hearts to repentance. Certainly an interpretation along these lines makes excellent sense from a Girardian point of view, especially when combined with the "Christus Victor" view of atonement which interprets Jesus' death as a means of defeating Satan.

Combining Girard, Abelard, and Christus Victor, I would say that by nonviolently expressing limitless compassion and forgiveness in the face of human abuse, Jesus exposed the scapegoat mechanism and made himself the model for a new humanity. Imitation of Christ rewires our violent neuro-circuitry, links us together in community, and reconciles us to God. In the process, the Satan of anarchic mimetic rivalry and the Satan of sacred violence are both cast out. Christus Victor!

Jesus' death was indeed essential to God's purpose of liberating humanity, and Jesus knew this. In the Gospels he is presented as knowing crucifixion to be his Father's will, and his desire was to please that will. "For this reason the Father loves me, because I lay down my life, that I may take it again. No one takes it from me, but I lay it down of my own accord." (John 10:17-18) Among the olive trees on the night he was betrayed, when Jesus prayed that his Father would "let this cup pass from me" (i.e., the cup of human wrath), he added: "Nevertheless, not my will but thine be done." His own deliberate actions had brought him to this dilemma. When he overturned the tables of the moneychangers, bringing the sacrificial operation of the Jerusalem temple to a halt for a few minutes, he placed himself "purposely and calculatedly in the cross-hairs" as Anthony Bartlett puts it.[169] It was his high profile, anti-sacrificial performance in the temple that sealed Jesus' fate in the eyes of the authorities. His willing surrender to the arrest that followed soon after was an act of self-giving deliberately undertaken as a means of revealing the true God, the God who has nothing in common with the gods of sacred violence, the God Jesus loved to call his "Abba" – the nonviolent, compassionately forgiving God. As Girard has famously written, "A nonviolent deity can only signal his existence to mankind by having himself driven out by violence – by demonstrating that he is not able to establish himself in the Kingdom of Violence."[170]

The word *atonement* first appears in print in Tyndale's 1526 translation of the English Bible. It means, literally, "at-one-ment," being a contraction of "at" and "one." In other words, it means reconciliation. But we must bear in mind that while Jesus effected a reconciliation of humanity to God, God had no need to be reconciled to us. The rivalry had been all on one side; from God's side there had always been unconditional love. Jesus' death and resurrection has given us access to that love, as a result of the opening of our hearts in response to his infinite forgiveness. In the place where our envy and anger should have been met with reciprocal violence, it encountered instead an absolutely unlimited font of compassionate forgiveness. As Paul wrote, "God's love has been poured into our hearts…" (Romans 5:5) It was a great victory over the devil of mimetic rivalry and the satanic scapegoat mechanism. Something like this, I believe, is the meaning of "atonement."

Chapter Twelve

Apocalypse and the Contemporary Situation

[T]he lesson of the Bible is precisely that the culture born of violence must return to violence.

René Girard, *Things Hidden* [171]

[T]he nonviolence of the cross pushes the envelope of the world in a completely new direction and we live in the space of its pushing.

Anthony Bartlett, *Virtually Christian* [172]

‡‡

Apocalypse: Human, All Too Human

We have looked at the massive inertia of sacred religion carried into Christianity by those who could not or would not be transformed by the full, radical implications of the gospel. Thus the church set itself up to be reviled. We can agree with Anthony Bartlett when he describes the history of Christianity as one continual, protracted "mimetic crisis." As he puts it, "...the history of Christianity is a history of crisis, provoked by its own internal struggle and frequent failure before the figure of the Crucified. Thus it stands historically under judgment from its own central motif and message."[173] This crisis can be described as a kind of ongoing sacrificial crisis because it stemmed from the inability of the church to establish the monolithic, totalizing presence that sacred violence achieved for ancient civilizations. Those cultures did not have to cope with the nagging, contrary presence of the Crucified. That victim stood nakedly revealed at the very heart of the church's life and message, even when the church turned it a blind eye. To do that, the church had somehow to suppress its own "central motif and message," which proved ultimately impossible. No matter how dramatically the church resorted to sacred violence, it could not credibly give Jesus an "extreme makeover" as a mace-wielding knight-in-arms. Even a venture in sacred violence as dramatic as the Crusades could not achieve for Christendom the monolithic stability of the ancient civilizations, no matter how badly Urban II's Vatican wanted to imitate Caesar's Rome. For the church was inwardly conflicted. If it refused to become what God had called it to be, neither could it become completely what it desired. Says Bartlett, "[T]he institution of Christendom is a sophisticated reculturation of the gospel Passion within the forces of sacred violence… [B]ut cultural Christianity was unable to sustain its foundation thus constructed; precisely, and above all, because of its *own* central symbols and texts, its sacrificial reformulation was always undermined from within."[174] Thus, as Bartlett indicates, Christendom turned to "greater and greater paroxysms of violence" as it sought to solve its own inner contradictions by recourse to the violent scapegoating of Jews and Muslims.

Nevertheless, the yeast's transforming work in the dough could not be impeded. The nonviolent Christ had entered deeply into Western consciousness, sometimes producing meteoric effects through the likes of a Fabiola or a St. Francis, other times becoming a thorn in the flesh of violent ambitions that had to work overtime to suppress the sting of conscience. The gospel was in the culture-altering business, whether it was accepted or rejected. Either way it produced results. Either way, a dynamic process was introduced into what was once a timeless, stable structure. We can hardly imagine what a dramatic cultural transformation Gerasene society would have experienced had they welcomed Jesus. But the fact that they didn't does not mean they were left unaffected. Their rejection of Christ would come back to haunt them through the presence of their transformed demoniac, and where stable relations once existed, a dynamic dislocation now intruded. Following this cultural path, leavened by the gospel to produce both positive and negative effects, we have arrived at our present age, inheritor of two thousand years of Christian history and influence. And we must ask where all this leaves us today. It is when we pose this question that we begin to see the (potentially terrifying) relevance of Girard's work.

Considering Girard's status as one of France's most esteemed intellects, inducted in 2005 into the Académie française (along with the likes of Voltaire, Racine, and Victor Hugo), it is remarkable to read a statement such as the following, which an unsuspecting reader might deem to have come from the mouth of a Fundamentalist Christian: "For me, any understanding of the contemporary world is mediated by the reading of Matthew 24."[175] Chapter 24 of Matthew's Gospel is sometimes called the "little apocalypse" (a version appears also in Mark). This is where Jesus answers his disciples' questions about the end of the world, filling them in on what to expect from the future. Girard is no Fundamentalist, yet he takes Matthew 24 with utmost seriousness, and believes in the possibility, even the probability, of an eruption of apocalyptic, end-of-the-world violence. The key point for Girard, however, in contradistinction to typical religious readings of Matthew, is that the apocalyptic violence will not be God's work, but entirely *our own*. It will be the result of an escalation to extremes, provoked by the mimetic mirroring of rivals no longer capable of resolving disputes at the expense of sacrificed scapegoats. In a world where nobody can be sacrificed for the sake of the general good, the general good will destroy itself unless it can find an alternate way to resolve rivalries.

Before we flesh this out with a fuller discussion of the contemporary situation, we need to answer a question which might already have occurred to some readers: "What about all those biblical texts that show *God* as the one who ends history, destroying the world in a fit of apocalyptic rage?" Since this question may nag some readers throughout the rest of this book, it is as well to deal with it here. Of course there is no space in a book of this size to examine all the texts that come to mind in this connection, but a brief look at Matthew 24, which Girard said must be taken into account in any evaluation of the contemporary situation, and perhaps a glance at Revelation, will at least give the reader a flavor of some Girardian approaches to the question of such texts.

The Matthew 24 discourse begins with the disciples asking Jesus, "Tell us, when will this be, and what will be the sign of your coming and of the close of the age?" They are asking two big questions about the end of history: *when* will it happen, and *what* will be its signs. Jesus answers by warning his disciples not to be led astray, since many false Messiahs will appear, and then says, "And you will hear of wars and rumors of wars; see that you are not alarmed; for this must take place, but the end is not yet. For nation will rise against nation, and kingdom against kingdom, and there will be famines and earthquakes in various places: all this is but the beginning of the birth-pangs." (24:6-8) In other words, what is to come is "business as usual": natural disasters and human violence. The violence will both persecute, and infect, Jesus' followers: "Then they will deliver you up to tribulation, and put you to death; and you will be hated by all nations for my name's sake. And then many will fall away, and betray one another, and hate one another. And many false prophets will arise and lead many astray." (24:9-11) Jesus indicates a kind of cumulative effect through time: "And because wickedness is multiplied, most men's love will grow cold. But he who endures to the end will be saved. And this gospel of the kingdom will be preached throughout the whole world, as a testimony to all nations; and then the end will come." (24:12-14)

The important point to note is that Jesus has said nothing in any of this to implicate God in the violence. In Jesus' presentation of history, even earthquakes and famines are desacralized. He does not say that God will send famine and earthquake as prosecutors of his vengeance and wrath. For Jesus, *these are just things that happen.* It is as though he is saying to his disciples what we have all read on bumper stickers: Shit Happens. Don't sacralize it. Don't invest it with mythological significance.

Jesus does indicate two things, however, which are *not* business as usual, but truly unique occurrences in history: the gospel spreading throughout the world, and the world increasing in "wickedness," or violence. He then proceeds to give an ominous description of what appears to be the destruction of Jerusalem in 70 A.D by the Romans, mixed with a bit of poetic apocalyptic imagery about the sun being darkened and stars falling from the sky. Jesus makes use of the kind of apocalyptic imagery with which his listeners would have been familiar; but we must realize that at the same time *he is subverting it by draining it of sacred violence.* This subversion works because Jesus uses apocalyptic imagery in a context that subtly assimilates it to human rather than divine violence. (For another example in the New Testament of this kind of mixing of celestial apocalyptic imagery with a current, nonviolent event, see Acts 2:14-21, where Peter quotes a text from the prophet Joel about the sun turning to darkness and the moon to blood, and applies it to the phenomenon of Pentecost, even though, obviously, the moon was not literally bleeding on that day, nor was it dark.)

Jesus' discourse in Matthew 24 suggests the same scenario Girard sees unfolding in the contemporary world: *a waxing of human violence accompanying a waning of the sacred.* Being familiar with Girard, we should be able to understand why: when, thanks to the work of Jesus Christ, we can no longer project our violence onto the gods, or "God," when the sacred can no longer exercise monopolistic control over culture, keeping our violence at bay, that violence will erupt from its true source – literally "with a vengeance."

The Book of Revelation looms large in most people's imagination as undeniable proof of the violence of the Christian God, so it seems important at least to touch on the subject here. First, Revelation *does* contain tons of violent imagery. But why? Is it because the text wants to make a theological statement about God's violence against his enemies? Some interpreters believe the violent language is there for another reason. We have to remember that for all the amazing bravery and faith that many Christians showed in the Roman Colosseum and other similar situations of persecution, those who joined the ranks of the fledgling Christian movement were, after all, human beings like ourselves. No doubt they got angry and experienced outrage. No doubt they struggled with their desire for vengeance against their persecutors. At times they were terrified. They suffered extreme loss and grief. And some of them lost faith and fell away. Not everyone is a saint. (And as we learned from the recent publication of Mother Teresa's journals, the reverse is also true: saints are human!) The violence in Revelation, in other words, had a cathartic effect for the persecuted congregations to whom it was originally read. Oppressors are defeated and empires are crushed, allowing the listeners to blow off steam and get a hit of cathartic victory while imagining the defeat of their persecutors. *But at the same time the book is subtly subverting the violence inherent within all of that.* Revelation is really quite a masterpiece of subversion. It allowed early Christian congregations to experience a cathartic release of less than Christ-like emotions at an imaginary, poetic level, while at the same time structuring the whole work within a theological framework that undermines the violence from within through its ironic juxtaposition of images. Of course, John may have been no more consciously aware of this process than the book's first audiences – or most of those who have read and studied the book ever since.

What, for example, are we to make of the expression – a key one for Revelation – "the wrath of the Lamb?" Those who believe in a violent God always take "wrath" to be the controlling concept here, so that wrath comes to determine the nature of the Lamb. But what if it is meant to function the other way around? What if the Lamb determines the nature of the wrath? After all, the Lamb is the real "hero" of the book, mentioned twenty-nine times, and an obvious image of nonviolence. The idea of a lamb being wrathful is ludicrous. I once slit a sheep's throat during a survival trek I took in the mountains of Utah, the only animal I have ever killed in my life. It just stood there while I held the knife, its body trembling with fear, and waited for the end. I realized then the utter appropriateness of calling Jesus the "lamb of God" when he submitted himself nonviolently to human violence. What we really have in the phrase "the wrath of the Lamb" is an ironic use of language which is meant to subtly undermine the whole concept of a violent, wrathful God. Anthony Bartlett summarizes matters better than anyone else I have read on the subject:

> *We learn that the Lamb holds the key to human history, opening its seals to reveal its purpose and meaning, including its intense inner violence. The Lamb is able to do this because it represents a completely different human/divine way of responding, other than that of violence. At the same time, precisely because of this revelation, all hell (literally) breaks out around the Lamb. The old world system – the Beast – does not remain indifferent to the introduction of a new way and the absolute challenge it makes, but reacts with continually redoubled violence. At the end of the book there is a final battle when the Beast and the kings of the earth with their armies are all slain by a figure called the Word of God, by the sword which comes from his mouth. But directly afterwards the new earth and the city of the Lamb welcome and heal these very kings and nations which have just been slain! The only figures not to be restored are the Beast and its prophet which represent the system of violence, the imperial order with its ideological apparatus of cult and worship.*[176] (Underlining mine.)

Earlier I stressed how obviously ludicrous it would have been to represent Jesus wielding a halberd or a mace. The Revelation text Bartlett references does not contradict that. Jesus is indeed represented as riding into battle; but the sword comes out of his *mouth,* and is a symbolic representation for his nonviolent Word. As we all know, Jesus could get angry, and he could express himself with anger, but he was never violent, even in the temple. His wrath was the wrath of a lamb.

Now, we can do what interpreters throughout the ages have done with the book of Revelation. We can make God into Siamese Twins named "Lion" and "Lamb," reconstituting the Janus-faced God who is both "just" and "merciful," violent and loving, depending upon which face confronts us in the moment. We can keep the Father pure in his righteous wrath, uncontaminated by

Jesus' compassionate forgiveness, so that in the end we have a God who will forgive those like ourselves who deserve forgiveness because they accepted it, but who will also "kick butt" on our behalf. But when we are tempted to do this, we need to remember Philip's question to Jesus: "Lord, show us the Father and we shall be satisfied." With these words Philip was asking the same thing the early Christians for whom Revelation was first written were tempted to ask, and indeed what we are all no doubt tempted at times to ask Jesus: "Show us the Father!" This is a way of saying "When are you finally going to stop this forgiveness stuff, Jesus? We're ready to hear the *Father* say to our enemies: 'Go ahead, make my day.' Because we know what will follow then! And it's high time those unrepentant baddies get their comeuppance. When is the Father going to kick butt? We're not getting from you the satisfaction we crave from God. We want some serious bringing to justice. Show us the Father! We want a hearing with the Old Man!"

But here is Jesus' response: "Have I been with you so long, and yet you do not know me, Philip? He who has seen me *has* seen the Father. How can you say, 'Show us the Father?'" (John 14:9) Jesus' very presence among the disciples has been an ongoing subversion of their ideas about God. Most of the time he was patient with them. Occasionally, however, as in John 14:9, he seems to lose a bit of that patience: "Have I been with you so long...!" But of course Jesus had no illusions about what he was up against. He was up against the sacred, and everything that had grown from the founding murder and the scapegoat mechanism: the whole of human culture, including human language itself. And he could not overthrow it violently; he could not use Satan to cast out Satan. What he could do was allow himself to be violently expelled from the human world, so that the ghost of his presence, the Holy Ghost, could return at the chemical level like yeast in a lump of dough to slowly transform the world, subtly altering the chemical composition of the violent structures within which we live and move and have our being. Revelation is an example of the work of that yeast in progress. It uses violence the way the book of Hebrews uses sacrifice: to cut the branch from under itself.

This short review of Matthew 24 and Revelation have shown

two ways in which New Testament texts that seem to evidence God's sacred violence can really be about something else entirely. Some texts upon closer examination are discovered to have nothing to do with divine violence, and it is only because we come to them with preconceived theological notions that we think they attribute to God the violence of which they speak. In other texts, such as the book of Revelation, images of sacred violence are indeed present, but are used ironically, and are undergoing assimilation to a new perspective. Girardian scholars approach New Testament texts that seem to attribute violence to God in various ways, but these are two important ones to bear in mind.

Society Without Sacrifice: The Victim Revealed

Girard's understanding of apocalypse as *human,* not divine violence really begins with the elimination of ritual sacrifice. As we have seen, the gospel spectacularly ended sacrifice in the West, and then progressively in other cultures touched by missionary activity. "Wherever the Gospels take root, blood sacrifices disappear forever."[177] But, as we have seen, even when sacrifice was mostly eliminated in the West, sacrificial thinking remained. It took much longer for the gospel to deal with that, and in fact it is still a work in progress. However – and this is crucial – that work progressed spectacularly in the 20th century, especially after World War II, and has now spread far beyond the West to become a global phenomenon. The agent responsible for this worldwide challenge to sacrificial practice and thinking is the gospel's revelation of the innocent victim.

Knowledge of and concern for victims had been increasingly in play throughout the last few centuries, according to Girard, but was confused with the excess baggage of various ideologies (like Marxism, for instance) which have now been largely discredited. The idea of the victim *as such* has now come into its own as an *absolute, universal value*. The contemporary world is alive, like no other civilization in history, to the issue of victimization. We advocate for the rights of victims, we search out victims, we try to outdo one another in saving victims. We see victims everywhere, even in the animal and vegetable kingdoms. This is as true for nations as it is for individuals. When there is a natural disaster, all countries feel obliged to pitch in, sending aid, workers, psychologists, financial relief – whatever is needed. Even large corporate entities must pitch in and tout their humanitarian good will if they are to appear legitimate in today's world. In a 2006 interview with Krista Tippett, host of NPR show *On Being,* Harvard professor of business administration Rosabeth Moss Kanter pointed to the different atmosphere at the World Economic Forum in Davos in recent years. Companies were no longer boasting of their wealth and power, she said, but were in earnest to announce their contributions to the relief of world poverty, or assistance to victims of natural disasters.[178]

While victim-rhetoric has been associated with political liberalism, it is just as crucial to the political right as to the left. Both are fearful of appearing as persecutors of innocent victims. In Girard's words, "[T]he victimary principle or the defense of the victims has become holy: *it is the absolute.* One will never see anyone attacking it. They do not even have to mention it. So we can say we are all believers in the innocence of the victims, which is at the core of Christianity."[179] This is so true that it has become the object of jokes. A few days after writing the above lines, a friend sent me an email which had the following quote in small type at the bottom: *"No trees were harmed in the sending of this email. However, for a few nano-seconds, billions of innocent electrons were seriously inconvenienced."* From elephants to environment to electrons, we have become ultra-vigilant about victims.

Even the military is affected. Dave Grossman is one of the world's foremost experts on the psychology of combat. He is on the road, he says, 300 days a year training military units to have what he calls a "bulletproof mind." In his book, *Combat,* Grossman makes the following startling observation: "Men have been at war for millennia, but only today have we discovered, or been willing to talk about, the reality of combat."[180] What accounts for this watershed historical change, so that only now are people discovering and talking about the reality of war? What obscured that reality in the past? The answer is myth, which always hides the victim. But in our society, consciousness of the victim is overwhelming the last remaining vestiges of the mythology of war. And the victims Grossman studies and helps are the *soldiers themselves*: not just the wounded soldiers, or the slain soldiers, but all soldiers who participate in combat and must suffer and wrestle with the spiritual and psychological fallout.

It turns out that helping soldiers achieve a "bulletproof mind" is getting tougher. A recent article in Newsweek begins with the tag line: "Moral Injury. Soldiers are supposed to be tough, cool, and ethically confident. But what happens when they have seen and done things that haunt their consciences? New studies suggest that the pain of guilt may be a key factor in the rise of PTSD [post-traumatic stress syndrome]."[181] I am not suggesting that soldiers never had qualms about their actions in war before the twenty-first century. Of course they did. But something different is happening today, at least in the United States military. The article says that America's veterans are getting worse: "Self-harm is now the leading cause of death for members of the Army, which has seen its suicide rate double since 2004. . . ." Secretary of Defense Leon Panetta is quoted as saying, "It's an epidemic . . . Something is wrong." And we are told that the single greatest risk factor for PTSD – bigger even than heavy combat – is *killing.*

We must step back and try to appreciate, first of all, what it means to be a society that even *cares* about this kind of stuff. Of course, part of the concern comes from the very modern desire to maximize efficiency; but I believe that concern for veterans and soldiers is just one more instance of the endless ramifying within our society (and increasingly in the world) of victim-consciousness. And it is this same consciousness that is making the soldiers themselves more highly vulnerable to guilt. In the ancient and medieval worlds, the scapegoat mechanism largely took care of this kind of thing. But somebody threw a monkey wrench into that machine, and today even the Army is feeling is crunch.

While all over the world awareness of the victim grows, it is accompanied by the decomposition of hierarchies once held sacred, but now increasingly recognized as having been built upon the blood of scapegoats. The dissolution of *dharma* in India is just one example of what is becoming a worldwide phenomenon. Indian journalists and filmmakers are hacking away at the caste system, bringing its victims to light. A film like Lagaan (2001), for example, would have been inconceivable except in the light of the process we are examining here. It is a "Bollywood" film in which a group of Indian villagers defeat the British in a game of cricket during India's colonial period. Bhuvan, the village-team leader, has a hard time finding volunteers to play against the British; and when it comes to the point of needing just one more player, he invites Kachra, an untouchable(!), to join the team. The villagers refuse to play if Kachra joins, but eventually Bhuvan convinces them – and Kachra proves to be a crucial asset in the team's victory over the British.

Lagaan is just one example that could easily be multiplied a hundredfold. A controversy recently erupted in India over the Bollywood film "Aarakshan," which focuses on what the makers of the film perceive to be the shortcomings of the caste-based affirmative action policies put into place at the time of Indian independence. These policies require certain quotas to be met with respect to educational institutions, with a view to giving more opportunity to lower caste members and Dalits (untouchables). The filmmakers believe that the quota system has failed to create genuine equal opportunity for the unfortunates of Indian society, and the film proved highly controversial, sparking protests and general unrest throughout much of India.

Such phenomena are happening all around the world today. All commentators see this as the result of secularization and globalization; what is seldom acknowledged, however, is that what is being globalized is a secular culture that is itself profoundly a product of the Bible's revelation of the victim, its truth-telling exposure of the scapegoat mechanism, and its deconstruction of mythology – which led to the desacralization of nature and the rise of modern science. Observing such phenomena, Girard believes that we are approaching the culminating moment in the gospel's "leavening" of the world.

That does not mean, however, that this process has gone unchallenged. "Satan" has not simply folded his cards and quit the game in quiet anticipation of an outpouring of human compassion. There have been movements, most notably Nazism, which have been very aware of the world's waxing victim-consciousness, and have sought to stamp it out. With reference to the Third Reich, Girard writes, "I believe that the most plausible philosophical interpretation of the Holocaust, from my viewpoint, is that it was an attempt to divorce the West from its dedication to saving victims. . . . It supposed that the principle of the victim could be buried under so *many* victims that everybody would see that it was not true. The attempt failed."[182]

The Nazis wanted very badly to be able to do what the ancients did. They wanted to ignore the last two-thousand years of Christian influence (and the entire Hebrew tradition it built upon) – indeed, to bury it – erecting over its grave a sacrificial altar full of the bodies of immolated victims, in exaggerated caricature of the great pagan civilizations. The resolve, strength, and spectacle with which Hitler pursued his project is a measure of the depth and strength of the Judaeo-Christian witness he was trying to obliterate. He knew that reviving a kingdom like that of the ancients would require a bold and audacious spectacle capable of proving that God cherished no concern for the weak. He would murder on such a prodigious scale that nobody would ever again be able to credit the biblical witness, and the Will to Power would triumph. Biblical knowledge of the victim, Hitler knew, is not something that can simply be shrugged off, or politely ignored. Two thousand years after the death and resurrection of Christ it is too late for that. It must be willfully scorned, derided, trammeled, and shown to be false and worthless.

There has been another reaction, however, to the waxing consciousness of the victim. I am referring to what Girard calls "the other totalitarianism," or, even more radically, the spirit of Anti-Christ. This is the development with which we are all familiar in its aspect as what has come to be called "political correctness." It is an ideology that takes up the cause of the victim, but in a radicalized way that appoints itself as the power that will finally bring justice and freedom to the world, ridding the world of all victims. It uses the time-honored method of scapegoating in order to consolidate its base. Since it is no longer acceptable to scapegoat Jews (even if one can criticize the nation of Israel), it scapegoats Christianity, attacking it as the hypocritical source of all the violent and ugly history perpetrated by the West. Of course, it does not acknowledge the Christian source of the very values it uses to prosecute Christianity. In truth, it is in *rivalry* with Christianity, though it does not acknowledge the fact. This spirit of rivalry drives it to ever more strenuous and ingenious crusades to find and save victims, in an effort to outdo the old religion. And victims do indeed benefit. But at the same time it runs an inquisition that creates victims of its own, called "perpetrators." Spiritually speaking, it practices a form of imitation of Christ perverted by a rivalrous desire to usurp and replace the spirit of Christ in a struggle to rule this world (although the rivalry is entirely one-way: the spirit of Christ is in rivalry with no one).

Girard writes, "Of course, very often Christian principles are prevailing in a caricaturist form, whereby the defence of the victim entails new persecutions! One can persecute today only in the name of being against persecution. One can only persecute persecutors. You have to prove that your opponent is a persecutor in order to justify your own desire to persecute."[183] Looking to the future of this phenomenon, Girard says, "You can foresee the shape of what the Anti-Christ is going to be in the future: a super-victimary machine that will keep on sacrificing in the name of the victim."[184]

We have, then, several amazing things happening in the world. We have the explosion of victim-awareness on a global level that obliges even international corporate powers and governments to advocate and assist in the cause of victimized peoples regardless of race, class, nationality, and so on. "Victim" has become a *universal absolute* for the first time history. We also have backlashes, attempts to crush the Judaeo-Christian conscience to make way for an unapologetic apotheosis of the human will. And then we have the more insidious attempt to banish Christ by imitating his concern for victims in a spirit of rivalry that seeks to gain power and control in the name of the victim. This latter is also an attempt to make way for an unprohibited satisfaction of desire – and this is something we must now address in some depth.

The Unleashing of Desire and the Multiplication of Rivalry

Concern for the victim has finally thrown off all the qualifying limitations imposed by previous sacrificial ideologies, and has become a universal absolute, bringing about wonderful things for the world's peoples – miracles of compassion, one might justifiably say, incredible things never before seen in the history of the world: advocacy for Indian untouchables; labor movements and child labor laws; the renouncing of slavery; the search to develop a prosthetic tail for a wounded dolphin; an award winning documentary that casts compassionate eyes upon – even celebrates – forsaken Brazilian landfill workers; the Special Olympics – examples leap from every page of modern history and every contemporary media source. Obviously, we could fill pages. We take it all for granted. But these triumphs have been achieved in the wake of the gospel's eradication of sacrifice: *and this means that the modern world is without sacrificial protection*. Let me explain what I mean by "sacrificial protection."

When the murdered and resurrected victim Jesus Christ was identified by his followers with all victims, it put a stop to sacrifice. But, as we have learned, sacrificial ritual was the glue that held societies together, channeling self-destructive violence out of the community. We have already seen that long before Jesus Christ appeared upon the world stage ancient societies periodically faced what Girard calls a "sacrificial crisis"; i.e., a crisis of reciprocal violence within societies that could no longer rely upon sacrificial ritual to help their people rid themselves of mutual antagonisms. Such crises resulted in the sudden or gradual diminishing of belief in communal myths, lack of conviction with respect to the meaningfulness of rituals, and growing disrespect for sacred hierarchies and taboos. Such crises happened periodically to societies quite apart from the influence of the gospel because these rituals, beliefs, and hierarchies were, after all, a structure of lies (what Girard calls the "order of false transcendence"[185]), and thus always vulnerable to stress and rupture. But societies could often bounce back from the brink of self-destruction through an extra high voltage of violent scapegoating that would "rally the troops." Or a founding murder could raise a new culture from the ashes of an old one. Once the gospel penetrated a culture, however, it inaugurated a more-or-less permanent, more-or-less acute state of sacrificial crisis within that culture, because it revealed the victimary mechanisms and violence upon which the sacrificial rituals, myth, and taboos of the society were based.

Now, sacrificial crisis means "leakage" of desire. This is the crucial point, and what follows will unpack it. We must remember that underneath the spectacle of the founding murder and all the sacrificial rigmarole built upon it and maintained through generations of faithful repetition – underneath all of this lurked the terrifying specter of *desire.* It was mimetic desire, the imitation of the other's acquisitive desire, that created the first rivalries that resulted in the horrific scenes of bloody anarchy just prior to the founding murder. Founding murders were the spontaneous discovery of a way to put a lid on the terrifying specter of desire. Sacrifice was the repetition of that murder, allowing rivals to temporarily suppress their mutual hostilities. Prohibitions/taboos were also put into place, sanctioned by terrible punishment, in order to lock-down the provocative and threatening mimetic desires that had fueled the rivalries in the first place. *When sacrifice no longer works, that mimetic desire "leaks" out, is freed from constraint, and flourishes in the form of multiplying rivalries.*

Without sacrifice, societies have to rely more and more heavily on prohibitions to block desire and keep rivalries in check; but in advanced stages of sacrificial crisis even taboos begin to lose their power of conviction, along with the cultural hierarchies that once kept people segregated according to class, race, status, and so on. People traditionally prohibited from imitating the desires of their superiors now experience the welling-up of new desires, or the liberation of suppressed old ones, based on a newfound freedom to imitate desires that were previously off-limits to them. This means the outbreak of new conflicts as liberated desirers come into direct rivalry with their one-time superiors.

A southern black, for example, was not even supposed to *desire* to drink from the white man's water fountain, or even *desire* a white man's woman. And, indeed, slaves rarely allowed themselves the luxury of imitating their master's desires because of the numbing hopelessness of their situation, and the cruelness of the consequences. Consciousness of the victim, however, eventually began to overwhelm and dissolve the ability of whites to achieve union at the expense of sacrificed slaves. It was hard to maintain the scapegoat mechanism in a nation so self-consciously steeped in the Bible, despite the insidious efforts to use biblical texts to justify slavery. Just as in the Middle Ages it was impossible for Christendom completely to remake Jesus in the image of a Saxon warrior (though it surely was tried, with horrible consequences), so it later proved impossible to remake Jesus as a slaveholder. The New Testament was there. The Gospels were there. And their proclamation of the victim could not be impeded.

When as a result of the Civil Rights Movement the southern taboos and sacred hierarchies gradually began to dissolve, *desire began to blossom* with new vigor for African Americans. This played itself out in thousands of ways (and continues to unfold). It has led, on the one hand, to a violent clash of classic rivalry, with each side denying that it is imitating the other's desire; and it has led on the other hand to some African Americans entering the arena of rivalrous contention within mainstream American consumer society, from whose game they had previously been expelled. (More on this culture in the subsection below, "The West's Temporary Solution.")

The point is that one way or another – and without attempting to trivialize the strides made by African Americans – the breakdown of sacred hierarchies and taboos, which comes about as a result of the loss of the ability to sacrifice victims, leads to the liberation of desire and the multiplication of rivalries. We are seeing this happen over and over and over again in today's world, whether we are talking about women, gays, or previously disenfranchised minorities in big city shanty towns. And, again, this is not to diminish the achievements of these groups. I too want to be on the side of the victims. But Girard is taking a step back and looking at the larger picture. Quite apart from the actual gains in human rights and prosperity that any particular group might achieve, it does not arrive at a human utopia, and the larger picture is not utopia. It is a picture of multiplying and splitting rivalries that as the ability to sacrifice diminishes, societal conflict increases: and there is no sacrifice to stop the escalation.

I need to make it clear that what I have been saying so far does not mean that there is less scapegoating in the world today. Scapegoating continues at all levels: individual, communal, national, corporate, religious, and so on. *But its violence is no longer generative.* Once upon a time in the world, violence was indeed generative – of order, of culture, of communities and civilizations. Through the action of the scapegoat mechanism human beings could turn their victims into gods and create mythological cultures from the stories of their immolation. But that depended on a collective, unanimous blindness which thanks to Jesus (and the Hebrew Scriptures in which he steeped himself), we no longer possess. Human beings are now conscious enough to spoil the party. We know too much what we do. Therefore *scapegoating today does nothing but escalate the violence and fuel the contemporary explosion of rivalry.* It is generative of nothing, and testifies only to degenerating order and peace in the world. The kind of scapegoating that litters the modern landscape reminds me of a car that will not start, although the engine turns over and over. It is the useless thrashing about of the Beast of Revelation, all the more frustrated and enraged because of the impotence of its violence to generate again the likes of "eternal" Egypt or Rome.

The result of all this is that the world is splintering into more and more microcosmic groups butting heads in rivalrous conflict with one another. This includes the rise of religious fundamentalisms, both within the United States and abroad. Some of these groups, like the Islamic extremist factions, are trying to revivify sacred violence, promoting a heavily sacrificial ethic even to the point of self-sacrifice through suicide bombing. These groups are exerting spectacular efforts to make violence generative once again, trying to use it to cast out what they consider to be the more heinous violence of secularization. But what happens to efforts like this in a world super-saturated with knowledge of the victim? They become just another part of the landscape of rampant mimetic rivalry. They become co-opted by the very mimetic desire they seek to suppress. They are not immune; on the contrary, they are expressions of the same sacrificial crisis that is engulfing the entire world, as knowledge of the victim spreads relentlessly into every corner of the planet, rendering the ancient generative possibilities of violence more and more inert, and giving rise to a worsening reciprocal violence among multiplying rival groups.

To understand this, we must look not at the differences, but at the essential unity of the rivals. To use Girard's example in *Evolution and Conversion,* the conflict between the West and Islamic extremism cannot properly be explained by pointing to the differences between the two cultures. That is how we usually try to explain it, of course, by pointing to differences of religion, cultural values, goals, interests, and the like. But Girard sees that the basic motive force giving rise to terrorism does not lie in such differences. These are not without importance from the point of view of certain analytical purposes, but the essence of the conflict derives not from difference but, Girard says, from "the desire for convergence and resemblance."[186]

> *Human relations are essentially relations of mimetic rivalry. What is experienced now is a form of mimetic rivalry on a planetary scale. When I read the first documents of Bin Laden and verified his allusions to the American bombing of Japan, I felt at first that I was in a dimension that transcends Islam, a dimension of the entire planet. Under the label of Islam we find a will to rally and mobilize an entire third world of those frustrated and of victims in their relations of mimetic rivalry with the West. But the towers destroyed had as many foreigners as Americans. But in their effectiveness, the sophistication of the means they employed, the knowledge that they had of the United states and their training, were not the authors of the attack in a sense at least partly American? Here we are in the middle of mimetic contagion.*
>
> *Far from turning away from the West, they cannot avoid imitating it and adopting its values, even if they don't avow it, and they are also consumed like us by the desire for individual and*

collective success. This sentiment is not true of the masses but of the ruling classes.[187]

As we have seen, rivalry is inherently mimetic: rivals end up looking very much alike in the end. The case is no different with modern religious fundamentalisms: they are reactions, all the more virulent by virtue of the exponential increase in the mimetic passions they judge dangerous. Yet the more they manifest the spirit of sacred violence, whether acting it out with literal bombs, or political crusades, or simply pulpit pounding which damns the "other" to hell, the more certain it is that they are struggling with their own internal mimetic desire.

At the same time that they attempt to prohibit desire by the revivification of sacred violence, and consignment of their rival to the realm of the profane, they are not immune to infection by those same desires. And when the "profane" forces react against fundamentalism by ardently defending their right to desire, the rivalry is engaged still more intransigently. Then for both sides the "other" comes to possess an unavoidable fascination, and the rival inevitably becomes the model. Thus the seeming paradox of the fundamentalist drive to master technology as seen among Islamic terrorists, as Girard pointed out above; but one could also point to the example of American televangelism. There is more going on here than a mere practical use of "profane" technology for the sake of "kingdom building." There is a real fascination with it, and a desire to wield it efficiently in order to wrest power from the rival whose mastery of it is envied, resented, and imitated. Naturally, Fundamentalists have their justifications and theological rationalizations for what they do; but the spirit of envious rivalry is all too evident in the desire for success, power, political control, moral and intellectual triumph over the enemy – the same desires, naturally, that their rival/models possess.

The documentary film "Waiting for Armageddon" illustrates this perfectly. The film interviews many Evangelical Christians, including a group of folks on a tour of the Holy Land led by an Evangelical guide. When they arrive at a hill overlooking the valley of Armageddon, where they suppose the final apocalyptic battle will happen, one of the group says:

> *In the tribulation this will be the final battle ground. . . . As a believer in our Lord Jesus Christ we'll have the greatest seat of all to watch it. That's something that's fantastic to me. We will not be here, but we'll be able to watch it. There is an ultimate final battle. It will be, I think, a lot of fun to watch, you know… not, not fun in the sense of knowing that people are dying without having received Christ as their savior, but at the same time, you know, seeing the prophecy fulfilled, seeing God's work come out.*[188]

The comment betrays an astonishing numbness to actual violence. The speaker's main concern is not the horrifying brute reality of violence per se – watching the battle is almost fun – but the fact of dying without having received Christ as savior. This spiritual concern overwhelms and completely denies the decimating horror of violence itself. Comments like this also make it obvious that despite belief in their own uniqueness, and their wish to sit in elevated judgment above the profane world, Fundamentalists are no more immune to the contagion of mimetic rivalry than anybody else. Fundamentalism's attempt to stop the spread of mimetic desire by resorting to sacred violence only results in adding yet another outcropping of mimetic rivalry to the modern landscape.[189]

And there is no way back from the uninhibited outbreak of contemporary mimetic rivalry. Unless knowledge of the victim were to be utterly stamped out of human consciousness, it is impossible to turn the clock back to pagan times. That would only be possible if the entire world could once again lose itself in the blinders of sacrificial ritual, murdering victims and turning them into gods, creating mythologies to glorify the deed, and growing enduring and stable cultures from the victim's ashes. But that process only works when *everyone* believes in it, and we live in a world in which almost everyone no longer believes in it. Even in Third World countries where scientific skepticism has not yet penetrated to a grassroots level, globalization has rendered people no longer capable of the kind of collective unconscious needed to build gods and cities out of lynched victims. The lynchings continue, but new gods no longer come into being. (Cases like that of Roop Kanwar, cited earlier, notwithstanding; hers is a very watered-down form of divinity, and when such rare events happen, even if they establish some kind of small local cult, they do not possess the kind of collective power that could found a new culture.)

No, we cannot turn back the clock as if Christ never lived. The old world, the pre-Christian world, certainly had rivalries; but sacrifice contained them, and taboos controlled desire. In our contemporary world mimetic rivalry is breaking out all over, like June. The collective "Legion" has lost its power to sacrifice the demoniac, and as a result has become a multiplicity of frightened and violent, charging swine.

We cannot even turn the clock back one thousand years, much less two. On November 27, 1095, Pope Urban II made a speech which roused all of Europe: a call to war against Muslims to reclaim the Holy Land. The West was still raw enough, still enthralled to enough sacrificial thinking to respond to Urban's rousing attempt at generative violence. In *Cross-Purposes,* Anthony Bartlett analyzes the chaotic conditions of Europe at the time, and demonstrates how Urban's move was a prime instance of scapegoating.[190] Urban tried to rally a decaying Europe and revive Christendom through the bonding power of spilt blood. Ultimately, Urban's scapegoating did not unify Europe; but in the short term his summons was so effective that men couldn't wait for the announced date of departure for Jerusalem before taking up arms in high righteous (and riotous) spirit, and initiating pogroms against the Jews; and we all know the horrors perpetrated by the Crusaders in Jerusalem during the first Crusade. Even after a thousand years of gospel influence Christendom was still capable of blinding itself to the reality of the victim – at least for a short while.

A thousand years later, however, and the situation is quite different. In 2001, after the September 11 attacks, George W. Bush tried to do something similar. He announced an Eastern "axis of evil" and hoped to rally the entire country under his leadership for a concerted effort at "bringing terrorists to justice." At first the sheer horror of the attacks on the Twin Towers, replayed thousands of times by mass media, swept much of the country into an anti-terrorist mania. As Susan Faludi points out in her book *The Terror Dream,*[191] popular media revitalized old myths about America being a nation of macho cowboy heroes protecting their women. There was a revival of John Wayne rhetoric, while Time and Newsweek, among other publications, told women to stay at home sewing and cooking – and actually predicted a spike in sewing machine sales! *But*… none of this lasted very long. It certainly did not sew America back together, heal the American "culture wars," quell the mimetic rivalry of political parties or inner city gangs, or restore faith in the righteousness of government. Very quickly questions began to be asked, uncomfortable questions about victims. Not only those victims of the falling towers, but the victims America had created overseas. Questions about the motives of the Bush administration were raised, along with questions about America's involvement in the affairs of other nations. It soon became evident that the country could not be rallied in a scapegoating scenario which sought to paint the world in simple black-and-white categories. Urban's effort fell apart in the long run; but Bush's attempt barely made it out the gate.

What I am saying here is not meant to excuse the terrorists, of course, or to minimize the tragedy of 9-11. I am as sensitive to victims, American or otherwise, as most other modern persons. But the fact that there were real victims in the Towers, and that the attack can with real justification be called evil, does not lessen the reality of the scapegoating machinations that tried to take advantage of those terrible facts. But such machinations (and this is the point) have to be carried out in a Western culture now far more alive with consciousness of the victim than Urban II's Europe ever was. *Everyone who had an opinion about the "war on terror" – whether they were critiquing the Bush administration or defending it, sought to justify their position in the name of victims.* Even if their professed concern was little more than a hypocritical guise for partisan politics, they were nonetheless obliged to make the profession of a concern for victims, and had to work overtime to disguise their real motives and goals. Because today, "the whole world is watching," and it is watching for victimization. As Girard said, *victim* is the absolute universal value in the world today, the only ethic unchallengeable even by the would-be Nietzschean superman. Thus the war on terror only contributed to the violence that is enveloping the world in a conflagration of mimetic rivalry. It has generated, and will generate, nothing – except more and more intense and escalating rivalry.

In sum, "the time is out of joint," as Hamlet said. The world is becoming more and more mimetically unstable. Unleashed desire and the proliferating rivalries that result can no longer find sacrificial resolution, and are turning the world into a bouncing crate of nitroglycerin.

The West's Temporary Solution

The explosion of desire and rivalry we are witnessing today began in the West, because the West bore the primary impact of the gospel, and has been steeped in it for two thousand years. But we have to face a curious fact. Even though the West is the world leader in unleashed desire, it seems to have learned ways to absorb the rivalries and most of the violence that Girard's thesis predicts should follow in the wake of the demise of sacrifice and prohibition. In fact, the Western economy actually seems to have learned how to stimulate mimetic desire and exploit it for profit! How is this possible? Why didn't the West's experience of extreme sacrificial crisis lead directly to self-destruction? Before moving on we need to take a look at a few possible answers to this seeming contradiction to the Girardian expectation.

One reason is that our economy is the most fruitfully creative in the history of civilization when it comes to inventing an endless series of identities, fads, crazes, and so on, as paths for the flow of mimetic desire. The mobility and interchangeability of options help to prevent confrontations from coming to a head. As an example, every young girl whipped by mimetic desire into a frenzy of coveting Hannah Montana backpacks or tennis shoes is the implicit rival of each of her peers who participate in the same craze. The camaraderie they all feel together, the sense of security they take from "fitting in," is in reality highly tenuous and unstable in the absence of mitigating factors that might elevate the relationship to a higher level. Their stability as a peer group is based on the sacrifice of those who are not "cool" enough to join the Hannah Montana bandwagon. It is a form of scapegoating, but unable to generate enduring effects. For the craze will soon pass, and the "mob" will break up. Then the rivalries which were implicit all along, but deferred, may break out. Girls who had bonded over shared Hannah Montana moments may well be at each other's throats just weeks or months later. However – and here is my point about "mobility" in our culture – by that time it is just as likely that they will be on to something else. A young girl for whom Hannah Montana has lost her glow can simply leave that world behind and deal with her disaffection by gravitating, for example, to female "Twilight" character Alice Cullen, striking up friendships and online associations with others who reinforce and escalate this new mimetic attraction.

In this way our culture keeps people in a mode of constant leaping from one desire to the another, thus managing for the most part to deter real violence and create a workable situation within which mimetic desire can be both highly stimulated and economically exploited. We might call this a kind of "identity mobility." Because of the fluidness of mimetic passion, its easy attachability and detachability, a disaffected individual has extraordinary mobility in shifting from subculture to subculture, each time finding a new and different satisfaction, vitiating any clash with previous cohorts. One simply leaves them behind and moves on when tensions arise, before violence explodes. (We are however seeing more and more of those occasions when for one reason or another the system stops working, and an individual gets "stuck" in a particular identity: a situation of extreme Girardian *scandal* in which one is paralyzed by obsessive fascination with former models who have become rivals, and ends up gunning them down. Such incidents demonstrate the tenuousness of consumer culture's ability to defer violence.)

Modern consumer identities have a short half-life before they segue to the next model/obstacle, and this scenario is constantly repeated in the lives of consumers as individuals flit from one in-group to the next, all the time driven by a haunting sense of lack that they believe they are alone in experiencing. This is the unrest at work in the West, and exported to the world.

So far we have been able to cope with the toxic levels of mimetic desire that fuel the free market economy, and I have described "identity mobility" as one reason it works. Another is the sheer abundance of mass manufactured goods. It is true that no one feels like they "have it all," and advertising is always stimulating desire for the new and the better, and more of it; but at the same time we are not in a situation of general scarcity of goods. When there is only one "Helen," violent confrontation among rivals for her affection is inescapable. But with an economy grounded in the technology of mass manufacturing, enough people can have enough of what seems desirable enough of the time, while still allowing for the amassing of exceptional wealth in the hands of a few individuals. For the majority, iPods, laptops, automobiles, and what-not are available, and there are many ways even for those who cannot afford them to go about laying hands on them, including the use of credit cards, eBay, cheaper generic brands, and theft. In this way, while still nursing plenty of cravings for objects of desire just beyond our reach, we are kept basically satisfied – and this keeps most of the violence deferred.

Then again, geographical mobility – not the identity mobility described above, but the possibility of actual geographical movement – also assists in deferring outbreaks of real violence. When the heat, emotional or otherwise, gets too bad, people can up and move (witness "white-flight" in urban neighborhoods). We also have a degree of upwardly social mobility unprecedented in the history of civilization, which defers outbreaks of violence by imparting the hope that ambitions can be realized through accepted channels which minimize violence. Our form of economic competition allows people to play hard without getting bloody. As Girard put it, "...normally businessmen who compete do not shoot each other (although sometimes they shoot themselves). Why are we able to use mimetic competition positively? Because we trust that we can keep competition from becoming violent. Capitalistic competition would be impossible were it not restrained by moral rules, which ultimately come from Christianity."[192]

Finally, should all the above fail and frustrations rise to meltdown levels, the technology of mass media is always there to provide all the narcotic dreaminess a civilization could possibly desire for keeping violence in the cage. People can watch escapist shows and read escapist fiction, satisfying their need for revenge and celebrating their achievement of victory over rivals, all vicariously without risking the spillage of actual blood. Sadly, this also produces passionless individuals[193] who, pacified by an endless stream of fantasy, take vicarious possession of that which they are too timid to fight for in reality.

But the big question in all of this is: *how long will this relative stability last?* The system has opened the Pandora's box of mimetic desire and learned how to whip it into a frenzy in order to exploit it economically. But the system is obviously vulnerable in hundreds of ways, dependant as it is upon the technological grid. And how long will we be able to exercise that extraordinary phenomenon of *trust* based upon our inheritance of Christian values that Girard mentioned, which allows us to compete without coming to blows? Everywhere we see trust breaking down, violence breaking out, and suspicion and fear increasing. People feel it. Just last week I reconnected with an old college buddy after a hiatus of several decades. He works as an auditor for various food chains, and was on his way to examine the books at a Pizza Hut. He said that its employees were robbing it blind, and that this was not at all an uncommon situation. "It's not the same world I grew up in," he lamented. Over and over again we see trust being broken, from the grassroots level to national sports and politics.

And, of course, crime is increasing. According to Dave Grossman, the violent crime rate in America today is *five times* greater than it was in 1957. But it's not just America. Per capita assaults have quadrupled in Canada since 1964. Since 1977 it has doubled in Belgium, Denmark, England-Wales, Germany, Hungary, Netherlands, Scotland, and Switzerland; tripled in Sweden, Austria, and France; quadrupled in Australia and New Zealand, and quintupled in Norway and Greece. (Grossman took these figures from national reports made to InterPol.) Grossman says that "It is not just happening in traditional 'Western' nations. Brazil, Mexico, and all of Latin America are seeing an explosion of violent crime, while nations like Japan and Singapore are also experiencing unprecedented increase in juvenile violent crime."[194]

In America, a traditionally moderate state like New Hampshire that has always insisted on politeness and manners in political discussion has become so polarized that political rancor in state government has risen to the height of mistrust: state representatives actually passed a law to permit themselves to carry firearms onto the House floor! Commentator Sarah Koenig tells the story of how representative Kyle Tasker accidentally dropped his gun in the middle of a criminal justice and public safety committee hearing![195]

At the federal level, senators claw and bite each other across polarized political divides that are no longer mitigated by personal relationships. According to Republican senator Pete Domenici, and Democratic economist Alice Rivlin, in a recent Brookings Institute interview with Krista Tippett, senators no longer develop personal relationships with their opponents as they once did. Ms. Rivlin noted that senators used to live in Washington and would socialize with each other. Their kids played on the same soccer team, their wives knew each other, and this made it much more difficult to call an opponent a bad person, as commonly happens today. Then Domenici adds, "I tell you, it was important that we know each other, and whatever can be done to tell the institutions of this country make your institutions more habitable for the elected officials and their families so they get to be a little bit intimate. So you're talking about Senator Nunn to your wife and you talk about Sam and she knows who Sam is. You wouldn't dare go to the floor of the Senate and say anything about him other than I don't agree with him. And he could be right but I'm just not on the same side and I'm going to try to convince you he's wrong. But he's a terrific guy." In the current atmosphere of mimetic rivalry in American politics, this all seems rather quaint.[196]

Of course, taken by themselves these examples might indicate nothing other than random outbreaks of typical human conflict, specific to their time and place, and which could be on the mend tomorrow. After all, hasn't everybody, at all times in history, had plenty of complaints about their contemporary generation? Yes, but we have to see the big picture that Girard is sketching. So before I get carried away citing more and more examples that would fill up the rest of this book, let us return to the main point. Mimetic desire fuels our consumer society, but because it is inherently rivalrous it does not create stable bonds. The free market system, which is now envied and imitated with varying degrees of success by the Third World and other parts of the planet, is looking like the skin of a balloon, stretching and stretching as it tries to contain the expanding hot air caused by intensifying mimetic desire and rivalry. The slightest needle prick could explode the whole thing. "[T]his system," says Girard, referring to the free market, "is also protecting us, albeit temporarily, from the explosion of even greater violence."[197] An economic downturn, a scarcity of necessary goods, or some other monkey wrench thrown into the delicately balanced wheel, and all the mimetic rivalry that has heretofore been more or less channeled into economic competition, or shifted from fad to fad, or place to place, or numbed by television, or distracted by technological toys, will overflow the channels within which its mad rush has been contained.

So we have an intrinsically rivalrous consumer-technological culture at war with itself but tenuously deferring violence through the narcotic of mass media, the ready availability of desired objects, and the mobility of social identity and geographical location (among other factors). That deferral seems less and less effective, however, as horrific violence spontaneously erupts in places as unlikely as the Post Office, MacDonald's, and schools – even an Amish schoolhouse. We also have this same culture locked in intense rivalry with religious fundamentalisms that blame it as morally degenerate. They seek anachronistically to revivify the sacred by mustering massive violence in the name of holiness, while refusing to admit their own envious passions. Their project is raised to a hysterical pitch by the fact that it is impossible to turn the clock back to a time when sacred violence could operate in a world unconscious of the presence of the victim, and by the fact that Fundamentalism knows itself at some level to be infected with what it condemns in its rival. As the remnants of sacrificial thinking continue to decay in the modern world despite Fundamentalism's attempts to revive it, and more sacred hierarchies collapse, liberated mimetic desire erupts in rivalrous factions across the planet like bubbles in boiling water. Liberated from confinement by top-down definitions, no longer frozen in societal roles accepted as the permanent will of the gods, the untouchable "Kachras" (*Lagaan*) of the world now step into a new and mimetically seething realm, subject to the stimulation of new desires inspired by the imitation of models whom they would previously have been afraid even to look in the eye, much less imitate. And in this new landscape, everyone seeks to satisfy their passions with an arsenal of technology undreamed of in ages past, and available to everyone. There is no permanent stability in this modern game, nor can there be, short of surrender to the spirit of Christ. There can only be violent escalation of rivalries without the brake peddle of a founding murder to stop it. The only thing that is certain so far is that we continue to look to some form of violence as the solution to the problem of rivals and enemies. And when we stare that enemy in the face, we refuse to see our own. Apocalypse from a Girardian perspective is a strictly human, not a divine, affair.

A Contemporary Effort to Revive Pagan Polytheism

Before moving into the final section of this book it may prove illuminating to take a quick glance at a contemporary pitch for an alternative solution: or, rather, a very ancient solution decked out in new garments – namely, polytheism. The testimony of the authors whose work we will be discussing is powerful because without realizing it they have observed some of the same phenomena Girard has emphasized; but they put it together in a framework that completely misses the mark. It will be fascinating, after having come so far in our exploration of Girard's perspective, to see how two philosophers from two of the grandest institutions within American academia inadvertently confirm some of Girard's major themes, yet completely misunderstanding the meaning and significance of their observations.

There are many intellectuals who understand Christianity's role in the "desacralization" which has come to characterize Western civilization, but see this as an unfortunate development that has stripped nature of its "magic." They call it "disenchantment," and contrast our modern ennui with the vitality of ancient peoples, who lived in a nature perceived as magical and awe-inspiring, and who lived lives imbued with meaning. The most recent development of this theme is by Hubert Dreyfus at Berkeley, and Sean Dorrance Kelly at Yale. These philosophers make many observations that indirectly support Girardian themes: the mimetic phenomenon and its contagious transference (which they describe perfectly, but without grasping that the phenomenon is mimetic); the connection of such phenomena to the sacred (which they romanticize); the idea that Jesus reconfigured the world with an extraordinary new vision of what it means to be human (and yet they reject that vision); and the way in which his vision desacralized the world (but they want to re-sacralize it). They propose polytheism as a way back to a nobler, more meaningful experience of life, and this is a good place to examine their proposal before we make our concluding clarification of the only real choice facing us in the future.

All of this can be found in their recent book, *All Things Shining,* which seeks to address the modern individual's lack of mooring and inability to "tell a coherent story about the meanings of our lives."[198] We have gotten to this unfortunate state, characterized by boredom, ennui, depression, numbed meaninglessness, and other similar states, because we live in a civilization that has lost any sense of the sacred. We no longer find meaning and fulfillment by responding to powers greater than ourselves. Homer's Greeks lived intense and meaningful lives, while moderns live boring, meaningless lives distracted by media, trivialized by daily trips to the convenience store, and numbed by paper-pushing office jobs. We are threatened by nihilism, and Dreyfus and Kelly want to recover the sense of "magic" that animated the ancients, their openness to the wonder of the world and to being carried away by forces greater than themselves that elevated them to peak experiences and made life "shine."

Aside from a token acknowledgement of the risks involved in their view (since being carried away by powers greater than oneself can just as easily refer to the Third Reich as to the Kingdom of Heaven!), Dreyfus and Kelly consistently avoid a hard look at the reality of life among the Greeks, and what it really meant to be enslaved to the sacred: something that Girard has done with unsparing realism. Girardians must leap out of their skin upon reading something like the following passage, in which Dreyfus and Kelly analyze sporting events as moments when "the sacred shines," explicitly connecting such moments with the influence of the crowd:

> *It is not that sports are sacred to the culture in any absolute sense. But there are moments in sport – either in the playing of them or in the witnessing of them – during which something so overpowering happens that it wells up before you as a palpable presence and carries you along as on a powerful wave. At that moment there is no question of ironic distance from the event. That is the moment when the sacred shines.*[199]

The irony in this observation, of course, is that when the authors describe what we have called a "mimetic wave," and connect it with the moment when the sacred shines, *they are actually describing the mimetic force behind the creation of the sacred itself.* But they have no understanding of that, or of its connection with violence. They see this "overpowering" as something wonderful and positive. They possess a complete lack of appreciation for (or perhaps any knowledge of) the analysis Girard has given of the mimetic phenomenon's connection to founding murders and the scapegoat mechanism in generating the sacred. Their use of sports as an example makes the comment even more ironic, since sports are in fact devolved sacrificial ritual. Competitive games run in channels deeply cut by the sacred, all the way back to the original Olympics and beyond. Opposing teams mirror each other as rivals, their rivalry making them virtually indistinguishable except for arbitrary and superficial differences marked on their costumes. The game basically simulates a sacrificial crisis in which everything is reduced to a mirroring sameness as the rivals imitate each other's desire to win. In order to resolve the crisis, one team must distinguish itself: that is, expel ("sacrifice") the other team. And the whole thing functions to release pent-up aggression in a controlled, safe, and manageable way, just as ancient sacrificial rituals did. (Although just as in ancient times, the carefully controlled ritual occasionally malfunctions and real violence erupts at sporting events!) Dreyfus and Kelly, therefore, do not realize how accurate they are when they call overwhelming moments in sporting events "sacred." Nor do they realize how terribly wrong they are when they describe it as a wonderful lifting out of oneself, and prescribe more of the same as an antidote to modern anemia.

Their ironic and unconscious interface with Girard continues when they indicate a few pages later that the meaning one derives from such "sacred" moments in sporting events is only temporary. "It wells up and carries you along as on a powerful wave... but when the wave passes, nothing but its memory survives."[200] In Homer's world the things considered most "real" were born of those moments when something would well up, take possession of the hero, then let him go. Dreyfus and Kelly call this process "whooshing" or "whooshing up." And they think we need to allow the same thing to happen to us. They are like philosophical surfer dudes, paddling their boards to hold position while waiting for the next big wave to come and "whoosh" them, so their lives can feel truly meaningful. But, as they indicate, waves come and go and nothing remains but the memory – so the ride must be constantly repeated. Once again they have hit upon the truth of the sacred, this time with respect to sacrifice. For we have seen how the mimetic wave that channels all aggression against the victim in a founding murder is a one-time event that, as it slips into the past as mere memory, must be evoked again and again: thus the need to induce the efficacious "whoosh" of that moment on a regular and controlled basis as sacrificial ritual, along with the use of mythological tales to keep the memory alive. For when the survival of society is at stake, merely treading water waiting for the next wave is not good enough: the next wave must be manufactured, so the group has a periodic release for mimetic violence.

Furthermore, "When something whooshes up it focuses and organizes everything around it."[201] That states the precise truth of a founding murder, which generates an entire sacred cultural order, including sacrificial ritual, mythology, prohibitions and taboos, and cultural hierarchies. Everything is focused and organized around that original, murderous "whoosh."

Dreyfus and Kelly do acknowledge the need to impose some moral controls on the "whooshing" they advocate; and this is not surprising because, as Charles Taylor points out in his response to the book (see below), like all of us Dreyfus and Kelly have internalized the "Axial" perspective of the last 2,500 years. They cannot and do not pretend to ignore the moral values that have grown out of the great post-Axial religions, and which now infuse our very being. But their presentation creates an unresolved and dangerous tension in the relationship between whooshing and moralizing. Most important, however, is the fact that they seem to have no grasp of the connection between the polytheism they advocate, and the power of mimesis to create the sacred through the scapegoat mechanism (let us remember that the gods were originally murdered human victims).

Charles Taylor, one of the most eminent philosophers of our time, has written a response to *All Things Shining,* in which he says the following:

Life under "polytheism" was… also a matter of meeting the demands of the gods, whether this meant facing insoluble dilemmas, or making the necessary sacrifices. And these always fell in unequal manner, whether on the prisoners sacrificed on Aztec pyramids, or the slaves working the mines at Sounion, whether on those selected as scapegoats, or on the neglected or exploited: slaves, women, or the 'widows and orphans' invoked by the Hebrew prophets.

Taylor continues a bit later:

In order to see dilemmas and conflicts here, one had to adopt another standpoint, one of wider concern, in which the fate of the sacrificed began to matter.[202]

Indeed! That is a fair summary of the process I have been delineating in this final section of the book, the process whereby "the fate of the sacrificed began to matter." It is because the fate of the sacrificed once did *not* matter that Greek philosophers scoffed at Paul in Athens when he preached to them about his worship of a crucified God. And two thousand years later it is a fair statement as to why a film like *Gran Torino* would have been incomprehensible to ancient Greeks and Romans, who would have had no framework within which to grasp the "dilemmas and conflicts" which that film evokes. For to them, not only did the fate of the sacrificed not matter: it was axiomatic that it shouldn't.

Yet two eminent philosophers from Berkeley and Yale can actually write:

> *To lure back these Homeric gods is a saving possibility after the death of God: it would allow us to survive the breakdown of monotheism while resisting the descent into a nihilistic existence.*[203]

They do not mean to imply that we moderns, who live in a secular scientific age, could ever believe in the existence of supernatural gods. But they want to "lure them back" in the sense of using them as metaphors for the kind of "whooshing" experiences we have been talking about, and as inspirations to a kind of human excellence that depends upon the ability to greet life in all its manifestations and moods with gratitude and wonder. This, they believe, is impossible for monotheism, which hard-headedly seeks to reduce life to one single, ultimate meaning. They feel caught (to use an appropriate image from Greek myth) between the Scylla of contemporary nihilism and the Charybdis of Christianity which unnaturally imposes a "secure and final and certain foundation." The religion of Christendom is to them as it was to the Melville they admire: the worst kind of narrow-minded fanaticism, a "misguided passion for monotheism."[204] (Although, to their credit, Dreyfus and Kelly are careful to distinguish Jesus, whom they like, from the religion built around his worship.) Monotheism is misguided because it closes off all other avenues of possible meaning in the universe in single-minded pursuit of the one and only final answer. To resolve this dilemma they propose a return to a kind of polytheism, understood not literally, but as a kind of openness to all the experiences life is capable of providing once we give up the conceit of a single transcendent meaning to reality. We should imitate the Greeks. And they quote Nietzsche: "Oh, those [Homeric] Greeks! They knew how to live."

It seems that in some ways pop culture is following their advice. There is growing nostalgia for a romanticized version of the ancient sacred. Mass media is popularizing the old gods in numerous books and films. If it were not for the fact that he goes to a Catholic school and has Christian parents, my eight year old son would know far more about the Greek gods than about Jesus Christ, thanks to the Percy Jackson book series. I am not condemning the series as a piece of entertainment. In fact, I read the first book to my son and enjoyed it myself, and we're now reading the second book. I am simply observing the enduring and newly revitalized popular appeal of the old myths. If the old gods are returning, however, it is only as images that take their place in the post-modern flux, the "blur," as Bartlett has called it.[205] Dreyfus and Kelly also perceive that blur, I think, and are concerned that it is leading us to nihilism. They are trying to find an alternative, something to lift us above its deadening effects, something that will not be just more of the "same old, same old" but constitute a true point of difference. And they almost found it – in Jesus! The kicker is that Dreyfus and Kelly come within inches of grasping the real meaning of Jesus. To reprise the lines I quoted earlier:

> *As he is described in the Gospels, Jesus totally transforms people's understanding of what it is to be a human being. This is a superhuman thing to do. Like a god the biblical Jesus reveals a new Christian World. … The central movements of the next nearly two thousands years of history in the West can be understood as attempts to spell out Jesus' understanding of human existence.*[206]

Dreyfus and Kelly also understand that the thrust of Jesus' concern centered on *desire*:

Jesus transforms radically the whole Hebrew understanding of human being and of what counts as a life worth living. Instead of outward actions, Jesus organizes the worthy life around private, personal, inward desires. . . . This makes the inner desires of the heart more important than outward actions.[207]

Most amazing of all, when Dreyfus and Kelly touch upon the issue of salvation, they hit pay dirt in terms of the Girardian understanding of mimesis:

When you are reborn then Jesus lives in you; you put on his body. But what does that mean? It might well mean that Christian salvation occurs by catching Jesus' contagious new mood of agape love. … Your desires are still out of your control, but entering this mood by hanging out with Jesus and his disciples, you are reborn a joyful new being with pure desires.[208]

This is an almost perfect description of the process of "contagious" mimesis, conceived positively as the imitation of Jesus. (Although positive mimesis does not guarantee anyone "purity.") And it shows how "salvation" is not an intellectual matter of confessing certain dogmatic beliefs, but an experience grounded in the same mimetic capacity that built the old sacred world, but now modeling itself on Jesus. As Dreyfus and Kelly quite accurately see, this is an experience which really does occur "contagiously" (a favorite word of Girard's). Christian conversion, after all, has always been something that happens in *relationship with others,* not in a vacuum. Saint Paul had a vision, but it was – and needed to be – immediately followed up with a visit from Ananias, who provided the concrete model, the "mood of agape," for Paul to "catch." And this of course would have been reinforced many times over in the following three years that Paul spent among the Damascus followers of Jesus.

This mood [of agape love] cannot be captured in universal principles that one can discern by philosophical contemplation. It is a way of being attuned to what matters that one can get in touch with only by being around those who exemplify it. This embodied aspect of Christianity is essential to its understanding of the saving mood of agape love, and therefore essential to the notion of salvation itself.[209]

They only need to reframe "mood" as "mimesis" for this portrait of Christian conversion to make complete Girardian sense. Nevertheless, Dreyfus and Kelly end up advocating a return to pre-Christian paganism because they believe that Jesus' inward focus, and Paul's deepening of it, ultimately led us down the wrong path. Augustine combined that inwardness with Platonism, and ended up with the idea that the saving truth is accessible as a kind of knowledge within one's own heart. "Human being" becomes an essentially inner domain: all you need to discover the truth is your own inner self. This "over-the-top" valorization of the individual eventually flowers into Descartes' self-sufficient ego, which thinks that by isolating itself in a room and doubting everything it can arrive at the truth. And this in turn leads to Kant and the Enlightenment idea of human beings as fully autonomous selves. The fuller, richer life is the one lived, shall we say, more "on the surface," in grateful connection to life as it grabs us ("whooshes" us) from the outside.

Frankly, I think Dreyfus and Kelly have not adequately explained their reasons for wanting to imitate the Greeks rather than Jesus. Personally, I would sooner entrust my life to Jesus' "mood of agape" any day than to Achilles' whoosh of anger, of which the Iliad sings. It is nonetheless stunning how close these philosophers veer to the Girardian perspective, and how close they get to realizing the only genuine alternative to the modern dilemma they set out to fix. But, sadly, they miss the mark by a thousand miles. Instead of taking their cue from Jesus as the real place for a new beginning, they try to strain the old sacred through a modern sieve, hoping to create at a product that will re-enchant the universe.

Finally, it must be said that the real heart of the problem with *All Things Shining,* I believe, is that it does not grasp the real *problem,* and so does not ask the important question. The authors have written an existential lament on the superficiality of modern souls, and express concern with the modern anemia, boredom, weakness of spirit, ennui, and nihilism. But they seem entirely oblivious to the basic and most urgent modern problem, which is *violence.* Once we grasp that, the impotence of their proposed solution becomes immediately evident.

It is clear that the way forward, if we are going to deal with the real problem before we destroy ourselves, does not lie through the graveyard of dead and divinized Greek victims. Romanticizing the sacred world of ancient polytheism, and trying to revive it in diluted measure to meet the problem of modern nihilism, is a testimony to the lengths to which we can be driven in our attempts to conjure a genuine alternative to the choice that lies before us: a choice from which, ultimately, we cannot wriggle free.

Compassion and Forgiveness: Adjusting Our Perspective

Must there be a human apocalypse? As Scrooge said to the Death spirit, "Before I draw nearer to that stone to which you point, answer me one question. Are these the shadows of the things that Will be, or are they shadows of things that May be only? Men's courses will foreshadow certain ends, to which, if persevered in, they must lead. But if the courses be departed from, the ends will change. Say it is thus with what you show me!"[210]

Thus we arrive at the height of dramatic tension in dealing with the apocalyptic theme. Girard's analysis has led us to the precipice of a monumental choice:

> *The Cross has destroyed once and for all the cathartic power of the scapegoat mechanism. Consequently, the Gospel does not provide a happy ending to our history. It simply shows us two options (which is exactly what ideologies never provide, freedom of choice): either we imitate Christ, giving up all our mimetic violence, or we run the risk of self-destruction.*[211]

Girard's own projection at this point is very bleak. His latest book, *Battling To The End,* an analysis of the work of the great Napoleonic military strategist Carl von Clausewitz, can be a depressing read. Clausewitz grasped the principle of mimetic escalation to extremes in modern warfare, but without Girard's full-blown insight into mimetic theory. Mimetic escalation becomes apocalyptic when the rivals are possessed of nuclear weapons and other instruments of terminal terror – thus the urgency of the crossroads toward which we are rapidly accelerating, and the choice we have to make.

I have no intention of diluting the sobering impact of these meditations, for the situation is indeed dire and the possibilities horrific. We need to come off our addiction to violence and vendetta. In this connection, what worked for Bill Wilson, co-founder of Alcoholics Anonymous, may be an important approach. In his letter to Carl Jung, Bill wrote, "In my case the dilemma had been created by my compulsive drinking and the deep feeling of hopelessness had been vastly deepened by my doctor. It was deepened still more by my alcoholic friend when he acquainted me with your verdict of hopelessness respecting Rowland H." For Bill Wilson, that sense of the hopelessness of his condition, demonstrated to him "scientifically" by his friend and physician, Dr. Silkworth, and by Carl Jung's work with another hopeless alcoholic, Rowland H., led to a final surrender of ego, which sobered him up and laid him open to a transforming spiritual experience. Then he had the idea: "If each sufferer were to carry the news of the scientific hopelessness of alcoholism to each new prospect, he might be able to lay every newcomer wide open to a transforming spiritual experience." "This concept," Bill claims, "proved to be the foundation of such success as Alcoholics Anonymous has since achieved."[212] Perhaps Girard saw himself as doing something similar when he published *Battling To The End,* hoping to sober us up by demonstrating the hopelessness of our dilemma. If so, he would be acting like an A.A. sponsor, according to the Alcoholics Anonymous publication, "Twelve Steps and Twelve Traditions," when it says:

> *Our sponsors declared that we were the victims of a mental obsession so subtly powerful that no amount of human willpower could break it. There was, they said, no such thing as the personal conquest of this compulsion by the unaided will. Relentlessly deepening our dilemma, our sponsors pointed out our increasing sensitivity to alcohol - an allergy, they called it.*[213] (Underlining mine.)

I think that we are, in a sense, *addicted* to violence: its dividends as a short-term, fast fix for problems, its exploitation as cinematic glamour, its drama, its adrenaline, its promise of glory and heroism in military contexts. And so perhaps it is wise to learn from the foundational experience of Alcoholics Anonymous, and not be in too great a rush to escape the emotional valley of death into which Girard's latter meditations have led us. It may well be that only from the perspective of that valley will we ever be able and willing to ask Scrooge's question with the radical earnestness required in order to invoke the only real salvation that exists.

Having said the above, I must now note that this book (mine, not Girard's) has a fault that has not yet been addressed. I have presented matters almost as if it were the gospel's primary intention to destroy, to announce, as it were, "bad news." This of course is not the case. If the gospel brought about the destruction of ancient civilizations, it did not do so with a destructive spirit (I am talking about the gospel itself here, not Christendom). And if we are threatened now with apocalypse, it is not because the gospel desires it. The story of the *good* news should not be told in a way that makes it seem as though Jesus came to destroy us. As Jesus himself says in John 12:47, "I did not come to judge the world but to save the world." The gospel is positive, and its primary thrust is creative. Jesus wanted to *liberate* human beings. Naturally, that meant challenging the powers that enslaved them, and so we find in Jesus' work an aspect of criticism – sometimes quite angry criticism. But he never opposed the powers with violence. His work was always creative, not destructive, a work of pure compassion. It is the story of something wonderful and new arriving, and its rejection by vested interests that refused to accept it. In their flight from it they destroy themselves. It is, in other words, the story of Legion, with its attitude of "What have you to do with me, Jesus, Son of the Most High God?" Rather than accept the liberation that Jesus brings, Legion prefers self-destruction.

The advent of the gospel brought a new humanity. The fact that it is still a work in progress is no fault of the gospel, but due to the recalcitrance of hearts that will not open with a sweep wide enough to let Jesus enter fully. We might remind ourselves once again of Peter's experience with Cornelius. The Holy Spirit fell upon the impure and profane centurion and his family, causing great joy and delight. It was a thoroughly positive and joyous, creative experience. That the old authorities should be left, as Alison put it, "muddled," and pained at the deconstruction of their sacred distinctions, is no fault of the gospel Peter preached. It is important to remember Jesus' embracing love for the world, which stretched all the way from the lilies of the field to the crowd that crucified him – but to which he still offered forgiveness. The gospel undid humankind's bondage to the sacred, but we use that freedom to continue the age-old practice of modeling our rivals' acquisitive desires, rather than Christ's non-acquisitive desire to please his Abba. The consequences are a direct result of our rejection of Christ's compassion, and our refusal to make it the model for our own humanity.

The story that runs all the way from the demise of the old sacred religions to the contemporary explosion of mimetic rivalry is the story of what happens when Life enters the realm of violence and exposes it for what it is by allowing itself to be cast out. "He was in the world, and the world was made through him, yet the world knew him not. He came to his own home, and his own people received him not." (John 1:10-11) The death-machine knew that with its hidden mechanisms exposed, its efficient functioning would be crippled, and it hoped to avoid that fate by burying that Life under a shroud of death. But the death-machine did not expect that, once killed, this Life would return – and with even more clarity (Emmaus) and abundance (Pentecost). And this Life just kept on coming, "with a vengeance," one might say; but only jokingly of course, because this is the "vengeance" of infinite forgiveness, infinite compassion, infinite self-giving love.

It has been the goal of at least one recent Girardian writer to highlight the positive nature of Jesus' work, and to remind us of the Christian faith's anchorage in hope. In his latest book, *Virtually Christian,* Anthony Bartlett agrees that Jesus' death and resurrection has undermined the old sacred, and set societies on a path of unraveling into mimetic anarchy that could prove apocalyptic. In this he is at one with Girard and the picture I sketched earlier. Bartlett, however, is at pains to show how the entirely positive forgiving compassion of Christ, which unexpectedly and miraculously erupted from the very abyss of human violence (the cross), has an almost irresistibly *attractive* quality which grows in luminosity and clarity the more we reject it.

According to the Gospel of John, just before the Last Supper, in anticipation of his crucifixion, Jesus said to his disciples, "Now is the judgment of this world, now shall the ruler of this world be cast out; and I, when I am lifted up from the earth, will draw all men to myself." (John 12: 31-32) In an earlier digression I talked about how the crucifix as an icon became one carrier (among many) of the gospel, a sign with the power to move hearts, breaking open a new sense of compassion for victims, while at the same time ironically undermining the sacrificial Christianity which exhibited it often for the wrong reasons. That was just one example of an unlimited number of ways in which the compassionate nonviolence of Christ infiltrated the realm of human culture, which is always a construction of symbols, words, images – basically, what scholars call "semiotics," meaning the study of signs. Bartlett is an earnest and acute observer of the ways in which our contemporary world expresses a cultural environment inescapably altered by the gospel. Here are some words about it from his blog, which he writes for "Theology and Peace," a Girardian organization:

> *In my book "Virtually Christian" I described a world radically infected by Christ. There has been a two millennial drip, drip, drip that has soaked our culture in the compassion and forgiveness of Christ, like soaking a Christmas cake in brandy!*
>
> *You don't see it? You think things are worse, more violent,*

more unjust, than they have ever been? And has not Christendom (Christian Culture) been one of the main culprits of the heedless violence in the world?

But how would you know that unless a source of compassion had made you exactly that degree more aware?

My argument is not that things are objectively better or worse. My argument is that our minds have been changed by Christ. And now because of that things can and may become better![214]

Far from secular culture being a heathen landscape only, Bartlett sees it full of observable signs of Christ. But as inheritors of all this, we are like fish that have lived in the lake all our lives, oblivious to the existence of water all around us. We take our perspective on life for granted: our acute awareness of victims, our commitment to human rights, our deep compassion for suffering, our ability to criticize Christianity or any other ideology for oppressing the weak, the poor, the untouchables of the world... and so on. But we are able to think, feel, and do all this because Christ's self-giving compassion has infiltrated the human realm of violence to the point that it now surfaces as a bona fide part of the secular culture it helped to create.

And it is crucial to understand that Christ's work in exposing the scapegoat mechanism did indeed create the conditions that allowed secular culture to develop, for it marked the beginning of the end for the sacred and its powerful grip on the mind and heart of humanity. For Bartlett, therefore, the picture looks dim only on the surface. He believes that at the same time mimetic rivalry is on the rise, our awareness is also growing that Christ offers the only real alternative to the terminal violence that will surely erupt from what I earlier called the "foaming froth of mimetic passion," momentarily held in check by a market economy and technology, but slipping more and more out of control every day. Bartlett calls that foaming froth a violent "blur." The world is full of alternatives – various political, religious, social, and economic agendas, philosophies, dogmas, creeds – all in rivalry with one another, all broadcast within the post-modern flux of words and images that dance daily across television screens, hum through the internet, and parade willy-nilly through the pages of magazines and books.

But more and more all this appears to be resolving into a kind of conflictual blur; the kind of thing one might experience watching television news continually for forty days and nights. (Could even Jesus have handled that?) After a while, one senses the sameness of it all, as one watches rivals exchanging hostilities in back-and-forth, reciprocal interaction across all walks of life and around the entire globe. Reciprocal exchanges of hostility take place so fast, with such lightening speed, that it all begins to blur. One begins to despair of a solution, sensing that there is no *essential* difference to be found among this kaleidoscopic onslaught of world events – *until the essential difference really does emerge, dramatically differentiating itself from the crowd. That essential difference is Christ, the nonviolent, forgiving, compassionate, self-giving Christ.* Now that is something truly different! And the faster and thicker the blur becomes as it reaches extreme intensity before exploding, the more clearly and attractively Christ's compassionate forgiveness is beginning to stand out as the only genuine life-giving alternative.

This "standing out" is not happening as a result of the preaching of pastors, or the publishing of Christian books, but is happening organically, within so-called secular culture itself as a result of the gospel's leavening of history. This is not something that requires a church. It is the "leavening" of which I have spoken many times in this book. In many ways Christ comes to be expressed more clearly and powerfully in the culture than in the church. For it is not a matter of dogma, but the Spirit of Christ. For that Spirit to be present there need not be explicit theological reference. Bartlett believes that this is how Christ is working in the world, and his hope is that it will pull us back, ultimately, from the brink.

I will give one example to illustrate how Bartlett understands this leavening of culture by Christ. In *Virtually Christian,* he mentions *Gran Torino* but does not expound on it. Here is a film produced and directed by, and starring, Client Eastwood, after a 53 year career as an actor, and 37 years directing (winning two Oscars for directing and two for best picture!). Despite the actor's 78 years of age, the plot seems to unfold in the same direction as so many other younger Eastwood films, in which he played the kick-ass, "make my day," Dirty Harry tough guy. In *Gran Torino* he plays Walt Kowalski, a growly racist Korean War vet whose wife has just died, and who ends up befriending his Hmong neighbors, whom he had previously despised. When their daughter is beaten and raped by a local gang, Kowalski ratchets up the action by making plans for what we think is going to be a wild west, shoot-'em-up climax in which one old man takes down the entire gang Rambo style.

But the film takes a surprise turn when Kowalski shows up alone, standing on the gang's front lawn. Stepping out onto the porch and leaning from upper story windows, the gang members aim guns and automatic weapons at Kowalski, who nonetheless continues to hurl tough talk and insults at them. Kowalski puts an unlit cigarette between his lips, then in a brazen mock gesture makes his hand into a gun and aims at each guy in turn, "pulling the trigger" to suggest what he plans to do to them. We wonder what in the world he has up his sleeve.

We know that he has taken all day to plan this confrontation very carefully. And we strongly suspect that he plans to die, since he made the first confession of his life to a priest earlier that day, bought his first tailored suit, and refused to allow his young Hmong friend (who is craving revenge) to accompany him on the mission. But what is he planning on doing, standing out there on the lawn making himself a sitting-duck target? The most he could be carrying under his jacket is a gun, which is obviously inadequate to the situation. Or maybe he has a grenade? Or dynamite? Maybe he is planning to light the cigarette, then use it to light dynamite? Like Samson who killed himself along with the Philistines when he broke the pillars of the temple, is Kowalski planning to bring down the whole house and gang on top of himself? Whatever the plan, we expect the same kind of fireworks that have thrilled us in other Eastwood climaxes.

Finally, with the unlit cigarette dangling from his lips, Kowalski reaches slowly inside his jacket, ostensibly going for a lighter, but possibly for a gun – then suddenly whips out his hand. Immediately the gang opens fire, hitting him from all angles with a hail of bullets worthy of Bonnie and Clyde. Soon the police are on the scene taking the gang bangers into custody. Kowalski, it turns out, was unarmed. The gang will be spending a lot of time in prison for killing an unarmed man – just what Kowalski had planned all along. His Hmong neighbors, once his enemies, won't be troubled by those gang bangers for a long, long time.

Kowalski's act can hardly be called a manifestation of the forgiving compassion of Christ. He hates those gang bangers. Nevertheless, as many reviewers have remarked, *Gran Torino* stands out from Eastwood's other films, with its stunning nonviolent twist and refusal of blood-vengeance. The film shows quite clearly that vengeance leads to escalation. When the gang burns the cheek of Kowalski's young Hmong friend with a lit cigarette, Kowalski finds one of them and beats the crap out of him, threatening worse should they lay hands on his friends again. Yet Kowalski's act of retaliation directly provokes the gang to rape Sue.

The vengeance theme is explicitly addressed in the film's dialogue when Kowalski discusses vengeance with a young Roman Catholic priest he mockingly calls "Padre," and the priest is convinced that Kowalski is going to cause major bloodshed. But the climax of the film is a self-conscious break with insidious cycles of vengeance. From the midst of the same old life of resentment, anger, vengeance-seeking and violence, there emerges a new solution, an idea of how to solve the gang problem for his friends in a way that will not require him to take blood vengeance, and will not lead to escalation. But it will require a Christ-like giving of his own blood: not as sacrifice to a wrathful God, but as compassion for his friends (if not his enemies). Within the limitations of his own narrow perspective, Kowalski became an imitator of Christ without ever invoking the name. As he lies dead on the lawn, eaten up by bullets, the camera begins with a close-up of his right hand. Blood trickles out from under his coat sleeve and runs down into his open palm still holding the cigarette. The way the cigarette is laid across his palm, in combination with the trickle of blood, makes it look uncannily like a nail driven through his hand. Then the camera pulls up and away to reveal his arms outstretched so that his body forms the perfect shape of a cross.

Let me emphasize, however, that the main point is not the rather self-conscious allusion Kowalski's dead body makes to the crucifixion. Nor are Client Eastwood's personal beliefs at issue here. The main point is that *we have developed a cultural context within which a film like Gran Torino makes sense and is well-received,* a story of how violent vengeance is rejected as a solution in favor of nonviolent self-giving. As mentioned earlier in this book, a film with a theme like this would have been derisible, if not downright incomprehensible, in the ancient world of epic heroes. They understood and lauded the self-sacrifice of the warrior; but the nonviolent Christian alternative would have appeared as ridiculous to them and worthy of scorn as Jesus must have seemed to the mob of Roman soldiers who scourged him.

Gran Torino is a kind of "text in travail" because the main character is not able to embrace any concept of forgiveness for the enemies he tricks. (Though it should be noted that the Hmong neighbors for whom Kowalski compassionately gives his life had also been his despised enemies at one time. Kowalski has come a long way!) The film thus represents a stage in the process of leavening whereby contemporary culture is becoming more and more aware of the Christ-alternative. Jesus haunts this film from beginning to end, sometimes with overt references and images, and sometimes through the theme of renunciation of vengeance itself.

Bartlett believes that in films like *Gran Torino* see we the Christ-alternative emerging into sharper focus *as cultural expression,* quite apart from any direct contextualization within the church, or any relation to church dogma. It is becoming increasingly evident to many artists, writers, song writers, and other expressive and forward-looking individuals that nonviolent, compassionate forgiveness is the only real alternative we have, the only genuine difference within the post-modern "blur." But artists do not operate in a vacuum: they reflect the larger cultural context within which they work. Even works criticizing the culture could not be understood unless they shared a common sign-language with their public. Bartlett believes that the Christ-alternative is emerging more and more clearly within our cultural sign-language, not as religious doctrine, but as "sign," as image, as something felt as inner prompting towards compassion and forgiveness as the world plunges deeper and deeper into mimetic chaos. The more that chaos intensifies, the blurrier the blur, the more bubbly the churning froth of our violent cultural ocean – the sweeter and louder the clarion of Christ's truly radical alternative will become. At the extreme point of this development, Bartlett believes, humanity will accept the imitation of Christ as the model for a new humanity. This need not mean conversion to Christianity as a religious practice and doctrine; it means humanity's surrender to the spirit of Christ, working anthropologically through compassionate forgiveness, which speaks louder than dogma.

In a way, we are back at Gerasa once again. Legion had recognized Jesus immediately upon seeing him: "What have you to do with me, Jesus, Son of the Most High God? I adjure you by God, do not torment me." That was Legion speaking in its capacity as organized, sacred structure over against the victim. The Legion we see in the world today, however, is much more like the herd of pigs: Legion as shattered unity thanks to the victim restored; Legion as multiplicity cut loose from sacred structure and thus overtaken by mimetic desire, everyone imitating everybody else's fear and violence as they rapidly approach the edge of the cliff. The question now becomes: Will our Legion, manifest as anarchic multiplicity, stop long enough in their rush towards the cliff to recognize Jesus again, surrender to him, and imitate him rather than each other, thus saving themselves from the plunge? It is Bartlett's hope and belief that they will.

Christ versus Dionysus: The Final Choice

There was one man who longed for a reinstatement of the ancient sacred, not as a "whoosh" to restore meaning and excitement to a technologically numbed world, but as an affirmation of the violence he understood was intrinsic to the sacred. Friedrich Nietzsche claimed to affirm life; but his vision of life was quite different from the "abundant life" the Fourth Gospel has in view. It was the life, rather, of the jungle, which includes violence and sacrifice. As a philologist and scholar of classical antiquity, Nietzsche was under no romanticizing illusions about the

Greeks – at least in this respect. He knew the dark side of pagan life but he exalted it because he believed it was an affirmation of natural harmony. In nature the strong survive and the weak fail, and so it should be. Greek literature is full of heroes, men whose lofty tough-mindedness earned them a position at the noble pinnacle of humanity for their great deeds of strength and courage. But the weak and the slaves were jealous; and such as these created Christianity, the religion of resentment. I necessarily oversimplify here, but for Nietzsche, Christianity was the great enemy of civilization. It was an attempt by the weak to get back at the strong by creating the dubious values of compassion and love – which produce nothing noble and strong in the world, but are useful as weapons to make the strong feel guilty and to depose them from their deserved positions of superiority.

Nietzsche saw himself as Christianity's archenemy. And yet at the same time, he was in some ways one of philosophy's most perceptive interpreters of Christianity. Girard has shown how Nietzsche understood the gospel perfectly with respect to sacrifice, and what was at stake in the encounter between Christ and the old sacred. He understood it with a clarity unsurpassed in the history both of philosophy and theology. But he understood from the wrong side of the divide.

What was it that Nietzsche perceived so clearly? He saw that the real spirit of Christ was anti-sacrificial and pro-victim. He was not thrown off, like so many other critics of Christianity, by sacrificial versions of Christianity which mingled the gospel with violence. He knew that the gospel opposed sacrifice, and that it had challenged and destroyed the old and noble religions in the name of "good news" addressed to slaves, women, children, the sick, poor, ignorant, and other marginalized unfortunates. And that is why he despised it. To Nietzsche, sacrifice was absolutely necessary to the furtherance of life; and the strong man, while occasionally indulging in aristocratic displays of mercy, does not hesitate to sacrifice the weak when necessary.

Girard has called our attention to two quotes in particular from Nietzsche's *The Will To Power*. In the first quote Nietzsche invokes the ancient god Dionysus as the desirable (and only) alternative to

Christ, whom he calls the "Crucified." The ancient Greek god Dionysus was murdered as an infant by being dismembered by the Titans. But to Nietzsche, Dionysus represents "the religious affirmation of life, life whole and not denied or in part"[215] Here is the first quote:

> *Dionysus versus the "Crucified": there you have the antithesis. It is not a difference in regard to their martyrdom – it is a difference in the meaning of it. Life itself, its eternal fruitfulness and recurrence, creates torment, destruction, the will to annihilation. In the other case, suffering – the "Crucified as the innocent one" – counts as an objection to this life, as a formula to its condemnation.*[216] (Underlining mine.)

We must recognize at once the tremendous insight this quote represents. Nietzsche completely "gets it" that there is no difference between the martyrdoms of Christ and Dionysus at the structural level: Christ and Dionysus both died similar painful deaths involving mob lynching. "It is not a difference in regard to their martyrdom." Nietzsche realizes, however, that there is a difference – in fact, an absolute *antithesis* – at the level of *meaning*. For Dionysus' death means affirming life in its aspect as torment and destructiveness, which is a natural part of the creative process; it has nothing to do with questions of innocence or undeserved suffering. Christ's death, on the other hand, is all about raising an objection to suffering, violence, destruction, and torment on the basis of the innocent victim. For Nietzsche, this means that Christ poses an objection to life itself, and is therefore hateful.

Nietzsche is certainly right that the crucifixion of Jesus Christ counts as an objection to the suffering which violence inflicts upon the world. And in the next quote, he gets to the heart of the issue:

> *Through Christianity, the individual was made so important, so absolute, that he could no longer be sacrificed; but the species endures only through human sacrifice . . . Genuine charity demands sacrifice for the good of the species – it is hard, it is full of self-overcoming, because it needs human sacrifice. And this pseudo-*

humaneness called Christianity wants it established that no one should be sacrificed.[217]

There it is. Nietzsche has just put his finger on the heart and soul of Girard's message: *Christianity wants it established that no one should be sacrificed.* Not misled by Christendom's centuries long adoption of the sacrificial thinking inherited from its pagan past, and not misled by the church's terrible and heinous practices of scapegoating against Jews, Muslims, and others, Nietzsche grasps the fact that genuine Christianity, or what I have been calling the gospel, *wants it established that no one should be sacrificed.* He grasps with stark clarity the new humanity that Girard, Bartlett, Hart, and many others have stressed emerged from the gospel influence, a humanity in which every individual is absolutely important, and in which victims, even one's *enemy* victims, are . . . I almost said "sacred." But of course that is exactly what they no longer are thanks to the gospel (unless we care to use the word with a highly diluted meaning). Perhaps it would be better to say something like infinitely precious.

Nietzsche doesn't see how the Dionysus myth fits the pattern of collective violence from which the gods were created. The myth may well have originated from the mob lynching of a helpless infant. Dionysus is more than the god of wine: he is the literal divinization of mob violence. It is the spirit of Dionysus that "whooshes" the women of Thebes and drives them into the hills to celebrate the first bacchanal festival – which becomes what Girard calls a "bloodthirsty nightmare"[218] as the delirious women start ripping men and beasts apart barehanded. Christianity does indeed refuse to accept this as part of the natural process of life. The gospel wants to save, help, heal, restore, valorize, celebrate, forgive, and love every overlooked and wretched victim ever oppressed, hurt, or lynched by anything from ancient religion to Marxism to Capitalism to Christianity itself.

Nietzsche has put the antithesis starkly and bluntly, but honestly. And this is the crossroads at which we now stand in the contemporary world. The struggle between Dionysus and the Crucified is the paramount choice of modern life. Whether

Dionysus takes the form of Hitler's mobs dismembering the Jewish community of Europe in a frontal assault on Judaeo-Christian values, or the form of the "super-victimary machine" that Girard calls the Anti-Christ, which seeks to outflank the work of Christ on the left by perversely imitating him, affirming the rights of victims while scapegoating Christianity and creating heaps of new victims by wreaking vengeance on those accused of being perpetrators – either way leads to apocalypse. For there is no way, as we have seen, to back out of the contemporary sacrificial crisis by resurrecting the ancient solution. And certainly the violent crisis we face is not even addressed, much less helped, by anemic philosophical attempts to revitalize the gods of polytheism as metaphors for peak psychological states. The dough has been far too fully leavened; we are living on the wrong end of history to invoke ancient religion. We are now at the place so vividly described by William Butler Yeats in his famous poem, "The Second Coming":

Turning and turning in the widening gyre
The falcon cannot hear the falconer;
Things fall apart; the centre cannot hold;
Mere anarchy is loosed upon the world,
The blood-dimmed tide is loosed, and everywhere
The ceremony of innocence is drowned;
The best lack all conviction, while the worst
Are full of passionate intensity.
Surely some revelation is at hand;
Surely the Second Coming is at hand.

There is more to the poem, but for our purposes we need go no further. Yeats was of course not a Girardian, and I am not going to attempt an exegesis of his poem as such. I ask the reader to bear in mind that throughout what follows I am not attempting to uncover Yates' meaning; I am simply using the poem for the sake of its imagery, which is wonderfully appropriate for allowing us to sum up the end point to which we have arrived.

The centre cannot hold and *things fall apart* because in a world leavened with consciousness of the victim, the scapegoat mechanism is no longer powerful enough to divinize the victims it creates and make them ground zero for a sacred center. Today the world sallies forth to meet the future without sacrificial protection and the timeless stability conferred by the sacred centers of old. When we use violence to try to establish a center, it escapes from us like a falcon from its falconer, becoming nothing more than one more instance of the anarchy of violent rivalry being loosed upon the world. *The ceremony of innocence is drowned* because we can no longer protest our innocence in the slaying of sacrificial victims.[219] We can no longer naively proclaim with the Babylonian priests cited earlier: "This deed was done by all the gods; I did not do it!"

The best lack all conviction because the old convictions are losing their authority. The hierarchical structures that gave them weight are being deconstructed as the victims upon which they were established and maintained are coming to light. (Note, for example, what the retelling of the Native American story from the point of view of the victims has done in recent years to undermine the "God is on our side" conviction of American manifest destiny.)

While the worst are full of passionate intensity. As old prohibitions are debunked, passions of mimetic desire explode into violent rivalries, and we find ourselves approaching a worldwide sacrificial crisis, a confused, blurred confrontation of all-against-all. Exchanges of reciprocal violence quicken and intensify throughout the world and we dizzy watching it, as we would if we tried to follow the back-and-forth volleys of a tennis match in a film played on fast-forward. And we cannot reign the expanding violence back in and constrain it around a sacred center. In today's atmosphere, the attempts of fundamentalist religion to cap mimetic desire and restore order become themselves nothing more than contributions to the frantic landscape over which they presume to sit in judgment.

Surely some revelation is at hand; Surely the Second Coming is at hand. Once again, putting aside Yeats' meaning and simply using the poem as it stands as a way of explicating the sum of what has been said in this book about our contemporary dilemma, it is stunning that suddenly, in the midst of "the worst," the Second

Coming occurs, in conjunction with some revelation. We are reminded of Anthony Bartlett's perspective, who sees the "loosed anarchy" of the soaring falcon becoming so blurred that the Spirit of Christ (whose gospel created the conditions for this anarchy in the first place) must burst clearly from its midst as the only real point of difference, the only genuine alternative – a new starting point for an old humanity. After almost two thousand years of partial occlusion by remnants of the old sacred, the gospel's full and unalloyed revelation of the victim is attaining unprecedented consciousness in the world. The "Crucified," whom Nietzsche saw as the great enemy of human progress, is coming. He comes as the innocent victim. In South Africa, in India, in Thailand, in Mongolia – everywhere across the planet the voice of the victim of human violence is being heard as never before.

Were he coming to seek vengeance, he would be no real, fundamental threat; for in that case he would be part of the sacred system itself, just another formulation of the immemorial "old time religion." But then there would be nothing divine about him, nothing breaking in from outside the realm of reciprocally violent relations. But Christ is not coming with Thor's hammer, Diana's bow, or Zeus' lightning bolt. He is coming with nails in his hands – or at least the marks of those nails. That is why he stands out, more and more, as the only true alternative for the world today.

This revelation that Bartlett sees springing up within modern culture itself, quite apart from established church environments (although it is happening there, too) indicates that people are gaining a new awareness, which is the first condition for change. Bartlett wants to believe that we are moving toward a time when human beings, faced with ultimate self-destruction, will carry that awareness into action, moved, not by a preacher, but from within their own burgeoning cultural consciousness, resigning their rivalries, forsaking vengeance, and forgiving their enemies – in whose face the compassion of Christ has taught them to see themselves. As "the worst" gets worse and worse, Christ looks more and more attractive, and will draw all people to himself (John 12:32), the Crucified: "When they shall look upon the one whom they have pierced, they shall mourn for him..." (Zech. 12:10) As the falcon of violence flies farther and farther beyond the falconer's control, the attraction of the cross and its power of compassionate forgiveness will emerge from the anarchic blur with simple brilliance (Bartlett calls it the "photon of compassion"), evoking a mimetic response of compassion from the human race.

Girard's own vision is grimmer. If Jesus comes again, it will probably be as witness to the human race's self-destruction, as he once witnessed the destruction of Legion when the Gerasenes refused the liberation he offered them. Like the herd, we are racing toward a historic crescendo which will plunge us into a sea of anarchic violence. Even if the Christ-alternative is recognized, that does not mean it will provoke a transformative imitation of Christ. As Anti-Climacus (Soren Kierkegaard) wrote, there is such a thing as demonic rage, which becomes all the more defiantly scornful as it becomes more directly aware of the truth. Against Bartlett's optimism we must balance Girard's warning that "When sacrifice disappears, all that remains is mimetic rivalry, and it escalates to extremes."[220]

> *Divinity has appeared and it is more reliable than all the earlier theophanies, but no one wants to see it. Humanity is more than ever the author of its own fall because it has become able to destroy its world. With respect to Christianity, this is not just an ordinary moral condemnation, but an unavoidable anthropological observation. Therefore we have to wake up our sleeping consciences. Seeking to comfort is always to contribute to the worst.*[221]

Whether one shares Girard's pessimism or Bartlett's optimism, we should remember that what is called for from the Christian is imitation of Christ. As we saw in chapter three when examining this idea in the New Testament, imitation of Christ as the model for a new humanity means learning a whole new kind of relationality based not on acquisitive desire, but on giving to the other, on humility, compassion, forgiveness, and love. And the imitation of Christ means that there is no end to these qualities. They do not suddenly exhaust themselves in the face of an overwhelmingly stubborn opposition.

Then Peter came up and said to him, "Lord, how often shall my brother sin against me, and I forgive him? As many as seven times?" Jesus said to him, "I do not say to you seven times, but seventy times seven." (Matt. 18:21-22. Jesus is probably alluding to Lamech in Genesis 4, who wanted to take seventy times seven vengeance against his enemies.)

"Seventy times seven" is not meant as a literal limit of 490 repetitions of forgiveness, but as a way of specifying limitlessness. Christians are called to imitate the unlimited love and compassion of their Lord, even to the point of death, if necessary, in the face of persecution. This must seem like foolishness to those who have not chosen to model their lives after Christ's, yoking themselves to Jesus as their Rabbi and following him wherever he may lead. But Paul knew that for those who have made this choice, Christ is the very "power" of God. Not indeed the kind of power the world understands, but the real power to break the hold of Satan at its crux: the bonds of scandalous mimetic entanglements, and the escalation of violent reciprocity into which they lead us.

Again, whether one shares Girard's pessimism or Bartlett's optimism, it is helpful to bear in mind the following wise comment by Drasko Dizdar, since in either case the world can still appear a terrifying place.

Maintaining peaceful balance in a storm of contagious violence is Christ's gift: the victim surrounded by the expulsive tempest of the sacrificial system bestows peace on all who seek him . . . undisturbed, untouched by terror, free from fear. Freedom from fear is the freedom that the contagion of violence cannot touch. [222]

And, finally, let us not forget the words of the Master himself:

My peace I leave with you; my peace I give you; not as the world gives do I give to you. Let not your hearts be troubled, neither let them be afraid. (John 14:27)

I have told you these things so that in me you may have peace. In this world you will have trouble. But take heart! I have overcome the world. (John 16:33)

Endnotes

[1] Jacques Ellul, *What I Believe* (Grand Rapids: Eerdmans, 1989), 60-61.
[2] Gil Bailie, *Violence Unveiled: Humanity at the Crossroads* (New York: Crossroad Publishing Company, 1999).
[3] See, for example, the work of James G. Williams, *The Bible, Violence, and the Sacred: Liberation from the Myth of Sanctioned Violence* (San Francisco: Harper Collins, 1991). Williams, a scholar of the Hebrew Bible, uses biblical criticism throughout his work.
[4] Frederick Copleston, S.J., *A History of Philosophy,* Vol. VII (New York: Doubleday, Image Books, 1994), 332.
[5] Ibid. 333.
[6] Rudolph Steiner, *The Education of the Child* (NY: Anthroposophical Press, 1996), 55.
[7] Jean-Michel Oughourlian, *The Genesis of Desire,* Trans. Eugene Webb (East Lansing: Michigan State University Press, 2010), 89-91.
[8]See Marco Iacoboni, *Mirroring People: The Science of Empathy and How We Connect With Others* (New York: Picador, 2009), and Giacomo Rizzolatti, *Mirrors in the Brain: How Our Minds Share Actions, Emotions, and Experience* (New York: Oxford University Press, 2008).
[9] Oughourlian, 85.
[10] Certain famous individuals seem to possess, all by themselves, the same power of mimetic attraction as large crowds. But, in fact, their "charisma" is their fame, which is, in fact, the crowd. They are instantiations of the admiring gaze of thousands or millions, and their power of attraction generally increases in proportion to their fame: that is, in proportion to the number of their admirers.
[11] Oughourlian, 17ff. See the whole chapter, "Psychological Movement."
[12] Comment made in the History Channel's "The True Story of Alexander the Great" (2004).
[13] See René Girard, *A Theater of Envy* (South Bend: St. Augustine's Press, 2004).
[14] "The Rape of Lucrece" in *The New Cambridge Shakespeare: The Poems,* ed. John Roe, (Cambridge: Cambridge University Press, 1992), 144-145. First quote from lines 15-21; second quote lines 29-35.
[15] All biblical citations in this book are Revised Standard Version unless otherwise indicated.
[16] II.iv.192-194.
[17] René Girard, *The Scapegoat,* trans. Yvonne Freccero (Baltimore: Johns Hopkins University Press, 1986), 165.

[18] Oughourlian, 43-80. This section on the interpretation of Gen. 2 and 3 is only part of the riches contained in *The Genesis of Desire*. This is a particularly valuable book for those seeking insight into the psychological dynamics of mimetic rivalry among couples, and how that can be handled within the context of counseling and therapy.

[19] To relate this to the discussion of mimetic desire in the previous chapter, just as the tree of knowledge is not exceptional among the other trees in the garden by virtue of some more beautiful display or tastier fruit, so in *Two Gentlemen of Verona* Silvia is no more lovely than Julia – a fact recognized by Proteus when he says: "She is fair; and so is Julia that I love, That I *did* love. . . ." The choice, ultimately, is not based upon a desirability intrinsic to the object.

[20] Oughourlian, 71.

[21] Ibid. 65.

[22] Compare Jacques Ellul's *To Will And To Do* (Philadelphia: Pilgrim Press, 1969). Ellul says, "[S]ince man is separated from God and in that situation defines the good for himself, he is radically incapable of discerning, loving, and willing God's good. That is why man is guilty whenever he pretends to do good, and why he is idolatrous whenever he pretends to be religious." (17) "When Cain is told to 'do well,' that is not an objective and impersonal formula. It is God who says to him 'do well,' and hence who initiates the dialogue; and it is only in this dialogue that Cain learns what is the good for him." (21) Ellul goes on to quote Micah 6:8 – "He has showed you, O man, what is good" – and says that this is "exactly the opposite of the knowledge obtained by Adam." (21) Morality, Ellul likes to say, is "of the fall." "Morality is part of the world. It goes to make up part of the world of sin. It is within that which is sin. It is not a judge of it, in the position of an arbiter who stands above the conflict. To suppose that morality, enunciated by man, or felt by him in his conscience, or obeyed by him in his behavior, could, when all is considered, be the will of God, is to suppose that man has not lost all in the fall, that a little something is still in the Eden situation." (42)

[23] The Code of Hammurabi King of Babylon, Trans. Robert Francis Harper, Ph.D. (Chicago: University of Chicago Press, 1904), 3.

[24] Girard, *The Scapegoat*, 165.

[25] Michael Hardin, *The Jesus Driven Life* (Lancaster, PA: JDL Press, 2010).

[26] René Girard, *I See Satan Fall Like Lightning*, Trans. James G. Williams (Maryknoll, NY: Orbis Books, 2001), 16.

[27] As we will see further along, scandal constitutes only *half* the picture of human enslavement to violence. In the situation the New Testament calls

"sin," human beings experience a *double* bondage. First, scandalized relationships constitute a force of violence in human affairs by whipping up and intensifying emotional fury as rivals lock horns in mutual imitation. But there is also the violence by which human beings overcome the rivalries that destroy community. Girard calls it the scapegoat mechanism (to be examined in the next chapter), and it pulls society together by discharging the violence of rivals onto an innocent victim. Gil Bailie sums up this double violence nicely by playing on the difference between the Greek term, *diabolos,* usually translated as "devil," and the Hebrew term *Satan,* meaning "accuser." For Bailie, *diabolos* connotes the force of mimetic rivalry as it tears human relations apart, pitting rivals against one another; Satan, on the other hand, indicates the scapegoat mechanism, the moment when rivals band together to accuse a victim. As Bailie puts it: "At the critical moment, when these passions have sown enough frenzy and reduced a society to pandemonium, the *diabolos* changes its modus operandi. The *diabolos* becomes the *Satan*. Suddenly, the accusing finger points, and a violent avalanche is set in motion, the end result of which is a pile of stones, a glorious memory, and the rudiments of yet another of the kingdoms of 'this world.'" (Bailie, 206) At present, our concern is only with the first part of this double process, the force Bailie calls the *diabolos*. This footnote is simply to alert the reader to the fact that the clash of mimetic rivals constitutes only half the problem of human bondage to violence.

[28] James Alison, *Prayer: a case study in mimetic anthropology* (Article taken from Alison's website, http://jamesalison.co.uk/pdf/eng54.pdf, and specified as the tentative text of one of the twelve sessions of "The Forgiving Victim" – an Adult Introduction to Christianity), 9.

[29] Ibid. 8

[30] Ibid. 8

[31] Williams, 6. (Italics in original.)

[32] Phil. 2:5-8. I am using the translation of this text provided by Michael J. Gorman, *Inhabiting the Cruciform God: Kenosis, Justification, and Theosis in Paul's Narrative Soteriology* (Grand Rapids: William B. Eerdmans Publishing Company, 2009), 11.

[33] The material here about first century Rabbis is taken from a sermon by Rob Bell, "Covered in the Dust of Your Rabbi!" available at http://www.jayzinn.com/uploads/dust_rabbi.pdf. Thanks to Dr. David R. Leaman, who alerted me to this source.

[34] In what follows I am indebted to the research of Willard M. Swartley, "Discipleship and Imitation of Jesus/Suffering Servant: the Mimesis of New Creation," in William M. Swartley, ed., *Violence Renounced: René*

Girard, Biblical Studies, and Peacemaking (Telford, PA: Telford, 2000), 218-145.

[35] René Girard, *Violence and the Sacred* (Baltimore: Johns Hopkins University Press, 1979), 306.

[36] Walter Burket, *Creation of the Sacred: Tracks of Biology in Early Religions* (Cambridge: Harvard University Press, 1996), 151-152.

[37] Walter Burkert, *Homo Necans* (Berkeley: University of California Press, 1983), 2.

[38] Ibid. 10.

[39] Ibid. 10.

[40] Walter Burkert, *Ancient Mystery Cults* (Cambridge: Harvard University Press, 1987), 6.

[41] Ibid. 11.

[42] cf. Illiad, Book I, lines 442-474, Lattimore translation, for a Greek example.

[43] John Hick, *An Interpretation of Religion: Human Responses to the Transcendent*, 2nd Ed. (New Haven: Yale University Press, 2004), 27.

[44] Gregory Batson, *Naven*, 2nd ed. (Stanford: Stanford University Press, 1958), 56, note 1.

[45] Girard, *Violence and the Sacred*, 52-54.

[46] Dr. Seuss, *The Butter Battle Book* (New York: Random House, 1984)

[47] Fyodor Dostoevsky, *The Possessed*, Trans. Constance Garnett (New York: Barnes & Noble, 2005), 606.

[48] Fyodor Dostoevsky, *Demons*, Trans. Robert A. Maquire, Ed. Ronald Meyer (London: Penguin Classics, 2008), 428.

[49] II.ii.83-90. See Girard's entire discussion of Shakespeare's *Julius Caesar* in *A Theater of Envy*, pages 185-226.

[50] There is no doubt that religion is prehistoric. "[T]here are clear traces of religious practice since the Upper Paleolithic that can be brought into line with attested religious phenomena. Still earlier, Neanderthals practiced ceremonial burial of the dead; many think that religious ideas must have accompanied such activities about 100,000 years ago." Walter Burkert, *Creation of the Sacred*, 12.

[51] The "defeat" of nondifferentiation, accomplished by the entire group projecting its violent "sameness" upon the murdered scapegoat, is the historical basis for the hundreds of mythologies from around the world known as "foundation myths." These myths recast the lynching in poetic, imaginative form in a way that preserves the perspective of the lynchers, and justifies the whole event. We will examine this is some detail in a later chapter, when we look especially at the Babylonian creation myth, *Enuma Elish*, in which we hear the story of how the god Marduk slew the Tiamat,

the god of chaos, and cut her up to create the cosmos. Such myths are about the leap from the state of chaos and nondifferentiation to an ordered, differentiated cosmos. Huge numbers of myths testify to the ancient savvy regarding the connection between murder and the "defeat" of chaos and the beginning of the world.

52 Among Girardians there is a competing view that should be mentioned here, in which the sacred is not *created* by the founding murder, just distorted by it. In other words, original humans experienced the sacredness of creation, which really was/is there; but through their violence and lies they distorted it into something violent and threatening, and lived in fear of it. This view usually goes hand-in-hand with an effort to preserve the theological doctrine of the "fall," which sees humanity's historical condition as a fall from a paradise of sacred beauty and wonder. This is in opposition to Girard's own evolutionary view, which posits no original, paradisal state, and no original harmonious relationship between the human and the divine. For Girard, our knowledge of God comes to us as a maturing revelation throughout the course of history. The experience of the "transcendent" which has been the major emphasis of most religions, is for Girard a projection of human subjectivity, not a genuine experience of God. An important exposition of the view opposed to this, which advocates for an original and harmonious human experience of genuine transcendence is the forthcoming book by Ceṣáreo Bandera, "Refuge of Lies," which I have been privileged to read in manuscript form. See also, however, Bandera, *The Sacred Game: The Role of the Sacred in the Genesis of Modern Literary Fiction* (University Park: The Pennsylvania State University Press, 1994).

53 Mircea Eliade, *Patterns In Comparative Religion,* Trans. Rosemary Sheed (Lincoln: University of Nebraska Press, 1996), 33.

54 Hick, 23.

55 Walter Burkert, *Creation of the Sacred,* 19.

56 See the dialogue in *Violent Origins: Walter Burkert, René Girard, and Jonathan Z. Smith on Ritual Killing and Cultural Formation,* Ed. Robert G. Hamerton-Kelly (Stanford: Stanford University Press, 1987). Burkert prefers to trace the development of religion to humanity's more general, biological inheritance, seeing religion as a "hybrid" of cultural and biological traditions, and links the development of sacrifice in particular to prehistoric hunting, killing of the animal, and subsequent feasting. He admits that these topics are beyond the reach of the scientific methods of strict sociobiology, but insists that this fact does not give us license to separate culture/religion from biological substructures formed by the evolution of life itself. In discussions of these matters, he says,

"Probabilites, selective observations, and hunches" will have to take the place of a precisely, mathematically modeled sociobiology. (*Creation of the Sacred,* 20.) That is also true, of course, for the Girardian interpretation; but mimetic theory also offers a coherent and insightful interpretation of the Bible, opening up new vistas in the text and solving some thorny theological problems relating to violence.

To some extent, the persuasiveness of Girard's thesis depends upon how much of a role, and what kind of role, one is willing to accord mimesis and mimetic violence in human origins. Commenting on Girard in a footnote in *Creation of the Sacred,* Burkert writes, "Instead of competition and 'mimetic desire' as construed by Girard, I prefer to emphasize the situation of anxiety and the characteristic reaction to it of 'abandoning'." (201, n.68) In other words, Burkert wants to credit anxiety in the face of predators in primitive survival situations as a formative agent for sacrifice: fear leads to abandoning something of the kill so that the predator will take it and leave you alone. This forms the matrix that becomes ritual sacrifice. But from a Girardian perspective, fear of an animal predator, while no doubt common for early hominids, was not a formative factor in the generation of sacrifice. Fear of the *human* predator – the *rival* – was a far more ubiquitous, universal, and ever lurking anxiety; and it was exacerbated due to the (no less biological) explosion of mirror neurons, leading to an exaggerated capacity for copying the other's desires and entering into reciprocal rivalries.

[57] Hick, 25. (Citing Eric Hornung, *Conceptions of God in Ancient Egypt: The One and the Many,* Trans. John Baines (Ithaca, NY: Cornell University Press, 1971), 179-180.

[58] Burkert, *Creation of the Sacred,* 34-40.

[59] Ibid. 37.

[60] See James Alison's excellent exposition of this text in the DVD series "Discovering the Nonviolent God: Eight Sessions for Adult Education," published by Preaching Peace (www.PreachingPeace.org).

[61] Burkert, *Creation of the Sacred,* 39.

[62] Robert Hamerton-Kelly, *The Gospel and the Sacred: Poetics of Violence in Mark* (Minneapolis: Fortress Press, 1994), 3.

[63] Girard, *Violence and the Sacred,* 3.

[64] To mention again a point made previously, monsters are embodiments of nondifferentiation. Elements considered fundamentally distinct in creation are blended in the monster, which, for example, may combine a human head with a lion's body. The popularity of monsters in world mythology bespeaks violent social conditions which inclined the mind

toward imaginative blendings. Under conditions of sacrificial crises, people had "monsters on the brain," as it were; they wanted stories in which the monster, as representative of the nondifferentiation into which they feared their culture was devolving, is slain, and order restored. This seems not dissimilar to the appeal of horror and fantasy scenarios in stories and cinema today, in a violent world in which differences are rapidly disappearing on a global scale.

[65] Eliade, 71, 74.

[66] Girard, *Violence and the Sacred,* 219.

[67] Ibid. 221.

[68] Girard, *I See Satan,* 9.

[69] Robin Lane Fox, *Pagans and Christians* (San Francisco: Harper & Row, 1996), 109-110.

[70] Ibid. 117.

[71] Walter Burkert, *Creation of the Sacred,* 89.

[72] Ibid. 30 - 31.

[73] Girard, *Violence and the Sacred,* 31.

[74] Girardian treatments of this theme often portray the full ambivalence of the victim – and thus of the sacred – as arising immediately, fully formed, at the moment of the victim's death. Certainly, the group would have realized that the "god" had created peace among them, and they would seek to placate and appease that god in an effort to continue realizing the blessing. So, yes, in that sense there would have been a "positive" side to the sacred from its very inception. But this is still a long way from the sense of a god who desires to bestow blessings, who has a truly generous face in addition to its evil face. We have to allow for a probable lapse of time (perhaps many thousands of years) before the positive face of the gods fully emerges, even though its seeds were planted in the founding murder. Michael Hardin has made this point in *The Jesus Driven Life,* 98. All these attempts at reconstruction are of course highly speculative, and one need not spend time worrying about the details in order to appreciate Girard's basic thesis.

[75] The question might arise in the reader's mind as to why we don't see this god-creation business happening in the world today. White racists, for example, never turn their African American victims into gods. The reason is that the modern world is no longer capable of founding murders. We have come too far and learned too much, thanks to the Judeo-Christian tradition, and particularly the New Testament Gospels, which have been a juggernaut of deconstructive force leveled against the sacred. Thanks to this deconstruction, and the inculcation of a conscience with regard to

victims, especially in the West, we are no longer capable of falling for the kind of powerful group delusion that created the old gods. To be sure, we can still *demonize* people, but we can no longer deify them: at least not in the literal sense in which a dead victim can become a foundational god giving rise to a new culture. (But the see the paragraph that follows in the main text for a discussion of deification in India. This is not a founding murder in the sense of being capable of giving rise to an entirely new culture; but it is certainly a devolved holdover of the phenomenon.) We live in a secular world in which "sacred" means little more to most people than "precious." There are few communities in the world today in which sacred notions survive in all their ancient purity and potency. This is due to the influence of globalization, which has carried not only technology but the values of Western culture which have been steeped in 2,000 years of Christian influence.

[76] Girard has argued that Hitler's Reich was, in fact, an attempt to revive the old sacred. Jewish genocide was an all-out attempt to pulverize the Christian ethic of sympathy for victims. It attempted to create a spectacular ocean of victims, from whose carnage the Reich would "suck reviving blood." (See Girard, *I See Satan,* 170-176.)

[77] Thanks to Paul Nuechterlein for calling my attention to this phenomenon in his lecture at the 2012 "Theology and Peace" conference.

[78] See New York Times article at: http://www.nytimes.com/1987/09/20/world/india-seizes-four-after-immolation.html. See also: http://www.hinduismtoday.com/modules/smartsection/item.php?itemid=472

[79] Wikipedia at http://en.wikipedia.org/wiki/Roop_Kanwar

[80] Wikipedia at: http://en.wikipedia.org/wiki/Sati_%28practice%29#cite_note-autogenerated3578-30 (Citing "Revival and Spread of Sati Huma Khan", *Economic and Political Weekly,* Vol. 34, No. 51 [Dec. 18-24, 1999], 3578. Published by: Economic and Political Weekly.)

[81] The illusion of the happy and willing sacrificial victim dominates Joseph Campbell's conception of sacrifice. In his discussion with Bill Moyers for the PBS series "The Power of Myth," Campbell cites the ancient Mayan soccer games, in which the winner (yes, the *winner!*) was sacrificed, and notes how the victim went gladly and joyfully to the sacrificial altar. If the victim himself is in joyful agreement with his lynching, reasons Campbell, what could be wrong? Never has propaganda won such a triumph over the human mind: both the mind of the victim who no doubt did actually

sometimes march willingly to his or her death in imitation of the desires of the group, or the mind of modern scholars who allow themselves to be seduced by the same lie.

[82] Cesáreo Bandera, *The Sacred Game: The Role of the Sacred in the Genesis of Modern Literary Fiction* (University Park: The Pennsylvania State University Press, 1994), 50-63.

[83] Ibid. 52 (See Bandera's entire discussion of Plato at 50-63, section titled "Plato's Sacred Anxiety," for an intriguing and penetrating interpretation.)

[84] Berkert, *Homo Necans,* 11. This remark is doubly interesting because of the reference to "all the gods," in which we can perhaps glimpse the *collective* nature of the violence which is the origin and essence of sacrifice.

[85] Bandera, *The Sacred Game,* 53.

[86] Louis J. Martyn, *Galatians: A New Translation with Introduction and Commentary,* The Anchor Yale Bible (New Haven: Yale University Press, 1997), 588. It should be noted that, in addition to Greek philosophy, prior to Christianity other attempts were made to purify the sacred of its ambivalence (as well as to critique the practice of sacrifice). Examples include the Hebrew religion, and Zoroastrianism. However, even when Zoroaster separates Ahura Mazda (the good God) from Agra Mainyu (the evil spirit), and when Israel elevates Yahweh as the supremely good Creator far transcending the power of evil, traces of the old sacred continue to play a role in the deity, who is still considered violent – although the violence now takes on an ethical tonality.

[87] Bailie, (139-140).

[88] The Cain and Abel story preserves the general memory of murder, but it does not preserve the *collective* aspect of the violence against Abel. Girard has shown that the reason murder generates culture is due to the unanimous participation of the entire group in the persecution of the scapegoat. We recall that the murder becomes *foundational* due to the experience of polarization against the scapegoat, which creates a powerful group identity that had not previously existed.

[89] Livy, *The History of Rome,* Vol. I.

[90] James Alison, *Raising Abel: The Recovery of the Eschatological Imagination* (New York: The Crossroad Publishing Company, 2000).

[91] Bailie, 134-135.

[92] Hardin, 98.

[93] Raymund Schwager, S.J., *Must There Be* Scapegoats*? Violence and Redemption in the Bible* (New York: The Crossroad Publishing Company, 2000), 135.

[94] Cf. the discussion in Bruce J. Malina, *The New Testament World: Insights*

from Cultural Anthropology, Rev. ed. (Louisville, KY: Westminster/John Knox Press, 1993), 166-172.

[95] Cf. Girard's discussion of plague in "The Plague in Literature and Myth," *To Double Business Bound: Essays on Literature, Mimesis, and Anthropology* (Baltimore: Johns Hopkins University Press, 1978), 136-154.

[96] See *Chicago Tribune* article "Pride On!" by RedEye, June 28, 2008.

[97] Hamerton-Kelly, *The Gospel and the Sacred*, 15.

[98] What does the text mean when it says that David consulted the Lord, and how did the Lord "speak" to him? The reference is probably to some form of lottery or chance-based divination. David is scapegoating Saul in this passage, and the choice of scapegoat, as we learned earlier in this book, is essentially arbitrary. (For a particularly vivid example of the use of lottery to designate a victim-scapegoat, see the story of Achan in Joshua 7.)

[99] See Girard's discussion of Greek tragedy in *Violence*, passim.

[100] Alfred Edersheim, *Bible History of the Old Testament*, Vol.5, Chp.3.

[101] This is not to say that Fundamentalists and Evangelicals are always complete literalists (though some Fundamentalists do carry the literal interpretation of the Bible to amazing extremes). They are capable of making interpretative allowance for such things as metaphor, symbol, rhetorical patterns, and so on. But once allowance has been made for such things, everything the Bible asserts about God must be true, and every theological statement in the Bible is given the same "weight." (Indeed, for most Fundamentalists and Evangelicals every *historical* statement the Bible makes must be true as well.) The idea that the Bible could manifest error in any of its statements about God is anathema. There is little sensitivity to the idea that *the Bible critiques itself*, and that it is from within the pages of the Bible itself that we glean the criteria that allow us to separate biblical chaff from biblical wheat.

[102] James Alison expounds on these passages, as well as several other related texts, in the series of lectures mentioned earlier, "Discovering the Nonviolent God: Eight Sessions for Adult Education," published by Preaching Peace.

[103] René Girard, *Things Hidden Since the Foundation of the World*, Trans. Stephen Bann & Michael Metteer (Stanford: Stanford University Press, 1987), 156.

[104] Ibid. 156.

[105] Williams, 158, sees God speaking in 52:13-15 and 53:11-12, and the people speaking in 53:1-10.

[106] Schwager, 129.

[107] There are many difficulties both of translation and interpretation of the

fourth Servant Song, and there are ambiguities about the role of God with respect to the sufferings of the servant, as well as other issues which I do not have space in this book to develop. Interested readers may consult, for starters, Schwager, 126-135; Williams, 158-162; Girard, *Things Hidden,* 155-158; *I See Satan,* 28-31.

[108] Schwager, 135.

[109] Cf. Bandera, *Sacred Game,* 1-11. (An interesting discussion, which Bandera entitles, "On 'Sacred Allergy' in Its Modern Form.)

[110] See Girard, *The Scapegoat,* 49-61, for his powerful exposition of this biblical text.

[111] Stephanie Dalley (translator), *Myths from Mesopotamia: Creation, The Flood, Gilgamesh, and Others* (New York: Oxford University Press, 2008), 261. "Cut off his blood" probably refers to cutting his arteries.

[112] Ibid. 228.

[113] Few scholars deny a relationship between the two texts, though debate continues as to which borrows from which, and the precise nature of the relationship.

[114] See *Satan,* 107-115; René Girard, *Oedipus Unbound* (Stanford: Stanford University Press, 2004), 107-113.

[115] Girard is using the word "religion" here as synonymous with sacrificial "sacred religions," which manifest the sacred/profane distinction and its concomitant exclusions.

[116] Girard, *Things Hidden,* 164.

[117] The reading, "you do what you have heard from your father" makes much more sense and flows more easily within the context, than the alternative reading, "you should do what you have heard from the Father." Both possibilities are attested by ancient manuscripts, but given the context of the entire debate, the former seems more likely the original.

[118] There is scholarly debate about who exactly "Zechariah" is, but it seems likely he is the last prophet whose murder the Hebrew Scriptures record, so that Jesus is referring the first and the last murder of the innocent victim in the scriptures, thus indicating a totality.

[119] One is reminded of Kierkegaard's way of putting it: "The crowd is untruth." Soren Kierkegaard, *The Point of View for My Work As An Author: A Report To History*, ed. Benjamin Nelson (New York: Harper & Row, 1962), 109-120. These pages constitute the first "Note" in SK's treatise "The Individual," and it is one of the most powerful critiques of crowd mentality every penned.

[120] S. Mark Heim, *Saved From Sacrifice: A Theology of the Cross* (Grand Rapids: William B. Eerdmans Publishing Company, 2006).

[121] Bruce Chilton, *Rabbi Jesus: An Intimate Biography* (New York: Image Doubleday, 2002), 12. Chilton makes it clear that the issue was not being born out of wedlock, which is what we mean by the term "bastard" today; the stigma had to do rather with the mother's having sex with the wrong man: "An unmarried woman impregnated by a man outside her own community was in an invidious position, suspected of illicit intercourse. Unless she could bring witnesses to show she had been in the company of a licit father, it was assumed she had been made pregnant by a *mamzer* or another prohibited person, so that her child was a *mamzer* (Mishnah Ketubot 1:8-9). Mary's sexual relations with Joseph had not been prohibited, but given that Joseph had lived in Bethlehem and she in Nazareth when she became pregnant, it was virtually impossible for her to prove that he was the father. In the absence of proof, Jesus was considered a *mamzer:* what the Mishnah at a slightly later period calls a *shetuqi*, or 'silenced one'... without a voice in the public congregations that regulated the social, political, and religious life of Israel (Deuteronomy 23:2)." (Chilton, 13.)

[122] James Alison, *Knowing Jesus* (Springfield: Templegate Publishers, 1993), 7.

[123] Girard, *The Scapegoat,* 172.

[124] The sermon is called "Embodying God's Earth-Shaking Mercy," and the video is currently available online in the National Cathedral archives at http://www.nationalcathedral.org/learn/recentLectures.shtml

[125] Girard, *The Scapegoat,* 181, 182.

[126] The historical-critical observation that the actual town of Nazareth has no steep cliff is not relevant to the kind of literary approach to the Gospel narratives adopted here. As mentioned earlier in the book, Girard believes that the New Testament Scriptures contain revelatory truth *as the text stands,* quite apart from the kind of precise historical accuracy that Evangelicals and fundamentalists think important.

[127] It is James Alison who has brought to the fore the significance of Jesus sending the man back to his own people. His entire sermon in the Washington Cathedral, alluded to previously, is an extended meditation on this aspect of the story.

[128] James Alison, *Faith Beyond Resentment: Fragments Catholic and Gay* (New York: The Crossroad Publishing Company, 2001), 131.

[129] Ibid. 128.

[130] Robert G. Hamerton-Kelly, *Sacred Violence: Paul's Hermeneutic of the Cross* (Minneapolis: Fortress Press, 1992), 63.

[131] Ibid. 63.

[132] Ibid. 66-67.

[133] Ibid. 69-60 for the 2 Cor. 5:14 text, and 77-78 for the Gal. 4:4-5 (which is my second example).
[134] Ibid. 78.
[135] In later rabbinic traditions, the technique of associating texts together based on certain hook-words was called *gezera shava.* It is quite commonplace in the New Testament. See H.L. Strack, *Introduction to the Talmud and Midrash* (New York, 1959), 94.
[136] Those who think that Romans 1-3 gives the lie to this statement should investigate Douglas Campbell's mammoth work, *The Deliverance of God: An Apocalyptic Rereading of Justification in Paul* (Grand Rapids: William B. Eerdmans Publishing Company, 2009). Campbell mounts an argument sustained through over 1,000 pages (several hundred of which involve close exegetical work with the Greek text) seeking to show that the passages in Romans 1-3, which have traditionally been interpreted as Paul lambasting Gentiles, are actually the words of Paul's opponent (given as an ancient rhetorical device called "speech in character"). This character is a Jewish or Jewish-Christian teacher whose merciless lambasting of Gentiles is precisely what Paul is critiquing!
[137] Literally in the Greek "scandalize" them. This is not the place, nor do I have the space, to elaborate on this passage in Girardian terms. But the Girardian concept of "scandal," which was examined in an earlier chapter, is exactly what Paul is talking about here. It was rampant in the Corinthian congregation, spreading contagiously as people formed themselves into rival factions.
[138] Williams, 5.
[139] Anthony Bartlett, *Cross-Purposes:A Grammar of Christian Atonement* (Harrisburg, PA: Trinity Press International, 2001), 23.
[140] James Ailson, *Knowing Jesus* (Springfield, IL: Templegate Publishers, 1993), 78.
[141] James Alison, *On Being Liked* (New York: The Crossroad Publishing Company, 2003), *ix.*
[142] Ibid. *x.*
[143] Ibid. *x – xi.*
[144] Ramsay MacMullen, *Christianizing the Roman Empire A.D. 100-400* (New Haven: Yale University Press, 1984).
[145] Hubert Dreyfus and Sean Dorrance Kelly, *All Things Shining: Reading the Western Classics to Find Meaning in a Secular Age* (New York: Simon & Schuster, Inc., 2011), 105, 108.
[146] David Bentley Hart, *Atheist Delusions: The Christian Revolution and Its Fashionable Enemies* (New Haven: Yale University Press, 2009), 163.

[147] Ibid. 163. The short phrases marked by quotations in this paragraph are Hart's.

[148] Ibid. 158.

[149] Ibid. 167.

[150] Ibid. 167.

[151] Ibid. 169.

[152] Susan Wessel, "The Morality of Disgust in Jerome and John Chrysostom" *Augustiniaum,* 50 (1):147-162.

[153] Ibid. All Jerome quotes in this discussion are citied by Wessel.

[154] See Girard, *Things Hidden,* 224-262.

[155] René Girard, *Evolution and Conversion: Dialogues on the Origins of Culture* (London: Continuum International Publishing, 2007), 259. (Emphasis mine.)

[156] Burkert, *Homo Necans,* 8,9.

[157] Girard, *Evolution and Conversion,* 259.

[158] Ibid. 260.

[159] Girard exposed and addressed the issue of sacrificial Christianity, but seemed reluctant to hold the church completely responsible for the incorporation of violence into its practice and theology, wanting to see this in some sense as an almost necessary development. "But this very demonstration [i.e., of God's nonviolent nature] is bound to remain ambiguous for a long time, and it is not capable of achieving a decisive result, since it looks like total impotence to those who live under the regime of violence. That is why at first it can only have some effect under a guise, deceptive through the admixture of some sacrificial elements, through the surreptitious re-insertion of some violence into the conception of the divine." (*Things Hidden,* 220) Girard seems to be saying, in other words, that the gospel truth will necessarily have to be mixed, "deceptively" as he puts it, with sacred religion, so that it can begin to change people almost without their realizing it; for otherwise people addicted to the power of violence would not even give the gospel a moment's hearing, looking as it does like total impotence. Now, there is no doubt that something like this is indeed what happened in the history of Christianity. But there is a thin line between recognizing that as a historical fact, and positing its necessity in such a way that a thorough-going critique of the church's irresponsibility seems unnecessary. In *Cross-Purposes* (see earlier footnote), Anthony Bartlett used mimetic anthropology to mount a full-fledged critique of historical Christendom's intercourse with violence, particularly with respect to its doctrine of atonement.

[160] Girard, *Things Hidden,* 225.

[161] Readers interested in pursuing critiques of violent atonement theories from a Girardian point of view should consult Anthony Bartlett's *Cross-Purposes,* referenced above, as well as Brad Jersak and Michael Hardin, *Stricken By God? Nonviolent Identification and the Victory of Christ* (Grand Rapids: Wm. B. Eerdmans Publishing Company, 2007); S. Mark Heim's *Saved From Sacrifice* (cited earlier); J. Denny Weaver, *The Nonviolent Atonement* (Grand Rapids: Wm. B. Eerdmans Publishing Company, 2001. (Weaver does not anchor his critique in Girardian terms, but he comments on Girard, and his book is highly compatible with the Girardian perspective of the other writers mentioned above. Bartlett blogs at *www.WoodHathHope.com* and *www.TheologyandPeace.org*. Hardin's website is *wwwPreachingPeace.org*.

[162] Stephan Finlan, *Options on Atonement in Christian Thought* (Collegeville: Minnesota, Liturgical Press, 2007), 47-48. See also Michael Hardin, *Sacrificial Language in Hebrews: Reappraising René Girard,"* in Swartley, ed., *Violence Renounced,* 103-119.

[163] See Bartlett's *Cross-Purposes* for a full and insightful account of the history.

[164] Ibid. 95-97.

[165] Ibid. 95.

[166] Ibid. 102.

[167] Ibid. 103.

[168] Anthony Bartlett, *Virtually Christian* (Winchester, UK: O-Books, 2011), 9.

[169] Ibid. 9.

[170] Girard, *Things Hidden,* 119.

[171] Ibid. 148.

[172] Bartlett, *Virtually Christian,* 16.

[173] Bartlett, *Cross-Purposes,* 138. By "under judgment" here, Bartlett does not mean condemnation. "[J]udgment in the light of abyssal compassion is something other than condemnation. It is a profound invitation to change."

[174] Ibid. 135.

[175] Girard, *Things Hidden,* 234.

[176] Bartlett, *Virtually Christian,* 10.

[177] René Girard, *Sacrifice,* Trans. Matthew Pattillo and David Dawson (East Lansing: Michigan State University Press, 2011), 87.

[178] National Public Radio, *"On Being,"* with Krista Tippett, episode entitled: *Globalization and the Rise of Religion.* The program is archived for downloading at:
http://being.publicradio.org/programs/globalization/index.shtml

[179] Girard, *Evolution,* 257.
[180] Grossman, Lt. Col. Dave, *On Combat: The Psychology and Physiology of Deadly Conflict in War and in Peace* (USA: Warrior Science Publications, 2008), xi.
[181] Tony Dokoupil. "Moral Injury." *Newsweek* 10 Dec. 2012: 40.
[182] Ibid. 236.
[183] Ibid. 258.
[184] Ibid. 236.
[185] Ibid. 235.
[186] Ibid. 238.
[187] Ibid. 238.
[188] *Waiting for Armageddon,* Dir. Kate Davis, David Heilbroner, Franco Sacchi. Q-Ball Productions, Inc. and Eureka Film Productions, LLC, 2008.
[189] I know I am painting with a very wide brush here. I have lumped Evangelicals and Fundamentalists into the same camp, even though they often distinguish themselves from one another. I am also aware that Evangelicalism has developed many sizes and shapes in recent decades, including a left-wing, nonviolent variety. I am only concerned here, however, with the vast majority of Evangelicals, and what they hold in common with Fundamentalists: namely, the "Janus-faced" God of love and violence. And if the sixteen novels of the "Left Behind" series which has sold over 65 million copies is any indication, the voyeuristic thrill of playing spectator to massive and sickening violence when it means the trouncing of one's rivals is something modern Evangelicals and Fundamentalists seem to be well at home with. Attempts to restore sacred religion to the modern world will not solve the problem of mimetic rivalry; on the contrary, they are just another manifestation of it.
[190] Bartlett, *Cross-Purposes,* 104-110.
[191] Susan Faludi, *The Terror Dream: Fear and Fantasy in Post 9/11 America* (New York, NY: Henry Holt and Company, LLC, 2007).
[192] Girard, *Evolution,* 242.
[193] Ibid. 251.
[194] Grossman, *Combat,* xx.
[195] The story of New Hampshire's political polarization was told by Sarah Koenig for NPR's "This American Life," episode titled "Red State Blue State," available for streaming (and transcript) at: http://www.thisamericanlife.org/radio-archives/episode/478/red-state-blue-state
[196] Interview conducted by Krista Tippett for her NPR show, *On Being.* Episode titled "Political Bridge People," available for streaming at

http://www.onbeing.org/program/political-bridge-people-pete-domenici-and-alice-rivlin/4892 (Transcript also available on the website.)

[197] Girard, *Evolution*. 247.

[198] Dreyfus and Kelly, 25. (See footnote 144 for full book citation.)

[199] Dreyfus and Kelly, 194.

[200] Ibid. 200.

[201] Ibid. 201.

[202] Charles Taylor (2011): "Recovering the Sacred," *Inquiry*, 54:2, 120.

[203] Dreyfus and Kelly, 61.

[204] Ibid. 161.

[205] Bartlett, *Virtually Christian*, 50.

[206] Ibid. 105, 108.

[207] Ibid. 109.

[208] Ibid. 111-112.

[209] Ibid. 113-114.

[210] Charles Dickens, *A Christmas Carol* (Textbook Classics, 2012), 97-98.

[211] Girard, *Evolution*, 237.

[212] Quotes from Bill Wilson's letter to Carl Jung, Jan. 23, 1961, taken from the website: http://www.barefootsworld.net/wilsonletter.html

[213] *Twelve Steps and Twelve Traditions* (New York: Alcoholics Anonymous World Services, Inc., 1952), 21.

[214] http://theologypeace.blogspot.com/2011/10/living-in-luminous-shadow.html

[215] Friedrich Nietzsche, *The Will To Power*, Trans. Walter Kaufmann (New York: Random House, Vintage Books Edition, 1968), 542.

[216] Ibid. 542-543.

[217] Ibid. 142.

[218] Girard, *Violence and the Sacred*, 126.

[219] Again, I recognize that Yeats was not a "Girardian." I am not exegeting the text. I am using the words of the poem as an elegant and poetic way of summing up the essence of our contemporary situation from a Girardian point of view. For Yeats himself the phrase "ceremony of innocence" most likely referred to the European world of peace and good times which was stunned into chastened silence and a guilty conscience by the horrific events of World War I. However, if this was Yeats' meaning, we can say that it is not entirely foreign to the Girardian interpretation of modern events. For it evidences part of the historical process of burgeoning awareness that has made it difficult in modern times to maintain a clean conscience about the victims we create.

[220] Girard, *Battling To The End*, 198.

[221] Ibid. 217.
[222] Drasko Dizdar, "Leaving The Temple," *Australian eJournal of Theology* 3 (August 2004), 3-4.

CHRISTIAN
ALTERNATIVE

Throughout the two thousand years of Christian tradition there have been, and still are, groups and individuals that exist in the margins and upon the edge of faith. But in Christianity's contrapuntal history it has often been these outcasts and pioneers that have forged contemporary orthodoxy out of former radicalism as belief evolves to engage with and encompass the ever-changing social and scientific realities. Real faith lies not in the comfortable certainties of the Orthodox, but somewhere in a half-glimpsed hinterland on the dirt track to Emmaus, where the Death of God meets the Resurrection, where the supernatural Christ meets the historical Jesus, and where the revolution liberates both the oppressed and the oppressors.

Welcome to Christian Alternative... a space at the edge where the light shines through.